SHAKESPEARE SURVEY

ADVISORY BOARD

Aspects of *Macbeth*
Aspects of *Othello*
Aspects of *Hamlet*
Aspects of *King Lear*
Aspects of Shakespeare's 'Problem Plays'

SHAKESPEARE SURVEY

AN ANNUAL SURVEY OF

SHAKESPEARE STUDIES AND PRODUCTION

41

with a General Index to Volumes 31–40

EDITED BY

STANLEY WELLS

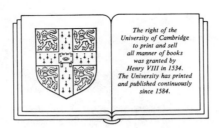

The right of the
University of Cambridge
to print and sell
all manner of books
was granted by
Henry VIII in 1534.
The University has printed
and published continuously
since 1584.

CAMBRIDGE UNIVERSITY PRESS

CAMBRIDGE

NEW YORK   NEW ROCHELLE   MELBOURNE   SYDNEY

Published by the Press Syndicate of the University of Cambridge
The Pitt Building, Trumpington Street, Cambridge CB2 1RP
32 East 57th Street, New York, NY 10022, USA
10 Stamford Road, Oakleigh, Melbourne 3166, Australia

First published 1989

Printed in Great Britain at the University Press, Cambridge

British Library cataloguing in publication data

Shakespeare survey: an annual survey of
Shakespeare studies and production. – 41:
[Shakespearian stages and staging].
1. Drama in English. Shakespeare, William –
Critical studies – Serials
822′.3′3

Library of Congress catalogue card number: 49–1639

ISBN 0 521 36071 4

Shakespeare Survey was first published in 1948. Its first
eighteen volumes were edited by Allardyce Nicoll. Kenneth
Muir edited volumes 19 to 33.

EDITOR'S NOTE

Volume 42 of *Shakespeare Survey*, which will be at press by the time this volume appears, will focus on 'Shakespeare and the Elizabethans', Volume 43 on '*The Tempest* and After', Volume 44 on 'Politics and Shakespeare', and Volume 45 on '*Hamlet* and Its Afterlife'. Topics for Volume 43 may include Shakespeare's writings from *The Tempest* till the end of his career, the theatrical and publication history of his works up to the closing of the theatres in 1642, his posthumous reputation, and the afterlife of *The Tempest* in production, adaptation, and influence up to our own time.

Submissions should be addressed to the Editor at The Shakespeare Institute, Church Street, Stratford-upon-Avon, Warwickshire CV37 6HP, to arrive at the latest by 1 September 1989 for Volume 43, 1 September 1990 for Volume 44, and 1 September 1991 for Volume 45. Pressures on space are heavy; many articles are considered before the deadline, so those that arrive earlier stand a better chance of acceptance. Please either enclose return postage (overseas, in International Reply coupons) or send a copy you do not wish to have returned. A style sheet is available on request. All articles submitted are read by the Editor and at least one member of the Editorial Board, whose indispensable assistance the Editor gratefully acknowledges.

Unless otherwise indicated, Shakespeare quotations and references are keyed to the modern-spelling Complete Oxford Shakespeare (1986).

With this volume the Editor succeeds Nicholas Shrimpton, whom we thank for his services, as the reviewer of theatre productions.

In attempting to survey the ever-increasing bulk of Shakespeare publications our reviewers inevitably have to exercise some selection. Review copies of books should be addressed to the Editor, as above. We are also pleased to receive offprints of articles which help to draw our reviewers' attention to relevant material.

S.W.W.

CONTRIBUTORS

JOHN H. ASTINGTON, *University of Toronto*
JONATHAN BATE, *Trinity Hall, Cambridge*
SAMUEL CROWL, *Ohio University*
RICHARD DUTTON, *University of Lancaster*
RICHARD FOULKES, *University of Leicester*
ANDREW GURR, *University of Reading*
PETER HOLLAND, *Trinity Hall, Cambridge*
MACDONALD P. JACKSON, *University of Auckland*
JOHN KERRIGAN, *St John's College, Cambridge*
IAN KIRBY, *University of Lausanne*
WILLIAM MONTGOMERY, *Oxford*
N. RATHBONE, *Birmingham Shakespeare Library*
LESLIE THOMSON, *University of Toronto*
CLAIRE M. TYLEE, *University of Málaga*
STANLEY WELLS, *The Shakespeare Institute, University of Birmingham*
R. S. WHITE, *University of Western Australia*

CONTENTS

ILLUSTRATIONS

ILLUSTRATIONS

THE SHAKESPEARIAN STAGES, FORTY YEARS ON

ANDREW GURR

The year when Allardyce Nicoll published the last survey of studies in Shakespearian play-houses and their software, 1948, was a year of abrupt demolition. Along with Nicoll's over-view in the first *Shakespeare Survey* came I. A. Shapiro's study of the early Bankside engrav-ings, which cut the foundation from John Cranford Adams's long labour of recon-structing the Globe by showing that Cornelius Visscher's tall octagon published in 1616 was not an accurate depiction of Shakespeare's playhouse.[1] Adams's work had so dominated scholars of the theatre that its demolition might be said to have left a bombsite. This image, used by Herbert Berry for Chambers's *Elizabethan Stage* volumes and their service of 'marmorealising' the age of document dis-coveries,[2] applies more aptly to the multitude of attempts to reconstruct the physical features of the time than to the recording of its docu-ments. Even there it is not quite an appropriate image, because lifesize reconstructions based on the Adams model still stand at the Folger Shakespeare Library, at Hofstra College, and in San Diego, Ashland (Oregon), Cleveland (Ohio), Cedar City (Utah), and Odessa (Texas), together with several more removed Fortune-imitating structures. Nonetheless it is true that some of the debris from Shapiro's demolition is still in need of being cleared away (the shop at the Folger Shakespeare Library, that magnificent resource for book-scholarship, still sells paper cut-outs of the Cranford Adams Globe and pictures of Visscher). Debris from the old reconstruc-tions, whether in the form of inner-stages or angled entry doors, still causes the occasional stumble.

As students of the postwar Germanies know, demolition can be an invigorating prelude to reconstruction. Cranford Adams had set an important precedent with his exact work on his three-dimensional model, care-fully articulated and with each structural member tested against known techniques of Tudor building. His exemplar has prompted the construction and testing in the last forty years of models for the Fortune, the Boar's Head, the second Blackfriars, and the Inigo Jones Cockpit as well as the Globe. Even De Witt's teasingly graphic picture of the Swan has been adjusted to make a plausible struc-ture. With much of this painstaking detail being strongly confirmed by a reassessment of the significance of Hollar's drawings of the Globe, tangible, or at least plausible, models for the various physical playhouse structures are emerging as the most tangible product of the last forty years.

As points from which to measure the dis-tance which has been covered since Nicoll

---

[1] Allardyce Nicoll, 'Studies in the Elizabethan Stage since 1900', *Shakespeare Survey 1* (1948), 1–16; I. A. Shapiro, 'The Bankside Theatres: Early Engravings', *Shakespeare Survey 1*, 25–37.

[2] Herbert Berry, Introduction to David Stevens, *English Renaissance Theatre History: A Reference Guide* (Boston, 1982).

wrote his survey, two comments he made about the state of the business in 1948 stand out. First, he lamented that 'we do not possess a practicable stage of Elizabethan proportions on which the theories [about Elizabethan stage practices] can be worked out' (p. 10). Apron and thrust stages as large as the Globe's are not rare now. Moreover, while the London South Bank's Olivier stage may not resemble the Globe very closely in anything, even its dimensions, there is certainly now the prospect of a full-scale reconstruction of the Globe in Southwark where at least the dimensions and the weather, if not the acoustics, should provide the testbed for reconstructions of the original performances that Nicoll wanted. His survey ended with 'the dream of a practical stage for the trying-out of theories . . . it would appear as though only something of this sort can aid us towards fuller and further accomplishment in the study of the Elizabethan theatre' (p. 16). We have come some way towards realizing that dream.

And, to a degree, the dream has expanded. The complete scheme for the International Shakespeare Globe Centre is of course not only Globe-centred. It includes plans for a second theatre, a hall playhouse, based on the plans which Inigo Jones probably drew for Beeston's Cockpit in 1616. That enhancement of the original dream gives some sharpness to the second point made by Nicoll which can serve to measure our distance from 1948. This is his conclusion that in the period covered by his survey 'the preponderating interest of the Globe and its associates has tended to outweigh that of the indoor houses' (p. 10). In the last forty years, no doubt partly because of the bombsite, we have on the whole dwelt indoors. A full-scale reconstruction of a playhouse design (drawn in precise detail by Inigo Jones for a playhouse to rival the Blackfriars) is a more tangible prospect, a better, much more reliable basis for experimentation about the original staging, than anything that was on the horizon in 1948.

Slowly we are developing a sense of how the playhouse designs evolved historically and how they varied. The documentary evidence which Chambers made into marble has been evaluated, sifted, and used, on the whole, to good effect – a close imitation in plastic of marble, if not the real thing. But the documents of course cover a great number of matters besides the physical structure of the playhouses. It is the less tangible matters, the different repertories, the staging, the sociology, and the mental equipment of Shakespearian playgoers, that are still a long way beyond our confident grasp.

This is not for lack of work in the field. The forty years since 1948 have seen more than twice as many publications as the three hundred years before that date. We are much more sure now, you might say, about what we do not know. What we seem to be less sure of is why we are doing what we are doing. The recent upheavals over theory were inevitable, and not just because of the way they stimulated a necessary rejection of the innate conservatism inherent in the marmoreal views and their Tillyardian extensions. The more that the main facts are turned into marble, whether they affirm that the sacred canon is still chewing its cud or whether they are the products of archaeological and touristic enthusiasm for a lost idyllic past, the more they will prompt shifts in ways of thinking about them. The more fixed the so-called canon becomes, the more pressure there is to find new ways of looking at it.

Stephen Greenblatt's 'poetics of culture', and the 'New Historicism' to which his name has been attached, are rightly more concerned to alter the perspectives than the fixities. Indeed, this approach depends on the fixities to validate its basic premise of the need to re-set the texts in their original contexts. One still winces when the New Historicists write that Shakespeare's company staged *Richard II* on the *night* before the Essex rebellion, conjuring up images of an anachronistically floodlit

Globe, though they have a regrettable precedent in Nagler's chapter about the first night of *The Tempest*.[3] Such slips only emphasize the need to identify more facts and fixtures. The radical and alternative Shakespeares prevalent on the eastern side of the Atlantic have even more need to cultivate a strong sense of historical change and the distance between Shakespeare then and Shakespeare now.

The most rewarding developments in recent theoretical arguments may come, a little surprisingly perhaps, from semiotics. In particular the methods of Saussurian linguistics, with its concern for non-verbal signifiers and the complexity of speaker–audience interaction, have a great deal to offer the study of plays as performance texts. They avoid the difficulties inherent in thinking of the written text as a fixity, and emphasize the importance of iconic and emblematic visual signifiers, while demanding caution over any attempt to 'fix' the fluid intricacies of the intimate and constantly shifting exchange between actors and audience. Since the main thrust in the study of staging Shakespeare through these last decades has been towards identifying emblematic significances, this is potentially a powerful new tool.

The range of work done on Shakespearian staging covers a broad territory: from the fixities of the physical playhouse structures, at one end, to the wildest conjectures, unfixed in principle and place, about the significance (or even the presence) of iconic and emblematic devices, at the other. When work on the plans for the reconstructed Globe on Bankside turned up the point that the stage was placed with its back to the sun, for instance, putting the stage platform in permanent shadow, it prompted a flurry of questions and conjectures about such interpretational matters as the likelihood of *Hamlet*'s having been written for artificial lighting.[4] There is no easy separation between the tangible achievements of identifying fixities and the business of interpretation

and pattern-making which create the link between the timber of the playhouses and the texts of the plays performed in them. Since those links are the chief justification for the amount of attention paid to the timbers, and since they often influence profoundly any reading of the evidence about the fixities, it is necessary to cast a broad net in this survey.

The first major landmark to be set up after Shapiro's demolition was Walter Hodges's *The Globe Restored* of 1953. Hodges's elegant drawings created a vivid though still heavily conjectural history for the evolution of the amphitheatres. Backed by a combination of careful study of the evidence and an architect's eye for practical structures, they set down the first stones of the post-Adams path towards a fresh concept for the Globe. The linkage Hodges identified between the early booth stages and the later tiring-house structures finally closed down the long debate about inner and upper stages which formed the core of the Adams reconstruction. Richard Hosley's scrupulous studies of the structural evidence for the Globe and the other amphitheatres have developed the ideas of Hodges and have led to the concept, developed by John Orrell, on which the projected Bankside reconstruction is to be based. Hosley and Richard Southern have also been the principal advocates of hall screens as a model for both amphitheatre and hall playhouse tiring-house fronts. This is a dubious model, since hall

---

[3] Stephen Greenblatt, *Renaissance Self-Fashioning from More to Shakespeare* (Chicago, 1980); Leonard Tennenhouse, *Power on Display* (New York, 1986), p. 88; A. M. Nagler, *Shakespeare's Stage* (New Haven, 1958), chapter 13.

[4] The point was originally noted by Leslie Hotson in *Shakespeare's Wooden O* (London, 1959). Alan R. Young in 'The Orientation of the Elizabethan Stage: "That Glory to the Sober West"', *Theatre Notebook*, 33 (1979), 80–5, and John Orrell in 'Sunlight at the Globe', *Theatre Notebook*, 38 (1984), 69–76, present the evidence in full. One development was Keith Brown's 'More light, more light', *Essays in Criticism*, 34 (1984), 1–13.

screens for the most part appear to have been fairly passive bystanders when plays were staged in their halls. But they provide the only close analogy to use if we are to elaborate the raw evidence of De Witt's plain-fronted tiring house.

Anchored firmly in the physical features of the amphitheatre but floating freely among the plays, Bernard Beckerman's *Shakespeare at the Globe* has been consistently and widely influential since its publication in 1962. The first book on the original staging to confine itself scrupulously to the evidence about one playhouse and the plays written for it, and covering the whole array from the repertory to the acting, its sane and careful conclusions set the standard for subsequent studies of other playhouses. The principles first set out by George Reynolds in his classic study of the Red Bull repertory, with its careful evaluation of stage directions in relation to the playhouse for which they were written and a hierarchy of reliability based on how distinctly a play belonged to a particular playhouse at a particular time, are fully ratified by Beckerman's book.[5] What he added, though, was equally valuable. Along with the hardware of the building he looked at the software of players and their parts, their audiences, their repertory system, and the entire substructure of production and performance which put the playscripts onto the stage. Subsequent studies, including T. J. King's analyses of the stage directions in plays written for particular playhouses[6] and Richard Hosley's current massive project to survey and relate the stage directions of all the plays known to belong to specific playhouses to the relevant structures, have benefited from the breadth of Beckerman's conspectus.

In recent years narrowness of range has become a chronic problem in stage studies. The students of architecture are hesitant to make pronouncements about practical staging, the actor-directors import unspoken (and often unthought-of) assumptions based on modern stage structures. Growing enthusiasm for the principles of emblematic staging has intensified this problem, since the emblematists can approach the Shakespearian stages from so many different directions. The traditions of Elizabethan pageantry examined by David Bergeron,[7] and the mysteries of iconic devices exemplified in the masques, merge insidiously into Alan Dessen's study of popular stage devices used as shorthand signals, where the entry of a character wearing a nightcap makes a bedroom scene, or riding boots signify travel.[8] The difficulty lies partly in the impossibility of identifying the many contradictory demands on the original stagers, the constant choices they had to make between the urge to be lavishly expressive and the need to be practical and economical, the choice between expenditure on properties for the sake of realism, or reliance, conveniently cheaper, on traditional emblematic forms. It is a necessary caution to remember Reynolds's point about how easily, in the absence of the stage directions, we could have misread the Red Bull's presentation of a scene (in *The Two Noble Ladies*, 1619–23) in which two soldiers, trying to cross a river, are drowned on stage.[9] This mild challenge to stage realism the company answered in a strikingly non-realistic way by introducing two Tritons who enter and drag the soldiers off, sounding their trumpets. Whether this distinctive way of staging a fairly realistic event was chosen for emblematic purposes, out of a traditional

5 G. R. Reynolds, *The Staging of Elizabethan Plays at the Red Bull Theater* (Oxford, 1940); Bernard Beckerman, *Shakespeare at the Globe, 1599–1609* (New York, 1962).
6 T. J. King, 'The Staging of Plays at the Phoenix in Drury Lane, 1617–42', *Theatre Notebook*, 19 (1964), 146–66, and *Shakespearean Staging 1599–1642* (Cambridge, Mass., 1971).
7 David Bergeron, *English Civic Pageantry, 1558–1642* (Columbia, 1971).
8 Alan C. Dessen, *Elizabethan Stage Conventions and Modern Interpreters* (Cambridge, 1984).
9 Reynolds, *The Staging of Elizabethan Plays*, p. 13.

reluctance to offer the banality of mere realism, or because divine providence was expected to intervene at that point in the story it is impossible now to tell. That, perhaps, is one measure of how far there is still to go in the study of staging.

Most of the broad shape of stage studies in the last forty years has been dictated by the need to evaluate a limited body of familiar evidence and to re-use it with a sufficient amount of the especial caution which bomb disposal experts use after an explosive demolition. The general recognition after Reynolds that there was not any 'typical' playhouse, but a wide diversity, has had the effect of producing narrower and closer studies of particular areas. If we ignore the risks inherent in excessive specialization, it can be said fairly that the results have been uniformly beneficial.

That irritable reaching after fact and reason which Keats characterized as so unShakespearian has had significant victories in identifying the shape of several playhouses. Herbert Berry's work on the legal documents and land-maps has finally made possible a reliable reconstruction of the shape of the Boar's Head amphitheatre.[10] Richard Hosley's reconstructions of the Fortune and the Swan,[11] Janet Loengard's discovery of the legal papers about the Red Lion, precursor to the Theatre,[12] the identification of the Inigo Jones drawings in Worcester College as a set most likely made for Beeston's Cockpit[13] – studies such as these have both lengthened and broadened the perspective on theatre-building traditions as they developed between 1567 and 1616. By learning about particular playhouses we know more about the traditional building concepts, if not the playing traditions, which led James Burbage to the Red Lion and the Theatre, and eventually to the Blackfriars. Some of the playacting necessities which dictated the new shape when the Boar's Head was adapted from a tavern into a playhouse in 1601 are recognizable too. Most notably of all, John Orrell's analysis of Wenceslas Hollar's meticulous work with his perspective glass has finally justified Shapiro's conclusion that Hollar's is the only reliable view of the Globe, while taking the evidence Hollar provides a good way further towards a reconstruction of the shape of the first Globe than the sceptical Shapiro thought it could possibly go.[14]

A few more significant documents, supplied in accurate transcripts, have extended the Chambers and Bentley records. R. A. Foakes has done a great deal to make the Henslowe papers more accessible to the kind of scrutiny that is only now beginning to be applied properly to those unique records.[15] Herbert Berry's work on legal records has considerably clarified the available facts about the Theatre and the Boar's Head.[16] Ann Haaker's work on the legal tangles surrounding Brome's contracts with the players, extended in Bentley's book about the conditions under which the professional playwrights worked, has

---

[10] Herbert Berry, *The Boar's Head Playhouse* (Washington, DC, 1986).

[11] Richard Hosley, 'The Playhouses', in J. Leeds Barroll, Alexander Leggatt, Richard Hosley, and Alvin Kernan, *The Revels History of Drama in English*, vol. 3: 1576–1613 (London, 1976), pp. 119–235.

[12] Janet S. Loengard, 'An Elizabethan Lawsuit: John Brayne, his Carpenter, and the Building of the Red Lion Theatre', *Shakespeare Quarterly*, 35 (1984), 298–310.

[13] John Orrell, 'Inigo Jones at the Cockpit', *Shakespeare Survey 30* (1977), 157–68. The same author's *The Theatres of Inigo Jones and John Webb* (Cambridge, 1985) develops the case further and provides an effective history of early seventeenth-century theatre design.

[14] *The Quest for Shakespeare's Globe* (Cambridge, 1983).

[15] R. A. Foakes and R. T. Rickert, eds., *Henslowe's Diary* (Cambridge, 1961). Foakes also has edited a facsimile edition of the Henslowe papers (London, 1977). His *Illustrations of the English Stage, 1580–1642* (London, 1985) is another useful addition to the list of books reproducing the material evidence.

[16] Herbert Berry, ed., *The First Public Playhouse: The Theatre in Shoreditch 1576–1598* (Toronto, 1980). The same author's work on the Boar's Head is listed in note 10.

improved practical knowledge of the conditions for playwriting.[17] There is much more demystifying to be done even in the familiar documents, though. The Henslowe papers throw up more teases than answers, over such matters of staging as the occasional use of large scenic structures and backcloths or painted cloths depicting such things as the city of Rome. In the Henslowe records there is also the basis for a closer look at the techniques of collaborative writing, the standard timetable for the mounting of new plays in the 1590s, casting and doubling in plays, and above all the intricate business of distinguishing the finances of the financier from those of the playing companies he ran.

Facts are nothing without interpretation, of course, and interpretation has flourished even more mightily in the last forty years than it did under Cranford Adams. Perhaps these years have been notable above all for a swing of focus away from the Globe and the other amphitheatres to the hall playhouses. It was probably an inevitable process, since whatever the quality of the plays there is certainly much more useable evidence in the new area than the old. The swing seems to have begun about the time of G. E. Bentley's article suggesting that Shakespeare's last plays were written for the Blackfriars (it appeared in 1948 in the same *Shakespeare Survey 1* as Allardyce Nicoll's survey drawing attention to the generally Globe-centred emphasis and Shapiro's demolition of the credibility of the Visscher engraving).[18] This view was given some help by the presumed link between the hall or 'private' playhouses and court staging. It was ramified strongly by the coincidence of Glynne Wickham's long and meticulous labours, and the heightening of awareness of emblematic staging which they provided, with the Orgel/Strong work on iconic devices used in the court masques.[19] Supported by the completion of Bentley's *Jacobean and Caroline Stage* (which extended the Chambers marmorealizing from 1616 to 1642 and drew attention to the pre-

dominance of the Blackfriars over the Globe after 1608) and strengthened by a new enthusiasm for city comedy, especially the boy company plays, the real shift of focus has been from the amphitheatre plays to the hall playhouse plays.[20]

Even without Ann Jennalie Cook's demolition of Alfred Harbage's concept of a 'popular' audience at the Globe, this was in some ways bound to be the anti-Harbage or 'coterie' era.[21] His *Shakespeare and the Rival Traditions* (1952) was an awesome extension of his book about Elizabethan audiences, and its analysis of the evidence has lasted much better.[22] *Shakespeare's Audience* (1941) set up as an archetypal theatregoer the London artisan. Harbage's politics were democratic and populist, and he wanted his Shakespeare to be written for industrious workingmen. *Shakespeare and the Rival Traditions* developed the implications of that view by distinguishing two playwriting traditions, one for the populist amphitheatres and the other for the exclusive coteries in the more expensive hall playhouses. One was Shakespeare's, the other was satirical and elitist, inimical to all that Harbage thought Shakespeare stood for. Harbage's position, both as historian of the theatre and critic of the plays, was the dominant one in the

---

[17] Ann Haaker, 'The Plague, The Theater and the Poet', *Renaissance Drama*, NS 1 (1968), 283–306.

[18] G. E. Bentley, 'Shakespeare and the Blackfriars Theatre', *Shakespeare Survey 1* (1948), 38–50.

[19] Glynne Wickham, *Early English Stages, 1300 to 1660*, 4 vols. (London, 1959–81). Volume 5 on 'Plays and their Makers' from 1576 to 1660, is still to be published. Stephen Orgel and Roy Strong, *Inigo Jones: The Theatre of the Stuart Court* (London, 1973).

[20] Gerald Eades Bentley, *The Jacobean and Caroline Stage*, 7 vols. (Oxford, 1941–68), and E. K. Chambers, *The Medieval Stage*, 2 vols. (Oxford, 1903) and *The Elizabethan Stage*, 4 vols. (Oxford, 1923).

[21] Ann Jennalie Cook, *The Privileged Playgoers of Shakespeare's London, 1576–1642* (Princeton, 1981).

[22] Alfred Harbage, *Shakespeare and the Rival Traditions* (New York, 1952); *Shakespeare's Audience* (New York, 1941).

forties and fifties. Since then the shift of focus from populist theatre to coterie theatre has brought about something like a complete reversal of preferences, and indeed of priorities. In the study of the sociology of the theatre this shift went furthest with Ann Cook's *The Privileged Playgoers of Shakespeare's London, 1576–1642* (1981), which in place of Harbage's archetypal workingman playgoer established the typical playgoer as privileged and gentlemanly. Both Harbage's and Cook's studies, in their concern to identify a uniformly typical and unified audience, ignored most of the evidence for diversity and swift change which is emphasized in the more recent *Playgoing in Shakespeare's London*.[23] Taking social sides in this way is one of the more seductive ways of oversimplifying the evidence.

The chief reason for this general shift of focus towards the plays of the hall playhouses is, I suspect, that in the seventeenth century the hall playhouses had all of what academics are likely to regard as the most interesting plays. There were plays written for the boy companies, especially the satirical and parodic plays they staged at Blackfriars between 1600 and 1608; there was Shakespeare's own shift (according to Bentley) from writing for the Globe to writing for the Blackfriars in his last years; and the fact that almost all the new plays were written for the hall playhouses after *The White Devil* in 1611. There was the corpus of Middleton, Chapman, Webster, Beaumont and Fletcher, Massinger and Ford. Against all this the amphitheatres could offer nothing except the old and much-parodied populist favourites of Marlowe, Kyd, and Shakespeare. The hall plays, with their sophisticated theatre of estrangement replacing the amphitheatres' simple theatre of enchantment, also offered scholars vastly more work and more pleasure with their theatrical in-jokes, their webs of satirical allusions, and their intertextual cross-references.

At the same time, study of the plays and their staging at the hall playhouses gained what I think ought to be regarded as an illusory strength from the work done on court staging, both of masques and plays. Because the hall playhouse audience was assumed to be composed largely of the courtiers and the ladies and gentry who went to plays at Court, it was (and is) also assumed, all too easily, that the staging of the plays in the hall playhouses was more like the staging designed for court shows than like the amphitheatre tradition. The masque-like seductions of *The Tempest* have deluded many students besides Ferdinand and Miranda.

In some respects Glynne Wickham's monumental *Early English Stages 1300 to 1660* has been a party to this shift in perspective. Publication of this work began in 1959 and is still not yet complete; this has to be the main reason for not yet pasting a Wickham label over the anti-Harbage label for the period. Wickham's volumes have two massive advantages over the great works of Chambers and Bentley. First, as the product of a single mind, conceiving the whole period as a continuum, they enjoy a cohesion which is not available in the earlier works, even when Chambers's two-volume *Medieval Stage* is tacked on to the four volumes of his *Elizabethan Stage*. Secondly, freed by the existence of Chambers and Bentley from the marmoreal labour of supplying all the factual materials in accessible form, the Wickham volumes can afford to concentrate rather more on their own priorities and their own hypotheses. Wickham is a much more interpretative and more speculative scholar than Chambers. He is manifestly more intrigued and excited by his materials. He may go wrong in his theorizing at times, but the target is always the same, the changing traditions which dictated the staging of plays over a period of more than three hundred years.

---

[23] Andrew Gurr, *Playgoing in Shakespeare's London* (Cambridge, 1987).

Reading through the four books (which constitute three parts) of *Early English Stages* which have so far appeared, it is easy to see why scholarly attention has seemed to retrace the upward social path of the plays from the Robin Hood maygames of the country towns in 1400 to the masques at court in 1640. Playgoing itself did not move up the social scale in these centuries. It was, with some local variations, as much a popular feature at fairgrounds as it was at court throughout the whole period. What the early Stuarts helped to give it was a strengthened social cachet amongst the London gentry and courtiers, so that it came to flourish in print as never before. It is, I think, fair to say that the attention we give to the plays now reflects their availability in print much more than it reflects their currency on English stages. Gerald Bentley's dismissive attitude towards the Red Bull repertory in the later volumes of *The Jacobean and Caroline Stage* reflects the many stock expressions of contempt for the Red Bull players and audiences published by courtly and gentlemanly commentators. But it also reflects the fact that very few of the Red Bull or other amphitheatre plays ever got into print. From the second decade of the seventeenth century publishers were far more ready to claim on their titlepages that a play had appeared at the Blackfriars or Cockpit than that they were the products of the Red Bull or Fortune. Buyers of play-quartos were largely gentry and titlepages advertising what playhouses a play belonged to reflected their interests, which were not expected to be engaged by anything on offer at the amphitheatres. So we, inevitably, tend to follow the gentry interests with the kinds of play we have in our hands.

The chief work which has swum against this current is Robert Weimann's study of the 'popular' dramatic tradition.[24] On the whole it adds little to our understanding of staging that is not also present in Wickham, but it is invaluable in its analysis of the traditions out of which Shakespeare's culture emerged. This is something that cannot easily be done by reading the culture of Shakespeare's afterlife backwards into his plays and his staging.

Preoccupation with the interests of the gentry and the court has not greatly inhibited work on the traditions of staging at the amphitheatres and the halls. Thanks partly to the growth in confidence which Chambers and Bentley have given by their labours, ramified by Wickham's historical sweep, more than ten books on the original staging have appeared in this decade, three of them in 1984 alone. In the main their concern has been to apply the fixities about the playhouses and the consequent deductions about emblematic signifiers to the plays, so cementing the link between the archaeological study of the playhouses and the critical study of the playtexts.[25] More than most areas of current concern, though, studies of the staging seem prone to the danger of presuming that there was a 'typical' pattern. This is not a matter of allocating particular stage directions to particular playhouse structures. We know far too little, for instance, about the differences in staging between the amphitheatres and the halls. The Red Bull, with its 'drum and trumpet' plays, was evidently notable for staging plays with battles, while the Blackfriars preferred wit-combats. But were there no plays with battles in them staged at the Blackfriars? Did Shakespeare's company exclude any presentation of the English history plays, or *Macbeth*, or *Hamlet* with its dangerous duel, from the company's winter repertoire

---

[24] Robert Weimann, *Shakespeare and the Popular Tradition in the Theatre* (London, 1978).

[25] Besides Alan Dessen's *Elizabethan Stage Conventions* listed in note 8, the more rewarding books include David Bevington's *Action is Eloquence* (Cambridge, Mass., 1984); Jean E. Howard, *Shakespeare's Art of Orchestration* (Urbana, 1984); Ann Pasternak-Slater, *Shakespeare the Director* (Brighton, 1982); Warren D. Smith, *Shakespeare's Playhouse Practice* (Hanover, NH, 1975); and John Styan, *Shakespeare's Stagecraft* (Cambridge, 1967).

after 1608? Real fencing matches could take place on the amphitheatre stages, but the hall playhouse stages were much too dimly lit to allow the kind of swordplay popular at the Rose and the Theatre. So what did Shakespeare's company do with their repertoire when they made their annual transfer from the open air to the hall? There is room for much more study about possible variations in the staging of the same plays at different playhouses.

The area which is probably now the most ripe for further study, for several reasons, is the sociology of the theatre. All of Muriel Bradbrook's work, still flourishing fifty-five years after her first book, has justified her own calls in recent years for a shift from the archaeology of the Shakespearian theatre to its sociology. For their own different reasons the New Historians and the New Marxists support that call. The strongest justification of all is the semiotic principle that communication is a web of connections and exchanges within the dynamic entity of author, players, and audience. To a great extent it is the sociology of the Shakespearian theatre which is still the darkest part of the landscape, so it is to be hoped that enough light will come to help the ripening process.

What then, we might ask, is the state of the art now? The concept of the plays not as, or not just as, texts for reading but as scripts for performance has certainly taken a firm hold. Routledge's Theatre Production Studies under the general editorship of John Russell Brown have produced several volumes covering the Shakespearian period. Each one includes a general section on the specific kinds of theatre with which the volume is concerned and then analyses the staging of several plays written for it. Michael Hattaway's contribution proved the value of this approach for the early amphitheatre plays, particularly by its analysis of two Marlowe plays. Peter Thomson did the same, with rather less success, for Shakespeare, and

most recently Keith Sturgess has produced a book about the Jacobean and Caroline 'private' theatres. This last gives some impression of the state of the art, in its strengths and its concomitant weaknesses, as it seems to stand in 1987.[26]

Sturgess's title reflects the current shift of interest from amphitheatres to hall playhouses, though it does not precisely represent his contents. 'Jacobean private theatre' is examined through the staging of three plays at the second Blackfriars, one of which is a Caroline play, plus one play at Court and one masque. There is no analysis of any play staged at the first Blackfriars, Paul's, the Cockpit, or Salisbury Court. Even the Blackfriars instances are confined to plays written for and put on by the King's Company after 1609. Possibly the boy company repertory is being held back for another book in the series, though there is no mention of one in the publicity materials. More likely the choice simply represents the author's preferences (he has directed stage productions of all the plays he analyses, as well as constructing a model of the Blackfriars playhouse). But the preferences themselves are distinctive and say something about current priorities.

One suspects that Sturgess's choice began with the plays themselves, the central trio being *The Tempest*, *The Duchess of Malfi*, and *The Broken Heart*. There are no boy company plays, which might be considered a pity given how much plays like *Eastward Ho!* and *The Knight of the Burning Pestle* can tell about the second Blackfriars before 1608; though it might also imply something about how much more viable the adult company plays from the hall playhouses now are in the theatre than the boy company plays. It might be possible to suspect, even, that Sturgess reflects Bentley's anti-amphitheatre prejudice in the narrowness

---

[26] Michael Hattaway, *Elizabethan Popular Theatre* (London, 1982); Peter Thomson, *Shakespeare's Theatre* (London, 1985); Keith Sturgess, *Jacobean Private Theatre* (London, 1987).

of his perspective. He admits that he finds it difficult to imagine *The Duchess of Malfi* on the Globe stage, despite the claim registered on its 1623 titlepage that it appeared there as well as at the Blackfriars. He says that the Caroline John Ford is a quintessential private-theatre playwright, ignoring his Jacobean writing in collaboration with Dekker for the Fortune and Red Bull. In one breath he echoes Carew's description of the King's Men's acting as natural and unstrained, while contrasting it with the loud delivery at the Globe. It may be unfair to link this prejudice directly with the choice made in the third section of the book, where we are given analyses of the staging of a masque and a play at Court, but it reaffirms the uneasiness generated by the statement that masques had an 'emphatic effect' on the development of British theatre, and the tacit assumption which seems to accompany it, that the private theatres were a step away from amphitheatre staging towards proscenium arch staging.

This last point is inconspicuous in the text of the book, but it is nonetheless influential in its consequences. The perspective or audience-eye-position from which the staging is viewed is placed distinctly in the pit, or at Court at the royal 'state'. Sturgess makes the point that the oblong shape of the Blackfriars shifted the balance of the auditorium away from that of the amphitheatres. Amphitheatre acting took place in the centre of a round, whereas the main body of the audience at the private theatres was grouped in front of the stage. He actually says that the gallants sitting on stage stools 'broke the picture-frame'. His reading of the evidence reflects this presumption. Public theatres like the Hope, he several times contends, were arranged with their audiences on three sides, in an arc of 300 degrees around the stage, whereas the bulk of the Blackfriars audience sat out in front. He does not acknowledge the recently established evidence for the Blackfriars galleries being curved,[27] which would perhaps have emphasized a little

how easy it was for the private stage to appear as if it was the centre of a circular hall, rather than at one end. Compounding this distortion, he ignores the evidence about spectators sitting on the stage balcony, which appears not only in De Witt's Swan drawing of an amphitheatre audience but in what one would have thought was the unavoidable *Roxana* vignette of a private playhouse. There is enough evidence for both amphitheatres and hall theatres to suggest that audiences were in the habit of sitting (or standing) in a complete circle around the players. The only distinct and uniform exception to this rule was at Court. Even there, the chief evidence which exists about the disposition of the various auditoria is for the staging of masques, which uniformly and uniquely required a front-end perspective. Court staging can easily generate misleading impressions about commercial staging in this period. Presumptions based on modern staging and reinforced by knowledge of court staging can consequently become dangerously misleading.

This kind of assumption is not the only regrettable feature of this version of the state of the art in 1987. The book itself could do with sharper editing, of the kind which was routine in Chambers's day. It has dozens of misprints (though I must admit to being disarmed by the description of *The Tempest* 3.3 as having 'maned characters', and by the 'ariel machinery' at Court) and some inconsistent facts (Fitzgeoffery's *Notes* are correctly dated 1617 on one page, but 1620 on another, and Jonson allegedly got into trouble for writing *Westward Ho!*, not its parody). Worse, in terms of modern book design, is that the fashion for using unjustified right margins for indented quotations sometimes makes it unclear whether the passage quoted is verse or prose.

Ultimately, the real problem in a book, and a series such as this, is most likely one of an

---

27 John Orrell, 'The Private Theatre Auditorium', *Theatre Research International*, 9 (1984), 79–94.

excess of enthusiasm. The temptation, and even the need, to identify the precise details of the original staging of these plays would probably be unstoppable even if there were no great impulse from the theatre to rehabilitate the original concept. The plays, when presented as performance scripts, demand that the scholar provides the service of illuminating the staging. The trouble is that the basis for such reconstructions is still so very shaky. Sturgess may err simply out of his proscenium-arch preconceptions when suggesting that the banquet set on the table in 3.3 of *The Tempest* vanishes when it is flipped over by a stage-hand concealed behind the table upstage of the audience. But when he contemplates Prospero's appearance *'on the top'* in the same scene, he is baffled, as we all are. The trouble is that, with his model reconstruction to hand, he is not able to admit it. His answer to the question where 'the top' may be is that it cannot be the stage balcony. Prospero must stand in some place higher up, altogether perhaps twenty feet above the stage. No suggestion about what that place might be is given in the text. The model, shown in two photographs, has a kind of promenade at the same height as the second gallery, above the stage balcony, which is presumably where Prospero is meant to stand. This is pure conjecture, filling the presumed space up to the Blackfriars hall ceiling with guesswork. It fudges the issues both of the construction of the Blackfriars tiring-house front and of the interpretation of stage directions generally. We cannot afford such imprecision, or such overenthusiasm.

One final test-case may serve to indicate the scale of uncertainty that still hangs over the original staging and how little we still have to go on when we try to distinguish between the early staging conventions, basic preconceptions then and now, and the influence of such physical constraints on staging as practical convenience. In Thomas Heywood's amphitheatre play *1 If You Know Not Me, You Know Nobody* the royal throne is needed on stage at the beginning, in the middle, and at the end of the play. We do not know whether it remained on stage in between the three scenes when it was used, or whether it was taken off until the next time it was required. The throne was, of course, a substantial property, including a dais with several steps, the chair of state on the dais, a tapestry or cloth of estate behind the chair, and a canopy over it. In Scene 2 (Malone Society Reprint, lines 45–145) after a formal entry and procession Queen Mary sits on the chair of state:

> By gods assistance and the power of heaven,
> We are instated in our brothers throane.
> (lines 48–9)

In Scene 4, when Mary is joined by Philip of Spain, the players might have used two thrones, though the more mobile Philip could have saved them the trouble by remaining on his feet throughout the scene. In the final scene of the play, Scene 23 (lines 1511–1598), Elizabeth enters formally in procession, described in a long stage direction, which includes this specification:

> *Foure Gentlemen bearing the Canapy over the* Queene, *two Gentle-women bearing up her traine, six gentle-men* Pensioners, *the* Queene *takes state.*
> (lines 1514–17)

There is no doubt about the canonical imagery of royalty used in these scenes and the other processional scenes and dumbshows. Crown, sceptre, mace, and sword are brought on in procession ahead of the monarch, who instates herself on the throne at the end of the procession. Between the processions in Scene 4 and Scene 23, though, only one scene requires the use of a throne. The use in that one scene is so odd that it seems to indicate that the whole apparatus of the 'chair of state' – dais, throne, and cloth of estate – must have been kept on stage throughout the play.

The scene concerned is Scene 12 (lines 899–918) and involves Elizabeth's gaoler in a bit of foolery.

Enter Beningfeild, and Barwick his man.
Bening: Barwicke, is this the chayre of state.
Bar: I sir, this is it.
Bening: Take it downe, and pull of my boots.
Bar: Come on Sir.
              Enter Clowne.
Clowne: O monstrous, what a sawcy companion's this?
   To pull of his boots in the chayre of state,
   Ile fit you a penyworth of it.
Bening: Well sayd *Barwick*, pull knave.
Bar: A ha Sir.
   [*The Clowne pulls the Chayre from under him.*]
Bening: Well sayd, now comes.
Clowne: Gods pity I thinke you are downe, cry you mercy.   (lines 899–911)

I interpret this little piece of horseplay to entail actions rather more discreet than the sacrilege they seem to suggest. When Beningfield says 'Take it downe', Barwick must remove the chair from the dais to stage level, so that Beningfield can sit on it while his boots are removed without actually profaning the sacred throne. According to Sir Thomas Smith it was not the chair itself but the 'cloth of estate' behind the chair which was revered in the absence of the royal occupant. He described the ceremonial doffing of headgear as a ritual which had to be performed not only in the monarch's presence, but in the presence of the cloth when the monarch was not on the throne: '. . . in the chamber of presence where the cloath of estate is set, no man dare walke, yea though the prince be not there, no man dare tarrie there but bareheaded' (*De Republica Anglorum* (1583), ed. Mary Dewar (Cambridge, 1982), p. 88. If Barwick did remove the chair from its position on the dais in front of the cloth of estate, he, of course, made it easier for the Clown to pull it from under Beningfield. That much is clear. What is not clear is where on stage the dais was, nor why the whole chair of state and its apparatus should have sat there for the preceding 600 lines and the following 600 lines of a play lasting 1600 lines, through all of which it was not in use. The casual way Beningfield and his and his man refer to it indicates that it was already on the stage at their entry for them to come across it, and that it was not put out especially for this one short piece of knockabout. The problem which that generates is that if it did remain on stage throughout the play one is made to wonder how the players manoeuvred themselves around it for actions like Scene 3, when a stage direction reads 'Enter Elizabeth in her bed' (line 188), and in Scene 5 when the six commissioners and Elizabeth require a total of seven chairs on stage.

Altogether this play has a number of major processions, one of them by torchlight, one bed scene, several dumbshows, and one scene with a goat. Admittedly the goat is on a string, but it would have consorted even more oddly with the royal throne than Elizabeth's mobile bed if the throne was given the prominence on stage that thrones always have in illustrations of Elizabethan throne rooms. It might have been feasible to ignore the throne, for instance, if it were set back against the tiring-house wall, in front of the discovery space, or even inside it. That would leave ample space on the forestage, and the stage pillars would to some extent mark off the environs of the throne from the forestage area and its activities. But no extant illustration of a real Elizabethan throne on its dais shows it pushed back against a wall, still less screened off in an alcove. It always occupied the central position in the hall, dominating the whole space. The most appropriate position on stage would have been similarly central, midway between the stage pillars, and facing out from the tiring-house front towards the bulk of the audience. There is no way it could have been inconspicuous on the stage, unless it was moved around according to the needs of each scene. And that also makes Beningfield's fortuitous and casual use of it peculiarly difficult to manage. There is plenty of room for conjecture in all of this software about matters of ostensible fact.

THE ORIGINAL STAGING OF *THE FIRST PART OF THE CONTENTION* (1594)

WILLIAM MONTGOMERY

'The usefulness of QI is . . . that it throws light on the theatrical and textual history of Shakespeare's play. It suggests something of the performances . . . for which such a version was provided, and it tells us something of the performances which the actor-reporter had known . . . The stage directions indicate not what the author envisaged but what an actor remembered actually taking place.'[1] Though Harold Jenkins here has *Hamlet* in mind, his observation is valid of all reported texts. A reported text, or 'bad quarto', has as its textual authority not authorial copy, nor authorial copy adapted for use in the playhouse, but an actual production of the play, usually, we suppose, one which has been in performance for some time and has, therefore, been theatrically 'broken in'. An ideal bad quarto would be one which reported with absolute accuracy not a promptbook or any other written document, but what was said and what happened on stage, just as an ideal printed text would be one which reproduced its copy with total fidelity. But this is not an ideal world: reported texts are all mediated not only by the circumstances of their printing, but also by the memories of their reporters. This is at once their theatrical advantage and their textual downfall. A reporter who witnessed – and probably took part in – the performance he reports will recall with sometimes only indifferent accuracy what he heard said, but he will also recall what he saw and what sounds he heard, and he may preserve some of these non-verbal recollec-

tions in his report. So, while all bad quartos are no doubt textually corrupt to the extent that they will not report with consistent accuracy what was said on stage, they may nevertheless often be expected to come closer than authorial texts or even promptbooks to what actually happened in performance.

A bad quarto may, therefore, provide information about the kind of stage its original was performed on; about the minimum cast necessary to perform the play; about the costuming, properties, music, sound effects, special effects, and some of the business employed in the production reported; and, where an authorial text is extant as well, about the kind of theatrical adaptation the play had undergone.

Though editors have made use of bad quartos for details of staging or for selected passages of dialogue (as, for example, in *Hamlet* or *Romeo and Juliet*), scholars have seldom analysed the staging requirements of any particular reported text in an attempt to determine something about its provenance. This is what I propose to do with the 1594 bad quarto of *The First Part of the Contention of the Two Famous Houses of York and Lancaster*.[2]

---

[1] 'Introduction', *Hamlet*, ed. Harold Jenkins, the new Arden Shakespeare (London and New York, 1982), p. 36.

[2] I do not propose here to argue the case for *The Contention* as a bad quarto. I give my reasons for believing it to be a reported text in Stanley Wells, Gary Taylor, John Jowett, and William Montgomery, *William Shakespeare: A Textual Companion* (Oxford, 1987), p. 175.

Two hypotheses have been advanced for the provenance of this text. One holds that it is printed from a report of an abridged touring production[3] (as, for example, appears to be the case with the first editions of *Henry V* and *The Merry Wives of Windsor*[4]); the other, that it derives from a London performance of the play.[5] Which of these hypotheses one accepts has important implications. If we regard Q as a report of a touring production, then we have to accept that it probably reflects the adaptation that a play written for a London theatre would have to have undergone in order to be playable under the more straitened circumstances of a provincial tour. Many of its variations from the authoritative Folio text – particularly cuts and structural rearrangements – would probably have been enforced on it by the circumstances of that tour and could therefore have little claim to authority (though even such a document has textual value, as Gary Taylor has shown of *Henry V*[6]). If, on the other hand, we conclude that the report derives from a London performance of the play, its dialogue and structure may be regarded as perhaps coming close to an authorially sanctioned performing text, and so could be of immense value to an editor. Moreover, which of these hypotheses one adopts will to some extent determine the dating of the report.

The staging requirements one can infer from *The Contention* suggest that the production which this text reports was performed on a fairly well-equipped stage. The play, for example, clearly requires a trap door. In the conjuring scene (1.4/Sc.4) Bolingbroke says as part of the conjuration, 'Send vp I charge you, from *Sosetus* lake, / The spirit *Askalon* . . . *Assenda*, *Assenda*' (lines 501–2, 505);[7] this is followed by the direction, 'the spirit riseth vp' (lines 506–7). At the end of the ensuing supernatural conversation, the direction 'He sinkes downe againe' is followed by Bolingbroke's 'Then downe I say, vnto the damned poule' (lines 518–19). The presence of a trap door

means that the main acting area must have been elevated at least enough to allow access to and operation of the trap. As we shall see later, this platform stage also has to have been large enough to accommodate at least nineteen actors at once. *The Contention*, therefore, was performed on a fairly large platform stage equipped with a trap door.

This platform stage had at least two entryways. Five stage directions refer to this feature: '*Enter at one doore, King* Henry . . . *Enter at the other doore, the Duke of* Yorke' (lines 21, 24); 'Enter at one doore the Armourer . . . and at the other doore, his man' (lines 847, 849–50); 'Enter *Iacke Cade* at one doore, and at the other, maister *Alexander Eyden*' (lines 1927–8); 'Enter the Duke of *Yorkes* sonnes . . . at the one doore, . . and at the other doore, enter *Clifford*' (lines 2061, 2062, 2063); 'Enter at one doore, the Earles of *Salsbury* and *Warwicke* . . . And at the other, the Duke of *Buckingham*' (lines 2084, 2085–6). These directions clearly indicate the presence of at least two entry doors. While there may have been more than two, which either were not used in

3 Madeleine Doran, *Henry VI, Parts II and III: Their Relation to the Contention and the True Tragedy*, University of Iowa Studies: Humanistic Studies, 4 (1928).

4 Gary Taylor, *Three Studies in the Text of Henry V*, in Stanley Wells and Gary Taylor, *Modernizing Shakespeare's Spelling with Three Studies in the Text of Henry V* (Oxford, 1979), pp. 72–111; Gerald D. Johnson, '*The Merry Wives of Windsor*, Q1: Provincial Touring and Adapted Texts', *Shakespeare Quarterly*, 38 (1987), 154–165.

5 Scott McMillin, 'Casting for Pembroke's Men: The *Henry VI* Quartos and *The Taming of A Shrew*', *Shakespeare Quarterly*, 23 (1972), 141–59.

6 Taylor, *Three Studies*, pp. 124–61.

7 All the quotations from *The Contention* are taken from the first quarto edition of 1594; line references correspond to the through line numbers of the Malone Society facsimile of Q1 (*The First Part of the Contention 1594*, ed. William Montgomery, The Malone Society Reprints 1985 (Oxford, 1985)); act-scene references are those of the Complete Oxford Shakespeare and the through-scene numbers are those of the original-spelling version of this edition.

this production or whose use is not clear from the text, this seems unlikely. Each of the five relevant stage directions is in the form 'Enter at [the] one door, [and] enter at the other [door]'; that is, the second door is consistently referred to, when it is referred to at all, not as 'another' door or as one of 'several' doors, but as 'the other door', which suggests that it is the only other door. The platform stage on which the production of *The Contention* reported in the 1594 quarto took place, then, had at least two entrance doors and probably only two.

There is some reason to believe that the stage had a discovery space: 3.2/Sc. 10 begins, 'Then the Curtaines being drawne, Duke *Humphrey* is discoured in his bed, and two men lying on his brest and smothering him in his bed. And then enter the Duke of *Suffolke* to them' (lines 1188–90). Suffolk, after a few lines' conversation with the murderers, tells them, 'Then draw the Curtaines againe and get you gone' (line 1197). The King and others enter, and do not see the bed or Humphrey. Later, however, after the news of Humphrey's death, Warwick says to the King, 'Enter his priuie chamber my Lord and view the bodie' (line 1243), after which is the direction '*Warwicke* drawes the curtaines and showes Duke *Humphrey* in his bed' (lines 1146–7). The point at which the curtains are closed is not specified. The following scene (3.3/Sc. 11) begins, 'Enter King and *Salsbury*, and then the Curtaines be drawne, and the Cardinall is discoured in his bed, rauing and staring as if he were madde' (lines 1437–9). No further references are made to the bed; no further 'discoveries' occur in the text.

It is not necessary to postulate a discovery space for *The Contention*'s original stage on the basis of these scenes; the staging of both can be explained in terms of the already established features of the stage. In fact, two alternative methods of staging present themselves. The less likely requires that the bed itself be brought on stage and identifies the curtains referred to in both scenes with bed-curtains.

By this method the bed would probably have been carried on at the beginning of the earlier of the two scenes and have had its dramatic purpose immediately made clear to the audience by the drawing aside of its curtains and the dumb show of Humphrey's murder. It would be left on stage the whole of this scene and the next, when it would serve as the Cardinal's bed. The area near the bed would thus become in the earlier scene Humphrey's 'privy chamber', as Warwick calls it, and in the later scene, the Cardinal's bedchamber. The audience would have to accept this localization and that the characters on stage see the bed only when their attention is drawn to it, as when, for example, Warwick invites the King to view Humphrey's body (line 1243).

This method of staging these two scenes seems unlikely. In a text remarkable for the detail of its stage directions, it seems significant that no direction refers to the bed being brought on stage. Moreover, the bringing of the bed on stage seems unnecessarily cumbersome.

The presence of two doors, or entryways, to the stage has already been established. Only one of these is required for entrances and exits in these two scenes. An alternative method of staging the discovery moments would have been for one of the two entryways to have been curtained and the bed placed behind this curtain. This seems more in harmony with 'Then the Curtaines being drawne, Duke *Humphrey* is discoured in his bed' (lines 1188–9) and 'then the Curtaines be drawne, and the Cardinall is discoured in his bed' (lines 1437–8) than the bed-on-stage hypothesis, for these directions suggest that the curtains conceal both the character and his bed, rather than the character alone. Of course, this method requires the assumption that at least one entryway was generally visible from the audience. This assumption agrees with what we believe we know of the structure of playhouses in the 1590s and is therefore perhaps easier to make than to assume the presence of a separate discovery space, for which there is little unambiguous evidence, though this remains a possibility. I conclude, therefore, that one of the two entrance doors to the main acting area was generally visible to the audience, was probably located at the rear of the stage, was curtained (at least for these two scenes), and served as a discovery space in these two scenes.

The Contention's original stage had an upper acting area of some sort. In the conjuring scene (1.4/Sc.4) Eleanor says, 'And I will stand vpon this Tower here, / And hear the spirit what it saies to you' (lines 485–6); a line or so later she is directed to ascend: 'She goes vp to the Tower' (line 488). After York and his party have broken in on the conjurers and after he has addressed several lines to Eleanor, who is still aloft, comes the direction, 'Exet Elnor aboue' (line 533). Much later in the play (4.5/Sc.16) comes the final reference to an upper acting area: 'Enter the Lord *Skayles* vpon the Tower walles walking. Enter three or foure Citizens below' (lines 1727–9). A brief dialogue ensues between Scales and the first citizen in which it is made clear that Scales is within the fortifications of the Tower of London. The first citizen says to Scales, 'The Lord Mayor craueth ayde of your honor from the Tower, / To defend the Citie from the Rebels' (lines 1734–5), to which Scales replies in part, 'I am troubled here with them my selfe, / The rebels haue attempted to win the Tower' (lines 1737–8).

We begin with the assumption that we are dealing with the same physical structure in both scenes. Next, we notice that the stage directions in each scene refer to the upper acting area as a tower. This is less probably a description of the upper area's physical appearance, than the reporter carrying over into the stage directions the dramatic function of the upper area in each of the two scenes. In the earlier scene Eleanor calls the upper acting area 'this tower here' (line 485), and as we have seen, in the later scene the upper area is meant to be the walls of the Tower of London.

The upper acting area seems to have had a direct entryway from off stage: this much one can infer from Eleanor's exit, 'aboue' and from Scales's entry 'on the Tower walles'. In both cases the actor involved seems to have been able to move directly between the upper area and off stage without having visibly to ascend or descend. There may also have been some direct means of access from the main acting area to the upper area involving an ascent visible to the audience. Eleanor's going 'vp to the Tower' from the main stage seems to suggest this: if the only access to the upper area were from off stage, one would expect something like 'Exit Eleanor' followed by 'Enter Eleanor aloft'.[8] Therefore, though there is some circumstantial evidence for a direct means of access to the upper acting area from the platform stage – even if no more than a ladder – it is of insufficient strength to warrant our positing the existence of such direct means of access. To explain Eleanor's and Scales's activity in these two scenes the upper area need only have had one point of entry, and one point of entry has already been identified with some confidence: the one that leads directly from off stage. It is simpler to assume the direction for Eleanor's ascent is less precise than it might be – it is not, after all, inconsistent with an off-stage means of ascent.

---

[8] This form of direction, in fact, with regard to Hume's movements, is similar to what one finds in the parallel scene in the Folio (TLN 626–32):

Bullen.   . . . but it shall be convenient, Master *Hume*, that you be by her aloft, while wee be busie below; and so I pray you in Gods Name, and leaue vs.
                    Exit Hume.
Mother *Iordan*, be you prostrate, and grouell on the Earth; *Iohn Southwell* reade you, and let vs to our worke.
              Enter Elianor aloft.

If one accepts with most modern editors that Hume reenters with Eleanor aloft, then one sees that Hume's ascent is noted in the form of an exit direction.

The upper stage need not have been more than several paces wide. This much space, however, would seem to be necessary for Scales to convey the impression of walking on the Tower walls. Once he begins his conversation with the citizens below, he presumably stops walking; Eleanor is mute while aloft, and, her attention fixed with that of the audience on the conjuration below, is presumably motionless until her silent exit, 'aboue'.

Nothing can be said with confidence of the distance between the lower and the upper acting area, that is, of the upper area's height. Were there at some point a normal conversation between a character aloft and one below, one could say that the upper area must not be so high as to render implausible a normal dialogue in what should be interpreted by the audience as a normal tone of voice. An upper acting area four storeys high, to choose an extreme illustration, would make normal conversation between one 'above' and one 'below' appear ridiculous – the disparity between what the audience sees and what it is expected to believe would be too great. But *The Contention* offers no such normal conversation between levels. In each of the two scenes the upper area is clearly identified in the dialogue, and thus to the audience, as a tower – that is, a place of great height. There is no reason to expect dialogue of a conversational tone between characters aloft and below. Indeed, dialogue in raised voices between levels here would seem dramatically appropriate: York, below, to Eleanor on the tower after he has burst in, and between Scales on the Tower walls and the citizens outside the Tower at ground level. Such raised voices would work whatever the upper area's height: if not so high, they would help with the audience's imaginative leap to reconcile what they see and what they are asked to believe; if high, simply to correspond to the physical facts of the stage and the imaginative dramatic moment.

The Contention (if one accepts that, as a bad quarto, it reports an actual production of the play and that its stage directions are, therefore, at least consistent with, if not fully descriptive of, the stage facilities available in that production) seems to have been performed in a space which possessed a raised stage equipped with a trap door; two entryways to this stage, one of which, visible from the audience and capable of being curtained, sometimes functioned as a discovery space; and an upper acting area at least several paces wide with an entryway from off stage and possibly also with a direct means of ascent from the lower, main, stage.

Just as one is able to say something of the minimum stage facilities necessary to perform *The Contention*, one is also able from a close examination of the text to draw some conclusions on the minimum number of performers necessary to enact the play. Before beginning this cast analysis, however, it is interesting first to examine the number and size of parts in the play.

There are no fewer than 117 roles in *The Contention*. This includes both speaking and mute parts, and treats as separate roles choruses and similarly named minor characters who appear at different times – for example, the 'one' who appears at lines 545, 548 (1.4/Sc.4) I consider a different role from that who appears at lines 604–5 (2.1/Sc.5). I presume here, as I do throughout my examination of the cast, that all entry directions are accurate as far as they go, and to these I add only characters whose presence on stage is clear from the dialogue – for example, the blind man's wife in 2.1/Sc.5. I consistently equate 'others' and 'soldiers' and similarly vague indications of number with two, though of course this is only a lower limit and consequently yields in calculation a lower limit for the number of parts in the play.

Of the 117 definite parts, 69 speak and 48 are mute; 4 of the speaking roles are female. The 69 speaking roles vary greatly in length, from only 4 words (the soldier who enters at line

1753) to 1757 words (the King). Though there are 69 speaking parts to the play, 8 of these are dominant. Five parts – the King, Gloucester, Suffolk, York, and Cade – together share 51.4 per cent of the play's dialogue; the Queen accounts for a further 7.2 per cent; and Warwick and the Duchess together, a further 10.3 per cent.

These eight parts, then, occupy a total of 68.9 per cent of the play's dialogue. Cardinal Beaufort's part contains 3 per cent of it; each of the remaining 60 speaking parts contains less than 3 per cent of the play's total dialogue. *The Contention*, therefore, contains 8 principal speaking parts, at least 61 minor speaking parts, and at least 48 mute parts.

Scott McMillin has already investigated the size and nature of the company of actors necessary to perform *The Contention*,[9] and in general he and I approach the problem similarly, differing only in a few details. We both begin by determining which scenes require the greatest number of actors; we agree that the two points of greatest cast-demand come at the change of scenes between line 890 (2.3/Sc.7) and line 891 (2.4/Sc.8), and at the end of the scene which concludes at line 2110 (5.1/Sc.21). McMillin argues that of these two points the former makes the greater cast-demand, which he interprets to be no fewer than 20 actors; he accordingly uses this point as his starting place, takes 20 as the fewest actors capable of enacting the play, and within this boundary casts the play. I, on the other hand, believe that the cross-over between scenes 7 and 8 can be performed by 18 actors and therefore choose as my starting place scene 21, which McMillin and I agree requires at least 19 actors.

Scene 21 opens with York entering accompanied by drum and soldiers (line 1966).[10] Buckingham enters 4 lines later (line 1971). Though just possible – especially in the case of Iden's men and York's soldiers – there is no reason to suppose that any of these roles are doubled with Cade, Iden, or Iden's five men, all of whom exit at the end of scene 20 (line

1965). At line 2000 York's soldiers exit, freeing them for reentry in other roles at the end of the scene. Two lines later the King enters (line 2003), followed 9 lines later by Iden with Cade's head (line 2013). Iden exits 24 lines later (line 2037), freeing him, too, for reappearance as another character at the end of the scene. As Iden exits, the Queen and Somerset enter (line 2038). At this point there are 5 actors on stage: York, Buckingham, the King, the Queen, and Somerset. Somewhere between line 2039, in which the King addresses him, and line 2081, in which the King commands that he be summoned, Buckingham exits. Let us suppose that he leaves at line 2056. Four lines after Buckingham's exit, Edward and Richard are directed to enter at one door with drum and soldiers, and Lord Clifford and his son are directed to enter at the other door, also with drum and soldiers (lines 2061–5). Interpreting, as before, 'soldiers' to mean at least 2 actors, this directs the entry of 8 actors to the already present 4. Salisbury and Warwick enter 18 lines later at one door with drum and soldiers, while Buckingham simultaneously enters at the other, also with drum and soldiers (lines 2084–6). In other words, 7 more actors enter to the already present 12, bringing the total to 19. All exit 23 lines later (line 2110). The following scene opens with the reentry of Somerset and Richard and therefore makes no additional demand on the size of the cast. Since there is ample opportunity (57 lines) for the actors playing York's soldiers at the beginning of scene 23 to double as some of the soldiers who enter with Edward, Richard, and the Cliffords, and since there is also sufficient time (40

---

9 McMillin, 'Casting for Pembroke's Men'.

10 With regard to casting, 'drum' creates some problems. Are we to posit a separate drummer? Or should we assume that one of the characters of whose presence we can be certain also played the drum? Consistent with the 'most economical' approach to the cast, I have adopted throughout this study the second of these alternatives. In the present instance, for example, I assume that one of the soldiers carries the drum.

lines) for the actor playing Iden to double as one of the characters who enter with Buckingham, the 19 actors present on stage at the end of scene 21 are enough to stage successfully the preceding, the whole of the present, and the subsequent scenes. No point in the play requires more than these 19 actors.

The only moment that comes close, as I have said, is the cross-over from scene 7 to scene 8 which I believe can be acted by 18 actors, but which McMillin argues requires a minimum of 20 actors. Before proceeding, then, let us turn to a close analysis of the stage movements of these two scenes: I will make my case for 18 actors and relate McMillin's case for 20.

Scene 7 opens with the entry of the King, the Queen, Humphrey, Suffolk, Buckingham, Cardinal Beaufort, and Eleanor led by officers (lines 802–4). Immediately, York, Salisbury, and Warwick, whose departures had ended the previous scene (line 801), enter to the King and his party (lines 804–5). If we assume that no more than two officers accompany Eleanor, and that both the Queen and Eleanor are played by boys, then at this point there are 12 actors on stage, including two boys. Eleanor, with 'some' (=2), departs 10 lines later (line 816), freeing, as we will see, two of the three for reappearance later in the scene; Humphrey exits 23 lines after their departure (line 839). This reduces the number of actors on stage to 8. Only 7 lines after Humphrey's exit, but 30 lines after Eleanor's and the officers', a group of no fewer than 8 enters (lines 847–51): the Armourer accompanied by at least 3 neighbours (3 speak), and Peter accompanied by at least 3 apprentices (3 speak). This brings the number of actors on stage to 16. All exit 38 lines later, and the scene ends (line 890). The following scene opens with the entry of Humphrey and his men (=2) in mourning cloaks (lines 891–2). Eleanor enters 10 lines later accompanied by the two sheriffs of London, Sir John Stanley, and officers (lines 903–7). A herald who enters 41 lines later (line 949) presents no problems.

Humphrey cannot double as one of the 8 characters who enter at the end of scene 7. He exits just 7 lines before their entry and reappears, at the beginning of scene 8, immediately after their departure. Therefore, though at the end of scene 7 only 16 characters are on stage, Humphrey's inability to double as any of these 16 raises the cast requirement at this point to 17. Similarly, it does not seem likely that Eleanor doubles as one of these 8 characters either. While the boy playing Eleanor might just have time (30 lines) after his exit as Eleanor at line 816 to change into, say, one of the three apprentices, he would not then be able to change back into Eleanor in the 10 lines that would be available to him.[11] Here, then, we probably have another reserved actor who, with Humphrey, exits in scene 7 and only reenters in the same role in scene 8. This brings the cast requirement to 18. The officers who exit with Eleanor can easily reenter 30 lines later as any of the 8 characters who enter at line 847. The demand remains at 18.

This brings us to a consideration of who – if anyone – from scene 7 can play the men (=2) who enter with Humphrey at the beginning of scene 8. We found 18 actors necessary to enact scene 7. Of these, we can eliminate two from consideration: both Eleanor and Humphrey appear on stage with the men in question in scene 8. We are left with the 16 actors who exit at the end of scene 7 and with the choice of either believing, as I do, that two of these can double as Humphrey's men in scene 8, in which case the cast-demand remains at 18, or of doubting, with McMillin, that this is possible, in which case the cast-demand rises to 20.

The objection to this instance of doubling

---

11 Within the body of plays he examines David Bevington notes that costume changes involving a change of sex require far more time than simple male–male role changes. He goes on to observe that male to female changes take longer than female to male ones: *From 'Mankind' to Marlowe* (Cambridge, Mass., 1962), p. 96.

would seem to be that the actors involved have insufficient time to exit, change costume, and reenter as different characters. Immediate reentry in the same role raises no problems; *The Contention* supplies several examples of a character exiting and reentering as the same character with no intervening dialogue or business: York, Salisbury, and Warwick exit at line 801 (the end of 2.2/Sc.6) and are directed to reenter in the opening stage direction of the next scene; twice members of Cade's party exit and immediately reenter (line 1685, 1686–8; 1761, 1762–4); and Somerset and Richard, who enter at the beginning of scene 22, are among the large group that exits at the end of scene 21 (lines 2110, 2111–13).[12] If we can establish that whatever costume change is involved here does not take appreciably longer than the time required for a simple exit and reentry, we can plausibly argue that 2 of the 16 actors who exit at the end of scene 7 can reenter at the beginning of scene 8 as Humphrey's men.

The stage direction at the beginning of scene 8 reads 'Enter Duke *Humphrey* and his men, in mourning cloakes' (lines 891–2). If we imagine these to be fairly full cloaks, covering most of the actor's body, the casting problem would appear to be solved: very little more time would be required by an actor to exit, put a cloak on over whatever costume he was already wearing, and reenter than it would for him simply to exit and reenter. Moreover, we know that two cast members, Humphrey and Eleanor, are already off stage waiting to reenter; they could, if necessary, have the required cloaks ready. This simple costume change would be sufficient to transform two minor characters in scene 7, say the second Neighbour and the third Apprentice, into Humphrey's men at the beginning of scene 8, and could easily be accomplished in the time available. Nineteen actors, then, could enact the play.

Two further points that McMillin makes require attention here. First, he believes four boys necessary to enact the play. However, two boys can carry three of the four female roles in the play, and it is possible that a man – very likely a young man – may have played the fourth. One boy could play the Queen and several minor male characters (e.g. Emmanuel, one of Stafford's soldiers (line 1635), and one of Gough's soldiers (lines 1762–3)); another boy could have played Eleanor, the blind man's wife (assuming the 64 lines between Eleanor's exit at 533 and the wife's entrance at 608 to be sufficient time for the necessary costume change), and several other minor parts (e.g. one of the supernumeraries, or 'others', in the opening direction of 1.1/Sc.1, who exit, at the very latest, at line 178, the largely mute rebel Nick, and one of the mute soldiers who accompany York in 5.1/Sc.21. The actor, whom I envisage as a young man (though this is not necessary), could have played Peter, Dick, Walter, several minor characters (one of the mute officers at line 804, the Heralds (lines 949 and 983), the second murderer (line 1189), one of the mute soldiers who accompany York in 5.1/Sc.21, one of the carriers of Buckingham at the beginning of 5.4/Sc.24, and the witch, Margery Jordan. Perhaps I am in error here, but it seems more sensible to suggest that a man played this presumably old hag than to posit a third boy who would be required only for this scene to play a part which, though visually important, is only some 39 words long. However, for a man to play a female part in the early 1590s would be unusual, and is something for which

---

12 Reflecting as they do theatrical practice, these examples of immediate reentry tend to undermine the so-called 'Law of Reentry' which posits the need for at least ten lines between a character's exit from one scene and his reentry in the scene immediately following. See Irwin Smith, 'Their Exits and Reentrances', *Shakespeare Quarterly*, 18 (1967), 7–16 and John Cranford Adams, 'The Original Staging of *King Lear*', *Joseph Quincy Adams: Memorial Studies*, ed. J. G. McManaway, G. E. Dawson, and E. E. Willoughby (Washington, DC, 1948), p. 323.

there is no clear precedent.[13] If one is unwilling to accept this possibility, then it becomes necessary to posit a third boy. Certainly no more than these three are required.

The second of McMillin's points that I wish to discuss here concerns the rearrangement, relative to the Folio text, of quarto scene 3 which he argues was necessitated by exigencies of the play's casting. The net effect of the revision is to introduce some 40 lines between the exit of the Armourer, Peter, and their guard and the beginning of the next scene. McMillin argues (pp. 147–8) that this was necessitated by the actors playing the Armourer and Peter in scene 3 having to reenter at the beginning of scene 4 as, respectively, Hume and Bolingbroke. I agree that the actors playing the Armourer and Peter probably did double with two of the characters who enter at the beginning of scene 4 and that this very likely was the reason for the revision of scene 3. I do not believe, however, that it is possible to determine which parts in scene 4 they played.

What can we conclude about the text of *The Contention* from this analysis of its original staging? All our findings converge to support the view that this reported text derives from the memory of a London performance. First, the text reports a need for staging facilities of a degree of sophistication almost certainly unavailable in the provinces. T. J. King, in his analysis of 276 plays first performed between 1599 and 1642 – that is, from a period beginning half a decade after the publication of *The Contention* – finds that those plays whose staging requirements are similar to those I conclude are necessary to *The Contention* constitute the smallest and most complex of the four groupings (according to the level of complexity) into which he finds the plays of his period divide themselves.[14] If such complexly staged plays were common, we would be able to say little about whether or not the provincial venues were equipped to handle them; but King demonstrates them to be relatively rare,

and in this rarity I believe we find support for our intuitive presumption that, as a group, these plays were peculiarly London-bound. Second, the size of the cast required to enact *The Contention* – at least nineteen actors – militates against its being a touring company. Bentley's investigations suggest to him that the size of a touring company was usually somewhere between nine and fifteen men.[15] Finally, just as one is able to infer from the text of *The Contention* something of both the minimum staging facilities and the cast necessary to the production reported by this text, one also can say something of the minimum stage properties probably used in that original production. Such an analysis has yielded interesting results, but pertinent to the present enquiry are not so much the kinds and colours of costumes worn, or the number and variety of weapons and other hand-held properties carried, as the bulk or specialized nature of some of the required properties – a bed, two or more cannon, and thunder and lightning – which also tend to support a London production.[16]

We are now in a position to lay to rest the

---

[13] David Bevington notes (in *Mankind*, p. 110) that in *1 Tamar Cam* the actor Thos. Parsons in one scene doubles as Persian and guard (1.4), in another as messenger and guard (3.3), and in still another as nurse and guard (4.1). 'We have here', comments Bevington, 'either a man playing a woman's role or a boy playing a succession of adult roles . . . At any rate, the shift from male to female roles was not unknown.' See also P. H. Parry, 'The Boyhood of Shakespeare's Heroines' (forthcoming in *Shakespeare Survey 42*). Gerald Eades Bentley, however, in *The Profession of Player in Shakespeare's Time, 1590–1642* (Princeton, 1984), pp. 113–14, note 1, gives a cautionary view of men playing female roles.

[14] T. J. King, *Shakespearean Staging, 1599–1642* (Cambridge, Mass., 1971).

[15] Bentley, pp. 184–8. Most of the examples Bentley cites are of touring companies of between nine and fifteen men; there is one of sixteen, and one (to Plymouth sometime in the season of 1619–20) of twenty.

[16] *The bed* is explicitly called for in the opening stage direction of 3.2/Sc.10, 'Duke *Humphrey* is discouered in his bed, and two men lying on his brest and smothering

suggestion[17] that the report from which the 1594 text of *The Contention* was printed was put together from memory after an unsuccessful provincial tour by one or more members of the touring company and thus reflects the sort of abridgement and adaptation that plays underwent during such a tour. Had this been so, the reported text would surely have reflected in its staging the constrained theatrical circumstances of such a tour: it does not. Rather, the text as reported reflects the full staging facilities of a well equipped London amphitheatre or hall playhouse. The text of *The Contention* as it survives in the first quarto certainly may have been put together *for* a provincial tour, but it must have been put together while the London production of the play was still the dominant memory of its reporters – before, that is, a tour forced the company to adapt and simplify the play's staging.

---

him in his bed' (1188–9). A need for bed-clothes, too, is signalled in Suffolk's instruction to Humphrey's murderers to 'see the cloathes laid smooth about him still' (line 1193). The 'the' that precedes 'cloathes' in this line seems to eliminate any ambiguity over whether by 'cloathes' Suffolk means 'garments' (*OED*, 1) or 'bed-clothes' (*OED*, 3). (Had the meaning been 'garment', 'his' would more probably have preceded 'cloathes'.) That a pillow is also required, while probable, is less confidently demonstrated. The bed that is required here, for Humphrey's murder, is also necessary to the next scene, 3.3/Sc.11, for the Cardinal's death. From Vaux we first learn near the end of the present scene that the Cardinal is dying. Among the things Vaux says of the Cardinal is

> Sometimes he cals vpon Duke Humphries Ghost,
> And whispers to his **pillow** as to him,
>
> (1499–1; emphasis mine)

This strongly suggests that the Cardinal, in *his* death scene, has a pillow. Since it is almost certain that the same prop bed was used in both death scenes, it is reasonable to suppose that in both scenes the bed is similarly outfitted. The bed-clothes that I believe are 'laid smooth about' the dead Humphrey probably also cover the dying Cardinal and, similarly, the pillow to which the Cardinal whispers is probably present on the bed at Humphrey's death and may well be the weapon with which Humphrey is smothered (line 1189).

The bed is again specifically called for in the opening stage direction of 3.3/Sc.11, 'the Cardinall is discouered in his bed' (line 1438); the argument for the bed-clothes and pillow is made in the preceding analysis of 3.2/Sc.10.

The cannon are among the certain requirements of 4.1/Sc.12; off stage alarums and the discharge of probably more than one chamber are called for in the opening direction: 'Alarmes within, and the chambers be discharged, like as it were a fight at sea' (lines 1463–4). F. A. Shirley, *Shakespeare's Use of Off-Stage Sounds* (Lincoln, Nebr., 1963), pp. 3–4, points out that cannon are not sounded very often in Shakespeare, and goes on to observe that the 'cannon used by the theatre companies were the type of cast-iron chambers often fired in salute. They were without long barrels or carriages, and were loaded with blank charges and fired on signal.'

The phrase, 'like as it were a fight at sea' (line 1464), suggests that there may also have been, in addition to the cannon, particular sound effects associated with sea battles such as 'the rattling of chains and hawsers, cries of sailors, and the blowing of the boatswain's whistle', all sounds which would have been familiar to an audience of the day as peculiarly maritime. For a discussion of this possibility, see Louis B. Wright, 'Elizabethan Sea Drama and its Staging', *Anglia*, 51 (1927), 104–18, p. 110. On the other hand, this phrase may be the reporter expanding the stage direction for the benefit of a reading audience.

Thunder and lightning are required by 1.4/Sc.4 which contains a straightforward direction for thunder and lightning (line 506); since it relies on the reporter's visual memory of a relatively spectacular effect, I think we must credit this direction as accurate. Thunder could have been mimicked in the theatre by drums or, more likely, by rolling a cannonball on a wooden or metal surface; lightning, probably by the explosion of a squib, a kind of firework.

Ben Jonson, in the Prologue to the revised *Every Man in His Humour* (1604? but possibly 1606 (Chambers, *The Elizabethan Stage*, 4 vols. (Oxford, 1923), vol. 3, p. 360) or 1612 (most recently argued by G. B. Jackson, *Every Man in his Humour*, The Yale Ben Jonson (New Haven, Conn., 1969), pp. 221–39)) refers to the 'nimble squibbe', which Gurr, *The Shakespearean Stage: 1574–1642*, 2nd edn (Cambridge, 1980), p. 170, explains was used to create lightning effects; also, in the Prologue to *Every Man In*, Jonson associates the 'roul'd bullet' with theatrical thunder and the 'tempestuous drumme' with the rumble of an impending theatrical storm. These effects he juxtaposes with a reference to the Henry VI plays and, by so doing, implicitly associates the one with the other. See also Shirley, *Shakespeare's Use of Off-Stage Sounds*, p. 7, notes 15 and 16.

[17] Doran, pp. 154–5.

CHARLES CALVERT'S *HENRY V*

RICHARD FOULKES

It is an orthodoxy of theatre history that from the termination of Charles Kean's management at the Princess's Theatre in 1859 and that of Samuel Phelps at Sadler's Wells in 1862 the English classical theatre endured an interregnum until Henry Irving established his own regime at the Lyceum in 1878.[1] Exceptions are admitted: Charles Fechter's romantic *Hamlet* (1861 and 1864) and the Bancrofts' meticulously researched *Merchant of Venice* (1875), but for sustained continuity in Shakespearian revivals it is necessary to look north to Manchester, where the principles of Free Trade went hand in hand with the flowering of civic pride, creating, in Asa Briggs's words, the 'Symbol of a New Age'.[2] There, in 'Cottonopolis', between 1864 and 1874, Charles Calvert mounted a sequence of twelve Shakespearian revivals, which his friend and coadjutant, the architect Alfred Darbyshire, described, in the language of his profession, as 'the cope-stone of effort . . . placed upon the beautiful edifice raised by the metropolitan managers'.[3]

To Darbyshire, Calvert's productions excelled those of metropolitan managers – principally Charles Kean – being 'carried on in a provincial city in a superior manner, with increased knowledge, and unlimited finance'.[4] But in the arts of the theatre, as in architecture and design, what the provinces claim as the outplaying of the metropolis may amount to no more than the perpetuation of an outmoded style carried to an excess, which would never have been acceptable to more sophisticated tastes.

Charles Calvert's (1828–79) own roots did not lie in the north. He was a Londoner by birth, receiving a good education from his silk merchant father at King's College School. His father was something of a religious zealot, having his son baptized into four different denominations by the age of twelve. Charles developed a strong religious temperament and would have entered the church but for the collapse of his father's business; this obliged the young Calvert to earn his own living, which he did as a traveller for a city firm dealing principally in straw hats. The Bishop of Oxford, apprised of Calvert's condition, was willing to facilitate his admission to a seminary to train as a missionary, but by then

---

[1] George C. D. Odell, *Shakespeare from Betterton to Irving*, 2 vols. (New York, 1920), vol. 2, p. 358. Another provincial exception was Edward Saker in Liverpool; see Russell Jackson, 'Shakespeare in Liverpool: Edward Saker's Revivals 1876–81'; *Theatre Notebook*, 32, 100–9.

[2] Asa Briggs, *Victorian Cities* (Harmondsworth, 1968), pp. 88 ff.

[3] Alfred Darbyshire, *The Art of the Victorian Stage* (Manchester, 1907), p. 32. Darbyshire (1839–1908) was born in Salford, and was a nephew of George Bradshaw, originator of the railway guide. His theatre commissions included the alterations to the Prince's in 1869 and the Lyceum for Irving in 1878.

[4] Darbyshire, *The Art*, p. 32. Darbyshire had seen only one of Kean's Princess's revivals, *Henry VIII* (p. 12), but had seen the Keans in *Richard II* and *King John* when they played at the Theatre Royal, Manchester in 1867.

Charles had become deeply interested in the writings of the Swedish philosopher, theologian, and scientist Emanuel Swedenborg, whose views he felt were incompatible with a religious vocation. An earnest and thoughtful young man, Calvert 'cast about in his mind for a more congenial means of livelihood . . . [and] he resolved to try the stage',[5] considerably influenced by the work of Samuel Phelps at Sadler's Wells. From 1852 he performed in the provinces, making his London debut under Shepherd and Creswick at the Surrey in 1855. The next year he married Adelaide Ellen Biddles (1837–1921), daughter of a provincial actor, whose career had begun as a child actress with the Keans. She proved to be a stalwart partner, both on and off stage.

Calvert's association with Manchester began in 1859 as stage-manager and principal actor at the Theatre Royal. Then in 1864 (Shakespeare's tercentenary year) a group of prominent Mancunians, having raised £18,000, opened the Prince's Theatre of which Calvert was appointed manager, a position he retained, not without some altercations with the proprietors (The Manchester Public Entertainment Company Ltd), until 1875, returning briefly to the Theatre Royal in 1877.

Calvert certainly did not conform to the stereotype of the freewheeling, feckless, and reckless provincial actor. His religious disposition prevailed throughout his life, Darbyshire describing his mind as 'cut in a mystical and logical mould: this mental condition was fostered and cultivated by his study and contemplation of Swedenborg'.[6] Darbyshire's own religious upbringing and convictions were Quaker and, though Calvert did not join the Society of Friends, he cannot have remained totally immune to their pacifist beliefs especially when working with Darbyshire on such a militaristic piece as Henry V.

Socially Calvert became a prominent member of the Manchester community – a supporter of worthy causes; a member of the Brazenose Club; a friend of such local luminaries as the Irelands, Charles Hallé, Tom Taylor, and several Owen's College professors. In his own profession J. L. Toole, Helen Faucit, the Honourable Lewis Wingfield, Arthur Sullivan, Frederick Clay, Charles Reade, and his mentor Samuel Phelps were amongst his circle. Calvert brought to his profession a reflective mind and an elevated sense of purpose. How he would have fared had he essayed a career on the London stage must remain uncertain, but undoubtedly he manifested artistic, managerial, and personal qualities which imbued his achievements in Manchester with more than merely local significance.

Calvert quickly signalled his intentions to the proprietors of the Prince's Theatre, and the playgoers of Manchester, by opening with a production of The Tempest on 15 October 1864. The play was chosen because it was relatively cheap to mount: 'The scenery is merely landscape and seascape, all thoroughly useful for other plays, – only five or six nobles' dresses need to be costly, and no armour is required',[7] so Calvert reassured his directors. The playbill for The Tempest reveals a blend of proven (if somewhat superannuated) London talent, some up-and-coming names, and Calvert's own partnership with his wife. Julia St George, 'Who is expressly engaged for this character', appeared as Ariel, a part she had played for Phelps at Sadler's Wells seventeen years earlier at the rather more appropriate age of twenty-three. At sixty-four years of age J. L. Cathcart was a mature Caliban. The act drop was provided by William Beverley,

---

[5] Mrs Charles Calvert, Sixty-Eight Years on the Stage (London, 1911), p. 19. Mrs Calvert's autobiography and Calvert's DNB entry are the principal sources of biographical information.

[6] Darbyshire, The Art, p. 48. Emanuel Swedenborg (1688–1772) died in London, where the Swedenborg Society was founded in 1810. Swedenborg was reburied in Uppsala Cathedral in 1908.

[7] Mrs Calvert, Sixty-Eight Years, p. 67. The playbill for The Tempest is reproduced on p. 71.

whose long career encompassed most of the leading London theatres; and Walford Grieve, whose family had contributed much to the success of Kean's revivals at the Princess's, was responsible for three of the seven sets. More originally, Calvert used incidental music by the young Arthur Sullivan, music that had first been performed at the Crystal Palace in 1862.[8] Calvert himself took the traditional actor-manager's role of Prospero and Mrs Calvert assumed Miranda.

The Tempest ran until the end of November, terminated only by preparations for the Christmas pantomime. Clearly Calvert's formula was greatly to the liking of Mancunian theatregoers. The London names, albeit somewhat passé, impressed them; the locally well-known partnership of Calvert and his wife reassured them; and the sprinkling of – in this case musical – innovation gratified their capacity for experiment. Alfred Darbyshire hailed *The Tempest* as an 'event . . . of vital importance in the history of our local and national stage. That night inaugurated a policy from which, in spite of adverse criticism and prophecy of financial disaster, Manager Calvert never swerved or departed in the slightest degree.'[9]

Shakespeare was to remain the cornerstone of Calvert's regime at the Prince's; *Much Ado About Nothing* and *A Midsummer Night's Dream* in 1865; *Antony and Cleopatra* in 1866, acclaimed by both Tom Taylor and Helen Faucit; *The Winter's Tale* in 1869; *Richard III* in 1870; more adventurously in 1871 *Timon of Athens*, but using *The Winter's Tale* set for economy and eliminating the women's parts as too objectionable; *The Merchant of Venice* in 1871, four years before the Bancrofts and anticipating them by making a preliminary trip to Venice to collect material, including a gondola; *Henry V* in 1872; *Twelfth Night* in 1873; *Henry IV Part 2* in 1874; and *hors série Henry VIII* at the Theatre Royal in 1877. Of these revivals Alfred Darbyshire was unequivocal in singling out *Henry V* as 'Calvert's

greatest, and I think his favourite, work . . . In this revival he reached the zenith of his managerial efforts . . . he strove to make his revivals educational; consequently he found in "Henry V" an opportunity of illustrating the life and manners of medieval England.'[10] Clearly the antiquarianism of Charles Kean sustained his namesake and, even more intensely, Alfred Darbyshire, who played a key role in that production and, like Kean, duly became a FSA in 1894.

Darbyshire's contribution to the revival was twofold: 'he planned and designed the architectural scenes' and researched and executed all the heraldic devices, 'realising the correct blazon of the arms and banners, as they were actually used on the heroic field of Agincourt'.[11] Equally meticulous attention was afforded to the costumes by the artist and illustrator J. D. Watson, whose 'enthusiasm knew no bounds: he not only made his careful drawings from best authorities, but he would actually cut out the patterns to ensure correctness and exactitude; and personally superintended the works of the costumier'.[12]

Both Darbyshire and Watson would have worked closely with the impressive team of scenic artists assembled by Calvert: Briggs,

---

8 Arthur Jacobs, 'Sullivan and Shakespeare', in *Shakespeare and the Victorian Stage*, ed. Richard Foulkes (Cambridge, 1986), pp. 196–201.

9 Darbyshire, *The Art*, p. 32.

10 Darbyshire, *The Art*, pp. 41–2.

11 Darbyshire, *The Art*, p. 42. Darbyshire's heraldic designs (70 pages) plus 18 watercolour scenic designs are contained in two magnificent souvenir albums, presented by Mrs Calvert to Charles Flower, in the Shakespeare Centre Library, Stratford-upon-Avon. Watercolours of Kean's *Henry V* set designs are located in the Department of Prints and Drawings at the Victoria and Albert Museum; his promptbooks and other material are in the Folger Shakespeare Library.

12 Darbyshire, *The Art*, p. 43. J. D. Watson (1832–1892), born in Yorkshire, trained at the Manchester School of Art. He was the brother-in-law of Birket Foster. Sixty-two costume designs by him are included in the souvenir albums at the Shakespeare Centre Library.

Firth, Hann, Thomas Grieve and his son Walford, F. Lloyds, W. Telbin and his second son William. Frederick Lloyds and the elder Grieve and Telbin had all worked as scenic artists on Charles Kean's production of *Henry V* at the Princess's Theatre in 1859. Few of the Manchester critics were qualified to compare Calvert's production with Kean's and one that did undoubtedly overstated his case: 'he [Mr Calvert] has in no way, so far as we are able to recollect, imitated a single point of the work of Mr Kean'.[13]

Calvert's acting edition of *Henry V* cut 1200 of the Folio's 3380 lines (Kean cut 1550), but this is put into perspective by comparison with the Quarto's 1620 lines.[14] Several of Calvert's cuts coincided with Kean's and others with the Quarto. Calvert's textual sophistication must remain doubtful, but evidence of contemporary scholarly interest in the text is provided by Brinsley Nicholson's editions of the Folio and Quarto versions (both 1875) and parallel edition of the two (1877) for the New Shakespeare Society. A more attractive reference point, as Gary Taylor observes,[15] was the Chronicles upon which Shakespeare drew and to which both Calvert and Kean deferred in a number of cases.

The Chorus presented a particular problem to the illusionistic Victorian theatre, but for both Kean and Calvert its resolution also solved the difficulty of finding a suitable role for their respective wives in a play which lacks any female role of importance. J. W. Cole referred to the 'happy thought of individualising the Chorus as the Muse of History, and of securing the exalted talent of Mrs C. Kean, for the delivery of some of the most impressive poetry of description that Shakespeare ever penned'.[16] Cole regarded Mrs Kean's performance as the 'keystone' of the revival, but Calvert, who had seen the production, had less favourable recollections, as his wife recalled:

the Chorus of Mrs Charles Kean, clad in vivid blue and scarlet, and with her hair done in the Victorian style (from which she never deviated, no matter what part she was playing), had remained in his recollection as unpoetic, and slightly wearisome.[17]

His initial intention was to omit the Chorus (common practice until Macready), next he considered 'a man in the costume of a herald', discarding that in favour of 'a woman with a long flowing dress of white, large white wings, and a golden crown, with an intense white light thrown on her'. This proved to be ineffective and instead 'a scheme of grey was . . . used. Grey rocks, soft silk robes of a pale bluey grey, and a pale-blue light upon Chorus, who stood upon a clump of rocks'.[18] She appeared first as Rumour, adopting sword and shield for Harfleur and garlands of white roses for the concluding royal wedding.

In the view of the *Guardian*[19] Mrs Calvert's 'fire of declamation and classical boldness of gesture' lacked 'the requisite naturalness', but the variations in her attire were recognized as a means of involving Chorus in the different scenes which she described, and Mrs Calvert's uxorial determination to contribute to her husband's venture was commended: 'It seemed to

---

13 *Courier*, 18 September 1872. This and all other reviews quoted, except *Era*, are reprinted in *Shakespeare's Historical Play of Henry the Fifth, As Produced under the Direction of Charles Calvert at the Prince's Theatre, Manchester, September, 1872. Opinions of the Press* (Manchester, 1872).

14 Calvert's acting edition: *Shakespeare's Historical Play of* HENRY THE FIFTH *Arranged for Representation in Five Acts by* CHARLES CALVERT *and Produced under his Direction at the Prince's Theatre, Manchester, September 1872* (Manchester, 1872). Charles Kean's acting edition: *Shakespeare's Play of* KING HENRY THE FIFTH *Arranged for Representation at The Princess's Theatre, with Historical and Explanatory Notes, by Charles Kean, F.S.A.* (London, 1859), reprinted with an introduction by John Russell Brown (London, 1971).

15 Gary Taylor, ed., *Henry V* (Oxford, 1982), p. 48.

16 J. W. Cole, *The Life and Theatrical Times of Charles Kean*, 2 vols. (London, 1859), vol. 2, p. 342.

17 Mrs Calvert, *Sixty-Eight Years*, pp. 137–8. A photograph of Mrs Calvert as Chorus appears opposite p. 137.

18 Mrs Calvert, *Sixty-Eight Years*, p. 139.

19 *Guardian*, 18 September 1872.

us as if in doing what she had to do she was activated by the wish to contribute her full share to the success of the play, and she succeeded to admiration.'[20]

In her first speech Mrs Calvert fared worse than Mrs Kean, losing lines 9–18 ('this unworthy scaffold', 'on your imaginary forces') and the concluding two lines. Both Kean and Calvert cut 1.1, for which they could have claimed the validation of the Quarto; instead the action got underway with 1.2 with predictably heavy cuts of the Salic Law debate. Somewhat surprisingly, in view of the interpretations he developed, Calvert followed Kean in cutting Henry's anticipation of 'many a thousand widows' (line 284) having cause to curse the Dauphin's scorn.

In both acting versions 2.1 and 2.3 were combined as 1.2, but Kean's cuts (as with the 'Eastcheap' characters generally) were much more extensive. Of Calvert's cuts the most significant were the Hostess's 'the King has killed his heart' (2.1.84) and Nim's 'The King hath run bad humours on the knight' (2.1.116), the excision of which (for which the Quarto can be invoked) assist a more sympathetic portrayal of the King. Perhaps because of these cuts the Hostess's 'necrologue' on Sir John was deemed 'unaccountably flat' in the performance by Mrs Harker, an old Manchester favourite, though new to Calvert's company.[21] Calvert followed Kean and earlier precedent in concluding the scene with the Boy's (Miss Julia Stalman) speech 'As young as I am' (3.2.29).

The second Chorus speech came next, immediately preceding the conspiracy scene (Calvert's 1.3, Shakespeare's 2.2), thereby enforcing the link between Chorus's exposition of 'three corrupted men' (2.0.22) and their ensuing appearance, without the diversion to Eastcheap. Charles Kean had introduced a tableau 'representing the three conspirators receiving their bribe from the emissaries of France' (Kean's acting edition of *Henry V*, p. 24), but although Calvert used a tableau to great effect elsewhere, he eschewed such an obvious illustration here. He also departed from Kean in the setting for the conspiracy scene, which Kean had located in the 'Council Chamber in Southampton Castle'. Instead Calvert afforded the Grieves even greater scope by locating the action at 'THE BEACH AT SOUTHAMPTON. THE ENGLISH FLEET AT ANCHOR', thereby giving literal immediacy to King Harry's: 'Now sits the wind fair, and we will aboard' (2.2.12).

The Grieves, experienced hands in such matters, based the design upon the historical descriptions of ships culled from the archives by Calvert and his aides:

Mr Grieve's attempt to convey an accurate idea of the clumsy, high-pooped, but picturesque vessels that were moored at Hampton ready to convey Henry and his troop to the French coast, is highly successful and the landscape is introduced with a power that no artist can better wield. The Isle of Wight, we presume, with its Needles, is shown in the distance, and the observer loses sight with regret of a very fine display of scenic art.[22]

Fine though the scenic display was it did not detract from what one critic termed the 'judicious insight' of Calvert's performance: 'No one would mistake the royal indignation for personal vindictiveness. The King feels the State injured, not the man, and it is possible to observe even a touch of pity for the wretched conspirators beneath the stern and fixed resolution of the monarch.'[23] Another critic commended the contrast between 'the tone of melancholy sadness' with which King Harry rebuked Scroop (2.2.91) and his 'natural and unconstrained' delivery of 'Now lords for France' (2.2.179).[24] Already Calvert's delineation of Harry was revealing a reflective quality

[20] *Freelance*, 21 September 1872.
[21] *Guardian*, 18 September 1872.
[22] *Courier*, 18 September 1872.
[23] *Examiner and Times*, 18 September 1872.
[24] *Salford Weekly News*, 28 September 1872.

upon which he was to build as the play progressed.

Calvert's second act began with Shakespeare's 2.4 and, like Kean, he could not resist a footnote appealing over Shakespeare's head to the Chronicles, drawing attention to the French King's insanity, which the dramatist had chosen to disregard. Nevertheless F. Haywell as the French King, a part he had played for Phelps at Sadler's Wells some twelve years earlier, turned in a judicious and dignified account of the character 'with a force and emphasis that appear to be warranted by the text, though history suggests his incompetency to vigorously direct his affairs'.[25]

Mrs Calvert reappeared as Chorus to transport King Harry, army, and audience alike to France, though forbearing to exhort the latter to 'eke out our performance with your mind' (3.0.35). The ensuing siege of Harfleur was a celebrated high point of all nineteenth-century productions of *Henry V*, Macready's and Kean's in particular, and yet it was in these scenes that Kean's filleting of the text sank to its lowest depths. Kean's version jumped from 'Once more unto the breach, dear friends' (3.1.1), which he reduced from thirty-four lines to eighteen, straight to 'How yet resolves the Governor of the town?' (3.3.84), similarly cut by thirty lines. In comparison Calvert's treatment of the Harfleur sequence was relatively restrained textually and particularly interesting interpretatively.

The Victorian theatre's preoccupation with antiquarianism is often equated with a total inability to make links between contemporary events and Shakespeare's plays. But in 1872 not even the most blinkered antiquarian could have been unaware of the parallels between recent events and King Harry's expedition to France. The slender pretext upon which Bismarck induced Napoleon III to declare war has echoes of the Salic Law debate, but more significantly the Franco-Prussian war was characterized by sieges of considerable duration and great deprivation, first of Metz, then

Orleans, and finally, and most brutally, Paris. The British newspapers and illustrated journals kept the public well informed on these events, which were swiftly given dramatic expression in the theatre of the day. Tom Robertson's last play *War* (St James's Theatre, 3 February 1871) is an example of a contemporary drama on the subject, which, as Martin Meisel points out, used Millais's painting *The Black Brunswicker* for its principal situation.[26] The affinity between the theatre and painting in the realization of events of the Franco-Prussian war is further evidenced by a vogue for tableaux depicting incidents from, or associated with, the war which were mounted at theatres across the country.

Meisel (p. 48) cites a series of Illustrative Tableaux entitled *The Dove and the Olive Branch* at the Theatre Royal, Dublin on 27 February 1871. Earlier that month (6 February), as Darbyshire recounts, Calvert himself 'conceived the idea of Stage Tableaux or living pictures, which should illustrate the horrors of war, the sufferings entailed and the blessings of peace', the final tableau of which was entitled 'THE DOVE and THE OLIVE BRANCH'.[27] The individual tableaux in the two series differ in all but two cases ('Summoned by the War' and 'Another Sortie'). Interestingly two of Calvert's tableaux ('War' and 'Peace') were described as 'After Landseer' and constitute further evidence of the theatre's propensity to create stage-pictures based on original paintings.

Another instance of theatrical concern for the victims of the Franco-Prussian war was an amateur production of *Twelfth Night* in Newcastle-upon-Tyne arranged by Calvert's associate J. D. Watson in aid of the fund for victims of the war, for which Calvert's own tableaux raised £300. Although Darbyshire gave full credit for the tableaux initiative to

---

25 *Era*, 29 September 1872.
26 Martin Meisel, *Realizations* (Princeton, 1983), p. 358.
27 Darbyshire, *The Art*, p. 50.

Calvert, the architect's Quaker convictions were evidently influential: 'the proceeds, through Mr Darbyshire's influence, were handed over to the fund promoted by the Society of Friends'.[28] A man of Calvert's innate sensibility, whose awareness of the horrors of war had been raised so recently by the Franco-Prussian hostilities, was not going to present a simplistically heroic interpretation of King Harry's expedition to France, least of all the fate threatened the besieged citizens of Harfleur.

In contrast with Charles Kean's single conflated Harfleur scene Calvert presented three different locations. His 2.2 'THE ENGLISH ENTRENCHMENTS. WITHIN BOWSHOT OF HARFLEUR' by the Grieves, for an almost uncut (save 'now attest / That those whom you called fathers did beget you') rendition of 'Once more unto the breach' (3.1.1ff.); his 2.3 'THE NEIGHBOURHOOD OF THE MINES. THE DUKE OF GLOUCESTER'S QUARTERS' by Briggs for Shakespeare's 3.2; and 'THE SIEGE OF HARFLEUR. AT THE BREACH. SIGNS OF A SEVERE CONFLICT', again by the Grieves, for Henry's ultimatum to the Governor (3.3.84ff.).

Like Kean, Calvert prided himself on the marshalling of his supernumeraries, but in these scenes he exacted from them not merely precision, but also a realism grounded in truth and sympathy: 'the English soldiers have suffered more than one repulse and hesitate to renew the assault'.[29] King Harry's mettle was severely tested as he exhorted his 'jaded army' to assault the breach once more. The Grieves's set skilfully offset the noise and tumult of the hesitant English troops in the foreground with the 'quiet repose of the distant sea whose surface glistens in the midday sun'[30] and the anchored ships which had brought them thither. The retention of Shakespeare's 3.2, particularly since it lacked the Boy's deflating speech 'As young as I am' (3.2.29), already transposed to 1.2, heightened the human predicament of the English soldiers.

King Harry's ultimatum to the citizens of Harfleur is generally regarded as a barometer of how sympathetically he is being portrayed. Any line after the opening nine, save the last two, can be expunged by deference to the Quarto and no doubt the excision of the most extreme threats would have been in tune with Victorian susceptibilities. To his credit Calvert cut only nine lines (3.3.98–104; and 125–6) and rendered the remainder with such conviction that the horrors in store were powerfully impressed not only upon the inmates of Harfleur, but also the audience, many of whom must have found themselves recalling reports of the recent sieges in the Franco-Prussian war. It is a measure of Calvert's performance that the retention of so much of King Harry's ultimatum did not remove sympathy for him, but revealed his earnest desire to save the citizens of Harfleur from such extremities. Calvert's second act concluded with Shakespeare's 3.6 enforcing Harry's punishment of Bardolf with a Chronicle footnote on the King's scrupulous treatment of the French people and cutting the last three lines to end on 'We are in God's hand, brother, not in theirs' (3.6.169), a sentiment with which Calvert's personal religious convictions no doubt accorded.

Calvert's third act opened with the fourth Chorus ('Now entertain conjecture of a time'), omitting not only Shakespeare's redundant apologia 'four or five most vile and ragged foils' (4.0.50), but all of the concluding seventeen lines including the sympathetic description of King Harry himself 'A largess universal, like the sun' (4.0.43). This may be explained partly by the transposition of the scene in the French camp (3.7) to follow Chorus as 3.1 – 'THE FRENCH DAUPHIN'S TENT. NEAR AGINCOURT (NIGHT)', Calvert siding with the Folio against history and the

---

[28] *Manchester Weekly Times*, 17 December 1897. Darbyshire was turned out of the Society of Friends in 1879.

[29] *Freelance*, 21 September 1872.

[30] *Salford Chronicle*, 21 September 1872.

Quarto by having the Dauphin present at Agincourt, as even the history-conscious Charles Kean had done.

Calvert was restrained in his cuts of the eve of Agincourt scene (his 3.2, Shakespeare's 4.1), those made serving to play down any aspersion upon the ordinary soldier (4.1.154–75) including 'all unspotted soldiers', lines 159–60, and 'The slave . . . in gross brain', lines 278–9. Calvert's own performance here was uniformly acclaimed:

We must confess, however, to have liked Mr Calvert best in the night scene before the battle of Agincourt – the finest passage, perhaps, in the entire play, upon which he seems to have bestowed peculiar care and study. The varying mood of the care-oppressed monarch was represented with a fine free play of elocution and of action, and the splendid soliloquy in which he sums up the controversy between himself and two representatives of his army as to the responsibilities of warring monarchs, and finally appeals to the God of Battles, was an effort of declamation worthy of the subject. In this scene fortunately the King was thoroughly well supported, particularly by the two soldiers Williams and Bates – Mr Chapman and Mr Dixon.[31]

As with his tableau 'The Dove and the Olive Branch' Calvert combined his sympathy for the humbler combatants of war with his skill in picture-making, his pose for 'Upon the King' (4.1.227) reminding one critic 'of a famous picture of Frederick the Great'.[32] Music – solemn chanting – and lighting – the gradual break of day – also served to enhance the effect.

The action reverted to the Dauphin's tent for 3.3 (Shakespeare's 4.2) before moving to 'THE ENGLISH POSITION AT AGINCOURT' by Telbin Jr. Henry's Crispian speech (4.3.18) shed eighteen lines leaving, nevertheless, 'a fine scope for careful and good acting, and the half reproachful yet sanguine and vigorous answer of the King, is one of the gems of the play to which Mr Calvert did ample justice'.[33] Calvert retained Pistol's encounter with the French soldier (his 3.5, Shakespeare's 4.4) with

its important pointer to the boys left guarding the baggage (4.4.70–3), with all of which Kean had dispensed.

Like Kean, Calvert inserted a footnote into his printed text quoting Chronicle accounts of Henry's engagement with the Duke of Alençon (which, in the play, is only alluded to: 'When Alençon and myself were down together' (4.7.152)), developing the incident into a major tableau (illustration 1) encapsulating the whole of the battle of Agincourt:

an elaborate tableau, which fitly represents the Battle of Agincourt, where horsemen and footmen of the opposing hosts are inextricably mixed together in deadly conflict. There is no swaggering attempt to represent the dealing of actual blows, which often converts a bloody tragedy into an amusing burlesque: but a picture in still life is presented on a crowded stage of the very death grapple of two hostile armies – a picture so telling and effective, that the audience demanded its repetition thrice.[34]

Manifestly Calvert's experience in the previous year of bringing home the horrors of war through the tableau form stood him in good stead here. The audience's enthusiastic response owed as much to patriotism as to aesthetic appreciation: 'This spirit-stirring scene appeals to our national feeling . . . rejoicing in victory crowning the English arms'[35] and for all his apparent distaste for war Calvert was not above weighting the odds in King Harry's favour. This he achieved by a transposition (in his 3.7) which has tempted successive interpreters of King Harry: he inserted Fluellen's 'Kill the poys and the luggage! 'Tis expressly against the law of arms' (4.7.1–2) to precede Harry's 'Then every soldier kill his prisoners' (4.6.37), thereby providing justification for what otherwise appears

[31] *Examiner and Times*, 18 September 1872.
[32] *Guardian*, 18 September 1872.
[33] *Salford Weekly News*, 28 September 1872.
[34] *Examiner and Times*, 18 September 1872.
[35] *Salford Chronicle*, 21 September 1872.

1   *Henry V*. Prince's Theatre, Manchester, 1872. Battle of Agincourt: Tableau

to be a gratuitously ruthless act. Calvert's skill in striking the required tone here is evident: 'by sarcastically laying the stress on the word soldier in the order – "Then every *soldier* kill his prisoners", he makes the King and the audience at once draw a distinction between a useless massacre such as the French have committed, and a necessary military measure such as the King commands'.[36]

Harry's preoccupation with the victims of war prevailed with the return of the French herald, Mountjoy (Calvert's 3.8, Shakespeare's 4.7.66):

perhaps the finest example of his due observance of the comparative weight of conflicting emotions is when the King is mourning over the dead bodies of York and Suffolk. Instead of violently starting or standing on royal dignity, Mr Calvert delivers his lines 'How, now! What means this herald?' in tones of sadness still bending over the bodies of his friends. The grief is too profound to be suddenly checked, and the actor's self-restraint considerably increases the pathetic interest of the incident.[37]

A lighter note intervened with the resolution of the 'glove' episode before the scene, which absorbed Shakespeare's 4.8, ended with Harry's command for *Non nobis* and *Te Deum*: 'All Kneel and Join in the Song of Thanksgiving'.

The spirit of Charles Kean reasserted itself in Calvert's Act 4 in which the Chorus prefaced the 'HISTORICAL EPISODE' of Harry's return to London (illustration 2). J. W. Cole acknowledged that for Kean: 'The success of a somewhat similar episode in "Richard the Second", undoubtedly suggested the idea . . .' but, instead of the double focus of the usurping and usurped monarchs 'In "Henry the Fifth" we have the triumph of a popular sovereign, unmingled with painful associations.'[38] Although the set by Hann was highly imitative of Kean's, and Calvert's acting edition followed Kean's verbatim, the atmosphere created was by no means 'unmingled with painful associations'. Such was the rather

---

[36] *Guardian*, 18 September 1872.
[37] *Examiner and Times*, 18 September 1872.
[38] Cole, *Life and Theatrical Times*, vol. 2, p. 346.

2 *Henry V.* Prince's Theatre, Manchester, 1872. Historical Episode: Procession

muted response of some of the crowd (numbering 300) to King Harry's return that one observer speculated that they were either 'faithful adherents of Richard the Second . . . [or] members of the peace party'.[39] In Calvert's production the EPISODE was no indulgent, thoughtless escape into jingoism, but a judicious blend of rejoicing and sorrow. Thus the returning soldiers were 'war and weatherworn veterans' and 'A tragic interest of the most touching nature is given to the scene by the introduction of groups of anxious women [including the Hostess], who scan the faces of the returned warriors, to distinguish, if possible, a husband, son or brother'[40] – see the fainting female figure in the bottom-right-hand corner of illustration 2. Again Calvert had succeeded in enforcing a contemporary awareness: 'In those days when there was no telegraph or penny post to communicate to the anxious relatives of soldiers . . . no alternative was left but to await for the return of the army.'[41]

Nevertheless nothing could be permitted to cloud the brilliance of the play's ending, which Calvert contrived with stunning scenery and textual dexterity bordering on deviousness. Imaginatively he cast two French actresses, the Mlles Legrand as Princess Catherine (Eugenie) and her attendant (Louise), but delayed their appearance until the final act, which began with the English lesson (Shakespeare's 3.4). One critic doubted, patronizingly, whether the lesson conveyed 'as much linguistic knowledge to the gallery as it is supposed

---

[39] *Examiner and Times*, 18 September 1872.
[40] *Weekly Times*, 21 September 1872.
[41] *Salford Weekly News*, 21 September 1872.

3   *Henry V*. Prince's Theatre, Manchester, 1872. Interior of the Cathedral of Troyes

to furnish to the Princess herself'[42], but this piece of cosmopolitan casting was generally welcomed. Catherine's far-sighted interest in the English language was soon overtaken by the appearance of King Harry and her father with their respective attendants (Shakespeare's 5.2).

Their romantic entente was interrupted at 5.2.270 to revert to the leek-eating scene (Shakespeare's 5.1) between Fluellen and Pistol shorn of its last twenty lines. Although J. D. Stoyle as Fluellen and Wyke Moore as Pistol were commended for the genuine comedy of this scene, neither they nor their audiences can have been under any illusion that their function was primarily to make time for

the transformation of the scene to the Grieves's surpassing achievement, 'INTERIOR OF THE CATHEDRAL OF TROYES':

The final scene transcends description . . . The interior of the edifice disclosed to view, affords the audience a conception of the grand cathedral, with its stately pillars and noble architectural details, lofty in its height and expansive in its breadth and depth . . . The vastness of the interior is so apparent and the perspective is so effective that the scene realises the conception of the noblest productions of architectural genius that are to be found in the finest continental cathedrals, and fittingly closes the

[42] *Guardian*, 18 September 1872.

latest creation of Mr Calvert's Shakespearian re-vivals.[43]

Faced with such visual delights few members of the audience were likely to unravel the intricacies of Calvert's text: starting with Queen Isabel's 'So happy be the issue, brother England' (5.2.12–20) and King Harry's response 'To cry amen to that, thus we appear', lurching to the French King's 'We have consented to all terms of reason' (line 325); combining Harry's lines 352–3 and 365–9 into a single speech and appropriating the Queen's 'God, the best maker of all marriages' (lines 354–63) for her husband, before concluding with a resounding 'Amen' from all concerned.

Calvert's *Henry V* was reviewed almost exclusively in the local Manchester press, which inevitably displayed a measure of loyalty, claiming national indeed international importance for it. The latter was in due course fulfilled when, after seventy-six performances in Manchester and some in Birmingham, the whole production was bought by the New York management of Jarrett and Palmer. The production enjoyed a tremendous success in New York, where the part of Henry was assumed by George Rignold, who toured it all over the world, arriving at London's Drury Lane in November 1879.

Such a prolonged and widely travelled success, excelling Charles Kean's on both counts, undoubtedly lends substance to Alfred Darbyshire's claims for it.[44] That is not to deny Calvert's artistic debt to Kean in particular for the pervading antiquarian style, the treatment of Chorus, and the interpolated episode of Henry's return to London. But Calvert outplayed even his mentor in the attention accorded to heraldry by Darbyshire and the expansiveness of the settings, notably those by the Grieves for The Beach at Southampton and the Siege of Harfleur. For all its shortcomings Calvert's acting version was superior to Kean's on every count, preserving more of the text and allowing greater prominence to supporting roles, not least the East-cheap characters. However, Calvert's greatest achievement lay in the sensitivity of his interpretation of the play and its principal protagonist, infusing such key scenes as the siege of Harfleur and the eve of Agincourt with his own contemplative turn of mind and awareness of contemporary events.

In an address given at the Calvert Memorial production of *As You Like It* in 1879, the actor's old friend H. M. Acton wrote:

But none who Calvert knew
Will doubt his place amongst the foremost few.[45]

That place rests principally upon his *Henry V* and, weighed in the scales of theatre history, it is both deserved and assured.

---

[43] *Salford Chronicle*, 21 September 1872.

[44] Kean's production ran for eighty-four performances at the Princess's. It cost £3,000 to mount. The cost of Calvert's production is not known, but most likely at least equalled his £4,000 on *Richard III*. Seat prices at the two theatres were similar, the Dress Circle being 5s. in each case.

[45] Darbyshire, *The Art*, p. 63.

HAMLET, AN APOLOGY FOR ACTORS, AND THE SIGN OF THE GLOBE

RICHARD DUTTON

The question of whether the first (1599) Globe theatre had a sign, and if so what it showed, is one that has teased scholars for some time. Sir Edmund Chambers set a tone of scepticism when he concluded his account of the Globe with the comments: 'Malone conjectured that the name "Globe" was taken from the sign, "which was a figure of Hercules supporting the Globe, under which was written *Totus mundus agit histrionem*". I do not know where he got this information.'[1] Ernest Schanzer demonstrated that Malone in fact got his information from the great Shakespearian scholar, George Steevens, who in turn possibly got it from the antiquarian William Oldys (1696–1761), which does not establish it as fact but at least takes it out of the realm of pure conjecture, where Chambers seemed to imply that it belonged.[2] We do know that other contemporary playhouses boasted such signs. Johannes de Witt noted in 1596 that the two 'more magnificent' of the four theatres he saw around London were sited south of the Thames 'and from the signs suspended before them are called the Rose and the Swan'.[3] And a character in Thomas Heywood's *The English Traveller* (c. 1627, printed 1633) comments:

> I'le rather stand heere
> Like a Statue, in the Fore-front of your house
> For ever; Like the picture of Dame Fortune
> Before the Fortune Play-house.

Given the dating, the reference is to the second Fortune theatre, built to replace the one which burned down in 1621; it is perhaps reasonable to assume that this feature emulated something similar in the original, which of course was substantially modelled on the Globe, but we cannot be sure. J. C. Adams was, to the best of my knowledge, the first to mention the lines of an anonymous elegy on Richard Burbage in connection with the sign of the Globe, where his sad companions are bid:

> Hence forth your wauing flagg, no more hang out
> Play now no more att all, when round aboute
> Wee looke and miss the *Atlas* of your spheare.[4]

It is, of course, entirely plausible that there should have been some confusion between Atlas and Hercules in this connection. Again, given the date this would presumably relate to the second (post-1613) Globe and can only count as circumstantial evidence of something similar in the original. Ejner J. Jensen subsequently suggested there was an allusion to the sign of the Globe in the Induction to Marston's *Antonio and Mellida* (c. 1599–1600), where the Children of Paul's mock the preten-

---

[1] *The Elizabethan Stage*, 4 vols. (Oxford, 1923), vol. 2, p. 434.

[2] 'Hercules and His Load', *Review of English Studies*, NS 19 (1968), 51–3.

[3] Quoted thus, in his own translation, by Joseph Quincy Adams in his *Shakespearean Playhouses* (London, 1920), p. 167.

[4] J. C. Adams, *The Globe Playhouse*, 2nd edition (New York, 1961), p. 31.

sions of those who behave 'as if Hercules / Or burly Atlas shoulder'd up their state'.[5] Suggestive as all this evidence is for the existence and nature of the sign, it is all either inferential or at one remove.

To compound matters, it is far from clear cut what we are actually talking about in referring to the 'sign' of the Globe. J. C. Adams briskly asserted that: 'In common with other playhouses of the same type, the Globe had a sign prominently displayed over the main entrance' (p. 31). He cites de Witt on the 'signs [intersignia] suspended before' the Rose and Swan as authority for this, but that is not exactly what the Dutchman said. Moreover, most scholars now think there were *two* general entrances to the Globe, not just one.[6] Irwin Smith went so far as to offer a possible reconstruction of what Malone described, working on the reasonable but unsupported assumption that it was analogous to an inn-sign.[7] The allusion to the sign of the second Fortune in *The English Traveller* makes it very clear that it was a prominent feature and very probably near an entrance; 'picture' sounds conclusive until we remember that it could also mean 'statue' or 'image' (like 'the Queen's picture' in *The Winter's Tale*) and, looking at the context, Heywood might very well have had something like that in mind. But there is no way of knowing how unusual that might have been. The best documented means of advertisement and identification used in the Elizabethan theatres were the flags that flew above them during performances – something shown in many of the otherwise sparsely-detailed contemporary pictures. The most detailed of all such pictures, the de Witt drawing of The Swan, for example, clearly shows a swan on the flag flying there. Indeed, in Elizabethan usage, a flag might well itself have been described as a sign (ensign) and have given rise to the tradition reported by Steevens, without there ever having been an architectural feature as such.[8] So, while there may well have been a prominent picture,

statue, or carving outside the theatre, it is not essential to establish its existence in order to authenticate the tradition of the 'sign' of the Globe. What we need to consider here is the evidence for the nature of the emblem, almost certainly on the flag, if anywhere, and possibly elsewhere too.

There are, however, problems about what the sign as reported would *mean* if it did exist. Schanzer himself, for example, remained sceptical about the tradition, even though he was able to give it more substance, because he saw no link between the picture and the motto, and because 'a picture of Hercules carrying the terrestrial globe offends against both mythology and common sense' (p. 52). There is no problem about Hercules substituting for Atlas, since it is established in the mythology that he did so do in pursuit of the golden apples of the Hesperides; equally, it is understandable that some of the contemporaries quoted above might have been a bit confused about this. But Schanzer assumed (as most people do) that 'the Globe' was the terrestrial globe rather than the celestial one, and that it was illogical for the earth-bound Hercules to be supporting the earth itself. In fact, as he demonstrated himself, there was already by the late sixteenth century an iconographic tradition of depicting Atlas, if not Hercules, bearing the earth rather than (as in the myths) the heavens. So, while

---

[5] 'A New Allusion to the Sign of the Globe Theater', *Shakespeare Quarterly*, 21 (1970), 95–7.

[6] See, for example, Richard Hosley on 'The First Globe Playhouse (1599)', in J. Leeds Barroll, Alexander Leggatt, Richard Hosley, and Alvin Kernan, *The Revels History of Drama in English*, vol. 3: 1576–1613 (London, 1975), 175–96, p. 177.

[7] *Shakespeare's Globe Playhouse* (New York, 1956), pp. 50–1.

[8] See C. T. Onions, *A Shakespeare Glossary*, revised by Robert D. Eagleson (Oxford, 1986), under 'sign, 2'. G. Blakemore Evans has recently supported the idea that the 'Hercules' reference in *Hamlet* might relate to the sign *and* the flag of the Globe. See 'Two notes on *Hamlet*: II.2.357–58; III.1.121–31', *Modern Language Review*, 81 (1986), 34–6.

the emblem may have been illogical, or at best paradoxical, it *might* have served as the sign of the Globe. With such doubts and qualifications, it is perhaps not surprising that those who have recently been primarily interested in the physical characteristics of the Globe and its stage, such as C. Walter Hodges, Bernard Beckerman, and John Orrell,[9] have tended to ignore the sign altogether.

The issue has been kept alive, however, by apparent references to the sign in Shakespeare's own plays staged at the Globe. The most notable of these is the exchange in *Hamlet*, in which Hamlet asks, 'Do the boyes carry it away?' and Rosencrantz replies 'Ay, that they do, my lord, Hercules and his load too' (2.2.360–2). This exchange occurs only in the First Folio version of the play, which provides the control-text for the edition of the play in the Complete Oxford Shakespeare (cited in this article).[10] The passage as a whole is widely taken to be a reference to the popularity of the children's companies, in the re-opened private theatres of c. 1600–1, which were 'carrying it away' from their most formidable rival, the great Globe on the Bankside.[11] It is, apparently, an in-joke aimed at the Lord Chamberlain's Men themselves. The force of it would vary depending on whether the lines were delivered within the Globe itself ('We're still here, in spite of them') or elsewhere ('Look what we've been driven to'). There is no evidence to support the old contention that the Lord Chamberlain's Men actually were driven to tour the provinces by the competition from the 'little eyases' (2.2.339), but we know from the 1603 ('bad') first quarto that they did take *Hamlet* itself as far as Oxford and Cambridge, possibly during the heavy plague of 1603, so this *could* be a jocular 'explanation' for their travelling. We have ample evidence from the *Parnassus* plays of c. 1598–1602 that university audiences took an interest in what was going on in the London theatres, so they might have been amused by such matters and have recognized an allusion

to something prominent within the Globe. Equally, of course, Bankside audiences would have been totally familiar with these issues.

Despite the reservations voiced by Chambers and Schanzer, and the other problems I have outlined, editors of *Hamlet* such as Harold Jenkins (Arden), Philip Edwards (New Cambridge), and G. R. Hibbard (Oxford) continue to footnote the passage as a reference to the sign of the Globe, presumably because it helps to make sense of a line that is not obscure – the boys are triumphing over the strongest opposition imaginable – but seems heavily pointed. I should like to support them (and to counter suspicions voiced by Schanzer (p. 52) that Steevens could have invented the sign purely to make sense of the line), by considering the passage first as it occurs in context, and secondly in relation to a passage in Thomas Heywood's *An Apology for Actors*.

Shortly before the 'Hercules and his load' remark, in expressing his melancholy world-weariness to Rosencrantz and Guildenstern, Hamlet says: 'This most excellent canopy the air, look you, this brave o'erhanging, this majestical roof fretted with golden fire – why, it appears no other thing to me, than a foul and pestilent congregation of vapours' (2.2.300–4). I would not be the first[12] to suggest that

---

9 In, respectively, *The Globe Restored*, 2nd edition (London, 1968), *Shakespeare at the Globe* (New York, 1962) and *The Quest for the Globe* (Cambridge, 1983).

10 I have no wish to open up here the question of the relationship between the various early texts of *Hamlet* or their dating. For my purposes, it is sufficient to assume that the Folio text is an authentic version of the play, in the sense of having been written by Shakespeare (whether or not it contains additions by him subsequent to the version as originally staged) and of having been performed by the Lord Chamberlain's Men on some occasion (whether at the Globe or elsewhere).

11 See Harold Jenkins's new Arden edition (London, 1983), pp. 2–3, 257 (note to line 358) and 473 (longer note to 2.2.358).

12 See, for example, Nevill Coghill, *Shakespeare's Professional Skills* (Cambridge, 1964), pp. 8–9.

Shakespeare had in mind here the super-structure or 'heavens' (the 1603 ('bad') quarto even has 'spangled heauens' in its travesty of this passage, E2^v line 28) that covered most Elizabethan stages, including the Globe, and was commonly painted with astronomical, astrological, and mythological figures. Professor Jenkins doubts whether, in view of the commonplace nature of the thought and terminology, 'Shakespeare needed such inspiration'.[13] But this somewhat misses the point. The inescapable fact is that, during a performance at the Globe, Burbage must have been self-consciously gesturing at a piece of theatrical architecture which directly mirrors Hamlet's lines. It is perhaps worth noting that the Folio text omits the 'firmament' – familiar from the 1604/5 ('good') quarto reading – after 'o'erhanging', turning the latter into a noun. 'Canopy', 'o'erhanging' and 'roof' are indeed all stock metaphors in Renaissance descriptions of the sky; but the absence of 'firmament' tips the passage away from metaphor and towards physical description of the architecture. (This may well, however, be merely a compositor's error.)

Furthermore, I wonder what we are to make of the running banter at the beginning of the scene about the position of Rosencrantz and Guildenstern *vis-à-vis* the person of Fortune.

GUILDENSTERN
    On Fortune's cap we are not the very Button.
HAMLET Nor the soles of her shoe?
ROSENCRANTZ Neither, my lord.
HAMLET Then you live about her waist, or in the middle of her favour?
GUILDENSTERN Faith, her privates we.
HAMLET In the secret parts of Fortune? O, most true, she is a strumpet . . . Let me question more in particular. What have you, my good friends, deserved at the hands of Fortune that she sends you to prison hither?[14]   (2.2.230–43)

The passage of course reverberates on many levels, introducing Fortune as one of the play's many explanations of the inscrutable forces that govern human affairs and, in the bawdry,

broaching the question of the political 'prostitution' which Hamlet will soon suspect of his old companions, if indeed he does not do so already. The effect of the passage depends upon the audience's familiarity with the iconographic tradition of Fortune as a woman, which was extremely commonplace. I have not seen it remarked upon, however, that in other respects the implied description of Dame Fortune is at odds with what was normal. Fortune was commonly depicted naked (certainly without cap or shoes), as in George Wither's *Emblems*:

> A *Skarfe displayed by the wind*, she beares,
> (And on her *naked Body*, nothing weares)
> To shew, that what her *Favorite* injoyes,
> Is not so much for *Usefulnesse*, as toyes.
> Her *Head is hairelesse*, all, except before.[15]

Clearly, Shakespeare may simply have embroidered here for his own immediate purposes. But in 1600 in London (there or thereabouts – the point does not depend on an exact dating of *Hamlet*, or even of the Folio version) Fortune must surely have had the specific additional connotation of the Fortune playhouse, which was built during that year and opened for business in the autumn. As we have already mentioned, the second Fortune is known to have had a 'sign' depicting Dame Fortune; there must be every possibility that its predecessor had one too. Does this banter refer to its unusual features? Certainly, the Lord

---

[13] Jenkins, p. 468. Similar points have been made about the fact that Jaques's 'All the world's a stage' speech in *As You Like It* does not *need* to take its cue from the supposed motto on the sign ('All the world plays the player'). See Agnes Latham, ed., *As You Like It*, new Arden Shakespeare (London, 1975), p. 55 note. The existence of the motto is, of course, in doubt; that of the painted heavens is not.

[14] The last question is missing from the generally superior 'good' quarto text.

[15] George Wither, *A Collection of Emblemes, Ancient and Moderne (1635)*, Publications of the Renaissance English Text Society (Columbia, SC, 1975), Illustration XL in the Third Book, p. 175.

Admiral's Men exploited the name of their new theatre. Henslowe paid Dekker in September 1600 for a lost play, *1 Fortune's Tennis*, with which Chambers conjectures they opened the theatre;[16] and there is the plot, at least, of a sequel among Henslowe's papers. It is not impossible, moreover, that Dekker's *Old Fortunatus* of the previous year (at their old house, the Rose), considered worthy of performance at Court, was an early shot in this publicity campaign; that certainly contains a notable 'cap' – the wishing-cap given to Fortunatus by Fortune, which sends him on his profligate ways. All in all it is difficult to believe that Shakespeare did not expect his audience to pick up some allusion to the playhouse of his company's principal adult rivals, just as shortly thereafter he was to invoke the Children of the Blackfriars, the 'little eyases'. The association of Rosencrantz and Guildenstern in this way with the rival company would add a further dimension to Hamlet's suspicions about them as spies rather than friends. And it would deepen the joke about 'Hercules and his load too', which of course Rosencrantz voices: the Globe, like Hamlet, is assailed on all sides.

What I have been trying to establish is that the allusion to 'Hercules and his load' is not an isolated extra-textual reference but the culmination of a sequence of such references. Hamlet's whole conversation here with Rosencrantz and Guildenstern is built around allusions to the world of the theatre: the Admiral's Men at the Fortune, the 'heavens' of the Globe, the Children of the Blackfriars, and finally (just before the Players arrive and the conversation changes tack) the sign of the Globe. The references in this passage contribute to *Hamlet*'s sustained meta-dramatic self-consciousness, linking with the play's obvious concern about modes of theatrical representation and with several other apparent extra-textual allusions – I am thinking, for example, of Polonius' line: 'I did enact Julius Caesar. I was killed i'th'Capitol. Brutus killed me'

(3.2.99–100), which seems to be a public/private joke between John Heminges (Polonius/Caesar) and Richard Burbage (Hamlet/Brutus),[17] and the suspicion that Robert Armin's (the Gravedigger) unearthing of Yorick's skull must have evoked memories of the famous jester who 'adopted' him, Richard Tarlton.[18] All of these seem to be features of a play in which Shakespeare, perhaps under the pressure of intensified competition, was profoundly rethinking the fundamentals of his profession. None of the allusions is, as it were, redundant or arbitrary, though equally the meaning of each of the passages in which they occur is perfectly intelligible without its super-added sense; each can be seen as contributing an additional dimension or referent to the context in which it occurs. I suggest that 'Hercules and his load too', as a reference to the sign of the Globe, is altogether too appropriate in this broad context – and most particularly at the end of a passage which seems to begin with a reference to the sign of the Fortune – for Steevens to have conjectured it out of the blue in order to explain one not-so-troublesome line.

In support of this suggestion I would like to throw another, very different, piece of evidence onto the scales. In *An Apology for Actors* (published 1612, though generally believed to have been written c. 1608), Thomas Heywood described in some detail the great amphitheatre erected by Julius Caesar on the Campus Martius:

---

16 *The Elizabethan Stage*, vol. 2, p. 441.
17 See Philip Edwards's Introduction to his New Cambridge *Hamlet* (Cambridge, 1985), p. 5; he cites E. A. J. Honigmann, 'The Date of *Hamlet*', *Shakespeare Survey 9* (1956), 27–9.
18 The Second Part of *Tarlton's Jests*, which includes 'How Tarlton made Armin his adopted sonne, to succeed him', was entered in the Stationers' Register on 4 August 1600 (at about the time *Hamlet* was being played) and possibly published then, though no edition of the *Jests* is extant earlier than 1611. See *The Elizabethan Stage*, vol. 2, p. 299 and note.

the Basses, Columnes, Pillars, and Pyramides were all of hewed Marble, the coverings of the stage, which wee call the heavens (where upon any occasion their Gods descended) were Geometrically supported by a Giant-like *Atlas*, whom the Poëts for his Astrology, feign to beare heaven on his shoulders, in which an artificiall Sunne and Moone of extraordinary aspect and brightnesse had their diurnall, and nocturnall motions; so had the stars their true and coelestiall course; so had the spheares, which in their continuall motion made a most sweet and ravishing harmony: Here were the Elements and planets in their degrees, the sky of the *Moone*, the sky of *Mercury, Venus, Sol, Mars, Jupiter, and Saturne*; the starres, both fixed and wandering: and above all these, the first mover, or *primum mobile*, there were the 12 signes; the lines Equinoctiall and Zodiacal, the Meridian circle, or Zenith, the Orizon circle, or Emisphere, the Zones torrid & frozen, the poles articke & antarticke, with all other tropickes, orbs, lines, circles, the *Solstitium* & all other motions of the stars, signes, & planets. In briefe, in that little compasse were comprehended the perfect modell of the firmament, the whole frame of the heavens, with all grounds of Astronomicall conjecture. From the roofe grew a loover, or turret, of an exceedding altitude, from which an ensigne of silke waved continually, *Pendebant vela Theatro*.[19]

Heywood's purpose here, as it is through much of his treatise, is to emphasize the honour in which the theatrical profession was held in classical times, and so to imply that it deserves no less in his own day. Modern scholars, looking for allusions to the Jacobean stage, have found it frustrating that, while 'often he makes statements or implications about contemporary actors and theaters, histrionic ideals, and dramatic values', most of these occur in the last and shortest 'booke' of the treatise and between them they constitute no more than a quarter of the total work.[20]

But we perhaps take too narrow a view of Heywood's strategy in the *Apology* to assume that his lengthy citations from antiquity are all, as it were, pedantic bluster. As he says himself of the use of classical topics in contemporary plays: 'If wee present a forreigne History, the subject is so intended, that in the lives of *Romans, Grecians*, or others, either the vertues of our Country-men are extolled, or their vices reproved' (F3ᵛ). He hurries on to assure us that he means this only in the sense of offering abstract moral lessons, not making particular applications – a practice of which he explicitly disapproves, associating it with the children's companies. Yet it seems likely that some of the antiquarian examples in his thesis were offered not just as abstract historical data, but with an eye to modern conditions. When he mentions, for example, that 'an ensigne of silke waved continually' from a louvre or turret growing out of the roof, he and his readers knew very well that it was contemporary practice in public playhouses to fly such an ensign. In fact, Heywood had misread the passage in Ovid (*De Arte Amandi*, I) from which the quoted Latin tag comes. Early in the *Apology* he had translated the whole of that passage, the relevant lines being:

In those dayes from the marble house did wave
No saile, no silken flagge, or ensigne brave. (B4ᵛ)

As Chambers observed, he 'mistranslates';[21] J. H. Mozley's Loeb edition offers a more sober and accurate version: 'No awnings then hung o'er a marble theatre'.[22] It is tempting to suppose that the mistranslation might have been deliberate – a way of transferring the past into the present for the alert reader of Latin. It is more likely, however, that Heywood made a genuine mistake because he was looking at the classical text through seventeenth-century

---

[19] I quote from the Garland facsimile (New York and London, 1973), D2ᵛ–D3, only changing u for v, i for j, and modernizing s.

[20] To take G. E. Bentley's selections from *An Apology for Actors* in *The Seventeenth Century Stage: A Collection of Critical Essays* (Chicago and London, 1968) as a fair abstraction in this respect. The quotation is from Bentley's Introduction to the selection, p. 10.

[21] See *The Elizabethan Stage*, vol. 2, pp. 546–7, on the flags in general; the comment on Heywood's mistranslation is in a footnote spanning the two pages.

[22] J. H. Mozley, *Ovid: The Art of Love, and Other Poems*, revised edition (London and Cambridge, Mass., 1939).

eyes. Either way, the 'mistranslation' underlines the contemporary dimension Heywood obviously saw in this text, which is further apparent in other details. Though we know very little about the interior decoration of Elizabethan playhouses, we do know that at least one of them was painted to look like marble, the stone from which the Campus Martius theatre was built.[23] Heywood himself points to the correspondence between 'the coverings of the stage' and what 'wee call the heavens', and the use of these in both eras for descent machinery. Shortly after this passage he goes on to describe different Roman theatres: 'every such was called *Circus*, the frame Globe-like, & merely round' (D3ᵛ) – an analogy that can hardly be casual in this context.

Clearly Heywood is suggesting not only that the Romans had splendid theatres, but also that the public playhouses of London were not dissimilar to them in some respects – a point that had independently struck Johannes de Witt (see note 3). Some such correspondence had always been implied (or taken to be implied) in the use of the names *Theatre* and *Globe* for these buildings – a pretension jovially mocked by Thomas Dekker in *The Guls Horne Booke* (1609) and elsewhere.[24] I do not wish to argue from this, on the lines of Frances Yates in her *Theatre of the World*,[25] that Elizabethan public playhouses were consciously and deliberately Vitruvian in their construction, or that Heywood was implying as much in his *Apology*; they were too mongrel in their pedigree for that. We do know, however, that the playhouses were not only large and functional, but also (pejoratively) described as 'sumptuous' and 'gorgeous'.[26] Heywood's detailed description of Caesar's theatre on the Campus Martius must in part be an attempt to rebut such charges of extravagance, suggesting that their magnificence properly emulates that of their honoured, and even more splendid, counterparts in the classical past. If, therefore, this description is meant to be seen to correspond in some degree to that of the playhouses with which readers would be familiar, it must be possible that the item on which Heywood dwells longest – the stage covering – was particularly striking in this regard. As we have already commented, the painted 'heavens' was certainly a feature of the Globe (and of other theatres too), though we have no way of knowing if it was as elaborate as that which Heywood describes.

Which brings us to 'Giant-like Atlas'. Heywood suggests that this was an architectural feature of the Campus Martius theatre, one that held up the 'heavens' – an entirely appropriate mythological motif, with none of the apparent incongruity that disturbed Professor Schanzer about Hercules holding up the 'globe'. It is hardly conceivable that there was anything so elaborate in any Elizabethan playhouse, even the pre-eminent Globe. Had there been, one suspects that we would have heard about it, in the Fortune theatre contract, if not in the gossip of the day. Certainly there is no suggestion of anything like this in the best visual evidence we have concerning Elizabethan stage-coverings, the de Witt drawing of the Swan; the posts that rise from or through the stage to support the 'heavens' there show signs of decoration at top and bottom, but nothing like an outsize human figure. Indeed, recent scholars have worried about how much the posts as shown in that drawing would obscure the audience's view of the action behind them, to the extent sometimes of suggesting that they were exceptional and that other playhouses might not have had them at all, but supported the 'heavens' from

---

[23] See Richard Southern, 'Colour in the Elizabethan Theatre', *Theatre Notebook*, 6 (1951–2), 57–8.

[24] See *The Guls Horne Booke*, facsimile edition (Menston, England, 1969), p. 7.

[25] London, 1969. See particularly pp. 127–8 and 164, where Dame Frances invokes this passage from the *Apology*.

[26] See *The Elizabethan Stage*, vol. 4, Appendix C: Documents of Criticism, items xv and xvii, pp. 197, 200.

the galleries on either side, as we know they did at the Hope. So it seems unlikely that the Elizabethans would have used anything as elaborate or bulky as Heywood describes. This detail of Heywood's description did not, then, accord with contemporary theatrical structures. But it would have been suggestive if any of them had otherwise incorporated such a motif into their 'sign', as we have reason to suppose at least that the Globe may have done.

The Campus Martius theatre passage establishes at the very least that a seasoned Elizabethan man of the theatre, such as Heywood was, knew of a classical association between the Atlas-bearing-the-heavens motif and an actual theatre. It helps to confirm the inference to be drawn from the passage in *Antonio and Mellida* spotted by Ejner Jensen (which is not *conclusively* a reference to a theatre as such), and it makes it more likely that Burbage and his fellow shareholders might incorporate a variant on the theme in their own playhouse. We have that much less reason to suspect that the Steevens/Malone tradition was a fabrication based upon *eighteenth-century* scholarship, as Chambers half implies. I cannot, of course, rule out the possibility that Steevens knew of this passage and ingeniously adapted it in order to explain the lines in *Hamlet*, even though those lines do does not strictly need any such explanation. But this seems to me markedly less likely than that he was reporting a genuine word-of-mouth tradition. Indeed, I would suggest that, together with the evidence previously assembled, the two points I have advanced – that an allusion to the sign of the Globe would be highly consistent with other features of the passage leading up to the remark about 'Hercules and his load too'; and that a contemporary man of the Elizabethan theatre specifically and pointedly associates such a motif with a playhouse, albeit a classical one – put the burden of proof on those who would question the authenticity of the tradition of the sign, rather than those who accept it.

Granted that the sign existed, however, we must still consider what it signified. Many years ago, Mrs C. C. Stopes suggested that Hercules carrying the Globe pointed to the herculean task of carrying the Theatre over to the Bankside and there re-erecting it, on the analogy of theatre=world=globe, which is not implausible, though it does not take into account Ernest Schanzer's scruple about the illogicality of the earth-bound Hercules supporting the terrestrial globe.[27] Recently, in the course of a much broader discussion of theatre-as-metaphor, Kent T. van den Berg ingeniously suggested a resolution to Schanzer's worry: 'If Shakespeare's theater had this emblem . . . the globe carried by its Hercules or Atlas is the theater itself. The emblem symbolizes the achievement of the players in sustaining their own theatrical realm and holding it up as an equivalent of the real world. The motto – for it *is* appropriate – proclaims this equivalence: *Totus mundus agit histrionem.*'[28] Such ingenuity ought not to have been beyond Shakespeare and Richard Burbage, who were handsomely paid in 1613 for respectively devising and making an *impresa* and motto for the Earl of Rutland, which perhaps suggests that they had some reputation for composing such witty and complex devices.[29]

I have no wish to take issue with Professor van den Berg's very sophisticated and plausible argument, but I would like to advance another and simpler possibility, suggested by the description of the Campus Martius theatre in *An Apology for Actors*. While it might not be practicable, for reasons I have suggested, to support the 'heavens' of an Elizabethan theatre with an outsize statue of Hercules, it would be

---

[27] C. C. Stopes, *Burbage and Shakespeare's Stage* (1913; reprinted New York, 1970), p. 77.
[28] *Playhouse and Cosmos: Shakespearean Theater as Metaphor* (Newark, London, and Toronto, 1985).
[29] See S. Schoenbaum, *William Shakespeare: A Compact Documentary Life* (Oxford, 1977), p. 272 and note.

entirely feasible to incorporate a carving or painting of such a motif into the 'heavens' themselves – a kind of visual pun, which might then be reproduced on the flag and associated with the theatre as a whole. The sign as thus hypothesized would, by definition, be of the 'celestial' rather than the 'terrestrial' globe,[30] which is of course totally consonant with the mythology. It is, I think, modern popular sentiment that most wants to associate Shakespeare's Globe with the *terrestrial* sphere, whose shape had only been determined during the previous century, and which so strongly connotes the realm of human achievement, though Professor van den Berg has added powerful arguments based on the symbology of the Elizabethan theatre to reinforce this sentiment. I would point, however, to the rival operation at the Fortune for evidence that contemporary theatrical symbolism might gesture in other directions: their goddess was (to use a crude distinction) strongly Medieval rather than Renaissance in her connotations, an image of the forces beyond human control, and the celestial Globe would similarly suggest matters beyond merely human endeavour.

There is a point, however, where I think my suggestion and Professor van den Berg's argument converge, and that is in the person of Hercules. In either of our accounts, it is more fitting that he should bear the Globe (whether celestial or terrestrial) than Atlas, since he *chose* to take up the burden – a grand gesture rather than a punishment. It was, moreover, a decep-tion, a piece of play-acting. Atlas was the only person able to bring him the golden apples; Hercules relieved him of his burden so that he could do this and then tricked him into taking it back again – deception on a heroic, even cosmic scale, which is the stock-in-trade of the actors, who pick up the world/universe with every performance and then make those who regularly bear it (the audience) take it back again at the end. *Histrio agit totum mundum*. If we look to *An Apology for Actors* again, Heywood attests to the reputation of Hercules as a supreme hero on the Elizabethan stage, fit to be the embodiment of the actors' endeavour: 'To see as I have seene, *Hercules* in his owne shape hunting the Boare, knocking downe the Bull, taming the Hart, fighting with the Hydra, murdering *Gerion*, slaughtring *Diomed*, wounding the *Stimphalides*, killing the Centaurs, pashing the Lion, squeezing the Dragon, dragging *Cerberus* in Chaynes, and lastly, on his high Pyramides writing *Nil ultra*, Oh these were sights to make an *Alexander*' (B4ʳ). Holding up the world (earth *or* cosmos) was one labour better depicted by the artists or woodcarvers than by the actors themselves.

---

[30] As, indeed, Philip Edwards assumes it should be in his New Cambridge *Hamlet*: 'The emblem of the Globe Theatre is supposed to have been Hercules carrying the *celestial* globe on his shoulders' (p. 133, note to line 333; my emphasis). As Chambers puts it, I do not know where he got this information.

'HID INDEED WITHIN THE CENTRE': THE HALL/FINNEY *HAMLET*

SAMUEL CROWL

When Peter Hall assumed the directorship of Stratford's Memorial Theatre and founded The Royal Shakespeare Company in 1960 he established a bold new direction in the modern staging of Shakespeare. Hall came to Stratford committed to building a permanent ensemble of actors who, through intense training and discipline, could discover a contemporary approach to Shakespeare's rhetoric. As he explained in his 1964 essay, 'Shakespeare and the Modern Director', the core problem centred on Shakespeare's language and modern assumptions about meaning:

Shakespeare's language and his form are, of course, foreign to us. Modern actors naturally distrust words. They know them as grey soiled things and, as any politician will tell you, rhetoric is now suspect. Actors also (in a time when the artist's freedom of self-expression is canonised) resent the disciplines of blank verse or alliterative prose. Techniques have, therefore, to be learnt and developed until Shakespeare's form is a discipline which supports rather than denies self-expression.[1]

Hall struggled to find a way to respect the integrity of the plays *and* to make them meaningful to a modern audience; to provide both text and context:

I'm trying to express Shakespeare as I honestly understand him. And without going to the conscious excesses of performing in modern dress, or turning verse into prose, or re-ordering the plays in terms of psycho-analysis, I must admit that I am a modern. So are the scholars whose re-interpretations I study, so are the audiences who watch my productions.[2]

As Hall and his successor, Trevor Nunn, have repeatedly admitted, their tutor to the contradictions and ironies of the modern world was F. R. Leavis. Hall approvingly records in his *Diaries* the following paragraph from a *Time* magazine article about his leadership of the National Theatre:

By the time he finished Cambridge, Hall had already directed several plays and, perhaps more significant, studied English under F. R. Leavis. Even though Leavis hated theatre, he made a lasting impact on Hall with his scrupulous examination of a text, particularly for its ironies and ambiguities and the sense that a work of art must be placed in a social context. Hall more or less applied that lesson in his celebrated *Wars of the Roses* productions, where the protagonists were not seen as gallant warrior kings but as bloody power buccaneers. Hall clearly believes that to immerse an audience unforgettably in a play, the cast and directors must locate and pinpoint the vital element that T. S. Eliot once called 'the present moment of the past'.[3]

During his years at Stratford, Hall's search for 'the present moment of the past' did not preclude imaginative tampering with Shakespeare's text, as witness the immediate and

---

[1] *Royal Shakespeare Theatre Company: 1960–1963*, ed. John Goodwin (London, 1964), 41–8, p. 42.
[2] *Royal Shakespeare Theatre Company*, p. 41.
[3] *Peter Hall's Diaries: The Story of a Dramatic Battle*, ed. John Goodwin (London, 1983), p. 223.

lasting impact of the Hall/Barton *The Wars of the Roses*.

However, by the time Hall was named to succeed Olivier as the director of the National Theatre in 1973, he had revised substantially his methods of examining the present moment of the past in a Shakespearian text. Hall's post-Stratford directing of Shakespeare has been distinguished by two guiding principles: presenting the full text with no cutting, rearranging of scenes, or reassignment of lines, and without pointedly setting the play's action against a specific cultural or historical context outside the Renaissance. In his fourteen years with the National, Hall has directed six Shakespeare productions: *The Tempest*, *Hamlet*, *Macbeth*, *Othello*, *Coriolanus*, and *Antony and Cleopatra*. He plans an autumnal end to his tenure with productions of *Cymbeline*, *The Winter's Tale*, and *The Tempest* in the Cottesloe in 1988.

In general, critical response to Hall's work with Shakespeare at the National has not been as positive as that during his years at Stratford. Hall's directing triumphs have been outside Shakespeare: *No Man's Land*, *Volpone*, and *Amadeus*. These successes share, however, with his Shakespeare productions his determination to extend his Stratford experience by linking the star actor tradition with ensemble principles.

As the specific focus of this essay and to illustrate Hall's work with Shakespeare in the past fifteen years, I want to turn to an examination of his production of *Hamlet* which opened the South Bank building in March of 1976. Now is a fitting moment to look back on that production as the new building celebrates its tenth anniversary and as the Hall era comes to a close. The production is significant because while originally planned to open on the Olivier Theatre's thrust stage, delays in construction forced Hall to open it at the Old Vic (the National's home since inception in 1962) and then to move it first (in March of 1976) into the Lyttelton, the new National's

proscenium theatre. Eventually this *Hamlet* found its way to the Olivier's wide open spaces thus making it the production which literally straddled the transition from the Olivier era to the Hall era in British Shakespeare; from the Old Vic to the New National.

Hall was returning to this seminal text ten years after directing it at Stratford where, next to *The Wars of the Roses*, it was his most heralded and popular – particularly with the young – production. Stanley Wells has provided a full account of Hall's work in his *Royal Shakespeare*. Wells is quite correct in stressing the ensemble impact of the production where critical attention was drawn as often to Tony Church's Polonius, or Brewster Mason's Claudius, or to Glenda Jackson's Ophelia as to the title character. As Wells reports:

Undoubtedly the most significant, as also the most controversial, piece of casting was that of David Warner as Hamlet himself. He was only twenty-four years old, and at this time was very much a 'modern', as opposed to a classical, actor. He was exceptionally tall, but unheroic in build; his face, though expressive, was not conventionally handsome. He did not cultivate grace of movement or beauty of voice, and his verse speaking was a law unto itself. He had been very successful as Henry VI in Peter Hall's production of *The Wars of the Roses*, and somewhat less successful as Richard II. The roles are significant; both of them rather passive, languid, pathetic characters. To cast him as Hamlet was itself a major interpretative decision. It was obvious that this would be no princely, romantic embodiment of the role. Mr Warner was, frankly, a gangling, spotty young man with traces of a Midlands accent. No make-up artist would transform him into anything remotely resembling the young Gielgud, and it was clear that Mr Hall could not wish him to effect such a transformation.[4]

In 1965 Hall had selected a Hamlet to fit both his interpretation of the play and the larger conception of ensemble playing which he had already gone far in achieving at Stratford. By

---

[4] *Royal Shakespeare: Four Major Productions at Stratford-upon-Avon* (Manchester, 1977), p. 33.

contrast, in 1975 he was reaching out to link the tradition of star actor with that of the powerful director wedded to ensemble principles. Hall selected Albert Finney to lead the company into its new home.[5] Finney was the most explosive of the younger actors looked to as the heirs of the Olivier, Gielgud, and Richardson tradition. I found the production a compelling mix of ideas and passion, though many perceptive reviewers failed to see how Hall's ideas about the play and Finney's often startling performance meshed. The following account tries to establish the way in which Hall's design and direction worked to score ideas set in the play about how power, corruption, and fragmentation frustrate and crush individual sensibilities struggling to develop and cohere. The production, in retrospect, signalled a sea-change in Hall's approach to Shakespeare which he has followed during the past fifteen years.

The following entry from Hall's *Diaries* was dictated on the morning after the production opened and underlines his own high expectations:

This is the closest I have reached to the heart of a Shakespeare play in my own estimation; it is the production which over the last fifteen years has the least gap between my hopes and the facts on the stage. It is also pure and clear. And the production is the closest I've ever got to a unified style of verse speaking which is right. I feel now I know how the verse should be treated. In Stratford days what I did was intellectual. Now I have found a way of doing it which is based on feeling and passion. It has been a very satisfying experience.

The audience were very attentive and the actors did well. All in all it was our best performance. The last scene has never gone better and I felt an actual tragic purgation in the house. The reception was really thunderous. I've heard it as much for Callas, but that's about all. Everybody very elated. I believe we're going to have a contentious press, but on tonight's evidence we have achieved something big.

Man leaving performance (snorting): '*Hamlet* is not as contemporary as that . . .'[6]

As Hall anticipated, there were a few snorters among the critics as well. Some reviewers were enthusiastic about Finney's performance, calling it rough and electrifying; others felt he raced through the part with little indication of its range or complexity. Surprisingly, there was even less comment about Peter Hall's staging of the play, other than to note that he was presenting an uncut *Hamlet* and trusting his audience to sit still for a single intermission which did not come until 'How all occasions do inform against me.' Mel Gussow's remarks in the *New York Times*, Sunday edition, were typical: 'Somewhere in Peter Hall's weighty production, there must be a purpose other than to present a leading actor in an uncut *Hamlet* in the nation's first theater. Perhaps the director and actor envision a commoner prince. If so, the vision has not been realized.'[7]

Benedict Nightingale had a more positive response to Finney's performance, calling it 'passionate and powerful, full of scalding humor and savage contempt'. However, he joined Gussow in failing to see any design to Hall's direction: 'It is Finney's evening, partly because of his own magnetism, partly because Peter Hall is determined to allow him his head. In recent years we've grown used to seeing Shakespeare's plays tailored with little sermons on subjects dear to his directors. But Mr Hall's production excludes nothing, emphasizes nothing, refashions nothing. The actors are presented with a bare stage and a totally uncut text, and then more or less left to get on with their jobs.'[8] I believe Gussow and Nightingale missed much that Hall did with a stage which was undressed but hardly bare, and I want to describe what we saw as we entered the theatre and how it became the

---

5 Hall really wanted Finney for *Tamburlaine* – planned as one of six productions to open the new building: *Diaries*, p. 163.
6 *Diaries*, p. 199.
7 *Sunday New York Times*, 25 July 1976, p. 5.
8 *Sunday New York Times*, 28 December 1976, p. 5.

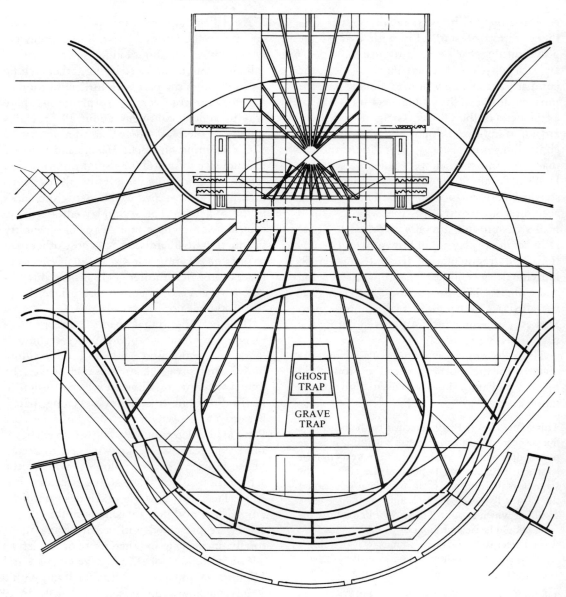

4   *Hamlet*. National Theatre, 1976. Stage Design, by John Bury

nutshell which bounded us all in Hamlet's bad dreams.

Hall's *Hamlet* incorporated three structural devices: a wall which ran across the stage approximately two-thirds of the way from proscenium to the rear wall and which was broken at its centre by a set of double doors topped by a triangular pediment, a white circle (some thirty feet in diameter) painted on the stage floor which ran from the double doors to the edge of down stage, and a series of eleven white lines which ran at radial angles from stage front through the double doors where they met and then fanned out again in mirror approximation to their position in front of the wall. Five of the lines intersected the circle. The audience became aware that the lines continued beyond the wall during the few scenes when the doors were open. The most effective use of our awareness of the lines' further path was during Hamlet's 'To be or not to be' soliloquy when Hall positioned Ophelia at the point where the eleven lines intersected while Hamlet, far down stage, confided his metaphysical dilemma to the audience. At such moments we were invited to see Hall's device as life-lines which could not flow and interconnect properly – the wall and double doors, symbolic of the larger political and mythic reaches of the play, reminded us of the formidable public issues and relationships at work in the text which deny the forms of contact, communication, and interchange which would be taken for granted in a world less out of joint.

Hall's use of these three devices universally failed to draw comment from the play's reviewers, yet my experience of the production found them central to his way of working with the text. Francis Fergusson, in his essay on *Hamlet* in *The Idea of a Theater*, comes to the play from a reading of *Oedipus Rex*. That context leads him to remind us that the play is not the prince. Fergusson repeatedly stresses the political and social ramifications and resonances of Hamlet's world as a means of correcting the Coleridgean or Freudian tendency to concentrate all our energies on Hamlet's inner drama. Two worlds, the political and the personal, are intimately intertwined in the play, constantly impeding and infringing upon each other, and Fergusson rightly reminds us of the larger dimensions of Hamlet's struggle.[9] The way in which Hall's simple but effective use of the wall and its centre doors was incorporated into our visual sense of the production worked to remind us of Fergusson's insight. The double doors and their triangular pediment were loaded with the suggestion of the House of Atreus. Nothing else in Hall's production was meant explicitly to invite parallels with Greek drama, but his determination to present the text without emendation supports the notion that this was meant to be not a tidy, but an epic *Hamlet*.[10]

It is instructive to note that Hall's interest in emblem and design had grown since his Stratford years. In his interview with Judith Cook just prior to directing *The Tempest* in 1973, Hall indicated that he had taken a six-year exile from directing Shakespeare and was coming back to him with a fresh perspective:

I've become very interested in emblematic theatre. And that has led me to the meaning of the baroque theatre, the baroque opera, the masque and the theatre of Inigo Jones. I think we are perhaps a little puritanical as a nation about the visual theatre. We are apt to think that as soon as Inigo Jones came into the Jacobean theatre, the writer was driven out. I don't believe that. The emblematic, visual side of the theatre – if you have a great artist doing it – is immensely potent.[11]

As a means of illustration let me cite three examples of the way Hall utilized the emblem he created on the stage floor. In both the nunnery and closet scene Hall and Hamlet use the obvious circle motif to its fullest. The periphery of the circle was, appropriately, Hamlet's territory. In both scenes he stalked and circled, probed and accused, the female figure planted in the centre. Neither scene was played with its potential for physical violence, as each is so often performed. Finney's Hamlet was too wary, too committed to his peripheral role as scourge and minister. He moved about the edge of Hall's circle throwing his taunts at the women who have been placed by others in a position they did not seek. Both Gertrude and Ophelia are central to Hamlet's deepest inner life provoking his outrage and disgust. In

---

[9] *The Idea of a Theater* (Princeton, 1949), pp. 103—12.
[10] Hall's plans to stage both *Tamburlaine* and *The Oresteia* during the National's first seasons on the South Bank underline his epic directional mood in the mid-1970s.
[11] Judith Cook, *Directors' Theatre* (London, 1974), p. 70.

this production, Hamlet's ambiguous relationship to both was made manifest by the way in which all three characters are seen to occupy an alien territory. The centre is rightfully Hamlet's. Claudius (Denis Quilley) and his Minister of the Interior, Polonius (Roland Culver), assign that space to wife and daughter as a means of determining why Hamlet's centre will not hold. But Hamlet avoided the centre, preferring to make his anguished rounds. Both women were fixed by Hall, Gertrude (Angela Lansbury) literally wedded to a chair, in a centre where their gestures repeatedly suggested they were nervous and uncomfortable – surrogate usurpers. Hamlet repeatedly moved in towards them and then, at the moment he discovered the hollowness of their centre – 'Where's your father?' 'At home' (3.1.132–3); 'What have *I* done, that thou dar'st wag thy tongue / In noise so *rude* against me?' (3.4.38–9) – he backed off from physical engagement to his distanced prowl.

In the nunnery scene Finney initially treated Ophelia (Susan Fleetwood) with great tenderness and his 'Where's your father?' was tossed off as a mad, almost comic, evocation of the silly old man rather than in response to any tell-tale movement in the wings. Hamlet took his cue for the scene's reality simply from Susan Fleetwood's guilty reaction. He immediately dropped her hands and retreated to the edge of Hall's circle where he made a complete perambulation as he delivered his stunning attack on the bewildered woman trapped in the circle's centre: 'If thou dost marry, I'll give thee this plague for thy dowry' (3.1.137–8). As this example serves to illustrate, I found Hall's use of such space repeatedly illuminating.

Another instance will serve as a further example of Hall's intentions about this centre space. In 4.5 Laertes charged in with sword drawn and assumed the centre of the circle. Claudius did not move in towards him but worked his way on the left edge of the painted circle. He lured Laertes from the centre to the periphery on 'Be you content to lend your patience to us' (line 208), skilfully having avoided a clash with Laertes' momentary appropriation of the centre. When we returned to the two poisoners in 4.7 their positions were reversed. Claudius was at the centre and Laertes *moved in* to join him on 'I'll anoint my sword' (line 113) – further proof that not only does the centre corrupt, but that the absolute centre corrupts absolutely.

Hall's use of the centre and the circle was repeatedly meant to remind us that those in *Hamlet* who comfortably assume the centre are feigners. As another instructive example, when Rosencrantz and Guildenstern entered through the open doors, in 2.2, Hamlet was on stage left of the circle as he began to unravel their clumsily weaved up folly. When he launched into the brilliant explanation of his loss of mirth, which quite escaped his obtuse and inept undergraduate inquisitors, he cut through the circle on 'What a piece of work is man' (line 304). This was another moment when Hall's staging subtly reinforced the intellectual motion of the text. As Rosencrantz and Guildenstern made the move to embrace Hamlet as, in Conrad's Marlow's phrase 'one of us', Finney's Hamlet stranded them on an empty island. By cutting through the circle he spatially cut them off at the same moment he offered his radical dismissal of the paragon of animals.[12]

Hamlet moved back into the centre, momentarily, at the conclusion of his inter-

---

12 Hall's diary entry for 7 October 1975 makes an interesting link between Hamlet's relationship with Ophelia and his Wittenberg friends: 'Important findings at rehearsal. Hamlet is not so concerned that Rosencrantz and Guildenstern are spies; nor is he concerned in the Ophelia nunnery scene that he is being overheard. The scenes are not about these discoveries; he knows them in a flash. He's concerned about the honesty of the characters in their replies when he charges them with duplicity, and both the scenes show him trying to demonstrate his own philosophy, anxiously, vigorously. They are a pattern of misunderstandings' (p. 188).

view with Rosencrantz and Guildenstern to proclaim that he was 'but mad north-north-west; when the wind is southerly, I know a hawk from a handsaw' (2.2.379–80), and then bolted towards the closed double doors to throw them open to welcome the players. Here came fresh air indeed. Hamlet led the player-king to the centre for their evocation of a previous fall and loss. This was one moment in the production when Hamlet seemed to revel in the centre. He could now momentarily enjoy that alien territory because he shared it with one who openly acknowledged that he was a feigner. The ability to weep for Hecuba was underscored several scenes later when Hamlet forced tears from his uncle-mother, our player-queen, when she occupied the same space.

I want to mention two casual props Finney used to create his Hamlet: a scholar's cloak and a sea-blue scarf. The cloak was used not only to identify the solemn black of mourning but also as an emblem of the Wittenberg Hamlet cannot discard once back in the provinces. Finney appropriated this common prop as an extension of his Hamlet which could be used to swirl out to threaten and estrange as well as curl in to hide and protect. He was most adroit at using his cloak to underline the expanse and impasse of Hamlet's nutshell. The scarf was employed to add a dash of romanticism. In the early scenes, it was tied rakishly around Finney's neck – the only spot of colour in his sombre demeanour or costume. The scarf was acknowledged, appropriately in the most self-conscious of Hamlet's soliloquies ('O, what a rogue and peasant slave am I' (2.2.551ff.), as Finney used it to deflate the exaggerated self-examination which concludes with 'Who does me this?' (2.2.576). When we saw the scarf next it was wrapped around Finney's forehead when he staged his performance of the mouse-trap: no longer an undergraduate's affectation but now a sign that Hamlet realized that he, too, was a player who must use his every resource 'to show . . . scorn her own image'

(3.2.22–3), including radical defiance. The scarf also served as a bandage for Hamlet's cerebral struggle with Claudius, a struggle which takes its toll and creates its own interior wounds: 'My wit's diseased' (3.2.308–9). At the conclusion of the play-within-the-play Finney untied his scarf and whirled it above his head as he leapt on to the raised platform where the *Murder of Gonzago* had been played out. I was reminded of Olivier's filmed leap into Claudius's vacated chair swirling a lighted torch; Finney's gesture here spoke to the play's move to strip away false faces and hidden realities while Olivier's intention was to extend the play's imagery of false fire and forced illumination: 'Lights, lights, lights!'

The play-within-the-play was staged with a deeply raked platform erected at the outer upstage edge of the circle. Three chairs were positioned in the centre of the circle in mirror approximation of their arrangement in 1.2 where the careful observer immediately noticed that the size of the chairs resembled those of the three bears: Claudius' was slightly larger than Gertrude's and Hamlet's was similarly smaller than his mother's, revealing Claudius' own strong sense of political geometry. The other members of the court were seated on benches on the edge of the circle. Hamlet, again uneasy with being positioned in Claudius' centre, moved his chair to stage left to join Ophelia. I mention this only as another example of the identification of the centre as Claudius' usurped province.

In the closet scene, Gertrude was seated on a chair at the centre of the circle in an interesting departure from traditional staging. As Hall commented about his decision to cut the bed:

A closet is a withdrawing room, a place for disrobing, not the bedroom. It's a stage tradition . . . to have a bed . . . but a bed is not really what the scene is about. It's difficult to play around it, and you rapidly get to Freudian images, but only Freudian images.[13]

---

[13] *Diaries*, p. 192.

As Hamlet verbally thrust and parried to uncover her culpability, the ghost rose from the elevator trap located immediately behind Gertrude's chair. The effect was astonishing because the audience shared Hamlet's perspective and his startled reaction as the ghost's silver helmet suddenly appeared as though sprung from Gertrude's head. Though Richard David's own fine analysis of the production takes issue with mine, we agree on the effectiveness of this moment. David's description vividly presents how Hall captures the Shakespearian resonances at work here:

> Growing more distraught, he [Hamlet] ranges impatiently about her chair; when, behind them both and masked by them, the Ghost rises from the trap. Now the Ghost had descended by the trap at the end of his interview with Hamlet, but that effect, in full view, had seemed contrived. His re-emergence in the closet scene was quite unexpected and a real piece of theatrical legerdemain. Hamlet, by now kneeling at his mother's knee, looks at the Ghost over her shoulder; she, all tenderness for her son suddenly seized in this paroxysm of madness, has no consciousness of his father's presence. The three reactions, Hamlet's intense, Gertrude's all maternal solicitude, the Ghost in painful hope against hope that sufficient memory of their bond may linger in his wife to make her aware of him, built up a strange chord, complex yet with each component note distinct and beautifully balanced; and the inspiration of this moment continued to inform the remainder of the scene in which the interchanges between mother and son, irretrievably separated yet bound by shared regrets, gently modulated into a sad autumnal calm.[14]

Here Hall's stage emblem vividly captured Shakespeare's exploration of the destructive consequences of this fatal family triangle and provided us with a startling Freudian image after all.

The only moments when the centre was held in steady focus were when it was occupied by the ghost and the gravediggers – the dead and the quick. Hall allowed the furious pace of his production to slow only at those moments when we were receiving the grave truth from king and clown.

In the final act the gravedigger digs Ophelia's grave in the circle's heart and Hamlet, in his wry banter with death's great clown, reveals his reconciliation with death's inevitability. A moment later, he strips off his grey seafarer's cloak to declare: 'This is I, / Hamlet the Dane' (5.1.254–5) as he jumps into the grave to acknowledge his love for Ophelia. These open declarations of public power (King) and private commitment (lover) at the very centre of a significant social ritual announce the end of his repressed struggle which had pushed him to the edge of personal and social alienation. Finney triumphantly appropriated the centre from this moment on and in the following scene he moved Horatio in from the periphery to the centre where he confidently confided to his friend his action in sealing the fates of Rosencrantz and Guildenstern. In the duplicitous fencing match, Hall provided a final original touch. Hamlet and Laertes were each provided a resin box into which they stepped before each play of the bout. The match was robustly staged to advantage Finney's vigour, but the consequences were to place white footprints, in helter-skelter fashion, all over the carefully conceived circle and its intersecting radial lines. 'Only connect' is what Hamlet cannot achieve except in death. Eventually the circle and the lines, Hall's design, were obliterated by the furious footsteps which led to the play's final devastation.

Hall's geometric understanding of Hamlet's fractured mind and world was beautifully mirrored in Finney's performance. His prince may have been soiled but was never sullen. All Hamlet's bitterness and disgust with Denmark's rank and gross unweeded garden were given full voice in a radical reversal from David Warner's 1965 interpretation. Finney's

---

[14] *Shakespeare in the Theatre* (Cambridge, 1978), pp. 81–2.

Hamlet was volcanic, wild, and whirling in and beyond words. Hall's own initial reaction to Finney as 'a powerful, passionate, sexy Hamlet, glowering with resentment', was an apt description of the performance as it matured through rehearsals.[15] What kept the performance focused was Hall's design, keeping this Hamlet persistently on the prowl of the periphery of the circle of Claudius' court until the interim, finally, became his.

Hall's subsequent work with Shakespeare has been unevenly received, but each of his productions followed the *Hamlet* pattern of linking a star actor with members of the regular National Theatre Company: Finney (again) in *Macbeth*, Scofield in *Othello*, McKellen in *Coriolanus*, and – most recently – Anthony Hopkins and Judi Dench in *Antony and Cleopatra*. John Peter's review of *Antony and Cleopatra* in *The Sunday Times* begins:

Golden ages of the theatre are usually in the past – but we may be living in one today. Peter Hall's production of *Antony and Cleopatra* (Olivier) is the British theatre at its spellbinding and magnificent best. This is a big, heroic play in every sense, and Hall's control over it is complete. The huge spans of the action tense up, arch and unfold like great symphonic movements and the poetry of this sensuous, athletic text tolls with burnished conviction. Hall reminds us, and we do need reminding, that the bedrock of classical theatre is the text; that the life of the play is first and most essentially in the words of the play, and that visual splendour and the excitement of action need to be justified by a sense that the words are both felt and understood.[16]

If Peter's assessment is correct, it appears that many of the virtues I found in Hall's 1976 *Hamlet* have come to full fruition in his final major Shakespeare production at the National.

---

[15] *Diaries*, p. 185.
[16] *The Sunday Times*, 12 April 1987, p. 55.

MALVOLIO AND THE DARK HOUSE

JOHN H. ASTINGTON

In writing the comic episode of Malvolio's imprisonment, in the second scene of act four of *Twelfth Night*, Shakespeare created an action which is not altogether easy to transfer to the stage. In his own time, if we are to believe the direction in the Folio ('*Maluolio within*' (4.2.20.1)), it was performed with Malvolio entirely out of sight and speaking from the tiring house, possibly from behind one of the stage doors; Feste would have had the entire expanse of the platform stage on which to play his games of changing identities, and we might imagine that the actor would naturally have broadened his antics to retain contact with the audience. In an Elizabethan public theatre, action near the stage doors was well removed from most of the spectators.

Staged thus, the scene does establish an important visual point, in that it is a reversal of the 'box-tree' scene (2.5), during which Malvolio holds the prominent downstage position while the conspirators spy on him from concealment upstage. The comedy of this earlier scene, a theatrical chestnut, depends on our being able both to hear and to see Sir Toby, Sir Andrew, and Fabian as they watch their gull take the bait; their stealth and circumspection are preposterously inept, and as a result farcical stage business has quite rightly been a tradition of the scene in performance. But on Shakespeare's stage Malvolio was not to be seen watching Feste in 4.2, or so the Folio implies, and although we must hear him, his voice would have reached an Elizabethan audience

from 'within' the tiring house, through the thickness of a fairly substantial wooden door, and across the depth of the stage, thirty feet or so to the first rank of standing spectators in the yard. Performance indoors – at Middle Temple Hall, for example – may have improved matters for the actor, although the scene is likely to have been staged in the same way: Malvolio's plaintive cries issued from the tiring house façade, at the upstage limit of the acting area. The central physical problems of the scene, therefore, are those of audibility and visibility, and so they have remained as the play has been translated into the conventions of the various kinds of theatre which have followed Shakespeare's own. This fairly short episode provides an instructive instance of how the bare modernism of post-Victorian staging, which liberated Shakespeare from pictorialism and supposedly rediscovered the original dynamics of the plays, might or might not reflect seventeenth-century stage practices.

The Old Vic director Harcourt Williams may speak for those who wrestled with staging the episode in the English theatre between the wars. His production of *Twelfth Night*, with John Gielgud as Malvolio, was seen at Sadler's Wells Theatre in 1931, and he writes thus of 4.2:

It is by no means an easy scene, and it would not go right. Eventually I had the Orsino couch stood up on end. It had rather the appearance of the base of a tower, and we thought that with a little grille and some kind of a roof, it would do. It had this advantage: it could be moved swiftly to the centre, and the other players could work round it with Malvolio raving inside . . . Alas it always looked like a tactlessly placed garden privy: and, what was worse, it so boxed in John [Gielgud]'s voice that he could not be heard in the stalls. What he really wanted himself was to be in an underground prison with just his hands waving up through the grid, but at neither theatre [Sadler's Wells and the Old Vic] is it possible to have a trap-door in the stage.[1]

In remounting the production, Williams adopted a third solution, which was as old as Rowe's edition of Shakespeare (1709):[2] 'I rearranged the Malvolio Prison as a divided scene such as was often used in old-time melodramas. One was able to see Malvolio in the "dark house" and the tormentors outside at the same time, which was an improvement.'[3]

Williams's difficulties make clear a central issue of the scene, over which most directors and designers will not be inclined to follow the Folio. In making Malvolio audible, one also renders him visible, and the appearance of a beseeching hand through the gap of a half-open stage door is the natural next step following the opening of the door to improve the projection of the actor's voice. Modern theatre-goers, I would guess, have never seen a production of *Twelfth Night* in which Malvolio remained entirely out of sight throughout the scene. In the Victorian theatre, as Williams suggests, the irony of the episode was presented with considerable visual elaboration. Irving's Malvolio lay in a straw-filled dungeon 'worthy of *Fidelio*',[4] on one side of the stage, separated from Sir Toby, Maria, and Feste by a wall with a prison door in it, which ran roughly at right angles to the front of the stage. One of the six settings for Augustin Daly's second production of *Twelfth Night* in 1877 was a 'Prison under the House of the *Countess*',[5] and such an arrangement is drawn in the Acting Edition of the play published by Samuel French (1931?). Most recently, the BBC Television Shakespeare (1979) treated the scene essentially in the Victorian fashion,

but the tradition has also continued on the stage in a modified form.

One important feature of the nineteenth-century dungeon scene was the dividing door, with a metal grille through which Malvolio could stretch his hands imploringly. In paring down the setting for his influential production of *Twelfth Night* at the Savoy Theatre in 1912, Harley Granville-Barker simply turned the Victorian scene through ninety degrees, dispensing with the door in favour of a large grille framework, painted in a light colour and emphasized with a white light, set centrally between black curtains. By standing to either right or left of this grille, Sir Toby, Maria, and Feste remained out of Malvolio's sight, while Feste and 'Sir Topas' could tantalize him by moving in and out of the area downstage of what the promptbook calls the 'prison window'.[6] Thus Granville-Barker restored the Elizabethan configuration, but in all other respects the Savoy staging had very little to do with the Shakespearian stage. The scene was played at the absolute downstage limit, on a shallow forestage which remained when the front curtains were closed on the scenic setting, and the imprisoned Malvolio remained visible, as he had in nineteenth-century productions, picked out with white light so that his sharp face and pale hands emerged startlingly against his black costume. The gaps between the bars were large enough for Henry Ainley, playing Malvolio, to poke

---

[1] E. Harcourt Williams, *Four Years at the Old Vic* (London, 1935), p. 103.

[2] See W. Moelwyn Merchant, *Shakespeare and the Artist* (London, 1959), plate 9, and the *New Variorum* edition of *Twelfth Night*, ed. H. H. Furness (Philadelphia, 1901), p. 261.

[3] Williams, *Four Years at the Old Vic*, p. 147.

[4] Quoted in A. C. Sprague, *Shakespeare and the Actors* (Cambridge, Mass., 1944), p. 10.

[5] William Winter, *Shakespeare on the Stage, Second Series* (New York, 1915; repr. 1969), pp. 64–5.

[6] Department of Rare Books, University of Michigan Library.

his head and arms through, so that the prison also became a pillory, as he struggled to reach out to 'Sir Topas' and to Feste.

Granville-Barker's simplification of the traditional pictorial prison, typically elegant and economical, allowed the ironic humour of the scene to emerge clearly. Such frontal treatment of the dark house, with Granville-Barker's bars, a door, or a window set between curtains, remained common at Stratford-upon-Avon between the wars, in the productions of William Bridges-Adams and Ben Iden Payne. Its chief disadvantage to those interested, as Harcourt Williams was, in maintaining a rapid movement from scene to scene, was that it remained tied to a fairly elaborate arrangement of the stage and to changing scenery. Occasionally the prison door has been built into a permanent multiple set,[7] but since it is used only once in the play it cannot be given either the prominence or the clarity within a single setting which Granville-Barker achieved with his downstage, spotlit grille.

The solution John Gielgud suggested in 1931 – to play the scene with Malvolio under the stage – retains the notion of the Victorian dungeon-prison, but rearranges its elements vertically rather than horizontally, and has the great advantage of economy. It uses a simple feature of most stages, including Shakespeare's own, and it is importantly related to the language of the scene itself. The prison is now commonly played in a trap, as John Russell Brown has pointed out in his discussion of *Twelfth Night*:[8] Gielgud himself, in directing the play at Stratford in 1955, had Laurence Olivier peering from a trap in 4.2, from which he was finally pulled out in the last scene of the play. Donald Sinden recently has described his performance for John Barton's production of the play with the Royal Shakespeare Company in 1969 as a Malvolio confined in 'some type of primitive septic tank'.[9] So well does the scene work with Malvolio imprisoned in the stage cellar that it is surprising to realize that as a tradition of staging it is still less than seventy-

five years old, and that its origins lie not in the English-language theatre, but in France.

Twelfth Night was never performed in the French theatre during the early part of this century,[10] so that when Jacques Copeau began to interest himself in the play, his imagination was not bound by any received manner of playing the scenes on the stage. Granville-Barker, reviewing a later revival of Copeau's version of *Twelfth Night*, remarks: 'French audiences, quite naturally, do not take their Shakespeare for granted as we do. So much the better; they are likely to get the more out of him.'[11] Copeau became attracted to the play through his general interest in the style of Renaissance drama, which to him constituted a rich and subtle range of theatrical effects achieved within a spartan simplicity of physical means; his interest had also undoubtedly been stirred by his having seen Granville-Barker's Savoy production in 1912. Although he remained a firm admirer of Granville-Barker throughout his life, he makes clear in writing to Duncan Grant, the English costume designer for Copeau's production, that his own conception was to be no slavish copy of another's work: 'Ce que je veux faire sera quelque chose de tout à fait différent de ce qu'a fait Granville-Barker. Et

---

[7] See the illustration of a setting by Roger Furse for a production at the Old Vic in 1950, in Hugh Hunt, *Old Vic Prefaces* (London, 1954).

[8] John Russell Brown, Introduction to *Twelfth Night, or What You Will*, in *Shakespeare in Performance: An Introduction Through Six Major Plays*, ed. John Russell Brown (New York, 1976), pp. 208–13.

[9] See *Players of Shakespeare*, ed. Philip Brockbank (Cambridge, 1985), 41–66, pp. 63–5.

[10] According to Helena Robin Slaughter, Copeau's production of *Twelfth Night* was 'la première fois qu'on la joué en France'. See 'Jacques Copeau Metteur en Scène de Shakespeare et des Elisabéthains', *Etudes Anglaises*, 13 (1960), 176–191, at p. 184.

[11] *The Observer*, 1 January 1922, p. 10. Reprinted as '*Twelfth Night* at the Vieux Colombier (1921)', in Stanley Wells, ed., *Twelfth Night* (New York, 1986), pp. 71–8.

d'ailleurs la très petite scène que j'aurai ne m'offira toutes les ressources que Barker avait à sa disposition au Savoy. Il nous faut user de toute notre habileté pour surmonter les difficultés auxquelles nous nous trouverons confrontés au Vieux Colombier.'[12] The scenic poverty of which Copeau speaks may have been imposed partly by means and circumstances, but it came to be a *desideratum* of his approach to the theatre, and naturally led him to a radical rethinking of staging. He distinguished firmly between staging which arises from discoveries made by working from within the text and that which is merely applied from without:

Par *mise en scène* nous entendons: le dessin d'une action dramatique. C'est l'ensemble des mouvements, des gestes et des attitudes, l'accord des physionomies, des voix et des silences, c'est la totalité du spectacle scénique, émouvant, d'une pensée unique qui le conçoit, le règle et l'harmonise. Le metteur en scène invente et fait régner entre les personnages ce lien secret et visible, cette sensibilité réciproque, cette mystérieuse correspondance des rapports, faute de quoi le drame, même interprété par d'excellents acteurs, perd la meilleure part de son expression.

A cette mise en scène-là, qui concerne l'interprétation, nous ne saurions apporter trop d'étude. A l'autre qui a trait aux décors et aux accessoires, nous ne voulons pas accorder d'importance.[13]

The production of *La Nuit des Rois*, first seen in the spring of 1914, was an outstanding success of the Vieux Colombier and it remained in the repertory of the theatre until 1923, being presented in New York between 1917 and 1919 as part of the Company's activities in the United States during the First World War. However, the post-war productions in Paris were perhaps those through which Copeau received most attention. Granville-Barker saw *La Nuit des Rois* late in 1921 and his review appeared in *The Observer* on New Year's Day, 1922; Kenneth MacGowan and Robert Edmond Jones surveyed the production as part of their view of *Continental Stagecraft* (1922). The grace and lightness of the performance impressed all those who saw the production: its musicality and rhythm were achieved partly by the actors' spoken style – greatly admired by Granville-Barker – and partly by a carefully measured physical pace, uninterrupted by scene changes: 'up and down the setting these players frisk, weaving patterns of beauty and fun that link them into the true spirit of the play. The curtain is there at convenient times to make the forestage into a neutral zone for duke or sea captain, and between this forestage and the balconied space behind there is room for all of Shakespeare's play to race along just as he wrote it.'[14]

For 4.2, Malvolio was confined to a trap in this forestage, from which he was allowed to peep in talking to Feste. Copeau prepared for the scene by connecting it thematically with 3.4, during which Sir Toby, Fabian, and Maria humour the supposed madman and lay plans for the 'dark room', by means of a 'pantomime' which preceded 4.1, and which may partly have been suggested by Granville-Barker's production.[15] It was a chase episode, in which Malvolio was pursued by his tormentors disguised as ghosts, ludicrously wrapped in sheets, and wailing, at the end of which he fell into the trap, which had been opened by Fabian.[16] Like a captured animal, Malvolio was now at the mercy of his hunters. Copeau's concern with simple theatricality led him to a staging of 4.2 which to a modern observer

---

[12] Jacques Copeau, in *Registres III: Les Registres du Vieux Colombier I*, eds. M.-H. Dasté and S. M. Saint-Denis (Paris, 1979), p. 192.

[13] Jacques Copeau, 'Un essai de rénovation dramatique', in *Registres I: Appels*, eds. M.-H. Dasté and S. M. Saint-Denis (Paris, 1974), 19–32, pp. 29–30. First published in *La NRF*, September 1913.

[14] *Continental Stagecraft* (New York, 1922), p. 181.

[15] Granville-Barker's promptbook notations for 3.4 indicate farcical pushing and shoving as Sir Toby, Maria, Sir Andrew, and Feste confront Malvolio.

[16] For information on Copeau's production I am grateful to Bill Peel, University of Toronto, for access to his notes on material in the Fonds Copeau.

seems obvious and unsurprising; it is difficult to imagine the novelty and revelation experienced by spectators who, if they had seen the play before at all, found its sense newly defined. Malvolio's prison was no longer a romantic cell, inviting pathos, but a frankly theatrical hole in the stage, in which the clever clowns catch the stupid one.

The precise influence of any production is difficult to trace and very few published notices of Copeau's *La Nuit des Rois* were specific about details of his staging – an exception is to be found in the remarks of Mac-Gowan and Jones in *Continental Stagecraft*, about which I have more to say below. Yet Copeau's treatment of 4.2, obviously enough, was copied in the English-language theatre, and has since become one of the commonest approaches to the scene on the stage. I have not attempted to trace Copeau's early influence in North America, where simply in terms of chronology one might expect English productions of *Twelfth Night* to be first to follow his lead. In general terms, however, it seems not entirely unfair to say that in the USA and Canada, Shakespeare production tended to be conservative and to defer to the English theatre, while the interests of the modernists of the American stage lay elsewhere. In England, Copeau's ideas about the scene were in the air at least by 1931 and probably had been for the preceding decade. Granville-Barker effectively had retired from the theatre in the period following the Great War, but his influence on other directors and on actors, including Gielgud, was considerable, and we may take it that his memories of *La Nuit des Rois* were communicated to others in conversation, as well as through his published notice of the production. The first English director to stage 4.2 of *Twelfth Night* in Copeau's manner was Bridges-Adams; he never saw the company of the Vieux Colombier, but he was regularly in touch with Granville-Barker throughout the 1920s.[17]

Bridges-Adams staged the play eight times at Stratford-upon-Avon, between 1920 and 1934, but it was only in 1932, following the opening of the new theatre, that he placed Malvolio in the cellarage during 4.2, by using the technical capabilities of the stage machinery to play a further visual variation on the divided scene. His earlier productions had used a sharply lit frontal prison which evidently derived from Granville-Barker's staging: the performances seen on the tours of the United States and Canada in 1928, 1929, and 1931–2 used a window set between 'blacks', through which Malvolio, in traditional fashion, reached his hands. On his return to the new building, with its elevating stage bridges, the director redesigned his production around two settings, one interior and one of a garden. The latter was used for 4.2, with a change which is described by a contemporary reviewer: 'Towards the end this garden scene is hoisted halfway up the proscenium, so as to reveal Malvolio imprisoned in a cellar underneath.'[18] Feste, playing from the raised portion of the stage above Malvolio, knocked on the trap at the line 'peace in this prison' (4.2.19), and thereafter teased his victim by alternately opening and closing the trapdoor, slamming it finally down on the groping hands at 'Pare thy nails, dad' (4.2.133); such byplay has since become traditional in staging the scene with a trap.

Bridges-Adams's treatment of 4.2 takes the simplicity of Copeau's version of the relationship between the two principals and translates it, through considerable elaboration of the stage, into the Victorian divided scene reworked: instead of adjoining rooms we are given an upstairs-downstairs cut-away and a restoration of the visual ironies consequent on a

---

[17] See Sally Beauman, *The Royal Shakespeare Company* (Oxford, 1982), chapters 4, 5, and 6 and Robert Speaight, *A Bridges-Adams Letter Book* (London, 1971), p. 51.

[18] *The Sheffield Telegraph*, 23 April 1934; *Theatre Records*, 28, Shakespeare Centre Library, Stratford-upon-Avon.

simultaneous view of the dark house and the world outside. It perhaps also restored sentimentality, since when the outside world is a garden Malvolio's gloomy confinement takes on a stronger contrast. The first English production to follow Copeau directly and to place Malvolio out of sight below the platform was that of Irene Hentschel, on the Stratford stage seven years later, in April 1939. The trap was placed centrally (it is referred to unceremoniously as a 'manhole' in the promptbook),[19] and it was also used, as it was in Gielgud's 1955 production, for Malvolio's entry into the final scene. One contemporary reviewer, twenty-five years after Copeau, was struck by the novelty of the idea: 'For Malvolio's incarceration the producer cleverly puts the prison below the stage and all one sees of Olivia's poor steward is an occasional hand or glimpse of his face.'[20] After the Second World War productions which adopted this staging became increasingly common: the Old Vic production of 1954, directed by Denis Carey and with Michael Hordern as Malvolio, placed the prison beneath an apron stage; it was followed immediately by the Gielgud–Olivier production at Stratford.

The tradition begun by Copeau is, it seems, strictly modern, yet it serves the essential purposes of the scene very well indeed, to the degree that flickers of doubt begin to play about the appropriateness of the Folio's stage direction, as it relates to the theatres in which *Twelfth Night* was first seen. Copeau's own approach to the text was to discover the requirements of a scene from the inside out, as it were, exploring the language and the rhythm to determine the appropriate physical expression of its sense. Malvolio's prison is, literally, simply a dark place, but figuratively it is a hell: full of anguish and torment for him, and for 'Sir Topas' a fitting location for one possessed of the devil and given over to spiritual darkness. From 'Fie, thou dishonest Satan' (4.2.32) to 'Adieu, goodman devil' (4.2.134) there are sufficient reminders of the old stage

location of the prince of darkness; Copeau, consciously or not, chose the theatrical hell to which Shakespeare is referring, in Feste's closing doggerel at the very least. For Robert Edmond Jones and Kenneth MacGowan it was clear that Copeau's production had stripped the Victorian varnish from the play and restored its natural sense: 'With the trap door in the forestage to act as a cellar, Malvolio can be incarcerated below-stairs and happily out of sight – much as Shakespeare intended.'[21]

Shakespeare's intentions may or may not be represented by the abrupt direction in the Folio; if they are not, the internal directions of his text, seen within the context of the theatre of his own time, point towards the staging later adopted by Copeau. Hell not only lay below the stage, but it was firmly associated with prisons in medieval and Renaissance art: a raised stage, with a prison door set in a recessed alcove below it, is shown in a representation of a street theatre in Antwerp in 1582.[22] Through a grille in the door a tormented demon grimaces at the observers. Thomas Dekker, mocking the foolishness of the devil in his satirical *Newes from Hell* (1606), imagines that he would not have enough foresight, if he ventured into the theatres, to avoid an old stage trick: 'because *Hell* being vnder euerie one of their Stages, the Players (if they had owed him a spight) might with a false Trappe doore haue slipt him downe, and there kept him as a laughing stocke to all their yawning spectators'.[23] The devil, imprisoned in the stage trap and visible, or at least audible, to a theatre audience, was therefore an old joke by 1606.

Prisons evidently were not invariably

---

[19] Shakespeare Centre Library.
[20] *The Evesham Journal*, 22 June 1939; *Theatre Records*, 33, Shakespeare Centre Library.
[21] *Continental Stagecraft*, p. 181.
[22] See Glynne Wickham, *A History of the Theatre* (Cambridge, 1985), p. 161.
[23] *The Non-Dramatic Works of Thomas Dekker*, ed. A. B. Grosart, 5 vols. (1884–6), vol. 2 (London, 1885), p. 92.

located in the stage cellar – that in *Measure for Measure* is not – but other seventeenth-century plays placed them there with reasonable frequency. Marston's play *Antonio's Revenge*, more or less contemporary with *Twelfth Night*, contains a scene in which the unfortunate Balurdo escapes from prison:

BALURDO
from under the stage.

Bal. Ho! Who's above there? Ho! A murrain on all proverbs! They say hunger breaks through stone walls, but I am as gaunt as lean-ribbed famine; yet I can burst through no stone walls. O now, Sir Geoffrey, show thy valour: break prison and be hanged. [*He climbs out.*]

> Nor shall the darkest nook of hell contain
> The discontented Sir Balurdo's ghost.
>
> (5.2.1–7)[24]

In Fletcher's *The Island Princess* (1621), acted at court and also by the King's Men at the Blackfriars and the Globe, we are given an indication of the partial appearance of the figure confined below the stage (as in many modern productions of *Twelfth Night*): in the second act of Fletcher's play the imprisoned king appears '*loden with chaines, his head, arms only above*'.[25] In two plays Massinger locates prisons under the stage platform: *Believe as You List* (1631), acted by the King's Men, survives in an important manuscript prompt copy which gives explicit instructions for opening the stage trap.[26]

Moreover, the simple notation 'within' is not always an indication that actors remained out of sight behind the tiring house doors. Beaumont's comedy, *The Knight of the Burning Pestle*, performed a few years after *Twelfth Night*, contains a scene which is partly a reversal of 4.2 in Shakespeare's play, in that the killjoy Mistress Merrythought attempts to gain entry to the house in which her carefree husband is carousing (Act 3). His mockery of her, which like Feste's of Malvolio is partly sung, almost certainly involves his appearance at the balcony of the upper level of the tiring

house. It was from there that the musicians, with whom he is drinking, produced their music for act breaks and songs, and it was the traditional position of the window, when the tiring house façade was used to represent a house. Mistress Merrythought, on the stage platform, is in the street attempting to open her door. The ironic ballad her husband sings to her, 'Go from my window, love, go', leads most modern editors to add a direction which embodies the sense of the words.[27] Such action would lead us to expect some reference to his being 'above', yet the 1613 quarto simply has '*Old merri⟨thought⟩ within*', repeated three times as a speech prefix – a very imprecise indication of what actually happened on the Blackfriars stage.

In Shakespeare's plays '*within*' most frequently means 'offstage', as it accompanies indications for shouts, cries, alarums, and other noises to be produced from inside the tiring house. Occasionally it specifies a position for the actor behind one of the stage doors, as it does for Lucio, for example, in 1.4 of *Measure for Measure*, when he calls out to be admitted to the nunnery. But there is one clear example, from an early play, where the term is used to mean 'not on the stage platform', and where the actors 'within' are in full view of the audience. In *1 Henry VI*, 3.5, the stratagem for taking Rouen concludes with the victorious French looking down from the walls on the expelled English commanders. The opening stage direction reads: '*An alarum. Excursions. The Duke of Bedford brought in sick, in a chair. Enter Lord Talbot and the Duke of Burgundy,*

---

24 *Antonio's Revenge*, ed. R. Gair (Manchester, 1978), p. 145.
25 *The Dramatic Works in the Beaumont and Fletcher Canon*, gen. ed. F. Bowers (Cambridge, 1966–), vol. 5 (1982), p. 570.
26 See Malone Society Reprints edition (Oxford, 1927), pp. 60–72.
27 See, for example, the editions of John Doebler (Lincoln, Nebr., 1967) and Sheldon P. Zitner (Manchester, 1984).

without; within, Joan la Pucelle, Charles the Dauphin, the Bastard of Orléans, [the Duke of Alençon, and René Duke of Anjou] on the walls.' Although *'without'* and *'within'* have reference to the fictional situation – inside and outside the town – the stage direction as a whole reads as an entirely practical clarification of movement, business, and the physical relationship of actors in performance: the theatrical sense of *'within'* seems to be thoroughly present.

A further instance from a late play may have more to do with the staging of Malvolio's dark house. In the long second scene of *The Tempest*, the impressive entrance of Caliban (line 323.1) is preceded by Prospero's increasingly agitated calls for him to appear and by one line of reply from somewhere offstage. In the Folio, it appears in this form: *'Cal. within. There's wood enough within.'* When read, the odd logic of this line stands out. If he is already *'within'*, why does he use the word as if it were somewhere else? The answer might be that he is *'within'* the sty of his hard rock, while the wood is *'within'* Prospero's cell, but such a distinction may reflect two theatrical locations. Although Prospero's calls for Caliban to *'come forth'* might have been directed at one of the stage doors, all the associations of the scene would have made it entirely appropriate for Caliban to have appeared through the stage trap. He is an earth-beast, a *'tortoise'*, a devil, and, at least before Stephano treats him as a pet dog, threatening and dangerous: the strenuous effort of making him appear, and the tense exchange of insults once he has done so, would have reminded a Jacobean audience of the popular devil-conjuring plays. His *'rock'*, indeed, is a kind of prison in which he is *'confin'd'*. The theatrical power of Caliban's first appearance may well have been emphasized by his crawling forth from the surface of the stage.

Such analogies can suggest only that an Elizabethan audience would not have found it surprising to see 4.2 of *Twelfth Night* performed as Copeau staged it; as to the authority of the Folio stage direction, we must remember that no notations to do with staging would be expected to cover every possible occasion on which the play might be performed. Scenes which in the playhouses used trapwork, flying machinery, or other special effects would frequently have been rearranged to suit the limited facilities of temporary performance spaces elsewhere – at court, or on the actors' provincial tours. Notations also creep into prompt copies haphazardly, and occasionally record contradictory instructions. A modern example is provided by the Bridges-Adams promptbooks for *Twelfth Night*: that for the 1932 production is simply the 1929 book with new notes added, and so in 4.2 it simultaneously records two distinct ways of staging the scene.[28] *'Maluolio within'*, therefore, indicates one treatment of the scene, but that is not to say that there was only one way in which Shakespeare's actors performed it. The house as dark as hell could quite appropriately have lain below the Elizabethan trapdoor, and Jacques Copeau should perhaps be regarded as the rediscoverer of a stage tradition.

---

[28] Shakespeare Centre Library.

THE TEXT OF CRESSIDA AND EVERY TICKLISH READER: *TROILUS AND CRESSIDA*, THE GREEK CAMP SCENE

CLAIRE M. TYLEE

It is perhaps because *Troilus and Cressida* raises the question of women's sexual identity that it was scarcely performed for three hundred years.[1] I am going to discuss ways in which Shakespeare's Cressida has been construed by recent critics, producers, and actresses, and how these interpretations might affect the understanding of the play by an audience in the 1980s. Until the 1970s most interpretations manifested precisely that coercive dominance of a particular set of cultural values which is the theme of the play. This was especially marked with respect to what G. Wilson Knight called 'the pivot incident of the play': Cressida's arrival at the Greek army camp.[2] My discussion will centre on this scene, to show how it is a key to the significance of one of the main questions posed by the play: whether a person's nature or identity is determined by the valuation set on that person by others. This question forms part of the general platonic scepticism which the play develops with regard to the possibility of anything's having absolute value or identity in a world subject to the digestive effects of time and human judgement. Within the world of the play Cressida is unable to maintain a sense of her own integrity. Similarly, in the course of changes in Western society, the character of Cressida in the text of the play has been subject to changing readings and widely divergent performances. This has inevitably affected the comprehension of the whole play.

*

From the first, Shakespeare's play deliberately counters the traditionally alluring vision of Helen summoned up by Faustus in Act 5 of Marlowe's *The Tragical History of Dr Faustus*; glutting his desire at the lips of this myth, Faustus takes Helen to be a worthy ground for war. But the seductive lips of the glamorous illusion suck forth Faustus's soul and charm it to hell. Pointedly Shakespeare's Prologue debunks his own high-flown eloquence about 'the princes orgulous' who are fighting the Trojan War, by explaining that: 'The ravished Helen, Menelaus' queen, / With wanton Paris sleeps – and that's the quarrel' (Prologue 9–10). Pandarus and Paris may call Helen sweet, but Diomedes speaks of her 'contaminated carrion' as 'bitter to her country' (4.1.73, 71). Even Troilus is cynical about her: 'Fools on both sides. Helen must needs be fair / When with your blood you daily paint her thus' (1.1.90–1). Hector puts it more bluntly: 'She is

---

[1] Compare 'a new play, neuer stal'd with the Stage', *The Epistle*, Quarto [second state] 1609 and 'The Stage History of *Troilus and Cressida*, pp. xlvii–lvi of Alice Walker's edition (Cambridge, 1957). Although a version of *Troilus and Cressida* was performed in Munich in 1898, the first recorded performance in English was a 'costume recital' in London in 1907. Around 1870, William Poel was recommended by his tutor never even to read the play, it was too 'improper' [Michael Jamieson, 'The Problem Plays, 1920–1970: A Retrospect', *Shakespeare Survey 25* (1972)].

[2] G. Wilson Knight, *The Wheel of Fire* (London, rev. edn, 1949), p. 47.

not worth what she doth cost the holding' (2.2.50–1). When finally we see 'the admirablest Lady that ever lived', 'that peerless dame of Greece',[3] 'love's visible soul' (3.1.32–3), we discover a silly, vain, petulant woman: spoilt into a mere 'Nell'. Her only asset is her painted flesh. She parallels that 'most putrifièd core, so fair without' (5.9.1) which tempts Hector and sates his sword. Although boasting about the possession of women is used as an excuse for the war in general, the duel between Hector and Ajax in particular, and the vendetta between Troilus and Diomedes, women are actually held in low esteem. Troilus despises his own weakness and vacillation, his prevarication, as 'womanish' (1.1.106–7). The first we hear of the great hero Hector is that 'he chid Andromache', his wife, because he had been struck down by Ajax (1.2.6). Women's opinions are neither sought nor listened to, although their future is at stake with the future of Troy. No one pays any attention to the prophecies of Cassandra, 'our mad sister' (2.2.97), despite her prescience. Cressida is truck for barter, without rights; her wishes are not considered any more than are Helen's. Women, prized solely as untainted, painted flesh, have no other worth.

However, although no doubt is ever expressed as to Helen's superficiality in Shakespeare's version of the myth, for the last century critics have been absolutely divided as to the nature of Cressida: from G. B. Shaw, who in 1884 found her 'most enchanting, Shakespeare's first real woman',[4] to Frederick S. Boas, who in 1896 considered her 'a scheming, cold-blooded profligate',[5] from Joyce Carol Oates, who actually called her 'evil' and 'villainous' in 1967 and assumed she was '"impure"' before becoming Troilus' mistress', 'an experienced actress in the game of love',[6] to Daniel Massa, who in 1980 found Cressida 'a fearful, loving innocent', and, although 'indecent', 'still a virgin', 'unpracticed'.[7] Oates completely ignored Pandarus' jokes about maidenheads (4.2.25–7) and

neither Oates nor Massa paid any attention to Cressida's soliloquy in which she claims that:

> Then though my heart's contents firm love
>   doth bear,
> Nothing of that shall from mine eyes appear.
>
> (1.2.290–1)

Yet, despite disagreements about the sincerity or virginity of Cressida when she makes love to Troilus (and thus about Troilus' naïvety), most commentators have agreed with Ulysses' judgement of her on the very next morning, at her arrival at the Greek camp, where he sets her down as one of the 'sluttish spoils of opportunity / And daughters of the game' (4.6.63–4).[8]

It should be noted that, as in modern English, 'daughter of the game' does not imply simply that she knows how to flirt and turn meetings into sexual encounters, but that she is 'on the game', a prostitute; that is: a woman who offers sexual intercourse for money.[9] The

---

[3] Christopher Marlowe, *Doctor Faustus*, in *The Complete Works of Christopher Marlowe*, ed. Fredson Bowers, 2nd edn, 2 vols. (Cambridge, 1981), I, 121–271, lines 1683–4 and 1685–6.

[4] G. B. Shaw, from *Transactions of the New Shakespeare Society* (report of a meeting on 29 February 1884); reprinted in *The Shaw Review*, 7 (1964), p. 16.

[5] Frederick S. Boas, *Shakespeare and his Predecessors* (New York, 1896), p. 376.

[6] Joyce Carol Oates, 'Essence and Existence in Shakespeare's *Troilus and Cressida*', *Philological Quarterly*, 46 (April 1967), p. 178.

[7] Daniel Massa, *York Notes on 'Troilus and Cressida'* (London, 1980), p. 29.

[8] For example Una Ellis-Fermor, *The Frontiers of Drama* (London, 1945), chapter 4; Kenneth Muir: 'Cressida's rapid capitulation stamps her as a daughter of the game so clearly that we hardly need the official portrait by Ulysses', in 'The Fusing of Themes' (1953), included in *Shakespeare 'Troilus and Cressida' A Casebook*, ed. Priscilla Martin (London, 1976), 82–95, p. 83; Robert Ornstein: 'a slut . . . She is a daughter of the game that men would have her play and for which they despise her', in *The Moral Vision of Jacobean Tragedy* (Madison, Wis., 1960), p. 244.

[9] *OED Supplement* (Oxford, 1972): '5f *the game*: prostitution; usu. in phr. *on the game*'. Compare *Collins Dictionary of the English Language* (London, 1979):

understanding and repetition of this expression by commentators seems to range from a weak sense, in which Cressida is simply an incurable flirt who is incapable of treating love as more than a game, to a strong sense, in which she is a nymphomaniac. If the phrase is taken to mean not that she sells herself (although she does call Pandarus a 'bawd' for bringing her a token from Troilus, 1.2.277), but that she is promiscuous, we should remember that Ulysses bases his judgement on a single meeting. This meeting, moreover, takes place on the very morning she left Troilus, before any assignation with Diomedes. Apart from which, being unfaithful to Troilus with Diomedes does not constitute either prostitution or promiscuity, nor does it prove she was insincere with Troilus. Unexamined emphasis on this part of the quotation has obscured the implications of the first part, where the sense of violent seizure implicit in 'spoils' suggests that men have made use of any available opportunity whatever to take advantage of her. Repeating the aggressive martial imagery, which is used to describe sexual intercourse throughout the play and which is responsible for Cressida's guardedness, 'spoils' hardly justifies the venom of Ulysses' choice of the word 'sluttish' or, at the beginning of the same speech, his use of 'Fie' to express disgust at *her*.

The problem with most scholarly interpretations of Cressida, as with Coghill's repetition of Alice Walker's solution that she is merely 'a chameleon' who reacts to her surroundings,[10] is not so much that they do not permit her to change in response to her experiences, as that they treat Cressida as if she had some essential integrity of personality to be found. In fact, whether or not she is sexually experienced, she seems to have had no opportunity to act autonomously, according to her emotions, and so she seems never to have been allowed to develop her own sense of herself, a sense of her own identity.[11] Repeating bits of acquired 'wisdom' to the effect that 'Achieve-

ment is command; ungained beseech' (1.2.289), in other words, that her only power lies in 'playing hard to get', and deciding that she will therefore 'hold off', she reveals in soliloquy that she bears firm love in her heart for what she herself sees in Troilus, but is determined to keep that emotion concealed. Nevertheless, perhaps influenced by Troilus' declaration of 'firm faith' (3.2.105), she goes back on that decision by usurping the 'men's privilege / Of speaking first' (3.2.125–6) to confess: 'Prince Troilus, I have loved you night and day / For many weary months', from 'the first glance' like all true lovers (3.2.111–12, 115). Then, she immediately remembers that now he 'will play the tyrant' for 'Who shall be true to us, / When we are so unsecret to ourselves?' (3.2.116, 121–2). Left briefly alone with him, she discloses her blind, but percipient, fears that lovers make promises that they cannot keep. In this she proves wise. She is still tentatively exploring her ground. Not so secure as Troilus, she is not so convinced of her whole-hearted commitment to him: 'I have a kind of self resides with you – / But an unkind self, that itself will leave / To be another's fool' (3.2.144–6). The implication of this paradoxical statement is that to be false to

---

'GAME 16. Slang, chiefly Brit. prostitution (esp. in the phrase ON THE GAME)'. Alan Sinfield glosses Ulysses' use of 'daughter of the game' in this sense in 'Kinds of Loving: Women in the Plays', in *Self and Society in Shakespeare's 'Troilus and Cressida' and 'Measure for Measure'*, eds. J. A. Jowitt and R. K. S. Taylor (Leeds, 1982), 27–44, p. 33.

10 Nevill Coghill, *Shakespeare's Professional Skills* (Cambridge, 1964), p. 107; Alice Walker, Introduction to *The New Shakespeare 'Troilus and Cressida'* (Cambridge, 1957), p. xii.

11 Compare Alan Sinfield: '[Cressida] is hardly allowed to exist as an independent person', in 'Kinds of Loving: Women in the Plays', *Self and Society*, p. 34 and Gayle Greene: 'Her fate is the working out of a character that lacks integrity or autonomy', in 'Shakespeare's Cressida: "A kind of self"', in *The Woman's Part: Feminist Criticism of Shakespeare*, eds. Carolyn Ruth Swift Lenz, Gayle Greene, and Carol Thomas Neely (Urbana, Ill., 1980), 133–49, p. 136.

Troilus is to be false to her own self. But how should she be committed to him, despite his adamant claim that he will be true to her? Even had he offered her marriage, Prince Troilus and his brothers show scant regard for the bonds of marriage.

In fact, Troilus has from the first demonstrated the typical bad faith of his culture with regard to both the war over Helen and his 'love' for Cressida. He has no 'appetite' to join the fools on both sides that fight over Helen, yet, since he cannot get 'better sport' with Cressida at home, he is persuaded by the alternative prospect of 'good sport' on the battlefield (1.1.113–15). Paris, who continues (in his own word) to 'soil' Helen in adultery, nevertheless encourages the others to see her as a source of their honour, and encourages her to use her beauty to disarm Hector's morality (2.2.145ff.). Hector is the most double-minded: a married man who treats his own wife like a piece of property, he is convinced that it is a moral law of nature and society, designed to curb 'raging appetites' (2.2.180), for a woman to belong to her husband. Yet he resolves not to return Helen to Menelaus. Apart from the besotted lover, Paris, and the warrior-husband, Hector, Troilus has one other elder brother on whom he might model himself as a man: Helenus, the priest, who recommends reason over desire. According to Pandarus, Helenus fights 'indifferent well' (1.2.119), but Troilus is contemptuous of him as lacking virility: 'Reason and respect / Make livers pale and lustihood deject' (2.1.48–9). In that martial culture rational judgement cannot prevail against the bull-headedness of physical energy; the Trojans share with the Greeks a system of values which equates sexual intercourse with armed combat, treating both as good sport, and proofs of manhood. Reasonableness is taken for virgin timidity in the face of 'manly' drives.

From the moment the Prologue speaks, until Pandarus' epilogue, the titillating idea of destructive blood-lust is the central image of the play: the sword and the arrow excitedly tickling like the erect penis, which 'kills' the lovers like the sting in the tail of the sweet honey-bee. Swords are addressed as if they were hungry, greedy for flesh and blood, and it is 'with a bridegroom's fresh alacrity' that Aeneas prepares to view the 'maiden battle' between Hector and Ajax (4.5.145, 4.6.89). Both Hector and Paris are governed by desire, raging appetite: Paris' sexual lust for Helen is paralleled by Hector's eager pursuit of military glory. And Troilus emulates them both. His 'love' for Cressida is a sexual gourmet's desire, painted up to look fair. Having awaited Pandarus' preparation of this delicacy, Cressida, he is fearful his palate may not discriminate finely enough, as a victorious soldier does not discriminate in his joy among piles of dead enemies. Cressida is surely right to be wary. Her gradual dawning that, 'O heavens, you love me not!' (4.5.84) is followed by two doubtful questions and then silence as Troilus, blithe about his own fidelity, self-importantly plays the comrade in arms with the blunt cynic, Diomedes. Too self-deceived to recognize his own sensuality, Troilus cannot foresee that it is not Greek gallantry, as he supposes, that will undo Cressida; she will be dominated by an unscrupulous bully who is frank about his lust.

Since J. L. Styan wrote his study of the relation between the criticism and performance of Shakespeare's plays, not many scholars would repeat Louis Marder's view that 'only the text can tell us what Shakespeare intended';[12] Styan believed that the text would not tell us much until it spoke in its own medium. On the other hand, the text itself does not dictate any particular theatrical mode and neither text nor medium can control interpretation. The problem Styan identified, that the producer and scholar both see what they interpret, before they interpret what they see, is the

12 Louis Marder, *The Shakespeare Newsletter*, 24 (February 1974); quoted in J. L. Styan, *The Shakespeare Revolution* (Cambridge, 1977).

problem inherent in *Troilus and Cressida*, which, as R. J. Kaufmann points out, 'provides no secure point of vantage from which to evaluate the action. There is no single, reliable choral observer within the play who can orient our responses',[13] although many commentators have treated Ulysses as just such a privileged observer. In a sense, Cressida *is* the text. Without responding to how she presents herself, without allowing her any autonomy, men impose on her their own evaluation; just as Cressida answers to people's expectations of her, so does the play. Cressida is not the self-assured young widow, Criseyde, but is she completely inexperienced, 'an unpracticed jilt' as Hazlitt called her, or an 'experienced actress' as Oates says? How artless might she be were Pandarus not around to chivy her and tease her into self-consciousness? The text is indeterminate. Neither can it determine the nature of the medium by which it will speak.

Struggling to remove the paradox of Cressida's submission to Diomedes, so that it should be only Troilus and not the audience to whom this is, and is not, Cressida, some producers have presented her as an artful bitch from her first appearance. This was taken to extremes in Tyrone Guthrie's production at The Old Vic in 1956, where Cressida was having an erotic liaison with her manservant before she seduced Troilus. Jonathan Miller's 1981 version for the BBC Television Shakespeare has a very young Cressida already licking her lips over Troilus in incipient lasciviousness even before the love scene. The famous production by John Barton and Peter Hall at Stratford in 1960 starred Dorothy Tutin, 'sweltering with concupiscence' in the words of *The Times* (27 July 1960), 'too early a seductress from an exotic film' in the opinion of John Russell Brown to make Troilus' belief in her 'winnowed purity' credible.[14] (This was one of a series of productions where 'antique' costuming accentuated the characters' physicality, although references in the text to a sleeve and glove suggest that, if the play was

ever staged in Shakespeare's time, it was performed in contemporary clothes.) Such interpretations falter on Cressida's grief at being cast out of Troy: 'No kin, no love, no blood, no soul, so near me / As the sweet Troilus' (4.3.24–5). Miller produced these scenes as the histrionic tantrums of a spoilt child, demanding attention and placated with a sleeve. (An experienced whore would hold out for more, one might suppose.) The parting became comic in Guthrie's production, with Troilus trying to pin Cressida into her clothes between her sobs, but this was part of an overall conception which diminished the love plot in order to show up the glamour of war and thus tended to obscure the relation between the two plots. Poel's production, staged in Elizabethan dress in 1912, had an opportunist Edith Evans already busy with her hat in the mirror while Troilus tried to gain her attention: 'But yet, be true' (4.5.73).

This 'business' with costume is a significant detail in the physical aspect of a total interpretation. In 1982 Valerie Smith questioned Seltzer's (1963) description of Cressida in Act 4 Scene 6 as a 'brassy slut':

When we last saw her, she was distraught and weeping, at her parting from Troilus. Is she still distraught? Or has she stopped crying, made up her face, and put on a new frock for the occasion? Does she kiss the Greek soldiers of her own free will, or is she simply pushed from one to the other without the power to refuse? Are her witty lines to Menelaus [37–46] spoken flirtatiously, or with sad resignation, as she tries to preserve some dignity in this humiliating scene?[15]

In Howard Davies's 1985 production at Strat-

---

13 R. J. Kaufmann, 'Ceremonies for Chaos: the Status of *Troilus and Cressida*', *English Literary History*, 32 (June 1965), 139–59, p. 156.

14 John Russell Brown, '*Troilus and Cressida* 1960', reprinted in *Aspects of Shakespeare's 'Problem Plays'*, eds. Kenneth Muir and Stanley Wells (Cambridge, 1982), 149–52, p. 150.

15 Valerie Smith, 'The History of Cressida', in *Self and Society*, eds. Jowitt and Taylor, 45–79, p. 62.

ford, which echoed Guthrie's by up-dating the play to the Crimean war, Cressida's grief-stricken refusal to leave Troilus led to her being bundled off in her nightie, her vulnerability never more clear. This was an interpretation in agreement with Jan Kott's view of the play: writing in Polish in the early 1960s, he considered Cressida to have been one of Shakespeare's most amazing characters. According to Kott, she is a teenager who has not yet been touched. Inwardly free, passionate, a would-be cynic, she defends herself by irony. On the night in which she comes to know the reality of love, 'she is violently awakened'.[16] Robert Wilcher found Juliet Stevenson's portrayal of this conception of Cressida completely sympathetic. Her arrival at the Greek camp was a 'brutal paradigm of how women are reduced to objects'.[17] It is here, perhaps more than anywhere, that the absence of stage directions in the text has allowed scholars to interpret what G. Wilson Knight called 'the pivot incident of the play' according to their preconception of innocent men tempted by a libidinous woman, rather than as a case of Susanna and the Elders. In 1931 W. W. Lawrence wrote: 'I do not see how anyone can be in doubt as to what Shakespeare thought of her, and meant his audiences to think, after reading the famous scene in which she kisses the Greek chieftains all round, and the scorching comments of the clear-sighted Ulysses.'[18] This conception of the scene was repeated by Oscar James Campbell in 1938: 'Cressida goes directly to the Greek camp, and kisses all the men, with an abandon much greater than the liberal customs of Elizabethan salutation prescribed. Ulysses . . . is conveniently at hand to keep the audience clear on that point';[19] and by A. P. Rossiter in 1961, when he wrote of the Cressida that Ulysses encountered, 'kissing the Greek generals all round as soon as she meets them'.[20] Although there are no stage directions at this point, it is clear from what Nestor says that it is *Agamemnon* that kisses *her*: 'Our General doth salute

you with a kiss' (4.6.20), and not the other way around. And in fact it is upon *Ulysses*' suggestion that everyone then kisses her: ''Twere better she were kissed in general' (4.6.22).

Although Daniel Seltzer recognized that it is she who is kissed, he insisted that 'Cressida must parade happily among the Grecian generals' while it happens, since 'she is now the brassy and degraded slut the Elizabethans had been taught to expect'. Yet he also felt that 'no simple reliance upon the Elizabethan rumor of Cressida's harlotry can explain her sudden and complete degradation'.[21] That Shakespeare might have been querying the dominant Elizabethan myths about both Helen and Cressida does not seem to have occurred to Seltzer. Although in 1980 Gayle Greene did not actually claim Cressida does it 'happily', she too thought that 'Cressida is quick to live down to [the Greeks'] view of her, allowing herself to be "kissed in general"'.[22] Boas agreed that 'on her arrival at the Greek camp she at once shows herself in her true colours. She allows herself to be "kissed in general" by all the chiefs'.[23] But does she? Very pointedly she asks Menelaus whether he is giving or receiving a kiss, and determines: 'Therefore no kiss' (4.6.40). And as for Ulysses, who set 'the game' up, she tells him to beg for one. Whether happy or quick, she does not just 'allow' 'all' the

---

[16] Jan Kott, 'Amazing and Modern', in *Shakespeare Our Contemporary* (London, 1965), p. 66.

[17] Robert Wilcher, 'Value and Opinion in *Troilus and Cressida*', an unpublished lecture delivered at the Royal Shakespeare Theatre Summer School, Stratford, 1985.

[18] W. W. Lawrence, *Shakespeare's Problem Comedies* (London, 1931).

[19] Oscar J. Campbell, *Comicall Satyre and Shakespeare's 'Troilus and Cressida'* (Berkeley, 1938), p. 215.

[20] A. P. Rossiter, *Angel With Horns* (London, 1961), p. 133.

[21] Daniel Seltzer, Introduction to the Signet Classic edition of *Troilus and Cressida* (New York, 1963), p. xxxi.

[22] Gayle Greene, 'Shakespeare's Cressida: "A kind of self"', p. 143.

[23] Boas, *Shakespeare and his Predecessors*, p. 376.

generals to kiss her, although I do not think that the text quite lends itself to the reading of Voth and Evans: 'She manages, with her wit, to keep most of the Greeks, including Ulysses, at arm's length for the entire scene'[24] since, according to the dialogue, out of the seven Greeks named as present at least four get close enough to kiss her, Patroclus twice. Howard Davies's production in 1985 showed Cressida being grabbed and flung from man to man until she recovered her self-possession by means of the same defence she had used against Pandarus: sarcasm. This conforms both to Luke Spencer's view in 1982, that: 'Cressida has been passed from hand to hand by the Greek generals in a ceremony that parodies their declared allegiance to collective responsibility'[25] as well as to Carolyne Asp's reading in 1977, that: 'as she is passed from man to man', Ulysses contemptuously 'emphasizes her weakness in this masculine world'.[26] It is somewhat different from Mark van Doren's conception of the scene as displaying the crude quality of Cressida's coyness, for 'each joint and motive of her body is so eloquent of the game as she passes down the row of Greeks lined up to kiss her'.[27] That view was clearly influenced by what Ulysses says ('Her wanton spirits look out / At every joint and motive of her body'), identifying her as one of:

> these encounterers so glib of tongue,
> That give accosting welcome ere it comes,
> And wide unclasp the tables of their thoughts
> To every ticklish reader.   (4.6.59–62)

Yet neither Pandarus nor Troilus was able to read Cressida's thoughts.

Ulysses has, of course, just been made to look a fool, and did not get the sexual thrill he had presumably hoped for in setting up the 'game'. The fact that he is 'ticklish' does not mean that Cressida is happy to tickle him. The suggestion that Cressida has somehow 'asked for it' obscures the grotesqueness of her being kissed full on the lips by Nestor, a man old enough to be her grandfather, and the disgust-ing innuendo of Patroclus' kiss (if Palmer is correct about 'popping'[28]). That this is not a 'ceremonial salute', as Yoder tried to redeem it,[29] is made quite clear when we see, almost immediately, the respect with which the chiefs greet Hector, in what might have been an

---

[24] Grant L. Voth and Oliver H. Evans, 'Cressida and the World of the Play', *Shakespeare Studies*, 8 (1975), 231–40, p. 236.

[25] Luke Spencer, 'Mediation and Judgement: The Challenge of *Troilus and Cressida*', in Jowitt and Taylor, *Self and Society*, 80–95, p. 88.

[26] Carolyn Asp, 'In Defense of Cressida', *Studies in Philology*, 74 (1977), 406–17, p. 413.

[27] Mark Van Doren, *Shakespeare* (New York, 1939), p. 207.

[28] 'IV.v.28. *hardiment*] act of daring; but I suspect Patroclus of an obscene allusion to tumescence (cf. *pop* = thrust in, or enter, suddenly and unexpectedly)': *Troilus and Cressida*, ed. Kenneth Palmer, the new Arden Shakespeare (London, 1982). At 4.5.61 Palmer chooses *ticklish*, which he glosses as 'easily aroused (especially sexually)', following the Q reading, rather than F's *tickling* which both Kenneth Muir and Alice Walker prefer. Alice Walker comments: 'Q has been widely approved, but it looks like a case of assimilation to "sluttish" in the next line and "tickling" gives perfectly good sense: C's wanton spirits are fully disclosed to any one who chooses to encourage them': *Troilus and Cressida*, ed. Alice Walker, New Shakespeare (Cambridge, 1957). Kenneth Muir, adopting *tickling*, suggests that Shakespeare may have altered *ticklish* (Q) to avoid the repetition of sound in *sluttish*: 'Both words make good sense: the admirers can be described as making lustful advances, or as being sexually aroused by daughters of the game': *Troilus and Cressida*, ed. Kenneth Muir, Oxford Shakespeare (Oxford, 1982), p. 62. Palmer adds: 'But since the *encounterers* are as active as their partners (compare to line 59), and since *the tables of their thoughts* may be presumed rather to tickle the reader, than to be tickled by him, I retain the Q reading. It is the reader (as Johnson observed of Lord Hailes) who is combustible.' It seems to me that in either case the onus is on the reader (to be tickling or ticklish) rather than on the text/Cressida, which conforms to the Prologue's reference to 'expectation, tickling skittish spirits'. The editors of the Complete Oxford Shakespeare (1986) read 'ticklish' without comment.

[29] R. A. Yoder, '"Sons and Daughters of the Game": An Essay on Shakespeare's *Troilus and Cressida*', *Shakespeare Survey 25* (1972), 11–25, p. 14.

identical welcome. The shock that this assault on Cressida might have given to Seltzer's assumed original Elizabethan audience may be gauged from the fact that earlier versions of the story still current, such as Caxton's, took pains to indicate how respectful the Greeks were toward Cressida, promising to 'hold her as dear as their daughter'.[30] They presumably did not mean 'daughter of the game'.

At the beginning of the play Troilus called on Apollo to tell him: 'What Cressid is, what Pandar, and what we?' (1.1.99). The question of the value and identity of the self is a constant query throughout the play: what's aught but as 'tis valued? Does anyone have an integral value or only by reputation?[31] It is a dilemma that both Hector and Achilles fall foul of. The question is raised particularly with regard to Helen, that 'pearl / Whose price hath launched above a thousand ships / And turned crowned kings to merchants' (2.2.80–2). Helen has been reduced to merchandise, second-hand goods, a soiled pearl whose only power lies in caprice. Ominously, Troilus answers his own query: Cressida is a pearl and he himself a merchant. Passed from Pandarus to Troilus, from Troilus to Diomedes, shoved from one general to another, then back to Diomedes who hands her to her father who passes her back again, she is a pearl cast before swine. When finally Troilus watches her capitulation to Diomedes, her behaviour confirms the valuation at which he already held women: that they were inconstant and could not match his own unquestionable integrity and truth. Yet at first he cannot believe the evidence of his own eyes: 'If there be rule in unity itself, / This was not she. O madness of discourse' (5.2.144–5) although at the very moment he was watching her, he himself was saying: 'I will not be myself, nor have cognition / Of what I feel' (5.2.64–5). The tragedy of Cressida is that she has no power to maintain any sense of her own value, her own identity, in the face of the way she is treated by both Trojans and Greeks. It might be she who says: 'I will not be myself, nor have

any cognition of what I feel', but she is already too far gone for that psychological movement to be a decision. Instead, her capitulation to Diomedes is also her capitulation to the male-dominated ideology: 'Ah, poor our sex! This fault in us I find: / The error of our eye directs our mind' (5.2.111–12).[32] Then, speaking for the play itself, a warning for Troilus and Ulysses, if only they could hear it: 'What error leads must err. O then conclude: / Minds swayed by eyes are full of turpitude' (5.2.13–14). Troilus himself, led by Ulysses, swayed by his eyes, finds his will distastes what it elected. From now on he is motivated by vindictiveness and the brutalizing nature of masculine rivalry becomes apparent.

It seems to me no accident that many critics and producers have taken what Alice Walker called Ulysses' 'realistic' view of Cressida as a guide to her nature, despite his duplicity and other unreliable judgements.[33] In much the same way E. M. W. Tillyard used Ulysses' speech on order to exemplify what he called 'The Elizabethan World Picture' as if there were unanimous agreement as to the nature of reality in Renaissance England. In fact, as we know, it was a time of increasing ideological conflict throughout Europe, resulting in the religious and political civil wars which took place in Britain between 1642 and 1691.[34] Ulysses' speech authoritatively validates auth-

---

30 Raoul Le Fèvre, *Here Begynneth the Volume Intituled and Named the Recuyell of the Historyes of Troye* (trans. W. Caxton (Bruges, c. 1475); compare the discussion by Valerie Smith, 'The History of Cressida'.

31 This question is discussed at more length in Terry Eagleton, *William Shakespeare* (Oxford, 1986), and in Kenneth Palmer's Introduction to his new Arden edition.

32 This point is further substantiated in Jonathan Dollimore, *Radical Tragedy* (Brighton, 1984), chapters 2 and 15.

33 Compare Voth and Evans, 'Cressida and the World of the Play', notes 11 and 12, p. 239.

34 E. M. W. Tillyard, *The Elizabethan World Picture* (London, 1943), pp. 17–20, and compare J. W. Lever, *The Tragedy of State* (London, 1971).

ority and hierarchy as fixed values in a play that constantly questions how values are determined; he delivers this speech during a debate amongst authority figures who mutually bolster each other's sense of self-importance while discussing how their pomposity is ridiculed. As part of their comforting myth of a natural order that guarantees social laws, these 'realistic' Greek men promote and share with the idealistic Trojan men a particular conception of manhood that defines men by contrast with women. This conception is implicit in the very first lines that Troilus speaks in the play. To be a man is to be virile, to be strong, brave and forceful; the most important value for a man is his honour, his reputation for strength and courage, which is determined by his physical prowess. A woman is expected to be weak, to lack courage, and to feel pity; to be 'tame'. She is valued by men for being fair. The value set by men upon male honour and their acquisitive attitude towards female beauty leads inevitably to envious rivalry amongst men, and is a source of the militarism that leads to war.

Despite the fact that for Ulysses, as for Hector, a stable social order based on natural laws is supposed to restrain men's base appetites (because, self-contradictorily, they believe that man is naturally bestial), their conception of manhood not only leads to the social instability of war, it also degrades women and brutalizes men. A man who will not fight is effeminate (i.e. less of a man and more of a woman), and is, in Patroclus' words, to be 'loathed' (3.3.211). A woman who is disrespectful of men's values, impudent, is mannish and equally loathsome. This emphasis on 'natural' sexual distinctions leads to brutish behaviour and denies individuality. It also denies men those responses that are classified as 'feminine' and prevents women from being assertive. Women are powerless in *Troilus and Cressida*: powerless to prevent war and death; powerless to prevent their own debasement into objects without feeling. In

Shakespeare's other plays of the same period it is the powerlessness of what are presented as 'feminine' qualities that leads to chaos and despair, but with the restoration of the feminine 'weaknesses' such as pity, courageous sympathy, and spontaneous generosity (which are the true milk of humankindness in men too) order and grace return. These are precisely the human qualities which find no place in war, and no grace or order blesses the aggressive world of *Troilus and Cressida*. Thus what appeared to Roger Warren to be a drawback in Howard Davies's nineteenth-century setting seems to me to be one of the vindications for updating the play in that way:

The very specifically nineteenth-century setting both helped and hindered Peter Jeffrey's Ulysses. He was given commanding positions behind tables that helped him to deliver the Degree and Time speeches with maximum clarity; but coming from a Victorian statesman in a frock-coat his wisdom sounded like a series of sententious platitudes.[35]

The programme notes, which include discussions by members of the cast concerning the hypocrisy of so-called 'Victorian values', indicate that this was deliberate.

As shown by the examples of Paris and Hector, the pursuit of female beauty or male glory for their own sake is delusive; an obsession with glamorous appearance actually converts the living reality into rottenness. But there is no naked eye available to Troilus to see this, or to see more *in* Cressida (as she sees in Troilus) than Pandarus presents:

PANDARUS I speak no more than truth.
TROILUS Thou dost not speak so much. (1.1.64–5)

Troilus can come to Cressida in Troy only by means of Pandarus; he can only get to her in the Greek army camp by following Diomedes with Ulysses as his guide. Both Ulysses and Pandarus use Troilus vicariously. Pandarus is the entrepreneur who titillates

---

[35] Roger Warren, 'Shakespeare in Britain, 1985', *Shakespeare Quarterly*, 37 (Spring, 1985), 114–20, p. 117.

Troilus by reiterating how 'fair' Cressida is ('fair' is almost the keynote of this play as 'honest' is of *Othello*). He is the showman who produces their first meeting as if it were a play: he interprets Cressida to Troilus, 'She fetches her breath as short as a new-ta'en sparrow' (3.2.31–2); controls and displays her, 'Here she is' (3.2.39); and prompts Troilus' response, 'Why do you not speak to her?' (3.2.44–5), commenting on the effect as he does so, 'Pretty, i' faith' (3.2.132), thus pre-empting all spontaneity. In the Greek camp Troilus watches Cressida flirt with his love-token, and as Diomedes 'tames' Cressida into submission to his will, so Ulysses 'tames' Troilus into patient resignation that Cressida is essentially fickle. Ulysses is already convinced that Cressida 'will sing any man at first sight' (5.2.10) – that she can sight-read a man like a sheet of music and respond immediately as if she knew him well, just as Ulysses could read her body like a text and be tickled by it on sight. Ulysses having been scorned publicly by Cressida is not the aid most likely to show sympathy for her predicament, nor to make it plain to Troilus. His irony to Troilus, 'You are movèd, Prince . . . May worthy Troilus e'en be half attached / With that which here his passion doth express?' (5.2.35, 164–5), is more than a little reminiscent of Iago's provocation of Othello's revulsion. Can the audience, too, only come to Cressida by means of the producer and the critic, those interfering go-betweens?

Pertinently, two actresses who have played Cressida recently have left us their responses to the coercive effect of male interpretations of their role.[36] Juliet Stevenson felt herself threatened by Howard Davies's interpretation of Cressida's relationship with Pandarus and Troilus for the RSC production in 1985. Davies wanted to create a sense of an intimacy between the three of them like the mutual affection in *Jules et Jim*. This went counter to Juliet Stevenson's understanding of the nervous defensiveness that Cressida displays against Pandarus at the beginning, and of her apprehension about Troilus' promises of constancy (which seems justified in the event by what Stevenson took for his betrayal of Cressida to Diomedes). Howard Davies's idea about this happy threesome echoes what Anton Lesser said in Fenwick's account of Jonathan Miller's 1981 production for BBC Television, in which Lesser had also played Troilus: 'It's an amazing triumvirate, Pandarus and Troilus and Cressida – what we discovered together was the mutual dependence that they had, which led to the emotional trauma when one of them is ejected and the triple relationship breaks up.' This does not cohere with what Suzanne Burden says about her understanding of Cressida in the same article: 'Taught by Pandarus, she's just about learned the ropes and she's quite aware that to him she's a puppet, a plaything he enjoys, but as soon as he's through playing that game he'll forget her . . . I felt she was a victim of states and men and rulers.' Miller himself sounds much more sympathetic to Cressida than Pandarus or Ulysses do, at first, but then he reveals himself as another ticklish reader: 'What we see is not the inevitable blossoming of a corrupt and sexually titillating girl, but the disintegration of a girl whose innocence is too inexperienced to handle the shock and the overwhelming stimulus of these rough attractive Greek warriors she comes across.' Under his direction Suzanne Burden played Cressida as sexually excited by being kissed, as thoroughly enjoying the game and her own power of arousal. She herself said:

I used to get terribly upset in the first days of rehearsal when people would say, 'She's nothing

---

36 Juliet Stevenson, 'Foolish Dreaming Superstitious Girls – Female Perspectives in the Plays (and in the Rehearsal Room)', an unpublished talk given at Royal Shakespeare Theatre Summer School, Stratford, 1985 and Suzanne Burden, in an interview for Henry Fenwick, 'The Production', *The BBC Television Shakespeare 'Troilus and Cressida'* (London, 1981).

but a tart and a sexual tease.' Instinctively I would feel quite angry but I couldn't explain why she wasn't. I saw her as a witty, intelligent young woman . . . just discovering herself . . . She's been brought up in a sophisticated man's world and she's enormously unprotected . . . She doesn't know what's happening and she's terrified, and her survival instincts come into play. She thinks, 'There's got to be a way out of this and if I have to use my sex I will'.

Juliet Stevenson managed to develop on the stage the idea of Cressida's vulnerability. She believed that, being hustled away from Troilus on the first morning after losing her virginity to him, Cressida is emotionally raw and experiences the kissing-game as a brutal sexual assault from which she defends herself by her only weapon: sarcasm. Stevenson's interpretation was partially successful for at least one other critic in the audience besides Robert Wilcher. Roger Warren saw that Stevenson's playing of a 'mercurial Cressida' in Act 1 was to use 'a brazen manner [as] a cover to protect herself from becoming a love-object like Helen'. But, after 'the generals subjected her to brutally violent kisses that amounted to assault', at first appalled, she then begins 'to play their game' and becomes a love-object like Helen after all: 'Ulysses made the parallel with Helen specific'.[37] It seems to me that Cressida was lost from the first moment she tried to take Troilus' sport seriously, but she is still demanding fair play at that moment of confrontation with Ulysses, a stalemate that is ended only by Diomedes' intervention. In the last analysis, women do not even have the power to play hard to get; they can be assaulted both physically and mentally, which is what Ulysses does make clear. Yet it is not until she is called out of her father's tent by her 'guardian' that Cressida finally succumbs to being a toy in a boys' game, treating Troilus' token for what it is worth. Stevenson acted the flirtation scene with Diomedes as if Cressida had been emotionally cauterized.

Juliet Stevenson's Stratford talk was ironically entitled: 'Foolish Dreaming Superstitious Girls' with the clear implication that some women, Cassandra-like, may have a true vision of the play which men might consider mad. Yet, as we can see from the example of Alice Walker and Joyce Carol Oates, most women's ability to see is as much conditioned as men's by the dominant values and conceptions of their culture.[38] The text cannot determine how either women or men read it, although editors, producers, and actors may incline our understanding towards their particular reading, since they control the medium by which we come to the text. Joyce Carol Oates, writing in 1967, was even more vehement than Victorian male critics had been in her denunciation of Cressida as 'villainous'. The one Victorian critic to speak up for Cressida was G. B. Shaw, who was vilified for the stand he took against war fever during the 1914–18 War. One of the first recorded English productions was mounted by the pacifist William Poel as that fever was gathering momentum in 1912; it was not a success, and the play only gained appreciative audiences from among the war-weary in 1920. Despite the wide regard for Jan Kott's views, the critical revision of Cressida did not gather strength until the 1970s.

The general move towards exonerating Cressida for inauthenticity (although there was still no agreement as to whether Ulysses was 'clear-sighted' or not) took place on both sides of the Atlantic. In a paper published in 1972, the time of the war in Vietnam, the American critic Audrey Yoder spoke of *Troilus and Cressida* as 'our play', because 'we know what this society and its war has done to

---

37 Roger Warren, 'Shakespeare in Britain, 1985', p. 17.
38 For other morally unfavourable judgements of Cressida by women see: Ellis-Fermor, *The Frontiers of Drama*; Winifred Nowottny, '"Opinion" and "Value" in *Troilus and Cressida*', *Essays in Criticism*, 4 (1954), 282–96; Mary Ellen Rickey, '"Twixt the Dangerous Shores": *Troilus and Cressida* Again', *Shakespeare Quarterly*, 15 (1964), 3–13.

our best youth'. Quoting with approval from Kott with regard to Cressida's 'rude awakening', Yoder said that 'among the Greeks [Cressida] is bound to be exposed and degraded . . . the Greek generals are taking what Cressida, essentially a captive, has no real power to refuse. She plays their game with wit and spirit, for that is her best defence . . . it is self-righteous for her world to judge Cressida. After all, she is simply practicing the way of that world.'[39] In a further sympathetic reading of Cressida published in 1975, not long after Watergate, Voth and Evans challenged the 'constant' critical judgement that Cressida is 'a mere prostitute, a cold and calculating woman': 'Insofar as her actions are determined by the real world of the play, a world which makes human attempts at ideals nothing more than attempts to give "fair" covering to sordidness and corruption, Cressida is not responsible' except for 'the "folly" of ignoring her knowledge of this world'.[40] By this date the women's movement in America was creating a new perspective on literature and expressly feminist criticism of Shakespeare was gaining official recognition.[41] However, in 1977 Carolyn Asp developed a view of Cressida which she had first indicated in 1971, contesting the general critical opinion that Cressida was 'either shallow or calculating, or both'. Asp claimed that the text will not allow us [sic] 'to dismiss her as Ulysses describes her, merely "a daughter of the game"'; rather, she shares 'the weakness of those who cannot see value in themselves independently of perceivers'. Conforming to Ulysses' insistence that 'it is public opinion that reveals the inner self', Cressida 'attempts to establish her value by the only way her culture allows. She uses her physical beauty to attract the praise of men.'[42] This interpretation not only ignores the sex and cultural power of 'the perceivers'; it slides over the particular vulnerability of women which is the 'weakness' Cressida shares. The first politically feminist interpretation of Cressida's character appeared in 1980: Gayle

Greene's 'Shakespeare's Cressida: "A kind of self"'. Commencing by stating that 'human nature is not "natural", but is, rather, shaped by social forces', Greene follows Raymond Southall's characterization of Cressida's society as 'a world informed with the "spirit of capitalism . . . busily reducing life to the demands of the belly"'. Cressida, treated as a cake or pearl, 'reminds us of the effects of capitalism on women'. Cressida is 'a cynical coquette' who treats 'love as combat' because she understands the principles of her society, 'though she is helpless to act on what she knows'.[43] It would have been interesting if Greene had made the connection between the greedy spirit of capitalism implicit in the play's language and the envious rivalry of militarism in the action of the play, to show how Shakespeare traces the source of war in the depreciation of women and 'feminine' values.

The general revaluation of Cressida in England seems to have commenced in 1975 with an article by John Bayley which suggested that 'When Ulysses calls her a daughter of the game we may feel obscurely that he is wrong.' Recognizing that 'Social exigencies compel [both Chaucer's and Shakespeare's Cressidas] to act in ways which society then condemns', he nevertheless considers that the play's action 'exhibits but does not explain' Cressida's predicament.[44] In 1978 Ann Thompson could still find Cressida 'repellant'[45] and in 1980 Kenneth Palmer was still

---

[39] Yoder, '"Sons and Daughters of the Game"', pp. 122–3.

[40] Voth and Evans, 'Cressida and the World of the Play', p. 237.

[41] Preface to Lenz, Greene and Neely, *The Woman's Part*.

[42] Asp, 'In Defence of Cressida', pp. 406–10 and also see '"Th' Expense of Spirit in a Waste of Shame"', *Shakespeare Quarterly*, 22 (1971), 345–57.

[43] Greene, 'Shakespeare's Cressida', p. 137.

[44] John Bayley, 'Time and the Trojans', *Essays in Criticism*, 25 (1975), 55–73, quotations from pp. 67, 68, and 69 respectively.

[45] Ann Thompson, *Shakespeare's Chaucer: A Study in Literary Origins* (Liverpool, 1978), p. 126.

speaking of Cressida as inexplicably 'trans-formed as she enters the Greek camp', and repeating, without qualification, Ulysses' judgement of Cressida as a whore.[46] Kenneth Muir felt that 'it should not be held against Cressida' that she is sensuous, or 'treated as a sex-object', but he also repeats the idea of her as a whore and speaks of her 'uninhibited behaviour on her arrival in the Greek camp'.[47] The views of Muir and Palmer are likely to be influential since their editions will be used in schools and universities. However, in 1982 a group of papers read at a conference in Leeds tried to explain Cressida's predicament in terms of the ideology of her society. Ironically, in view of the imminent Falklands conflict, Valerie Smith concluded:

Part of the change in critical attitudes towards the play has been brought about by a change in public attitudes towards war. Two world wars have made people wary of the public-school heroism of Hector and Achilles, who talk about the Trojan campaign as though it were an extended Test Match. More particularly, where Cressida is concerned, the new current of feminist thinking has led to a revaluation of traditional attitudes towards women.[48]

Jonathan Dollimore discussed *Troilus and Cressida* in 1984 as part of a general re-appraisal of sixteenth- and seventeenth-century drama in terms of the contemporary debate about natural law and concluded that: 'The discontinuity in Cressida's identity stems not from her nature, but from her position in the patriarchal order.'[49]

Such political radicalism may not be widespread, but after the powerful influence of the Women's Movement, Juliet Stevenson's audience in 1985 might have been less inclined to view the play through Troilus' eyes as directed by Ulysses. Ros Asquith, reviewing that production for *The Observer* (30 June 1985), thought that 'almost every woman on the planet' could have the insight to see Cressida 'as a human being torn between love and survival, rather than as a flirtatious plaything'. Perhaps now more women would consider,

apparently 'instinctively' like Suzanne Burden did, that Cressida may not behave as she does merely in order to tease, even if men find her tickling. Her attempts to gain the upper hand over Diomedes by playing hard-to-get are pitiful, but sympathy for 'her choice . . . between rapist or protector' as Asquith put it need not be sentimentalized. Burden points out that Cressida never tells Diomedes that she loves him. No, but she talks of giving her heart together with Troilus' love token, dangling it tantalizingly in a context that equates 'heart' with 'cunt'. If she has become emotionally 'hollow', that is because no real choice of emotional commitment has been left open to her. I think one difficulty for women in the audience now is that they may sympathize too much with Cressida, identifying too far with a feminist wish for female integrity to be able to acknowledge what she is finally forced to become. If she is not precisely a whore, she is synthetic. Ros Asquith found that: 'Juliet Stevenson is . . . a startling and forceful Cressida.' Someone who is as much in two minds as Cressida states herself to be, and as 'subject to exploitative definitions of her by men'[50] (which she is shown as powerless to control), can scarcely be forceful. In this play valuing is not detached appraisal; it is an active, dynamic process which affects what is valued. Pursued for her sexual allure, Cressida gradually learns to read her own self through the double-minded male discourse that dominates her by the end of the play; degraded, she becomes as it were a corrupt text.

Ros Asquith praised Howard Davies's production, describing it as 'visually seductive'. This statement pinpoints a problem inherent in most of this century's productions. If the text is now generally agreed to be concerned with

---

[46] Palmer, 'Introduction', p. 57.
[47] Muir, 'Introduction', pp. 36–7.
[48] Smith, 'The History of Cressida', p. 76.
[49] Dollimore, *Radical Tragedy*, p. 48.
[50] Sinfield, 'Kinds of Loving', p. 33.

the seductive process by which the pursuit of fair appearances corrupts reality itself, then producers and designers need to find a mode which will express this to the audience. Any mode chosen still has to overcome a pre-established adherence to the very values which the play exposes as inauthentic. Naturalism actually tends to reproduce the aggressively materialistic representations of women's sexuality which our culture enforces, along with the egoistic greediness which leads to rivalry and war. Making a production as glamorously 'realistic' as possible simply encourages the audience to read with its eyes only, superficially. Shakespeare's text tells us little about the theatrical conventions of his time, but certain scenes are pointedly non-naturalistic. Hector's encounter with the enticing corpse in armour is an example of such an emblematic scene.[51] My own feeling is that, despite the insight into the play to be gained from Juliet Stevenson's committed performance and Howard Davies's choice of a Victorian setting in 1985–6, modern audiences, both women and men, might benefit from the reintroduction of two non-naturalistic conventions of Shakespeare's time: doubling and the use of male actors for female roles. The way in which readers are influenced by their own sexual expectations might be better brought home if the female parts were played not by glamorous, nubile young women, but by men. The point that women are constructed by cultural values would be made more effectively if the two wives, Andromache and Helen, were played by the same actor, and if one other actor played both Cassandra and Cressida. Audiences, of course, do not much enjoy being estranged in this way. Like other readers, they prefer to be tickled pink by vicarious excitement.

---

[51] Significantly, this scene had to be omitted from Davies's modern dress production, see Alan C. Dessen, 'Price-tags and Trade-offs: Chivalry and the Shakespearean Hero in 1985', *Shakespeare Quarterly*, 37 (1986), 102–6, p. 104.

ANTONY AND CLEOPATRA, ACT 4 SCENE 16: 'A HEAVY SIGHT'

LESLIE THOMSON

Just how did Shakespeare intend the dying Antony to be raised to Cleopatra in her monument? By what means? By whom? How high? To where? Was there a balustrade to get him over? Was there a window to get him through? These questions have long puzzled theatre historians, and a variety of ingenious answers has been offered.[1] The text has become a basis for speculation on the physical characteristics of the Globe Theatre both because of and despite the fact that it provides no direction other than: '*They heave Antony aloft to Cleopatra*' (4.16.38.1). While it is usually assumed that more explicit stage directions are missing, it is also possible that what we have is sufficient and an indication that Shakespeare knew what he wanted and how it would be done. Certainly, given his theatrical experience, it is most unlikely that he would have created staging problems requiring complex and therefore expensive and restrictive solutions.

Emendations and additions proposed by most modern scholars are made in the belief that without them the raising of Antony would be disconcertingly and unsuitably awkward. Perhaps, however, we should consider whether Shakespeare intended exactly this effect, and we should begin by asking not 'how' but 'why' Antony is raised aloft. To suggest that Shakespeare was merely following Plutarch ignores alterations to his source elsewhere.[2] Furthermore, by 1606–8 Shakespeare would not have included staging diffi-

culties without a reason; if such difficulties had interfered with his intentions they would not be there. But possibly, rather than being directed by Plutarch and restricted by the Globe stage, Shakespeare saw a way to combine its physical properties with his interpretation of a famous love story so that one would complement the other. When the focus is shifted from how Antony was raised to why, it becomes apparent that the disturbing relationship between the manner and matter of this scene is similar to that in the play as a whole. And when the scene is no longer considered in isolation from the rest it is possible to perceive how it is prepared for both visually and verbally by what comes before it and is itself the beginning of what follows. Given the paradoxes that pervade the play, when we return to the question of how Antony was raised, the theories seeking to remove staging difficulties become less convincing and a solution that emphasizes the awkwardness rather than removing it seems worth proposing.

'I do not much dislike the matter, but / The manner of his speech' (2.2.116–17), says Caesar, the master of ceremonies, about Enobarbus, the plain-speaking observer. An audience is likely to have a similar response to

---

[1] Some of these will be discussed below.

[2] It is generally agreed that North's translation of Plutarch was Shakespeare's main source. See Kenneth Muir, *Shakespeare's Sources*, 8 vols. (London and New York, 1957), vol. 1, 201–19.

the raising of Antony in 4.16 and, just as Caesar's ability to manipulate responses should not be underestimated, neither should Shakespeare's. As observers of this love story we 'like', are emotionally engaged by, the romantic matter: the raising of Antony to join Cleopatra in a final embrace; but we 'dislike', are detached by, the realistic manner: the awkwardness of doing so insisted upon by the dialogue. We experience – and not for the first time – a sense of being pulled two ways in our response, as Antony is pulled between Rome and Egypt until this moment in the play. As has often been noted, Shakespeare's method throughout seems to have been to create as many disconcerting ambiguities for the audience as possible.[3] Especially for the seventeenth-century observer, expectations fostered by Plutarch's criticism of Antony for loving Cleopatra are countered by Shakespeare's refusal to condemn him. As well, while ostensibly a tragedy, the play is actually an inseparable mix of tragedy, comedy, history, and romance. And whereas we know that Caesar's Rome represents the time of 'universal peace', we cannot but regret the loss of the potentially anarchic life-force represented by Cleopatra's Egypt. These and consequent incidental ambiguities pull us, vacillating, through the play until the moment when Antony – the *de casibus* hero, the victim of Fortune[4] – does not fall as convention dictates but rises to die. That he is raised not only literally, visually, but also metaphorically, and that the raising is both physically awkward and accompanied by puns on heaviness is completely in keeping with the confusing juxtaposition of manner and matter throughout the play. Indeed, this scene is one of several emblematic moments and it works as a microcosm of the wider themes and effects. In particular, when Cleopatra refuses to descend from her monument and Antony must go to her, we see an ironic enactment of the first three lines of that characterizing and characteristic opening exchange between Antony and Cleopatra:

CLEOPATRA If it be love indeed, tell me how much.
ANTONY There's beggary in the love that can be reckoned.
CLEOPATRA I'll set a bourn how far to be beloved.
ANTONY Then must thou needs find out new heaven, new earth. (1.1.14–17)

Antony's condition in the fourth line is met by Cleopatra when she becomes 'fire and air' (5.2.284) and joins Antony in an imaginary realm beyond the power of the 'universal landlord' (3.13.72).

Antony's death scene is the last of a series in which Cleopatra causes Antony to move towards her and he willingly does so. In fact, Cleopatra's power to pull Antony to her, both physically and emotionally, can be seen as a key organizing principle of the language and structure of the play. In 4.16 this idea becomes almost farcically literal when Cleopatra refuses to descend from her monument and asks her women to help 'draw him hither' (line 14). The audience is confronted with a visual enactment of the duality characteristic of Antony from the start: as a soldier he is weak for allowing himself to be drawn, but as a lover he is admirable for being willing to go to Cleopatra. Through the play, Antony himself describes his predicament in terms that will perhaps have some bearing when we consider how he is raised to Cleopatra:

These strong Egyptian fetters I must break,
Or lose myself in dotage. (1.2.110–11)

I must from this enchanting queen break off.
(1.2.122)

---

[3] See Maynard Mack, '*Antony and Cleopatra*: The Stillness and the Dance', in *Shakespeare's Art*, ed. Milton Crane (Chicago and London, 1973), pp. 79–113. The whole of this study of the play's paradoxical nature provides support for the present analysis but section IV is particularly relevant.

[4] Mack notes that we are given the impression of 'a sort of paradigm or exemplum in the de casibus tradition', and also that '"fortune" . . . with its cognates and synonyms, appears some forty times in *Antony and Cleopatra* . . . and repeatedly in connection with Caesar', pp. 86, 87.

when poisoned hours had bound me up
From mine own knowledge.   (2.2.95–6)

While from the safety of the auditorium we might be inclined to agree with Antony's self-condemnation, we are repeatedly prompted to question our response when even Enobarbus and Caesar acknowledge Cleopatra's drawing power. Our expectations are countered when the Roman soldier, Enobarbus, departs from his characteristic cynicism to describe the Egyptian queen who has captured his captain's heart. But he immediately returns to his habitual irony when describing the first of many similar responses by Antony and again the language used and the description of the action prepare us for what we hear and see in 4.16. After impressing his listeners with his description of Cleopatra on the Cydnus, Enobarbus continues:

Upon her landing Antony sent to her,
Invited her to supper. She replied
It would be better he became her guest,
Which she entreated. Our courteous Antony,
Whom ne'er the word of 'No' woman heard
          speak,
Being barbered ten times o'er, goes to the feast,
And for his ordinary pays his heart
For what his eyes eat only.   (2.2.226–33)

Caesar, too, departs briefly from his characteristically business-like, unemotional mode of speech when he describes Cleopatra, and acknowledges a power that endures even in death:

but she looks like sleep,
As she would catch another Antony
In her strong toil of grace.   (5.2.340–2)

If the process that brings Antony to the monument to die is begun at Cydnus, so too is the corresponding one that causes Cleopatra to join him in death at the play's end ('I am again for Cydnus', 5.2.224). Indeed, the sequence of Cleopatra's retreat to her monument having told Antony she is dead, Antony's attempt to go to her by killing himself, Cleopatra's

message that she is alive, Antony's movement to the monument, their brief reunion, their separation by his death, and their final union at her death is prepared for by several similar sequences. Each time the two lovers move in tandem: Cleopatra initiating, Antony following, Cleopatra retreating, Antony following, Cleopatra finally moving to him; whereupon the whole process begins again. This is not merely a verbal separating and reuniting but also a physical one and thus visible throughout, culminating in the moment when Antony is lifted up to Cleopatra.

Antony and Cleopatra enter the action together. They argue and separate. In the second scene Cleopatra enters looking for Antony who she says has been struck by 'a Roman thought'. She asks Enobarbus to 'Seek him, and bring him hither', but even as Antony enters, Cleopatra leaves saying, 'We will not look upon him' (1.2.77–81). Her purpose in this perverse action is made clear in the next scene when Cleopatra again asks for Antony and sends Charmian to:

See where he is, who's with him, what he does.
I did not send you. If you find him sad,
Say I am dancing; if in mirth, report
That I am sudden sick.

Charmian protests, 'if you did love him dearly, / You do not hold the method to enforce / The like from him'. She advises Cleopatra to 'give him way; cross him in nothing'. Cleopatra scornfully replies, 'Thou teachest like a fool, the way to lose him', and immediately repeats her earlier action when Antony enters and she insists on their separation: 'Pray you, stand farther from me' (1.3.2–18). They argue about Fulvia's death and Antony's imminent departure, but as he is leaving, Cleopatra finally asks forgiveness for her 'idleness' (line 95) and wishes him a successful journey. They embrace, and Antony's response indicates that this first sequence has ended, as will the last, in a reunion that transcends the physical:

Our separation so abides and flies
That thou residing here goes yet with me,
And I hence fleeting, here remain with thee.

(1.3.103–5)

The long separation of Antony and Cleopatra in the present action, wherein Antony
seems to move away from Cleopatra by
marrying Octavia, is filled first with Enobarbus' description of the events on the Cydnus
that concludes with Maecenas saying, 'Now
Antony / Must leave her utterly', and Enobarbus' reply, which underlines Cleopatra's
ability to draw others to her:

Never. He will not.
Age cannot wither her, nor custom stale
Her infinite variety. Other women cloy
The appetites they feed, but she makes hungry
Where most she satisfies. (2.2.240–4)

We are not surprised when, just forty-three
lines later, Antony says, 'I will to Egypt; / And
though I make this marriage for my peace, / I'
th' East my pleasure lies' (2.3.36–8).

To keep the lovers' relationship in the fore-
front despite their continued separation in the
present, we are next given another suggestive
description of Antony and Cleopatra. For
Cleopatra it is merely a fanciful image, but the
echoes of Cydnus and the foreshadowing of
4.16 are surely deliberate on Shakespeare's
part.

Give me mine angle. We'll to th' river. There,
My music playing far off, I will betray
Tawny-finned fishes. My bended hook shall
    pierce
Their slimy jaws, and as I draw them up
I'll think them every one an Antony,
And say 'Ah ha, you're caught!' (2.5.10–15)

The sequences of separation and reunion are
played out in a minor key in the two exchanges
between Cleopatra and the Messenger – a
substitute for Antony – who comes to tell her
of Antony's marriage to Octavia (2.5, 3.3). In
passing, it is worth observing that, like the
first, this conflict ends on a hopeful note ('All
may be well enough', 3.3.46), arguably at the

last moment when hope for Antony and Cleopatra in the physical, political world is
possible.

The Actium sequence begins with Cleopatra
insisting that she join Antony in battle despite
Enobarbus' protests. And his fears are confirmed when Cleopatra,

        – i' th' midst o' th' fight –
When vantage like a pair of twins appeared,
Both as the same, or rather ours the elder –
The breese upon her, like a cow in June,
Hoists sails and flies . . .

        She once being luffed,
The noble ruin of her magic, Antony,
Claps on his sea-wing and, like a doting
    mallard,
Leaving the fight in height, flies after her.

(3.10.11–15, 17–20)

In the next scene, it takes some effort by Eros,
Iras, and Charmian to bring Antony and Cleopatra together again. A distraught Antony
asks, 'O, whither hast thou led me, Egypt?'
Cleopatra responds, 'Forgive my fearful sails! I
little thought / You would have followed'
(3.11.51, 55–6). This reply is frequently met
with hoots of derision and incredulity from
spectators and critics, and even Antony finds it
hard to accept:

        Egypt, thou knew'st too well
My heart was to thy rudder tied by th' strings,
And thou shouldst tow me after. O'er my spirit
Thy full supremacy thou knew'st, and that
Thy beck might from the bidding of the gods
Command me. (3.11.56–61)

The scene ends with their temporary reconciliation, but now there is a note of sadness –
Shakespeare invites us to say 'heaviness' – as
well:

Fall not a tear, I say. One of them rates
All that is won and lost. Give me a kiss.
    He kisses her
Even this repays me. (*To an Attendant*) We sent
    our schoolmaster;
Is a come back? (*To Cleopatra*) Love, I am full of
    lead. (*Calling*) Some wine

Within there, and our viands! Fortune knows
We scorn her most when most she offers blows.
(3.11.69–74)

The imagery used by Antony to describe Cleopatra's effect on him and the juxtaposition of their kiss with his defiance of Fortune anticipate the scene towards which Shakespeare is pulling them and us.

But this sequence of together, apart, together, apart, together is not yet complete. When Antony sees Thidias kissing Cleopatra's hand they draw apart once more until Cleopatra again initiates their reconciliation, whereupon Antony is 'satisfied' (3.13.170), and goes off to his final battle renewed as both lover and soldier.

The final sequence begins by both confirming and questioning this soldier–lover duality when Cleopatra and Eros arm Antony. After the first stage of the battle, a triumphant Antony meets Cleopatra at Alexandria. But the inevitable separation soon follows when, according to Antony, Cleopatra betrays him, and he is defeated by Caesar as a consequence. When Cleopatra enters he spurns her and she flees to her monument, sending the message that she is dead. Her command to Mardian – suggested, ironically, by Charmian – is a reminder of how she has toyed with Antony earlier:

> go tell him I have slain myself.
> Say that the last I spoke was 'Antony',
> And word it, prithee, piteously. Hence,
>   Mardian,
> And bring me how he takes my death. To th'
>   monument!   (4.14.7–10)

That she can do this and not be aware of the probable consequences gives us an important insight into the all too human motives for Cleopatra's actions. Here and earlier when she says, 'I little thought you would have followed', and 'Why is my lord enraged against his love?' (4.13.31), she shows how her need to exercise her power over others, especially Antony – to be loved in the most basic sense –

paradoxically blinds her to the effect that power has on others, especially Antony. She does not, or perhaps cannot, distinguish between the game of love and the game of war – it is all 'sport' to her, and because she conflates the two, so does Antony:

> I made these wars for Egypt, and the Queen –
> Whose heart I thought I had, for she had mine,
> Which whilst it was mine had annexed unto't
> A million more, now lost –   (4.15.15–18)

When he is told that Cleopatra is dead, Antony vows to 'o'ertake' (4.15.44) her by the only possible means: suicide. But the sequence is not complete: Cleopatra is alive and the dying Antony asks to be taken to her for the ritual embrace of reconciliation. When he dies they are separated physically for the last time but, also for the final time, it is Cleopatra who will make the movement towards Antony to finish the sequence and the play by dying herself and joining him in the world of myth.

Manner and matter conflict in Shakespeare's treatment of both Antony's and Cleopatra's suicides – one might say they die in the 'high Egyptian fashion'. As is the case throughout the play, what is said counters the effect of what is done so that our response is equally mixed. Cleopatra's suicide – made possible by a simple peasant whose unintentional puns prompt both our amusement and analysis – is prepared for when Antony bungles his suicide and must be cumbersomely lifted to a punning Cleopatra. But while on one level her puns are intentional, she, like the 'rural fellow' (5.2.229), says more than she knows.

For an audience whose ears have become attuned to the puns and paradoxes about the related ideas of weight, bearing, drawing, rising, and falling that fill the play,[5] both the action of raising Antony and the accompany-

---

[5] As far as I can discover, no studies of the play's imagery have analysed this aspect; indeed, it is rarely noted except in passing.

ing language should have implications that preclude any single, unambiguous response. As she will do at her own death, Cleopatra acts as both director of and commentator on the action: 'Help me, my women. – We must draw thee up. / Assist, good friends' (4.16.31–2). 'Draw' recalls the fishing image, already quoted, and stirs up other equally ironic echoes as well. When Agrippa is helping Caesar to manipulate Antony into marrying Octavia he argues, 'Her love to both / Would each to other and all loves to both / Draw after her' (2.2.141–3). And when Octavia is leaving her husband to return to her brother, Antony advises: 'Let your best love draw to that point which seeks / Best to preserve it' (3.4.21–2). As Enobarbus prepares to leave Antony he justifies himself by philosophizing about manner and matter, using imagery to present a negative view of Antony that will be challenged in 4.16:

> Yes, like enough, high-battled Caesar will
> Unstate his happiness and be staged to th' show
> Against a sworder! I see men's judgements are
> A parcel of their fortunes, and things outward
> Do draw the inward quality after them
> To suffer all alike. That he should dream,
> Knowing all measures, the full Caesar will
> Answer his emptiness! Caesar, thou hast
>   subdued
> His judgement, too.   (3.13.28–36)

'Staged' and 'show' are overt references to the theatrical element in the characterization and action important through the play, especially in the final act. As well, the metaphorical 'draw' is heard again. But even more significantly, Enobarbus contrasts a 'full' Caesar with Antony's 'emptiness'. In 4.16 Antony's weight, his heaviness, will be used visibly and verbally to counter this view, but not before a multiplicity of connotations has been brought to our attention. Frequently the implication is overtly bawdy, as when Charmian, having her fortune told, says 'Good Isis, hear me this prayer, though thou deny me a

matter of more weight' (1.2.61–2). Cleopatra imagining Antony on his horse exclaims, 'O happy horse, to bear the weight of Antony!' (1.5.21). This idea is twisted by various Romans into suggestions of Antony's effeminacy, as when Enobarbus riddles, 'If we should serve with horse and mares together, / The horse were merely lost; the mares would bear / A soldier and his horse' (3.7.7–9). The 'bearing' of things literally or metaphorically 'heavy' is referred to in other related contexts. Early in the play Cleopatra foreshadows the complexities of 4.16 by saying to Antony: ''Tis sweating labour / To bear such idleness so near the heart / As Cleopatra this' (1.3.94–6). Of Lepidus, and thus of Antony, Enobarbus says, 'A bears the third part of the world' (2.7.87). And after being defeated, Antony tells his men, 'The land bids me tread no more upon't, / It is ashamed to bear me' (3.11.1–2). Then, describing the consequences of Antony's defeat, Caesar says, 'the three-nooked world / Shall bear the olive freely' (4.6.5–6). In the scene just preceding 4.16, the dying Antony asks his followers to 'Bear me . . . where Cleopatra bides'; they cry, 'Most heavy day!' (4.15.129, 132), but Antony tells them and us how to respond to what will follow:

> Nay, good my fellows, do not please sharp fate
> To grace it with your sorrows. Bid that
>   welcome
> Which comes to punish us, and we punish it,
> Seeming to bear it lightly. Take me up.
> I have led you oft; carry me now, good friends,
> And have my thanks for all.   (4.15.133–8)

Finally, when Cleopatra tells Dolabella of her dream Antony, he replies: 'Your loss is as yourself, great, and you bear it / As answering to the weight' (5.2.100–1).

Cleopatra's comment as they begin to lift Antony to her, 'Here's sport indeed' (4.16.33), has puzzled, even offended many who think it out of place at this serious moment. Others, however, have perceived the allusion to

Charmian's earlier description of past sport with Antony:[6]

> 'Twas merry when
> You wagered on your angling, when your diver
> Did hang a salt fish on his hook, which he
> With fervency drew up.   (2.5.15–18)

As suggested above, Cleopatra's responses to Antony's accusation of betrayal invite us to conclude that it is all angling for attention, all sport to her; paradoxically, it is only when she is literally drawing up the consequences of her actions that she gains the inner strength to downplay the seriousness by making light of heaviness, as it were. Her punning words, 'How heavy weighs my lord! / Our strength is all gone into heaviness, / That makes the weight' (4.16.33–5) can be contrasted with Caesar's earlier criticism of Antony's indulgence in 'mirth' and 'sport', and his self-righteous warning: ' – yet must Antony / No way excuse his foils when we do bear / So great weight in his lightness' (1.4.18, 29, 23–5).

In the political world Caesar rises as Antony falls. But countering this, and complicating our response, is that as Antony falls in that context, he is raised, both literally and figuratively in another: the world of love.[7] When Antony asks the Soothsayer, 'Whose fortunes shall rise higher: Caesar's or mine?' (2.3.15), he prompts the audience to formulate an answer. After Actium, Antony describes himself as 'declined' (3.13.26) and speaks of his 'fall' (3.13.158, 4.13.48). In defeat he also speaks of his 'baseness' (4.15.57, 77) which, considering Shakespeare's use of 'base' in *Richard II* (3.3.175–93), probably has a similar significance here. But when he has regained his soldier's confidence he can conflate war and love: 'To business that we love we rise betime, / And go to't with delight' (4.4.20–1). And if the first words of Antony's men when they see he is dying are, 'The star is fall'n' (4.15.106), Antony's nadir as a Roman and a soldier coincides with the beginning of a process that seems intended to raise him in our estimation as a human being and lover.[8] From the point when Antony bungles his suicide, our appreciation of what makes him great, of his magnanimity and its effect on others, is fostered and we are prompted to agree that he 'do[es] . . . not basely die' (4.16.57). When he learns Cleopatra has lied about her death he unquestioningly forgives her and goes willingly to the new 'bourn' she has set 'how far to be beloved'. But it is especially after Antony has died that Cleopatra 'find[s] out new heaven, new earth' in the world of the imagination – hers and ours – where she establishes an Antony who 'grew the more by reaping' and rises to join him saying, 'I am fire and air; my other elements / I give to baser life' (5.2.87, 284–5).

---

6 For a survey of early opinion see *The Tragedie of Anthonie, and Cleopatra*, in the New Variorum Edition, ed. H. H. Furness (Philadelphia and London, 1907), vol. 15, pp. 318–19, note 43.

7 See David Bevington, *Action is Eloquence* (Cambridge, Mass., and London, 1984). Discussing 'ironies of visual hierarchy' in Shakespeare, he says they 'can be found in the monument scene in *Antony and Cleopatra* where the lifting up of the dying Antony to Cleopatra and her women simultaneously emphasizes his tragic failure (expressed in the heaviness of his body and the cumbersomeness of lifting him aloft right before the spectators' eyes) and his elevation to mythic greatness as the immortal lover of the Egyptian queen', p. 107.

8 See Robert Ornstein, 'The Ethic of the Imagination: Love and Art in *Antony and Cleopatra*', in *Later Shakespeare*, eds J. R. Brown and B. Harris, Stratford-upon-Avon Studies 8 (London, 1966): 'Whatever ironies attach to the manner of Antony's death, he is raised visually, and poetically, above the earth on which the melancholy Enobarbus sinks', p. 42. And Maurice Charney, *Shakespeare's Roman Plays* (Cambridge, Mass., 1961), notes that the fall of Antony is 'marked by a persistent imagery of vertical dimension'; that . . . Antony's place is an elevated one (both literally and figuratively) and in its own way defies the temporal height of Caesar. The note of fulfillment and reconciliation in this image places the fate of Antony outside the toils of tragedy', pp. 133, 135.

Since manner and matter, ideal and reality are never reconciled in any element of the play and our response is always equivocal as a consequence, it is not surprising that Cleopatra's motives are perhaps not as admirable as the actions and language they produce. From the moment she flees up into her monument until she escapes up into death she is acting to avoid being, in Antony's telling phrase, 'hoist . . . up to the shouting plebeians' by Caesar (4.13.34). From one perspective, Antony's death marks the beginning of a struggle between Cleopatra and Caesar to see who will direct and star in the rest of the show. In a way that Antony is not, both are consummate performers always playing to and conscious of an audience; neither would or could allow himself or herself to be 'hoist' anywhere as Antony so willingly does. But Antony senses Cleopatra's greatest fear and his angry threat is accurate: Act 5 is a contest between Caesar's desire to lead Cleopatra in triumph and her determination to stage a triumph of her own.

Cleopatra's immediate response to Antony's threat (4.13.32–9) is to flee to the safety of her monument. And when the dying Antony pleads for a last kiss, she refuses, revealing the fear his words have planted:

> Dear, my lord, pardon. I dare not,
> Lest I be taken. Not th'imperious show
> Of the full-fortuned Caesar ever shall
> Be brooched with me, if knife, drugs, serpents, have
> Edge, sting, or operation. I am safe.
>
> (4.16.23–7)

When Proculeius comes to persuade Cleopatra to surrender, she asks defiantly: 'Shall they hoist me up / And show me to the shouting varletry / Of censuring Rome?' (5.2.54–6). Later when a sympathetic Dolabella confirms Caesar's intention Cleopatra tells Iras:

> Thou, an Egyptian puppet shall be shown
> In Rome, as well as I. Mechanic slaves
> With greasy aprons, rules, and hammers shall
> Uplift us to the view . . .

> The quick comedians
> Extemporally will stage us, and present
> Our Alexandrian revels. Antony
> Shall be brought drunken forth, and I shall see
> Some squeaking Cleopatra boy my greatness
> I' th' posture of a whore.   (5.2.204–7, 212–17)

As many have noted, the phrase 'boy my greatness' is an overt reference to a theatrical convention of Shakespeare's theatre. As such the reference is daring since it makes the audience aware of their 'willing suspension of disbelief' and thus threatens to shatter it.[9] In a similar way, Quince's 'This green plot shall be our stage, this hawthorn brake our tiring-house' challenges the audience of *A Midsummer Night's Dream* (3.1.3–4). Not surprisingly, both plays use theatrical conventions to explore the illusions and delusions of love, their power to cause 'dotage', and the greater power of the imagination to foster belief in the literally unbelievable. Paradoxically the 'boy' reference in *Antony and Cleopatra*, like the green plot/stage inversion, does not break the illusion; rather it is strengthened by being challenged. As well it confronts us with the artifice of art – Cleopatra's and Shakespeare's – and prompts us to become aware of how art can mask a less than ideal reality.

'Boy my greatness' is perhaps the most striking theatrical self-reference in the play, but it is only one of many overt references which are, in turn, only a part of the concern with performance and performing that pervades it. Not just Caesar and Cleopatra, but virtually all the main characters are self-conscious role-players, concerned with 'earn[ing] a place i' th' story' (3.13.45); others are equally self-conscious observers and commentators; some, most notably Enobarbus, are both. Repeated commands to onstage observers to 'behold and see' or 'observe' make the off stage audience more aware of its role

---

[9] 'Artistic bravura' is the term used by M. M. Mahood, *Shakespeare's Wordplay* (London, 1957), pp. 127–8.

and thus of the difficulty of separating performance from reality, manner from matter, in politics and in love.

With this in mind it seems worth considering whether Shakespeare deliberately constructed the play to put such strain on the physical stage and its conventions that an audience cannot help but become conscious of its characteristics, limitations, and connotations. The multiplicity of locations is unusually and notoriously difficult to stage,[10] but this difficulty enhances our sense of movement, 'Like to a vagabond flag upon the stream, / Goes to, and back, lackeying the varying tide, / To rot itself with motion' (1.4.45–7). Oscillation, equivocation, and ambiguity characterize both the actions of Antony and Cleopatra and our response to them.[11] This disconcerting quality is made particularly apparent by the staging of 4.16. On the one hand, the three levels of the stage represent a hierarchy with the upper level often suggesting superiority – moral and political or social[12] – and by this point in the action we must question Cleopatra's, or anybody's, right to be there. On the other hand, the difficulty of lifting Antony 'aloft' gives visual form to the verbal redemption (one is tempted to say resurrection) of Antony achieved here by Cleopatra. These and similarly conflicting signals might prompt us to consider whether we are to see this emblematic moment as a celebration of the power of love or as a demonstration of stage management – or both.

Since neither the dialogue nor the stage directions in the Folio text of *Antony and Cleopatra* give any specific indication of how Antony was raised or to what, stage historians must speculate, basing their theories on what little is known about the physical characteristics of Shakespeare's stage in general and the upper area in particular. Some have been tempted to use the description in North's Plutarch as a starting point. In North's translation we are told that Antony is lifted by Cleopatra and her women using 'certaine chaines and ropes' which they cast down from above. Raising him was very difficult,

but Cleopatra stowping downe with her head, putting to all her strength to her uttermost power, did lift him up with much a doe, and never let goe her hold, with the helpe of the women beneath that bad her be of good corage, and were as sorie to see her labor so, as she her selfe. So when she had gotten him in after that sorte, and layed him on a bed: she rent her garments upon him, clapping her brest, and scratching her face and stomake.[13]

It is tempting to use this description to fill in what Shakespeare omitted; but if we follow North in this, why not also for the second monument scene (5.2) when Cleopatra is surprised and captured? In North's translation: 'Proculeius did set up a ladder against that high windowe, by the which Antonius was trissed up, and came downe into the monument.'[14] Following this would mean staging the second scene on the gallery, an idea which receives no support, either from Shakespeare's text or stage historians. Nevertheless, Shakespeare does use his source selectively throughout and it is possible that he intended the first monument scene to be staged as Plutarch describes it. Taken literally, this would mean the use of ropes and chains, the raising of Antony by Cleopatra and her women only, and the entry of Antony through a window to be laid on a bed within the monument. Most theories of how the scene was staged seem to be attempts to accommodate these details, often with elaborate solutions, the staging of which

---

[10] For a survey of this and other aspects of the staging see Margaret Lamb, *Antony and Cleopatra on the English Stage* (Cranbury, N. J. and London, 1980).

[11] For a perceptive analysis of this aspect and its effect on the observer see Janet Adelman, *The Common Liar* (New Haven and London, 1973).

[12] On the use and symbolism of the stage façade, especially the upper area, see Bevington, pp. 99–114.

[13] Geoffrey Bullough, ed., *Narrative and Dramatic Sources of Shakespeare*, vol. 5 (1964), pp. 309–10.

[14] Bullough, p. 311.

would have been difficult in a venue like the Globe and impossible in a provincial theatre.

There are two general theories about where the action of 4.16 takes place: on the upper playing area or on a specially constructed scaffold. Perhaps the most complicated version of the first theory is that of Bernard Jenkin. He argues that Shakespeare, having written a version that followed Plutarch, discovered that heaving Antony aloft 'could not be done without delaying the action of the play, distracting the audience, and dropping the performance to a plane far below that at which tragedy must be kept', so he wrote a second version using an 'inner stage' on both the main and upper levels. In Jenkin's view, Shakespeare solved the problem by having Antony seem to be raised to the upper area behind a curtain at the back of it, out of sight of the audience so that 'all delays, mechanical difficulties and devices have been swept out of the way'.[15] But for Dover Wilson, using the inner stages 'ignores the *textual* fact . . . that dead bodies have to be carried away at the end of both scenes, a thing unnecessary upon the inner stages with their curtains'. Citing Plutarch's description, Wilson suggests that the monument was specially constructed on the outer main stage, over the trap through which Cleopatra and her women entered, and below the 'heavens' which were equipped with a winch for lifting Antony.[16] Walter Hodges also postulates a special structure in front of the tiring house façade, but for him the main problems to be solved are in the distance Antony must be raised and the balustrade obstructing the audience's view of Antony once he is lying in the monument.[17]

Harley Granville-Barker and Bernard Beckerman both discuss these two problems but neither offers any specific solutions. Granville-Barker assumes the height of the upper area to be ten or twelve feet from the main stage, a distance that would be increased by a balustrade 'at least three feet high'. He continues:

Swinging a dying man over it and lowering him again asks some care. Granted this done with skill and grace, what of the effect of the rest of the scene, of Antony's death and Cleopatra's lament over him, played behind the balustrade as behind bars? Clearly it would be a poor one. The balustrade must, one presumes, have been removed for the occasion or made to swing open, if the ordinary upper stage was used.[18]

Beckerman, who thinks the scaffold idea unlikely since the stage direction specifically says 'aloft', a term never present when scaffolds are used elsewhere,[19] also addresses the distance and balustrade problems:

Neither 10' nor 12' are prohibitive heights although a railing would be difficult to work over. Perhaps it was possible to remove a portion of the railing. Despite the obstacles, however, Antony was raised in a manner which, we must suppose, was not ludicrous.[20]

In perhaps the most detailed study of the scene, Richard Hosley puts together a series of conjectures to develop a proposal for the lifting of Antony. Acknowledging that the text is not specific, Hosley says that Cleopatra and her women 'are presumably to be imagined as reappearing (as in Plutarch) in an upper window of the monument. I assume that, in the original production at the Globe (1607), the

---

[15] '*Antony and Cleopatra*: Some Suggestions on the Monument Scenes', *Review of English Studies*, 21 (1945), 1–14, pp. 4, 6.

[16] *Antony and Cleopatra*, ed. J. Dover Wilson (Cambridge, 1950), p. 230, commentary headnote to Act 4 Scene 15.

[17] *The Globe Restored*, 2nd edn (London, 1968), pp. 54–6.

[18] *Prefaces to Shakespeare*, 4 vols. (Princeton, N.J., 1952), vol. 1, pp. 404–5.

[19] And see Richard Hosley, 'The Gallery over the Stage in the Public Playhouse of Shakespeare's Time', *Shakespeare Quarterly*, 8 (1957), 15–31: 'Certainly the business of "heaving Antony aloft" poses a difficult problem in historical reconstruction, but regardless of the exact agency by which he was raised one is on pretty fair grounds (because of two directions calling for action aloft) in supposing what he was raised to was a gallery over the stage', p. 22.

[20] *Shakespeare at the Globe* (New York, 1964), pp. 230–1.

actors appeared in one of the windows of a tiring-house gallery over the stage generally similar to that depicted in the De Witt drawing of the Swan Playhouse'. Hosley again cites Plutarch in describing how Antony was lifted, saying that, 'Shakespeare's text . . . is consistent with Plutarch. . . . Clearly it is Cleopatra and her Maids who heave Antony aloft, in Shakespeare as well as in Plutarch.' Given this, and his belief that 'the barrier of the gallery would have been some fourteen feet above the stage', Hosley concludes that, 'Cleopatra and her Maids must effect the heaving aloft by means of a rope.' He goes on to suggest that Antony was not lifted in a reclining position, as is usually supposed, but seated in a chair attached to ropes on a winch.

Thus the three boy actors 'heave Antony aloft', swinging him and the chair into the gallery through its window when he has been hoisted to the necessary height. (The gallery windows at the Swan may be estimated as about six feet square.) They lower the chair to the floor of the gallery, and Antony then sits in the gallery window for his subsequent dialogue with Cleopatra, until carried away (still in the chair) at the end of the action.[21]

Margaret Lamb, in her appendix, 'Heaving Antony Aloft', describes Hosley's proposal as 'colorful but rather clumsy' and adds:

There is . . . only one other recorded contemporary theatrical hoisting, in which a boy was lifted only a few feet; and there is no conclusive evidence that the Globe had flying machinery in 1606. A gallery-and-winch arrangement could not have been used on tour; but in that case Antony could have been heaved up bodily from below and grabbed from above – the simplest, and in some ways the best, solution.[22]

However, whereas the earlier theories are largely attempts to accommodate Shakespeare to Plutarch, Lamb is arguing for a connection between Shakespeare's staging and Daniel's revised (1607) and vivid description of the same scene.[23] Thus she concentrates on fitting Shakespeare's dialogue to Daniel's description

and ignores the technical problems of height, balustrade, and window.

What it comes down to is that we may speculate as much as we please, but, given the text's vague dialogue and stage directions and our lack of knowledge about the Globe Theatre, we cannot come even close to being certain what was actually done. However, although it is true that metaphorical language is not always a reliable indication of physical action, it is at least worth considering whether a staging can be devised that does not go against the given stage directions on the one hand and complements the imagery and earlier action on the other. By disregarding Plutarch and by assuming that the various physical problems in using the gallery are real and were capitalized on by Shakespeare, one can arrive at a possible staging workable and effective not only at the Globe in 1607, but anywhere with a raised playing area.

Basically, what I want to suggest is that Antony is lifted up to Cleopatra in the gallery but not on to it, and that he is lowered again to the main stage after he dies to be carried out by his men at the end of the scene. While this may not have been the way it was done, it certainly could have been, and staging the scene this way would remove technical problems that have preoccupied directors and critics as well as adding a visual dimension to the dialogue. If this staging is used, the Folio text needs no emendations. The previous scene ends with the exit of Antony's men 'bearing' him and 4.16 begins: '*Enter Cleopatra, and her Maids*

---

[21] 'The Staging of the Monument Scenes in *Antony and Cleopatra*', *Library Chronicle*, 30 (1964), 62–71, pp. 62, 63, 64.

[22] Lamb, p. 182. And see Lamb's descriptions and illustrations of the various post-Renaissance stagings of this scene: pp. 58, 80, 88–9, 95–7, 141, 153, 168.

[23] Lamb bases her argument on an earlier article: Joan Rees, 'An Elizabethan Eyewitness of *Antony and Cleopatra*?' *Shakespeare Survey* 6 (1953), 91–3. And see Mary Olive Thomas, 'The Repetitions in Antony's Death Scene', *Shakespeare Quarterly*, 9 (1958), 153–7.

aloft, with Charmian & Iras' (TLN 2996–7). Diomed enters below (as the absence of a specific location indicates) as do '*Antony, and the Guard*' (4.16.6.1, 9.1; TLN 3005, 3010). Cleopatra asks Charmian, Iras, and 'friends below', presumably the soldiers carrying Antony, to 'draw him hither'. Antony's first word is 'Peace' and perhaps this stops them from raising him. Certainly they do not do so since when Antony asks Cleopatra for a last kiss she refuses to leave her monument and repeats her earlier request while also calling to Antony as she has so often done before:

> But come, come, Antony. –
> Help me, my women. – We must draw thee up.
> Assist, good friends.   (4.16.30–2)

Even without Plutarch's reference to 'chaines and ropes' as a suggestion, given the numerous earlier references to bonds, ties, and fetters to describe Antony and Cleopatra's relationship, it is quite likely that when the opportunity presented itself Shakespeare made the metaphor literal by having Cleopatra and her women lower ropes of some kind so that while the boy actors on the upper level would not actually bear any of the weight, they would seem to. Then, during Cleopatra's 'Here's sport indeed' speech, Antony's men lift him gradually and with difficulty towards Cleopatra, who is either in a window or behind a balustrade with her women, miming the action of pulling him to her.[24] 'Yet come a little. / . . . O come, come, come!' she cries and, as the Folio stage direction says, '*They heaue Anthony aloft to Cleopatra*' (4.16.37–38.1; TLN 3043–5). While this certainly can mean that they put him on the upper stage with Cleopatra, it is equally possible that all they do is raise him to her level. And, assuming that Cleopatra is reaching out of the window or over the balustrade in seeming to pull Antony towards her, the distance to be covered would be reduced to a mangeable ten feet or so. As discussed above, the action of the play is essentially a series of sequences ending with the two lovers coming together in an embrace, and Cleopatra's 'welcome, welcome' indicates that a physical union has been achieved once more.[25] The image presented would be satisfying and emblematic, reverberating as it does with connotations and allusions both specific and general. And, if Cleopatra is leaning out of and over the gallery and Antony is being held up to her, there would be no problems of visibility for the theatre audience.

The onstage audience cries 'A heavy sight' (4.16.42) and so it would be, not only figuratively but also literally if Antony is still being held up by those below. If this punning seems incongruous at such a moment we must remember that Cleopatra has just made the same play on words, and variations of it have run through the play. Furthermore, the mixture of humour with tragedy is quite in keeping with the ambiguous effect of Antony's bungled suicide attempt and Cleopatra's asp-bearing peasant. The manner of the scene – the action – would be, should be physically awkward, but as elsewhere this awkwardness is juxtaposed with the language of genuine emotion, neither cancelling the other, each pulling at us simultaneously, asking us to judge the matter, to assess the value, the meaning of what we are seeing.

In this staging, Antony would be held aloft only until he dies – just twenty-four lines of dialogue – and it is possible to speculate that his descent is also signalled by Cleopatra. Again, while acknowledging that dialogue is an unreliable indicator of action, I offer the following as a possibility, but a very real one since nothing works against it and the thematic implications are considerable. The Folio provides no stage direction for Antony's death, but as is often the case this job is left to the

---

[24] If the ropes are used for symbolic purposes only, no winch would be necessary.

[25] See Ornstein: 'Even the sorrow she feels in bearing his dying weight is transmuted by the memory of their earlier "dyings"', p. 35.

dialogue. Antony's words, 'Now my spirit is going; / I can no more' (4.16.60–1), are the signal and, if he is merely being held aloft rather than lying on the upper stage, perhaps Cleopatra's response is intended not only as a confirmation that he is dead, but also as a description of his physical descent and separation from her:

> O see, my women,
> The crown o' th' earth doth melt. My lord!
> O, withered is the garland of the war.
> The soldier's pole is fall'n. Young boys and girls
> Are level now with men. The odds is gone,
> And there is nothing left remarkable
> Beneath the visiting moon.   (4.16.64–70)

In passing it is worth observing that, as modern editors indicate, Cleopatra faints as she finishes this speech.[26] If, however, she is on a Swan-type gallery, behind a window or even behind a balustrade, she would have to collapse into the arms of her women or over the sill or railing if she is to remain in view for this brief, but important, moment when she seems to move toward Antony, but returns to take control once more. Similarly, if Antony's body has been lowered to the main stage it would still be visible, which it would not be if lying on the floor of the gallery. Surely the audience should be able to see the body as Cleopatra directs our attention to it when next she speaks?[27] The contrast between Antony dead below and Cleopatra taking control above would be an effective way to initiate the final movement of the play. And, as a last point, the Folio stage direction concluding the scene, '*Exeunt, bearing of Anthonies body*' (TLN 3107), needs no explication or emendation if he is lying on the main stage. Since it is the end of the scene the 'exeunt' applies not only to Cleopatra and her women, but to all on both levels of the stage; if Antony's body is below, his men bear him off to burial from there.[28]

Staged in this way, the fall of Antony the soldier is also the triumph, in its Medieval, visual sense as well as metaphorical, of Antony

the lover, a transcendence necessary for the presentation and acceptance of Cleopatra's dream Antony in Act 5. By contrasting the awkward physical action of lifting Antony, with Cleopatra's loving lament in 4.16, Shakespeare challenges us, as Cleopatra will later challenge Dolabella, to accept with our hearts what our minds resist. We are encouraged to suspend our disbelief, if you will, and perceive, with Hippolyta, 'something of great constancy': the power of love.[29]

Antony and Cleopatra is a study of human love in all its manifestations and at its centre are the title characters: not idealized lovers but fallibly human ones. The nature of their relationship is the organizing principle of the play: the generic mix and the shifting locales create a realistic context for the vacillation and paradox characteristic of love. Antony and Cleopatra may seem larger than life, but their relationship is a paradigm of the human struggle, and capacity, to love and be loved. And the play dramatizes the sad truth that the more intense love is, the more it is likely to reveal not only our best qualities but our worst flaws as well; indeed, that more often than not the two are inseparable. One way Shakespeare conveys this essential paradox is to combine romantic motives and language with realis-

---

26 See, for example, the Arden, Riverside, and Signet editions. The Oxford *Complete Works* has '*She falls.*' If this is meant to be taken literally, and if she did so on a Swan-type stage, Cleopatra would not have been visible to the audience. A few lines later the Oxford has her '*recovering*'.

27 Note that, while it cannot be considered a definite indication of location, Cleopatra says, 'The case of that huge spirit now is cold' (4.16.91), rather than the 'this' we might expect if he were above with her.

28 'We'll bury him', Cleopatra says (4.16.88), so presumably Antony is buried in some other part of the monument. Caesar's final words, 'Take up her bed, / And bear her women from the monument. / She shall be buried by her Antony' (5.2.350–2), do not help to clarify the matter.

29 The word 'love' and its forms occurs more than fifty times in the play.

tically awkward physical action, inviting us as well as the onstage observers to respond. On the face of it, Cleopatra holed up in her monument and Antony being hauled up to it prompt us to view her as selfish and him as effeminate; but the context and the language counter this view, making us aware of what is admirable: Antony's selflessness and Cleopatra's determination to survive. We are never allowed to remain passive observers complacently condemning Cleopatra for beckoning and Antony for coming. Unlike Plutarch, Shakespeare does not criticize Antony for loving her and Cleopatra for ruining him; rather, by setting up comparisons through the play he invites us to see that a great but flawed love is incomparably preferable to no love at all, or to a love that falters in adversity, or to one that is founded upon practical considerations. The disconcerting ambiguities are reminders that by its very nature human love is irrational, causing us to desire it even as we resist it. Antony's death scene, like Cleopatra's, is and should be troublesome and troubling, not because Shakespeare did not know what he was doing, but because he did.

THE TEMPEST'S TEMPEST AT BLACKFRIARS

ANDREW GURR

At one fairly inconspicuous moment in Heywood's play *1 The Fair Maid of the West*, the Chorus to Act 5, the Chorus says, of a shipwreck scene,

> Our stage so lamely can express a sea
> That we are forc'd by Chorus to discourse
> What should have been in action.   (4.5.1–3)[1]

The Fair Maid was moderately well known even before Heywood wrote a sequel for the Cockpit company who played it at Court in the early 1630s, when the two plays were first published.[2] It was probably originally written in 1609–10, because *The Roaring Girl* refers to it, and that play can be dated precisely in 1611.[3] The dating, very close to the time *The Tempest* was written, raises the question whether Shakespeare heard Heywood's lament before he wrote the shipwreck scene to open his play, or alternatively whether Heywood's Chorus was commenting on the failure of *The Tempest*'s shipwreck scene. Either Shakespeare was showing Heywood what a different playhouse could do on its not-so-lame stage, or Heywood was disowning Shakespeare's failure.

Another play of Heywood's, written rather earlier, *The Four Prentices of London*, has a broadly similar display of modesty, this time prescribing exactly what he would have liked his stage to show. The 'presenter' in the second scene of Act 1, like the Chorus in *Henry V*, asks the audience to use its imaginary forces to conceive a shipwreck:

[1] Thomas Heywood, *The Fair Maid of the West, Part 1*, ed. Robert K. Turner, Jr, Regent's Renaissance Drama Series (London, 1968), 1–90.

[2] Heywood published both plays together in 1631, when they were in the Cockpit's repertoire. The second play belongs stylistically to the 1630s, but the first has the characteristics of the 'citizen' playhouse repertoire of the first decade of the century, when Heywood was a 'fellow' of the Red Bull players. See G. E. Bentley, *The Jacobean and Caroline Stage*, 7 vols. (Oxford, 1941–68), vol. 4 (1956), pp. 568–9.

[3] A. M. Clark, *Thomas Heywood: Playwright and Miscellanist* (Oxford, 1931), p. 110, dates the first play called *The Fair Maid* after 1609, because it seems to have taken the name 'Muly-sheck' from a pamphlet published in that year. This dating is supported by Brownell Salomon in his edition of the play (Salzburg, 1975, pp. 3–13). Clark also dates the play before 1611 because of an apparent allusion to its subtitle, 'A Girl Worth Gold', in *The Roaring Girl*, which was on stage early in 1611, according to Cyrus Hoy, *Introductions, Notes, and Commentaries to Texts in 'The Dramatic Works of Thomas Dekker edited by Fredson Bowers'*, 4 vols. (Cambridge, 1980), vol. 3, p. 9. P. A. Mulholland, 'The Date of *The Roaring Girl*', *Review of English Studies*, NS 28 (1977), 18–31, affirms 1611 as the date for at least the main composition of the play. *The Roaring Girl*, performed at the Fortune, does have two other references in the same scene, 4.2, to early plays in the Henslowe repertoire which were being run either at the Fortune or Red Bull. After the references to 'brave girles: worth Gold' at line 166, there is an allusion to *Friar Bacon and Friar Bungay* at lines 171–2 and to *A Knack to Know an Honest Man* at line 264. The two unmistakable allusions make the third, to Heywood's play, much more likely. The phrase 'a girl worth gold' was not proverbial, at least in the strict sense, and some such allusion to a play fits the context in *The Roaring Girl*. That in itself does not of course prove that it was a new play in 1611.

Imagine now yee see the aire made thicke
With stormy tempests, that disturbe the sea:
And the foure windes at warre among
    themselves:
And the weake Barkes wherein the brothers
    saile,
Split on strange rockes, and they enforc't to
    swim.   (sig. C1r, lines 7–19)[4]

I have always been inclined to resist the idea that Shakespeare very often sat in on the plays of his rival playhouses. For one thing, he should have been busy performing his job as a player at his own playhouse when the rival companies were performing. He and Heywood were almost unique among the playwrights of their time in having an urgent contractual reason not to attend the plays of other writers. That is one minor cause for thinking that it was difficult for either of them to have observed the other's plays. But by 1610 Heywood may have been making his living from his 220 plays alone, and Shakespeare is widely assumed to have been retiring, at the grand old age of forty-six, to his home in Stratford, so for both of them acting may have ceased to be a daily necessity. Heywood does appear to have seen *Pericles* and *The Winter's Tale* before he wrote his first *Ages* plays.[5] Whether Shakespeare ever heard Heywood's plays at the Red Bull is a more doubtful question.

And yet there is another consideration which in the end might suggest that Heywood wrote innocently and first, and that it was Shakespeare who took note of Heywood's disclaimer rather than Heywood who mocked Shakespeare. *The Tempest* was the first play Shakespeare unquestionably wrote for the Blackfriars rather than the Globe. Much, probably too much, has been made about the possible effects on Shakespeare's writing when, after a thirteen-year delay, the Blackfriars playhouse finally came into the possession of Shakespeare's company in 1608 and they began to play at the hall venue through-

out the long London winters. *Pericles* and *Cymbeline*, as well as the post-1609 *Winter's Tale* and *Tempest*, have been claimed as distinctive in the canon partly because of the new playhouse and its more affluent customers. This is unacceptable if only because *Pericles*, for one, was on the Globe's stage more than a year before the company could have had any inkling that it was about to acquire the Blackfriars. Even *The Winter's Tale* has nothing that could not have been staged as easily at the Globe as at the Blackfriars. On the other hand, *The Tempest* is uniquely a musical play among Shakespeare's writings, and the consort of musicians at Blackfriars was justly famous. Under the boy company management before 1609 they offered concerts lasting an hour before the play began.[6] Of course the consort of Blackfriars musicians might easily have played through the summer, when the Blackfriars was closed, at the Globe in its newly installed music room on the stage balcony. If they were not to play there, the creation of a

---

[4] Thomas Heywood, *The Four Prentices of London* (London, 1615; *BEPD* 333a). *The Four Prentices* in its original form predates 1607, when it achieved a satirical mention at the Blackfriars in *The Knight of the Burning Pestle* (Francis Beaumont, *The Knight of the Burning Pestle*, in *The Dramatic Works in the Beaumont and Fletcher Canon*, gen. ed. Fredson Bowers, vol. 1 (Cambridge, 1966), p. 12. It was not printed, like *The Fair Maid of the West*, until 1632, and may have been revised by Heywood before its publication. In 1632 he claimed he had written it fifteen or sixteen years earlier, which must mean either a revision or plain misrepresentation.

[5] According to Ernest Schanzer, Heywood seems to have borrowed from, or at least have been familiar with, both *The Winter's Tale* and *The Tempest* in his *Golden Age* and *Silver Age*. See: 'Heywood's *Four Ages* and Shakespeare', *Review of English Studies*, 11 (1960), 18–28.

[6] Frederick Gerschow, visiting London in the train of the Duke of Stettin-Pomerania in 1602, wrote about the hour-long concert that preceded a play at Blackfriars. In later years the fame of the Blackfriars consort of musicians was attested by Bulstrode Whitelocke among others. See Bentley, *The Jacobean and Caroline Stage*, vol. 6 (1968), p. 32.

balcony music room at the Globe to match the Blackfriars music room would seem a redundancy.[7] The music, though, is not final evidence that Shakespeare wrote the play specifically for the Blackfriars. Much more significant is the fact that *The Tempest* is the first of his plays to show unequivocal evidence that it was conceived with act breaks in mind.

Plays on the amphitheatre stages ran non-stop, without pauses for an interval or between the acts. On the hall stages, however, either as an acknowledgement of the formal five-act structure or for the more practical purpose of getting time to trim the candles that lit the stage and auditorium, brief pauses between the acts were standard. In *The Knight of the Burning Pestle*, performed at Blackfriars by the boy company in 1607, there is an 'interact' between each act of the play, during which music plays and a boy dances. One of them features a burlesque 'Maylord' speech of a little over thirty lines. The audience on stools on the stage, some of them players disguised as audience, chat with one another during the pauses and comment on features such as the stage hangings. Some such pause, at least for music, must have been designed to intervene between Acts 4 and 5 of *The Tempest*.[8] Prospero and Ariel leave the stage together at the end of Act 4 and enter together again to open Act 5. Shakespeare evidently expected there would be a break between the acts. He has the same characters leaving and re-entering like this in none of his other plays. For that reason if no other it is clear that he had the Blackfriars in mind, not the Globe, when he wrote *The Tempest*.

Conceivably he knew his play would be first available for performing in the winter, between September and May when the company used the Blackfriars and the Globe was empty. But its unique exploitation of instrumental music as well as song, the plethora of magic and stage effects dependent on the music, makes the scoring for the hall playhouse a consequence of something more positive than the accidents of the seasonal timetable. It was not a fortuitous exercise, this scoring for the Blackfriars, and it certainly cannot be ascribed to Shakespeare's increasing distance from the stage, which is sometimes used as another way of explaining why the last plays are so distinct. It is, of course, rather too readily assumed that Shakespeare retired from the stage to Stratford in 1609, a year before he wrote *The Tempest*, and that he therefore withdrew from any direct engagement with the company's playhouses. His mother, who seems to have managed some of his business interests at home, died in September 1608 and left a number of matters which held his attention there.[9] It was nearly four years before he clearly reaffirmed his London interests by buying the Blackfriars gatehouse, in March

---

7 In the Induction to the 1604 version of *The Malcontent*, written for the Globe, the players speak of 'the not-received custom of music in our theatre': John Marston, *The Malcontent*, ed. George K. Hunter, The Revels Plays (London, 1975), Induction, line 84. After about 1608 the plays begin to require a music room on the upper level. See Richard Hosley, 'Was there a Music-Room in Shakespeare's Globe?', *Shakespeare Survey 13* (1960), 113–23.

8 If *The Knight of the Burning Pestle* is anything to go by, the length of the pause for an act-break amounted to not more than twenty-five or thirty lines of dialogue on the average, sometimes a little more. This amounts to less than two minutes and matches the thirty-three lines which Ariel might have needed between Acts 3 and 4. For the uniqueness of this act-break in Shakespeare, see C. M. Haines, 'The "Law of Re-entry" in Shakespeare', *Review of English Studies*, I (1925), 449–51. W. T. Jewkes showed that between 1583 and 1616 out of 67 indoor plays 59 mark act breaks, whereas out of 134 amphitheatre plays only 30 mark them: Wilfred T. Jewkes, *Act Division in Elizabethan and Jacobean Plays, 1563–1616* (Hamden, Conn., 1958). Even on these figures some of the allocations to types of playhouses are questionable. I cannot find any amphitheatre play which clearly calls for a pause between the acts.

9 Ernst Honigmann's paper, 'Shakespeare and Commerce', given at the World Shakespeare Congress in Berlin, April 1986, makes this point.

1613. That, as Schoenbaum suggests,[10] may have been no more than an investment, of the kind Richard Burbage was making in the same precinct at the same time, but its locality is nonetheless suggestive. I think there is a little evidence in *The Tempest*, besides the act-break, which indicates that he was definitely not remote from the new playhouse and its company when he composed the play for it. *The Tempest* was written with an exact knowledge of what the play's staging required, even to some precise line-counting to measure the time needed for different changes of costume.

Ariel's airy speed on stage is marked not only by his frequent boasts about how fast he can girdle the earth but by his rapid changes of costume. He goes offstage, for instance, for only sixteen lines in 1.2, when Prospero tells him 'Go make thyselfe like to a nymph o' th'Sea' (TLN 433–Exit 437[11]), before he returns in the new dress ('*Enter Ariel like a water-Nymph*' (TLN 453)). We can assume he retains this dress and the invisibility which is said to go with it through the scene with tabor and pipe, 3.2, which ends with him invisibly leading the comic conspirators offstage (TLN 1512). He then has seventy-one lines to dress himself with the Harpy costume and wings before entering to the courtiers and their banquet at TLN 1583, in 3.3. According to the stage direction '*He vanishes in thunder*' (TLN 1616), he then has another seventy-one lines before he returns without the Harpy costume and wings at TLN 1687, in 4.1. There is a difficulty here, since Prospero appears to address him at TLN 1619–20 after the stage direction says he has vanished – 'Bravely the figure of this *Harpie* hast thou / Perform'd, (my *Ariel*)' – and if he does remain on stage to hear this aside, as he hears all Prospero's other asides to him, he would not leave the stage until it is cleared at TLN 1649. This would allow him only thirty-eight lines to remove the wings and Harpy attire. But here too there is an act break. Either Ariel was allocated 71 lines to put on and 71 lines to take off the winged costume,

or 71 lines to put it on and 38 plus an act-break to take it off. Since act-breaks seem to have lasted the equivalent of about thirty lines of dialogue, Ariel would then have about seventy lines to change out of the Harpy costume, matching the seventy-one he was given to put it on. This apparent symmetry of time allowed for dressing or undressing in a particular costume is repeated, and I suspect confirmed as a carefully calculated feature of the staging, by Ariel's third change of costume.

In the masque in 4.1 Ariel takes the part of Ceres. This piece of doubling became a routine tradition in nineteenth-century productions, sound practical sense given the need of a good singing voice for the two parts. It was first proposed as an editorial interpretation by John Dover Wilson,[12] on the basis of Ariel's subsequent statement to Prospero that he 'presented Ceres' (TLN 1840), and is generally accepted by modern editors as the explanation for this phrase. As before, to change into the costume for Ceres, Ariel is allotted a strictly measured length of time. He gets 27 lines between his exit as Ariel at TLN 1706 and his entry as Ceres at TLN 1733, then has 29 lines, or 25 lines of dialogue plus some business, between his departure as Ceres at the end of the masque at TLN 1808 and his re-entry at TLN 1837 in 'Thy shape invisible', as Prospero calls it at TLN 1859. Altogether Ariel has four different costumes. The first, not an 'invisible' gear since Miranda has to be put to sleep before he enters, is only worn in 1.2 between his entry at TLN 299 and his exit at TLN 437. The

---

10 Samuel Schoenbaum, *William Shakespeare: A Compact Documentary Life* (Oxford, 1977), p. 273.

11 Through Line Numbers (TLN) provide a rough guide to the elapsed time in a performance at the Globe, and, with pauses added for the act-breaks, also at the Blackfriars. The TLN used here is that of the Norton Facsimile of the First Folio.

12 *The Tempest*, eds. A. Quiller-Couch and John Dover Wilson, The New Shakespeare (Cambridge, 1921), p. 81.

second is the '*water-Nymph*' costume which marks him out as invisible, and which he wears through the rest of the play, as we know from Prospero's order in 4.1 (TLN 1859) to remain invisible, and the reminder in 5.1 (TLN 2054), 'Invisible as thou art'. This takes sixteen lines to put on. The two changes from the water nymph costume are into the '*Harpey*' (3.3), with the wings he can clap over the banquet table, and into Ceres for the masque in 4.1. It is, I think, no coincidence that a similar number of lines should have been allowed for the changes into and out of these non-routine costumes, and it is hardly surprising that the Harpy's wings should have required nearly three times as long as the Ceres costume, and more than four times the original change into the invisible water nymph. All in all *The Tempest* lays down more exacting demands for its staging than any play in the canon, even without the special functions the music undertakes. Ariel's costume changes suggest that Shakespeare was calculating quite precisely what his company could be asked to do.

Even without Heywood's modesty to set against it, the shipwreck scene which opens the play is a remarkably bravura piece of staging. It could have been done more easily on an amphitheatre stage than in a hall, and was a feature more familiar at such venues than in the halls, though even there it was done more often by Chorus than in action, as in Heywood and *Henry V*. Storms like *King Lear*'s were not infrequent at the Globe, enough to make the opening of *The Tempest* quite disturbing to audiences accustomed to the quieter indoor conditions of the hall playhouses. And of course Shakespeare's play went further. There are no real precedents anywhere in earlier plays for mounting a storm complete with a shipwreck on stage. Indeed the musical effects, which do not appear until the second scene, might be considered the second and reassuring movement in a deliberate challenge to audience expectations. At the Blackfriars a wild

and stormy scene like the middle act in *King Lear*, with drums rumbling and bullets crackling to make thunder offstage, might deliver an initial shock to the routine musical expectations of the Blackfriars audience, expectations which would be only slowly eased by the announcement of Prospero's magical control of the storm and the music which follows. And yet even on the amphitheatre stage of the Globe Heywood's modesty indicates the size of the challenge. The technical aids available for creating a storm amounted to little more than the offstage noises. Thunder from a 'roul'd bullet' (a metal ball trundled down a metal trough) and 'tempestuous drumme'[13] were standard accessories on both types of stage. Fireworks or rosin for lightning flashes were available at the amphitheatres but unpopular at the halls because of the stink. The stage directions in *The Tempest* 1.1 call only for thunder and crashing noises offstage, not for flashes of lightning (the opening stage direction specifies a '*noise of thunder and lightning*' only). The Blackfriars stage and auditorium might have been dimmed a little by closing the hall windows, but there is nothing to suggest that the lights were dowsed, and nothing about the windows either. In fact it would have been uncharacteristic and cumbersome to pause while the windows were reopened after the storm and I doubt if that kind of atmospheric aid was attempted. The scene is the plainest possible confrontation, in the most unlikely setting, to the challenge implied in Heywood's disclaimer.

It is a bravura piece of staging not only in the way it deploys an outdoor effect at an indoor playhouse, but because that effect sets up the ruling conceit for the whole play. A thoroughly realistic storm, with mariners in soaking work clothes being hampered in their

---

[13] Jonson's terms, in the 1616 Prologue to *Every Man in his Humour: The Revised Version from the Folio of 1616, Ben Jonson*, eds. C. H. Herford and Percy Simpson, vol. 3 (Oxford, 1927), Pro. 18–19.

work by courtiers dressed for a wedding,[14] concludes in shipwreck for all. And immediately this realism is proclaimed to be only stage magic, the art of illusion. The courtiers, supposedly as soaked as the mariners, return with their clothes as fresh as ever. By the end of the play even the mariners are dry again, the joke about the realism of wet clothes being taken over by Stephano, Trinculo, and Caliban in Act 4. The whole play depends on the initial realism of the shipwreck scene. It is the verification of Prospero's magic and the declaration that it is all only a stage play. If we accept that its realism succeeds, it is also a supremely adroit and discreet upstaging of Heywood and the Red Bull's modesty.

Shakespeare, of course, had himself previously used a Chorus to 'waft you o'er the seas', as Jonson derisively described it.[15] The Chorus in *Henry V* which opens Act 3 names several of the features which appear in *The Tempest*. The later play did not actually show 'Upon the hempen tackle ship-boys climbing', but it does have mariners hauling on ropes, or orders for them to do so. You can certainly hear the Master's 'shrill whistle, which doth order give / To sounds confused'. The *Henry V* Chorus, as in Heywood, urges the audience to assume that the scene flies 'with imagined wing' and asks them to 'Suppose, that you have seen' and to 'Play with your fancies'.[16] Even without Heywood, it was an exceptional audacity in Shakespeare to launch a new play in a new playhouse on such a piece of realism, at the very beginning of the play, to a cold audience.

The Blackfriars, we know, had two entry doors and a central 'discovery space' in the tiring-house wall, a balcony above, flanked by the curtained music room, and a stage platform half the size of the Globe's with boxes along its flanks and up to fifteen gallants sitting on stools on the stage alongside the boxes. Apart from the cramping of platform space it was not dissimilar to the Globe's stage area and, in fact, the opening scene could have been

done equally well on either. Minimally, all the scene itself needed for the original performance was two doors. More use might have been made of the fringe areas, especially the balcony room, but reconstructions of early staging are wise to stick with definitions of the minimal requirements and leave extensions to speculation. At 1.1.6 the Master's shout for the Boatswain and the Boatswain's reply 'Heere Master' indicate that each of them comes on stage by a separate door. The Master then exits, presumably through the same door as he entered by, and the Mariners enter, presumably by the door the Boatswain appeared through, in order that they should not collide with the Master as he exits. The Master subsequently remains offstage, heard only by means of the whistle he must have round his neck. The only alternative way to do this, by no means impractical since this is the Master's only appearance in the scene, would have been for him to appear on the balcony and call to the Boatswain who stands below him at stage level. The Master's whistle could then be heard from the music room which we know was a curtained room on the upper level at Blackfriars. That would leave both doors free for the entrance of the mariners and courtiers, although the use of two doors would limit the effect of bustle and confusion which results from everyone fighting past one another for the same door.

There are some major uncertainties over the movements in the scene, chiefly because most of the exits are inadequately marked. Even multiple exits are scored in the singular and some are not marked at all. The worst uncertainty this creates is about the ropes. The

---

[14] Gonzalo in 2.1 (TLN 743–5) says their clothes are 'now as fresh as when we put them on first in Affricke, at the marriage of the Kings faire daughter *Claribel*'.

[15] Jonson, Prologue, *Every Man in his Humour*.

[16] *Henry V*, 3.0.1–10. Heywood must have written *The Four Prentices*, I suspect, with the *Henry V* choruses echoing in his mind.

question is whether realism went so literal-minded as to have real ropes dangling from the balcony for the mariners to haul on when the Boatswain orders them to 'Take in the toppe-sale' (1.1.12) and 'Downe with the top-Mast' (1.1.43). There is some emphasis on rope-hauling, since the Boatswain says sarcastically to the courtiers at 1.1.31, while the mariners are still on stage, 'wee will not hand a rope more'. Gonzalo's allusion at 1.1.39 to the 'rope' of the Boatswain's 'destiny' would also gain more pungency if a visible piece of apparatus was dangling like a noose from above. Ropes hanging from the music room would give the mariners something to do and also allow the courtiers to get visibly in their way. Unfortunately the deficient notation of exits leaves two distinctly alternative possibilities, one with ropes and one without.

The Boatswain's instruction 'Downe with the top-Mast' might be directed either at mariners onstage tailing onto real ropes or to offstage mariners on imaginary ropes. Striking the topmast in heavy weather was fairly new technology in Shakespeare's day, a practical piece of seamanship but one not easily realized on stage or recognized by a London audience, except through words. Paying out a rope to the music room might have given a visual indicator of the action of lowering the topmast to back up the words. If so, we have to assume two groups of mariners, one which exits with the Boatswain at 1.1.35, the other remaining to haul on the ropes at lines 43–4 when the Boatswain gives the order, and again at 1.1.57–8 when he shouts 'lay her a hold, a hold, set her two courses off to sea againe, lay her off.' The other group would be the one to return '*wet*' at 1.1.59. If, on the other hand, the ropes are imaginary and offstage, the whole body of the mariners would exit with the Boatswain at 1.1.35, justifying his order to the courtiers, 'out of our way, I say', on behalf of the whole crew as they all exit. The Boatswain would then re-enter *solus* at 1.1.42 as the courtiers leave, to shout his instructions

about the offstage ropes at 1.1.43–4 and 1.1.57–8 before all the mariners re-enter '*wet*' at 1.1.59. The absence of any *exeunt* for the mariners, or even some of them, leaves the staging of the rope-hauling unclear. Two considerations make the latter option more plausible. First, the relatively small number of supernumeraries likely to be available as crew would make their division into two groups less desirable. The smallish Blackfriars stage, already encumbered with fifteen stool-sitting gallants wearing ostrich-plumed hats and smoking long pipes, would not have taken large crowd scenes easily. The more the mariners were offstage and the fewer of them coming on stage the better. Secondly, the practical problem of how to make the ropes disappear after the topmast had been lowered – an action which required the ropes to be fastened to something after the hauling – would create too much risk of unhandy and possibly visibly ridiculous rearrangement. The ropes would have to disappear before Prospero and Miranda enter at the end of the scene, since they are supposed to be watching the ship-wreck from the island, which would not be encumbered with dangling ropes. The ropes could not be hauled up silently into the music room without someone first releasing them and making such a public and all-too-visible readjustment look silly. All the hauling, therefore, must have happened offstage.

The main action dramatized in the scene is the contrast between the bustling Boatswain and the rabble of unhelpful courtiers, at least seven of whom enter at 1.1.14. The offstage noises include not only the thunder and tempest but the Master's whistle, which *Henry V* tells us gives order to sounds confus'd. This offstage shrilling makes the Boatswain tell the mariners at 1.1.12 'Tend to th' Master's whistle' and makes King Alonso's question 'where's the Master?' when he enters at 1.1.14 emphatically redundant. It does of course indicate Alonso's ignorance of ships as well as the level of mastery that he, as king, prefers to converse with. When the Boatswain ignores him and Antonio angrily renews the question the Boatswain makes it clear the offstage whistle is still sounding – 'Do you not heare him?' The courtiers are in his way. His concern is with the crew, telling them 'cheerely, good hearts'. His only word for the courtiers is 'Out of our way, I say' as all the crewmembers rush off through the crowd of courtiers at 1.1.35.

The incomplete marking of the mariners' exits is matched by that of the courtiers' exits, though in the latter case it is easier to deduce the sequence of their movements. They all go off at 1.1.41, leaving the Boatswain briefly alone on stage to shout his orders. Theirs is the '*cry within*' at 1.1.45 before three of them re-enter to hamper the Boatswain for a second time – 'yet againe?' – at 1.1.47. On their re-entry the king is no longer with them. The three who speak are probably the only ones who return to the stage and they all help to identify themselves by speaking in the way the later development of their characters (in 2.1) would indicate. Sebastian and Antonio, the courtiers most likely to do so, angrily shout back at the Boatswain for his insolence. Gonzalo, who never speaks unselfconsciously in the king's presence – another reason for thinking that the king does not return – is more cheerful in adversity.

The second entry of the mariners at 1.1.59, their spectacular condition '*wet*' making a perfect contrast to the splendours of the courtiers' apparel, is the beginning of the end. The ship's business, from the Master's whistling to the attempt to set more sail and steer offshore, all happens offstage, if my conclusion about the ropes is correct. So the return of the dampened mariners is a token that disaster is looming for the well-dressed passengers. The Boatswain's second set of orders about rope-hauling is evidently too late to be of any help, and his directive 'off to Sea againe, lay her off', followed by the re-entry of the wet mariners, covers the ship's last moments before it is

disabled. That appears to be signalled by the '*confused noyse within*' at 1.1.70.

John Jowett[17] has proposed that several of the stage directions in *The Tempest* bear the signs of Ralph Crane rather than Shakespeare. Crane, a regular scribe for the King's Men in the 1620s, does seem on occasions to have used his memory of performances to supplement the stage directions of the texts he was transcribing. Descriptive stage directions, such as the '*queint device*' at 3.3.74 with which the banquet vanishes, are in the terminology of a spectator, innocent of stage mechanisms and incapable of being prescriptive as authors and playhouse book-keepers commonly were. The adjective used for the offstage noise of the apparent shipwreck at 1.1.70 has a similar air. 'Confused' might be the term a spectator not precisely sure what the crashing and banging is supposed to represent might give it. Possibly Crane, the scribe and spectator, was doctoring his text for the reader here.

There is also another possibility, which seems to me more likely, and which is also consistent with Jowett's reading of this passage. The Folio text appears to give the lines following the '*confused noyse*' to Gonzalo, who has spoken the preceding lines, and seems to go on to speak the odd gabble which follows. The Folio arranges the text as follows:

Gonz. Hee'l be hang'd yet,
  Though euery drop of water sweare against it,
  And gape at widst to glut him. *A confused noyse within.*
  Mercy on vs.
  We split, we split, Farewell my wife, and children,
  Farewell brother: we split, we split, we split.
Anth. Let's all sinke with' King
Seb. Let's take leaue of him.   *Exit.*
                                    (TLN 68–75)

17 John Jowett, 'New Created Creatures: Ralph Crane and the Stage Directions in *The Tempest*', *Shakespeare Survey 36* (1983), 107–20.

Editors since Theobald have given the lines from 'Mercy on vs' to the last 'we split' to voices '*off*'. Partly this is on the ground that Gonzalo has no brother on the ship to say farewell to, as the lines require, while both Sebastian and the offstage Alonso have. But Gonzalo, like the rest of the courtiers, has no wife and children on board either, so the cry is evidently not addressed to relatives present in the flesh. Children and brothers become important later in the play, of course, in Ferdinand and Miranda, and Antonio and Sebastian. I am inclined (like Jowett) to think that the three lines following from 'Mercy on vs' are the sounds made in the '*confused noyse*', and that they are offstage.[18] The positioning of the stage direction is similar to the conventional '*within*' which usually marks offstage voices. The scribe merely failed to detach them from Gonzalo's onstage lines. The question this leaves unclear is whether the '*confused noyse*' was only voices, or (as it might be if Crane was transcribing what he remembered of the performance) whether there was some more material sound of the ship striking and splitting.

For reasons that in part depend on a more general view of what this scene is meant to do, I think that voices alone make the noise here. This is a dangerous kind of assumption, because it quickly leads into circular arguments. It also assumes a deficient text. However, a full transcription of these moments at the end of the scene clearly is lacking, since no exit is marked for Boatswain and mariners, and therefore some interpretation of the evidence has to be made. Some offstage voices must have joined with Gonzalo's even if they did not replace him, since the main events are happening offstage, where the splitting would be most pointedly observed. The confusion would be the appropriate moment for the Boatswain and mariners to leave the stage, probably accompanied by Antonio and Sebastian as they say their exit lines. A mixture of mariners and courtiers

leaving together at this point would exemplify the general disaster. Gonzalo would then be left to speak the last four lines *solus*. The lines are not addressed to anyone and nobody answers him. Moreover his solo exit after the others by one door leaves the opposite door free for the entry of robed Prospero and the agitated Miranda for the start of 1.2.

That, in broad terms and with some necessary conjectures, is a reconstruction of the minimal staging that Shakespeare seems to have intended for the original performances. The supply of evidence is defective chiefly in the incomplete marking of exits. It is consistent with what we know about the material design of the stage at the Blackfriars. A. M. Nagler, who has given an account of how he thinks the whole play was originally staged, would accept this minimal rendering, only adding the possibility that more use was made of the balcony, chiefly for the Master.[19] The main features of this staging – bustle and agitation, the physical confusion in the clash of the busy mariners with the bothered courtiers, the noises off, the focus of everyone's attention on events happening just offstage signalled by the noises and the wet mariners – are utterly realistic, however slight were the devices used to create the realistic effects. The wetting of the mariners is a wonderfully literal-minded and yet strikingly minimal realization of the storm effects. Such realism is vital as a precursor to the revelation in the lines next following, when Prospero tells Miranda that the tempest and shipwreck are only an illusion of

---

[18] John Jowett sets out the text in precisely these terms in the Oxford *Complete Works* (Oxford, 1986).

[19] A. M. Nagler, *Shakespeare's Stage*, enlarged edition (New Haven, 1981), has a chapter entitled 'The First Night of *The Tempest*'. Apart from the fact that the first performance would have been in an afternoon, not at night, Nagler's deductions about the original staging of the opening scene are consistent with the version offered here. He assumes that the Master would definitely have been on the balcony and makes no mention of ropes.

his art, that the passengers and crew will be found safe, the ship trimly rigged, the wet clothes clean as if newly pressed.

There are a few points more which can be made about the necessary minimalism of this staging as it was designed for the Blackfriars. A criterion for it, and also perhaps an indication that Shakespeare was commenting on Heywood rather than the reverse, is Fletcher's imitation of Shakespeare's staging in the opening scene of *The Sea Voyage*.[20] Fletcher's play, written in about 1622, was also designed for the Blackfriars, since like *The Tempest* it has an act-break between Acts 4 and 5, where Crocale, Clarinda, and Julietta exit and then re-enter to start the final act. Fletcher's play generally overdoes Shakespeare's model. His play has two islands and two ships, though its stage effects are fairly similar, including '*Horid Musick*' before the reunions which bring about the happy ending, and a banquet. The banquet, however, which is watched over by an Amazon in Prospero-like fashion, is not transformed by any magic, and is amazing only in having potatoes included in the food and drink. The play has none of Prospero's magic, and no Caliban.

The tempest and the threat of shipwreck in its opening scene is a benign version of Shakespeare's subtle literal-mindedness. Its use of sea-terms suggests that Fletcher knew the idioms of the sea less well, but was deliberately trying to remind his audience of the earlier Blackfriars play before setting his off on a different course. The initial stage direction is '*A Tempest, Thunder and Lightning. Enter Master and two Sailors*'. The Master immediately delivers his echo.

Master.
  Lay her aloof, the Sea grows dangerous,
  How it spits against the clouds, how it capers.
  And how the fiery Element frights it back.
  There be Devils dancing in the air I think
  I saw a *Dolphin* hang i'th' horns o' th' moon
  Shot from a wave, hey day, hey day.
  How she kicks and yerks!

  Down with the Main Mast, lay her at hull,
  Farle up all her Linnens, and let her ride it out.

The Master goes on to talk about the risk of the ship splitting, and calls for the Boatswain, who suggests casting the lading overboard. This is eventually done, much to the dismay of the courtiers, whose valuables are thus lost. Altogether this scene does a good deal more to establish the plot-line than Shakespeare's does. At 180 lines it is well over double Shakespeare's 79 lines, much of it concerned with the passengers. All the sea-talk is covered in the opening 60 lines, including mention of leaks, the ribs being open, the rudder almost spent, and a proposal to hoist out the boat. The scene then moves on to the courtiers. The woman on board is the only one alarmed for her life. She is told 'We ha storms enough already; no more howling', and the Master threatens to clap her under the hatches. The focus settles on throwing everyone's treasure overboard at the demands of 'so rude a tempest', and there is talk of swimming. At the end of the scene the Master demands that everyone help – 'My life now for the Land. / 'Tis high, and rocky, and full of perils'. They all exit. Two men marooned on the island then enter, discussing the storm and the ship, and make it clear that the ship has safely made harbour.

Fletcher's scene is designed to be an immediately recognizable echo and development of Shakespeare's and therefore cannot be compared too closely with it. It alludes to its model and then moves smartly on along its own plot-line. Some use is made in a subsequent scene, for instance, of the wet clothes device, but probably not in the same literal fashion. At the beginning of 1.3 a courtier says, 'Wet come ashore my mates, we are safe arrived yet', and a little later, 'I'll dance till I'm dry.' I would doubt whether the players would want to afford the wetting of courtier clothes, as dis-

---

[20] I use the text first published in Francis Beaumont and John Fletcher, *Comedies and Tragedies* (London, 1647).

tinct from the working dress of the mariners, and there is not the need here of the striking appearance wet that Shakespeare's scene demands. Fletcher's play, being ostensibly realistic throughout, does not need the emphatic though momentary illusion of reality which Shakespeare's scene requires from the wet clothes.

Comparison with Fletcher's scene and its intertextual links clarifies two main features of Shakespeare's. The first is *The Tempest*'s refusal to indicate any plot-line. All we see is the shipwreck, with no indication of where the ship is going or who is on it, or why. Shakespeare's courtiers are only sketched in. Alonso is in authority, but helplessly lost. Sebastian and Antonio are sycophantic – as Antonio's angry renewal of the king's pointless question and later his 'Let's all sink wi' th' King' (1.1.74) show – and bad-tempered. Gonzalo is cheerful if verbose in adversity. Ferdinand is on stage for twenty-five lines and has no word to say. There are faint hints of what is to come in the king's helplessness when the Boatswain tells him 'Use your authoritie. If you cannot, give thankes you have liv'd so long and make your selfe readie in your Cabine for the mischance of the houre' (1.1.28–9). Even more obliquely, perhaps, the farewells to brother, wife, and children in the '*confused noyse*' hint at an element in the play to be developed later. These are all so fleeting and enigmatic that the effect is entirely given over to the tempest. After the wreck anything could happen.

For all the focus on the storm, very little action takes place on the stage itself. The offstage sounds, from the opening stage direction about the '*tempestuous noise*' and the Master's whistling to the confused hubbub of voices at the end, direct us to things happening tantalizingly out of vision. First one man, the Master, appears. He is joined by the Boatswain and a number of mariners, all in working clothes. Then at least seven gorgeously dressed courtiers enter, mixing amongst the men in working clothes and provoking four requests to go below from the Boatswain, increasingly curt: 'I pray now keepe below . . . Keepe your Cabines . . . to cabine, silence . . . make your selfe readie in your Cabine for the mischance of the houre.' The working men rush off leaving Gonzalo to try cheering the king up before all the courtiers leave and the Boatswain re-enters. He has hardly issued two orders when he is interrupted by an offstage cry from the courtiers and three of them re-enter. The Boatswain shouts at them and two shout back before the working clothes return, now wet, to announce the end. It is a scramble of anonymous functionaries and courtiers falling over one another in a limited space, calling to, or rather against, one another, their hubbub punctuated by entrances and exits and offstage thunder, whistling and cries of panic. It displays human helplessness in the face of natural violence.

The Blackfriars playhouse was the antithesis of disorder and natural storms. It was a candle-lit hall, with seats for everyone, exclusively an enclave for the leisured class of courtiers, gallants, gentry, and their ladies. None of its seats cost less than sixpence, the price of a box at the Globe, and even the sixpenny seats were banished to the furthest remove in the galleries. The priorities in its auditorium were the reverse of the Globe's. At the amphitheatre, in a tradition going back to travelling companies performing in market places, the first priority was standing room around the stage, the minimal pennyworth. If you paid more you removed yourself to a bench in the galleries behind the 'understanders o' th' yard'. You might do so for comfort – twopence for a gallery seat, threepence for one with a cushion – or for a roof to protect you from rain. Whatever extra you paid, you saw the play from behind the crowd standing in the yard and the rain. At the Blackfriars the opposite priorities prevailed. The more you paid the closer to the stage you sat, in a box along the flank of the stage for half a crown – ten times the price of a cushioned seat at the Globe – or on a stool on the stage itself. The Blackfriars was indeed playgoing for the privileged.[21]

If *The Tempest* truly was the first play Shakespeare planned for the Blackfriars, his opening scene was a model of how to *épater les gallants*. The shock of the opening's realism is transformed into magic the moment Miranda enters. Her first two lines are reassuring –

> If by your Art (my deerest father) you have
> Put the wild waters in this Rore, alay them.

She knows what Prospero is capable of, and her appeal tells the audience what his magician's robe and staff ought already to signify. It is not after all going to be a rough-and-tumble amphitheatre play of the kind Heywood was writing for the Red Bull. But its course still does not run smooth. It is a play which consistently arouses, challenges, and disappoints courtier expectations. Eventually Shakespeare does offer some satisfaction to the taste of the masque-hungry courtier, but even that belated spectacle is broken off in disharmonies by the cold reality of the conspiracy. The audience, quite specifically a Blackfriars audience of gallants and courtiers, is being kept in suspense. Like the courtiers in the shipwreck, the audience is not to know what it is in for.

---

[21] The contrasting conditions of the two auditoriums and audiences are described in the author's *Playgoing in Shakespeare's London* (Cambridge, 1987).

KEATS AND *LUCRECE*

JOHN KERRIGAN

Among the papers at Keats House, Hampstead, is a marked-up copy of Shakespeare's *Poetical Works*,[1] ignored, in large part, both by Keatsians and by students of his 'Presider'.[2] Caroline Spurgeon may give us, in her classic study, the gist of Keats's notes to the plays, *Venus and Adonis* and the *Sonnets*; but, like every other praiser of Keats's 'Shakespearian' qualities,[3] she neglects the marks and remarks which criss-cross *A Lover's Complaint* and *Lucrece*. The omission is a grave one, not only because it reinforces assumptions about what is distinctively 'Shakespearian' which Keats, allowed a hearing, might correct, but because the gathering of poems – a loan perhaps, then gift, from J. H. Reynolds[4] – was so constant a companion and informing an influence during Keats's productive years that it deserves the fullest attention from those who wish to understand the growth of his genius.

Perhaps the most surprising feature of this volume is the dense underlining it shows throughout *A Lover's Complaint*. The poem has been read closely and with enjoyment. Keats and Reynolds, parleying, it appears, through annotation, underline, endorse each other's underlining with verticals in the margin, redouble those, and add enthusiastic footnotes. Opening the book now, one seems to eavesdrop on literary conversation in the Keats circle – dialogue which continued until the circle broke and Keats set sail for Italy and death, taking this volume with him and inscribing, opposite the first stanzas of *A Lover's Complaint*, 'Bright star, would I were stedfast as thou art . . . ' The pleasure apparent in the Hampstead markings should give us pause.

---

[1] *The Poetical Works of William Shakespeare* (London, 1806), no editor cited, published for Thomas Wilson. Shakespeare's poems are quoted from this edition (long s modernized, as throughout the essay); for line references, and quotations from the plays, the Oxford *Complete Works* (1986) is employed. Thanks are due to the staff of Keats House Library, and to Anne Barton, Jonathan Bate, Jeremy Maule, Kenji Naito, Lucy Newlyn, and Stanley Wells for criticism and encouragement.

[2] *The Letters of John Keats 1814–1821*, ed. Hyder Edward Rollins, 2 vols. (Cambridge, 1958); vol. 1, p. 142.

[3] *Keats's Shakespeare, a Descriptive Study* (London, 1928). The critical tradition goes back to Woodhouse (letter to John Taylor, c. 27 October 1818, *Letters*, ed. Rollins, vol. 1, pp. 388–90). Furthered by Arnold's essay 'John Keats' (1880) and Middleton Murry's *Keats and Shakespeare* (London, 1925), it still offers insights (see, for example, chapters 8 and 9 of Jonathan Bate's *Shakespeare and the English Romantic Imagination* (Oxford, 1986) and R. S. White, *Keats as a Reader of Shakespeare* (London, 1987)).

[4] The title-page is inscribed 'John Hamilton Reynolds to John Keats, 1819' but, given the correlation between its marking and Keats's comments in letters written before that date, Spurgeon is probably right to suppose 'that Reynolds lent this volume to Keats some time before he actually gave it him for his own' (*Keats's Shakespeare*, p. 38). Certainly, the famous epistle from Burford Bridge, on 'beauties in the sonnets' and '"cockled snails"' (*Letters*, ed. Rollins, vol. 1, pp. 187–90), proves 'Shakespear's Poems' an inspiration by 22 November 1817, and a book worth mentioning to Reynolds rather than (in the same day's correspondence) to Benjamin Bailey.

Academic ears may judge the complaint 'from the same belfry' as 'Shall I die?', or damn it as 'ostensibly efficient',[5] but Reynolds will scribble, against an especially complex and heavily marked passage (lines 141–7), 'a very characteristic stanza', and opine of the lines 'O father, what a hell of witchcraft lies / In the small orb of one particular tear' (lines 288–9), 'perhaps as fine as anything in his plays'.

By no means all the underlining in this 'fine' and 'characteristic' poem can be attributed, but a continuity in practice with other parts of the book suggests that, as Spurgeon concluded of the volume's *Sonnets*, after a thorough examination of all Keats's Shakespearian notes, 'by far the greatest amount of marking is by Keats'.[6] Certainly, when the relaxed confidence of the pen-work – less crisply angular than Reynolds's – is added to the quality of what is underlined, it is impossible not to think the tracing of lines 29–35 and 101–3 Keatsian. Responding to the maid's abandonment, the poet of 'La Belle Dame sans Merci' would seem to underscore the description of her 'untuck'd' hair 'Hanging her pale and pined cheek beside'. Pleased by its fresh natural imagery, its figuring of moody weather, the poet of 'I stood tip-toe' picks out a passage on the youth's exquisite anger: 'such a storm / As oft 'twixt May and April is to see, / When winds breathe sweet, unruly though they be'. Even Shakespeare's interest in duplicity, which leads to an involution some find alienating, strikes a sympathetic chord. The image of letters 'With sleided silk feat and affectedly / Enswath'd and seal'd to curious secrecy' (lines 48–9), the stanza on poisoned yet restorative tears (lines 295–301), the lines on 'subtle matter' and 'tragick shows' (lines 302–8): these are respectively underlined, marked with triple and with single verticals in the margin.

Moreover – and this must particularly strike those who have, like the present author, sought to relate *A Lover's Complaint* to the *Sonnets* published with it in 1609 – the Hampstead markings reinforce the long poem's emphasis on persuasion by means of sexual charm, jewelled gifts, and derivative, panegyrical 'similies'. Picking out the stanza on the young man's 'browny locks' (lines 85–91), this book underlines 'paled pearls, and rubies red as blood', 'deep-green emerald', 'heaven-hued saphire' (lines 198, 213, 215), and the clause about 'deep-brain'd sonnets' (line 209). Indeed, not content with underscoring 'O then advance of yours that phraseless hand, / Whose white weighs down the airy scale of praise' (lines 225–6), it marks the second line with no fewer than eight parallel verticals in the margin. 'Whose white weighs down the airy scale of *praise*'. Everything one might readily say about Keats and the limitless founders on that final word. The poet may have been drawn to the 'phraseless hand' through a fascination with what cannot be circumscribed in verse, but the annotator's attention to the 'airy scale' shows us a reader discovering the pivot on which the lover's seduction, and the maiden's poem, revolve.[7]

---

5 Andrew Gurr, 'Mulberrying', *London Review of Books*, vol. 8, no. 5 (6 February 1986), quoting p. 20; Barbara Everett, 'Mrs Shakespeare', *London Review of Books*, vol. 8, no. 22 (18 December 1986), quoting p. 9.

6 Spurgeon, *Keats's Shakespeare*, p. 39.

7 Compare John Kerrigan, ed., *The 'Sonnets' and 'A Lover's Complaint'* (Harmondsworth, 1986), pp. 17–18. Also marked in the Hampstead copy: line 14 (underlined), line 17 (underlined), lines 22–3 (vertical in left margin), lines 27–8 (vertical in left margin), lines 29–35 (double verticals in left margin, trebled for lines 31, and the underscored 32), lines 58–60, 'Sometime . . . hours' (underlined), lines 71–7 (vertical in left margin, doubled for line 73, with 'tell your judgement I am old' underlined), line 82, 'Love lack'd a dwelling' (underlined), line 84 (underlined), lines 99–103 (vertical in left margin, trebled for line 100, and lines 101–3, with 'maiden-tongu'd' as well as 'was he such a storm . . . though they be' underlined), lines 120–6 (vertical in left margin trebled for line 126, with a cross against line 122 keyed to note 'himself'), line 132, 'dialogu'd' (underlined), lines 141–7 (vertical in left margin, quadrupled for line 147, with a squiggle beside line 144, and keyed to the comment 'a very characteristic stanza'), lines 162–8 (vertical in left margin), line 193 (underlined), line 196 (double

Interestingly, the lines marked most heavily in the Hampstead *Lucrece* – a text in which Reynolds's hand cannot be discerned – once more involve 'praise' and its Shakespearian corollary, 'fame'.[8] Tarquin, it will be recalled, rides 'From the besieged Ardea all in post' to the house of Collatine, where, encountering the chaste Lucrece, he is smitten. To ingratiate himself, Shakespeare says:

> He stories to her ears her husband's fame,
> Won in the fields of fruitful Italy;
> And decks with praises Collatine's high name,
> Made glorious by his manly chivalry,
> With bruised arms and wreaths of victory:
>> Her joy with heav'd-up hand she doth
>> express,
>> And, wordless, so greets heaven for his
>> success.   (lines 106–12)

The entire stanza is marked with a vertical line in the left margin, and five added verticals plus underlining – more emphasis than anywhere else in the poem – stress 'He stories to her ears her husband's fame . . . fruitful Italy'. That such an emphasis is justified becomes apparent when one considers the form of the whole; for this is another seductive moment on which a poem turns. Indeed, the passage should remind us of a disjunction in the *Sonnets'* and *A Lover's Complaint*'s account of praising fame, since both lie along a fault-line between a textual project and its operation.[9] In the original narrative, after all, recorded by Ovid and Livy and repeated in 'The Argument' to *Lucrece*, Collatinus and others at the siege of Ardea proclaim the 'virtues' of their wives 'in their discourses after supper'. To prove this virtue substantial they set out as a party for Rome, only to discover all the wives except Lucrece disporting themselves. Inflamed by 'Lucrece' beauty', Tarquin returns to Ardea with the other generals, but then steals back to Rome and commits the rape. In the poem, by contrast, there is no prior encounter, no occasion on which Tarquin might have been tempted by the woman. Instead, it is suggested, Collatine's 'boast of Lucrece' sover-

eignty . . . Braving compare', prompted Tarquin to gallop from the siege and pour his own venomous compound of praising fame into Lucrece' 'ears' (lines 33–42).

That this divergence from Ovid and Livy was deeply intended can be deduced from a play admired by the young Keats, *Cymbeline*.[10] There, once again, a husband's 'boast' precipitates tragedy; for it is Posthumus' public vaunting of Innogen's 'virtue' which prompts Giacomo to test her, creeping across the rushes of her bedchamber like, as he declares, Tarquin. Indeed, while Collatine becomes 'the publisher / Of that rich jewel', his wife (lines 33–4), Posthumus wagers with Giacomo a 'diamond' identified with Innogen (1.4.70–166). The Hampstead annotations should be recalled. By marking those jewels

---

verticals in left margin), lines 197–203 and 204–5 (vertical in the left margin, in addition to the underscored line 198), lines 211–17 (vertical in margin, in addition to the two underlined phrases), line 219 (underlined), lines 237–8 (vertical in left margin, doubled for line 238), lines 244–5 (vertical in left margin, trebled for line 245), line 261 (underlined), line 278 (underlined), lines 288–9 (four or five verticals in left margin, with a cross keyed to the judgement noted above, 'This is perhaps as fine . . . ').

8 The full list reads: lines 106–12 (vertical in left margin doubled with, with three verticals to the right, for the underscored lines 106–7), lines 141–2 (double verticals in left margin), lines 197–201 (vertical in left margin, with lines 197, 198, and 200 underlined), lines 211–17 (vertical in left margin), lines 568–71 (underlined with vertical in left margin), line 715 (underlined), lines 944–5 (double verticals in left margin), lines 946–52 (vertical in left margin, with lines 947–8 underlined), lines 1007–8 (vertical in left margin), line 1497 (underlined), lines 1835–41 (vertical in left margin and line 1835 underlined).

9 Kerrigan, *The 'Sonnets'*, pp. 21–9.

10 For his schoolboy enthusiasm see Charles and Mary Cowden Clarke, *Recollections of Writers* (London, 1878), p. 126. The continued significance of this play is attested by, for example, the letter to Woodhouse on 'the poetical Character' (27 October 1818, *Letters*, ed. Rollins, vol. I, pp. 386–8), in which 'as much delight in conceiving an Iago as an Imogen' points up in the contrast a link with *Othello* where both overlap with *Lucrece*.

which the youth received as love tokens, then purveyed to seduce the maid – the 'emerald', 'heaven-hued saphire', and 'diamond' – they alert us to a Shakespearian link between re-ification and sexual treachery. *Cymbeline* remains indicative. With the 'diamond' at stake, Giacomo climbs out of a trunk in which, he claims, his valuables are kept, and suggest-ively slips a bracelet from Innogen's wrist. It is this token, added to the news of his wife's birthmark, which pitches Posthumus into the world of *Othello*. The bangle and crimson mole, 'cinque-spotted', like the strawberry-spotted handkerchief, fetishistically translate the female body into its disposition and adjuncts, and advance a narrative of tragic deception inaugurated, for Shakespeare, in the soldiers' tents and 'at a feast' in Rome, with Posthumus' and Collatine's attempts to lend their wives' 'virtue' value.

For Collatine to 'boast of Lucrece' sover-eignty', in a text concerned, like *Julius Caesar*, with conflict between tyrannical and republi-can values, is ironic. By vaunting his wife's virtue, Shakespeare implies, Collatine puts it on a level with Tarquin's regal pride, and betrays the principles associated for Eliza-bethan readers with his house. But a secondary sense of the word, emerging as the poem unfolds, is at least as important. In the period, 'sovereignty' could mean 'the dignity attach-ing to certain dispositions of heraldic bear-ings',[11] and for Collatine to 'boast' his wife's 'sovereignty' is for him to blazon her in ways which tellingly anticipate the perceptions of his enemy. Even the blushes and pallor which greet Tarquin's arrival are gold and silver on the 'field' or background of the 'shield' of Lucrece' countenance:

> This heraldry in Lucrece' face was seen,
> Argued by beauty's red, and virtue's white.
> Of either's colour was the other queen,
> Proving from world's minority their right:
> Yet their ambition makes them still to fight;
> The sovereignty of either being so great,
> That oft they interchange each other's seat.
>
> (lines 64–70)

If the ambiguity of 'sovereignty' is productive here, less so, perhaps, is the association of blazoning with the narrator. Not for nothing has this passage become the focus of feminist commentary.[12] Yet the phrase 'was seen' should not be overlooked; coinciding with 'heraldry', it introduces Tarquin as perceiver. The whole encounter is shaped by the emer-gence of Sextus' gaze from Shakespeare's. To read from line 50, his arrival, to line 84, with its 'silent wonder of still-gazing eyes', is to find benign strife heightened into what is seen as self-division by a 'traitor eye' (line 73). While the narrator presents red and white as inter-mingled, with virtue never not governing beauty on Lucrece' 'shield', the rapist reads it as a sign of battle. The heraldic 'field' is, in his eyes, militarized and divided, a 'silent war of lilies and of roses / Which Tarquin view'd in her fair face's field' (lines 71–2). Like Thomas Heywood, in a congruent section of 'Oenone and Paris', Sextus finds in the 'strife' of 'white and redde' evidence of unconscious 'shame'.[13] He construes Lucrece' 'blushes' as sexual incitement.

If Tarquin misreads, Lucrece fails to inter-pret. Innocence makes her illiterate, incapable of discerning Sextus' intent. As the narrator remarks:

> But she that never cop'd with stranger eyes,
> Could pick no meaning from their parling looks,

---

[11] George Wyndham, ed., *The Poems of Shakespeare* (London, 1898), p. 227, quoting John Gwillim's *Display of Heraldrie* (London, 1610 [1611]), at p. 43, a passage which in turn invokes Gerard Legh's *Accedens of Armory* (London, 1562) as authority.

[12] See Coppélia Kahn, 'The Rape in Shakespeare's *Lucrece*', *Shakespeare Studies*, 9 (1976), 45–72, at p. 51, and Nancy Vickers, '"The blazon of sweet beauty's best": Shakespeare's *Lucrece*', in *Shakespeare and the Question of Theory*, eds. Patricia Parker and Geoffrey Hartman (London, 1985), pp. 95–115, an admirable essay which reached me too late to contribute to my argument.

[13] London, 1594, quoting Joseph Quincy Adams's edition, Folger Shakespeare Library Publications, 5 (Washington, D.C., 1943), p. 13.

Nor read the subtle-shining secrecies
Writ in the glassy margents of such books;
She touch'd no unknown baits, nor fear'd no
    hooks;
Nor could she moralize his wanton sight,
More than his eyes were open'd to the light.

(lines 99–105)

Tarquin is a learned edition or black missal. He carries notes in his eyes like comments in a margin; and they point, as index-fingered glosses did in Elizabethan books, towards dark matter, clear lust. The Princess in *Love's Labour's Lost* has Boyet on hand to interpret the King of Navarre's 'heart's still rhetoric dis-closèd with eyes' (2.1.229). Those 'eyes', he explains, 'glassed' and glossing the King's intent, 'Did point you to buy them', just as 'His face's own margin did quote such amazes / That all eyes saw his eyes enchanted with gazes' (lines 242–7). Unable thus to read, and lacking good counsel, Lucrece sees only eyes 'open'd to the light', glancing rather than 'parling'. Her failure to 'moralize' is a major lapse in the terms set by this poem, where the coding of character and its interpretation are decisive activities.

Hence the nature of Tarquin's self-doubt, a dozen stanzas later, as he contemplates the rape in prospect. Combining images from heraldry and the book, he says:

    my digression is so vile, so base,
    That it will live engraven in my face.

    Yea, though I die, the scandal will survive,
    And be an eye-sore in my golden coat;
    Some loathsome dash the herald will contrive,
    To cipher me, how fondly I did dote.

(lines 202–7)

The lines should remind us that blazoning constructed male as well as female identity. At once a means of maintaining ancient distinc-tions and of endorsing social advancement, heraldic ciphers articulated late Elizabethan and Jacobean culture to an extent it is easier to underestimate than analyse. Even those inclined to believe, with the King in *All's Well*, that 'honours thrive / When rather from our acts we them derive / Than our foregoers' (2.3.136–8), thought such 'nobility' worth 'display'. Henry Peacham, for example, insists in *The Compleat Gentleman* that 'meannesse of birth and beginning' are consistent with 'Honor' and 'Nobilitie', yet he goes on to elaborate, in loving detail, the principles 'Of Armorie, or Blazon of Armes, with the Antiquity and Dignitie of Heralds'.[14]

The fascination is understandable. In order to mediate between the self and society, her-aldry developed an idiom expressive enough to rival the language of the book. Indeed, the two modes are visibly continuous in Emblem Books like Peacham's *Minerva Britanna*, which includes devices used in late Elizabethan Accession Day Tilts. And it is in this context, with Sidney's device of '*Speravi* "dashed through, to shew his hope therein was dash-ed"',[15] that we should read the 'loathsome dash' in Tarquin's 'coat'. Dedicated to South-ampton – a direct descendant of the York Herald, William Wriothesley, and notable contributor to Accession Day tournaments – *Lucrece* is bound up with the Essex circle and their Sidneian world of Protestant knight-hood. It makes bookish heraldry the locus of serious concerns. When Collatine's wife meets an 'attaint' in rape (line 825), dishonour is registered in the chivalric image as surely as self-disgust in the idea of infection. Lucrece has been, the word suggests, touched by an oppo-nent's lance and disgraced in the lists.[16] Through her, she feels, Collatine's scutcheon is sullied, and a 'loathsome dash' has been marked in the family, as well as Tarquin's, face:

    O unseen shame! invisible disgrace!
    O unfelt sore! crest-wounding, private scar!
    Reproach is stamp'd in Collatinus' face,

---

[14] London, 1622, quoting pp. 3, 138.
[15] Cited by Roy Strong, *The Cult of Elizabeth: Elizabethan Portraiture and Pageantry* (London, 1977), p. 144.
[16] Compare, for example, the use of 'untainted' in Sonnet 19.

And Tarquin's eye may read the mot afar,
How he in peace is wounded, not in war.

(lines 827–31 [1806 italics])

Just what is at stake here becomes clear if one compares the stanzas from 'Saint Agnes' Eve'[17] which so impressed Hood, the Pre-Raphaelites, and, a few streets away from Keats House, Gerard Manley Hopkins.[18] Porphyro, of course, gains access to Madeline's chamber with the help of a Shakespearian nurse, old Angela. There he lurks in the cupboard, like Giachimo in the trunk, till his beloved arrives. 'A casement high and triple-arch'd there was', writes Keats,

> All garlanded with carven imag'ries
> Of fruits, and flowers, and bunches of
>   knot-grass,
> And diamonded with panes of quaint device,
> Innumerable of stains and splendid dyes,
> As are the tiger-moth's deep-damask'd
>   wings;
> And in the midst, 'mong thousand
>   heraldries,
> And twilight saints, and dim emblazonings,
> A shielded scutcheon blush'd with blood of
>   queens and kings.   (lines 208–16)

The 'colours' which *Lucrece* details with heraldic exactness[19] are blurred here in organic images of fruits and flowers and fabrics. Instead of Collatinus' 'mot' we find a '*moth*'s deep-damask', and the Shakespearian idea of damasking is steeped afresh in dappled pigment felt as texture. It is dimness which enthralls Keats, the tactile thickening of moon-beams, and the aura of an aristocratic past. Yet his responsiveness to this last does not subsume Madeline in her scutcheon. While the 'shielded' window records her nobility, like heraldic glass in Peacham,[20] an erotic warmth flushes those 'queens and kings' with a contrary Keatsian blush, and the casement casts images which cannot contain the body:

> Full on this casement shone the wintry moon
> And threw warm gules on Madeline's fair
>   breast,

> As down she knelt for heaven's grace and
>   boon;
> Rose-bloom fell on her hands, together
>   prest,
> And on her silver cross soft amethyst,
> And on her hair a glory, like a saint:
> She seem'd a splendid angel, newly drest,
> Save wings, for heaven: – Porphyro grew
>   faint:
> She knelt, so pure a thing, so free from mortal
>   taint.   (lines 217–25)

We are still in the realm of heraldry, but the 'taint' which St Agnes' eve may bring is far from 'attaint' at some Accession Day tilt. The identity granted Lucrece by the coincidence of body and blazon is here thrown free of symbolism. If the ruddy 'gules' which cast their light on Madeline's breast blush for her, they no more fix a meaning than they are her blood. The woman remains herself, and the 'Rose-bloom' is an intimation, almost an answer to her prayer 'for heaven's grace and boon'. What is in Shakespeare a matter of reading, here takes on depth and opacity. In *The Eve of St Agnes* character is sexualized by a bodying forth in light, not by interpretation.

Narrative objectivity of the kind projected by Beckett and Robbe-Grillet is hardly Keats's aim. Objects in his romance carry a strong affective charge, are felt out inwardly as the more significant for not signifying. Hence the palpable rightness of Porphyro's heaped and candied fruit, and there being nothing to make of it. What the draft accounts of Madeline's

---

[17] All quotations are from Jack Stillinger, ed., *The Poems of John Keats* (London, 1978), who notes on p. 629 Keats's invariable use of this title – also standard in the early transcripts – in his letters. The now-familiar title preferred in the first edition (1820) may have been provided by its publisher, Taylor; compare below, p. 114 and note 34.

[18] George H. Ford, *Keats and the Victorians: A Study of His Influences and Rise to Fame 1821–1895* (Yale, 1944), pp. 8, 85, 128–31; 'The Escorial', esp. stanza 6.

[19] For these 'tinctures' see *OED*: 'Colour', sb. 2b.

[20] See, for example, *The Art of Drawing with the Pen* (London, 1606), pp. 63–5 (I4ʳ–K1ʳ).

undressing reveal is the same instinct at work: a poet labouring to image the desirable 'object' without reduction, to celebrate eros without voyeurism. Whether Keats succeeds in this, any more than Shakespeare unambiguously distinguishes his narrator's attentive, from Tarquin's 'traitor', eye at lines 50–84, is debatable. He remains perhaps for most readers, 'the voyeur . . . also / somewhat embarrassed'.[21] But his intent seems clear in those revisions which remove, for instance, the strip-tease 'Loosens her fragrant boddice *and doth bare*' and wrong sort of physicality in 'Loosens her *bursting* boddice' (app. crit., lines 225/226), while developing the image, neither reticent nor fetishistic, so near yet removed from Shakespeare's 'emerald', 'saphire', and 'diamonds', of 'warmed jewels' unclasped 'one by one' (line 228).

Moreover, Keats sets up tremors of irony designed to unsettle an identification of rapt poet with desiring intruder. Thus, 'Seemed a splendid angel, newly dressed, / *Save wings*, for heaven' (lines 223–4) slyly rescues Porphyro's admiration, in the nick, for love. And it is the attempt to fictionalize Madeline which prompts this flicker of dissent. In Porphyro's effort to assimilate her to 'The carved angels' of her father's house, 'ever eager eyed . . . With hair blown back, and wings put crosswise on their breasts' (lines 34–6), we recognize the same claim that the scutcheoned window makes upon her, and which Keats denies. While Lucrece is 'a virtuous monument' under Tarquin's 'unhallowed eyes' (lines 391–2), a stony image of her own perfection that 'stories' her 'fame',[22] Madeline becomes 'a mermaid' or nesting bird (lines 231, 235–9) – vocal yet scriptless, anonymous creatures. It comes as no surprise, in this context, to find Keats varying an immediate source, Richard Polwhele's *The Fair Isabel*:

Thro' diamond panes of storied glass
Scarce could the light of morning pass.
Yet 'twas enough, through each dim pane,
The room with richer tints to stain;

Colouring, upon the shrine below,
The crucifix with finer glow,
And from its polish'd brilliance raying,
And on the Virgin's image playing,
But, where an amber radiance fell,
Illumining fair ISABEL!
No muse, in sooth, could paint it true –
So soft it was, and sombrous too![23]

That word 'storied' could not appear in Keats – does not appear, indeed, even in draft, among obvious echoes. Moonlight, in his poem, spreads the scutcheon's blush over Madeline without growing into meaning.

Likewise the obscurity of books. In *The Eve of St Mark*, which Keats began shortly after 'Saint Agnes' Eve', the omniscient narrator, with a more commanding pitch of address ('Upon a Sabbath day it fell'), places in his tale a heroine who reads while she is 'storied'. 'A curious volume, patch'd and torn' (line 25) prompts Bertha's fantasies, and, oddly, when 'she read[s] awhile', it's 'With forehead 'gainst the window pane' (lines 48–9). Thus drawn inside the frame of her intelligence, 'with bright drooping hair, / And slant book full against the glare', Bertha might escape us; but Keats brings the book to life in the 'monsters' and 'wildest forms and shades' which play about her in the lamplight as she reads, and then indeed quotes the volume – in the literated substantiality of pseudo-Chaucerian Englyshe (lines 67–114). By contrast, Angela's intelligence is glazed into opacity, 'Like . . . an aged crone / Who keepeth clos'd a wond'rous riddle-book, / As spectacled she sits in chimney nook' (lines 129–31), and Madeline,

---

[21] Amy Clampitt, 'Chichester', from 'Voyages: A Homage to John Keats', in *What the Light Was Like* (London, 1986), 57–9, p. 59.

[22] On the ambiguities of 'Monument' see *OED*, esp. 2, 4b, and 5c ('A written document . . . A piece of information given in writing . . . An enduring evidence or example . . . A carved figure, statue, effigy').

[23] Quoted by Ian Jack, in *Keats and the Mirror of Art* (Oxford, 1967), pp. 194–5. Also, compare Milton, *Il Penseroso*, lines 159–60.

Bertha's equivalent, is as obscure. The scutch-eoned window is a dense medium of annunci-ation, and not, like Bertha's textual metonym, a lucid barrier the mind is pressed against. You would not find, in *The Eve of St Agnes*, 'subtle shining secrecies / Writ in the glassy margents of such books', where glosses are glass for textual deciphering. Since the body in 'Saint Agnes' Eve' is illegible, Madeline lies between the sheets in bed 'Clasp'd like a missal where swart Paynims pray' (line 241). The image has given Keats's editors pause, but it is there to protect the girl from reading. She is, Keats tells us as directly as he could, a closed book. While Tarquin misreads, and Lucrece fails to moral-ize, *The Eve of St Agnes* removes its heroine from interpretation.

These texts might seem so different as not to be worth comparison. But *Lucrece* is, in my view, the missing source of 'Saint Agnes' Eve'. Traditionally, it has been supposed that a popular superstition, discovered in Burton's *Anatomy of Melancholy*, prompted Keats to write the poem. Local debts, like the one to Polwhele, and several involving Milton, were then incurred. But, while superstition explains Madeline's going to bed on this night to dream about her lover, Porphyro's unexpected arrival in her father's castle and his slipping to her room to ravish her when she is, at best, half-asleep, then the lovers' hasty departure before dawn – these structurally echo Shake-speare's poem. That Angela, the nurse, was inherited from *Romeo and Juliet*, along with the antagonism between the lovers' families, has been long accepted. The text is littered with ideas from *Hamlet*, *Measure for Measure*, and *The Tempest*. So why not a further, and informing, debt to Shakespeare?

Certainly, this would explain the sharing of motifs. When Tarquin creeps towards Lucrece' chamber, for instance, the doors grate accusingly and

As each unwilling portal yields him way,
Through little vents and crannies of the
    place

The wind wars with his torch to make him
    stay,
And blows the smoke of it into his face,
Extinguishing his conduct in this case;
    But his hot heart, which fond desire doth
        scorch,
    Puffs forth another wind that fires the torch.
                                        (lines 309–15)

In the rushes of the corridor he finds 'Lucretia's glove, wherein her needle sticks' and, drawing it out of the matting, he is pricked. By proso-popeia we learn, 'this glove to wanton tricks / Is not inur'd; return again in haste; / Thou seest our mistress' ornaments are chaste.' But Tarquin still misreads, and presses on to rav-ishment. As the narrator says:

He in the worst sense construes their denial:
The doors, the wind, the glove that did delay
    him,
He takes for accidental things of trial.
                                        (lines 317–26)

Shakespeare's implication is not Keats's, that objects are sensately realized in otherness, but that, in a discursive Rome, misreading is as guilty as not reading is ill-advised.

The Eve of St Agnes offers us, again, a 'gusty floor' and rhetoric of doors. Yet objects in this text are freed of meaning or inexplicably – like moonlight through dense glass – graced by it. When Porphyro follows Angela 'through a lowly arched way, / Brushing the cobwebs with his lofty plume' (lines 109–10), the lover's passage is fraught with suggestion. Youth, we might deduce, sweeps up Decay. Yet the event remains untranslatable. As Chesterton observed of the plume on Marmion's helmet, it is not described for the sake of what it tells us about Scott's hero but because the plume is a plume. Equally when Madeline leads Angela down the staircase 'To a safe level matting' (lines 190–6), or goes on to open her chamber door:

Out went the taper as she hurried in;
Its little smoke, in pallid moonshine, died:
She clos'd the door, she panted, all akin

KEATS AND LUCRECE

To spirits of the air, and visions wide:
No uttered syllable, or, woe betide!
But to her heart, her heart was voluble,
Paining with eloquence her balmy side;
As though a tongueless nightingale should swell
  Her throat in vain, and die, heart-stifled, in her dell.   (lines 199–207)

That self-communing which is an aspect of the St Agnes' eve superstition here underlines the contingency of what occurs. Where Tarquin's light is blown out as a warning, and rekindled in an Ovidian touch by his ardent breath, Madeline's gutters as event. Only in the side-long glance at Philomel's ravishment does Keats incite interpretation.

It is an important cue, and rare. Shakespeare boxes actions in with glozing, so that, though his poem unfolds in a narrative present, it feels distant from the reader. Keats employs a staple perfect, but the events of 'Saint Agnes' Eve' seem immediate and unfabled because objects are unglossed and because the narrator's few interventions suggest he does not control the outcome of his tale. 'Let no buzz'd whisper tell', he is wont to cry, when Porphyro enters the castle, 'All eyes be muffled, or a hundred swords / Will storm his heart' (lines 82–4). Engaged yet by no means omniscient, the Keatsian narrator brings these lovers to life by standing near the reader. Such tension as the plot evokes depends on this detachment – on an acted-upon resistance to storying, a relinquishment of narrative power. Hence Keats's deletion at an early stage of the push-start that the first Woodhouse transcript gave the fable: 'Follow, then follow to the illumined halls, / Follow me youth – and leave the Eremite' (lines 27/28). And hence the adding and subtracting of the preparatory stanza on Porphyro's heaped fruit (lines 54/55), as Keats seeks to reconcile narrative coherence with narratorial reticence. All of which calculated detachment makes the tongueless nightingale, dying in its dell, remarkable. For an allusion to Tereus' rape, and his cutting out his victim's

tongue, is unmistakable here, though it supplements event with story and merges Madeline with legend.

As it happens, the lines support the claim that 'Saint Agnes' Eve' is in debt to Shakespeare's poem. 'Come Philomel', Lucrece cries after the rape:

Come Philomel that sing'st of ravishment,
Make thy sad grove in my dishevel'd hair.
As the dank earth weeps at thy languishment,
So I at each sad strain will strain a tear,
And with deep groans the diapason bear:
  For burthen-wise I'll hum on Tarquin still,
  While thou on Tereus descant'st, better skill.

And whiles against a thorn thou bear'st thy part,
To keep thy sharp woes waking, wretched I,
To imitate thee well, against my heart
Will fix a sharp knife, to affright mine eye;
Who, if it wink, shall thereon fall and die.
  These means, as frets upon an instrument,
  Shall tune our heart-strings to true languishment.   (lines 1128–41)

This fable recurs, of course, in *Titus Andronicus*, where the tongueless Lavinia reveals her rape by referring to a copy of Ovid, and it returns much later in *Cymbeline*, where Giacomo discovers that Innogen before going to sleep has turned the leaf of her book down at the ominous tale. The story, as a story, seems to have been Shakespeare's familiar recourse when figuring rape. But the fable is not Keatsian, and the need to make sense of its presence in 'Saint Agnes' Eve' has provoked over-reading of the kind which might have been corrected by a glance towards *Lucrece*. To judge the poem a 'fantasy of eroticized destructiveness', because the myth of Philomel images 'shattering and loss',[24] is to mistake the work by neglecting not only Keats's humane particularity, but that of Shakespeare's mediating text.

---

24 Beverly Fields, 'Keats and the Tongueless Nightingale: Some Unheard Melodies in "The Eve of St Agnes"', *Wordsworth Circle*, 19 (1983), 246–50.

This is not to imply that a debt to *Lucrece* counts against 'dark' readings. Indeed, Keats deploys his nightingale in ways which support Jack Stillinger's description of Porphyro as 'villainous seducer'.[25] Emphasizing the bird's Shakespearian 'eloquence', and the 'Paining' of its 'side' as though 'against a thorn' – not a motif found in *Lemprière* or Ovid – Keats then calls her 'heart-stifled', choked, dumb. A violent side of the fable is invoked here, and, significantly, this transumption marks the first of several stressed allusions to Madeline's moaning, panting, weeping, or venting 'witless words with many a sigh' (line 303). Against this background of silence and incoherence, Porphyro's 'voice' becomes an image of erotic force. He may rouse Madeline with 'La belle dame sans mercy', but Chartier's fifteenth-century dialogue between hapless wooer and articulate lady is, for Keats, a foil to what occurs. 'Give me that voice again' is Madeline's first imperative on waking up (line 312). Like the author of *A Lover's Complaint*, Keats associates female responsiveness with a vocalism which is ultimately Echo's: iterative, insecure, and inclined to prompt, 'rape me with the musick of thy tongue'.[26]

But can there be rape by request, and are we dealing with *The Rape of Madeline*? Up to a point, both questions are the same. 'Wide awake', though 'still' beholding 'the vision of her sleep' (lines 298–9), Madeline cries 'Oh leave me not in this eternal woe' (line 314), and no resistance to Porphyro is recorded in any form of the text. Few juries would convict on such evidence. Yet it seems significant that, in revising the poem to 'remove an opening for doubt what took place',[27] Keats placed the word 'still' under such strain that its ambivalence – temporal yet adversative – was lost, and Madeline slipped back into sleep:

> and still the spell
> Unbroken guards her in serene repose.
> With her wild dream he mingled, as a rose
> Marrieth its odour to a violet.

> Still, still she dreams, louder the frost wind
> blows.   (lines 318–23, app. crit.)

In heightening the sexual explicitness (and making 'with the violet' more intrusively 'to . . . '), Keats did not need to seal Madeline in 'repose', returning her to those 'poppied' slumbers which Stillinger associates with the rape of Clarissa. It might be claimed that 'Still, still she dreams' adds a note of desire and assent, since it emphasizes wish-fulfilment in the wakeful-sleeping state. But our reading of this sequence has been more hindered than helped by that cliché, as it has become, of Keatsian criticism: 'The Imagination may be compared to Adam's dream – he awoke and found it truth.'[28] While there are Miltonic resonances at this point (not all of them reassuring), the most significant echo, ignored by Keats's editors, is Shakespearian and suggestive of deception, substitution, and sexual threat. For Innogen, waking among the bushes and herbs, finds dream life 'still', as though in sleep, melled with the real:

> The dream's here still; even when I wake it is
> Without me as within me; not imagin'd, felt.
> A headless man? The garments of Posthumus?
> I know the shape of 's leg; this is his hand,
> His foot Mercurial, his Martial thigh.
>   (4.2.308–12)

This woman thinks she wakes beside a lover and husband, but her partner is the man who, one scene earlier, vowed to rape her.[29]

---

25 'The Hoodwinking of Madeline: Scepticism in *The Eve of St Agnes*', *Studies in Philology*, 58 (1961), 533–55.

26 James Shirley, *Narcissus, Or, The Self-Lover*, in *Poems* (London, 1646), stanza 80. This is not the place to explore Shakespeare's use of Narcissus and Echo as a link between the early *Sonnets* and *A Lover's Complaint*.

27 Woodhouse to John Taylor, 19 September 1819, *Letters*, ed. Rollins, vol. 2, p. 163.

28 *Letters*, ed. Rollins, vol. 1, p. 185.

29 As R. S. White observes (*Keats as a Reader*, p. 82), the same sequence from *Cymbeline* lies behind Isabella's mourning for the decapitated Lorenzo (lines 393–472). Evidently 4.2.293–334 made a deep impression on the poet.

To look again at Woodhouse's report is to find Keats coming clean about the Tarquin streak in Porphyro. When his friend called the rewrite 'unfit for ladies', Keats declared that:

he does not want ladies to read his poetry: that he writes for men – & that if in the [original version] there was an opening for doubt what took place, it was his fault for not writing clearly & comprehensibly – that he sh[oul]d despise a man who would be such an eunuch in sentiment as to leave a ⟨Girl⟩ maid, with that Character about her, in such a situation: & sho[ul]d despise himself to write about it &c &c &c – and all this sort of Keats-like rhodomontade.

This is explicit and, even allowing for bluster, unlovely. 'With that Character about her' seems particularly dubious. It is what gets said about raped hitch-hikers, or women on the streets after nine. Angered by the threat of censorship, Keats has lined up behind Porphyro and obscured his own position by clarifying the poem. As always, the verse is more subtle than Keats in its defence. But some of the same problems as arise with Shakespeare's blazoning cling to Porphyro's reduction of Madeline, after their 'Solution sweet', to 'beauty's shield, heart-shaped and vermeil dyed'. Is this flimsily the language of heraldry ('N.B. the *heart* in blazon is . . . called a *body heart*'), or richly the idiom of Spenser?[30] How much interpretative weight should be attached to the line's completing a set of rosy guled images assembled by Keats with deliberation and meshed with the narrator's 'voice'?[31]

In *his* handling of ravishment, Shakespeare is unflinchingly responsible. Though Lucrece blames herself for being raped, the poem makes it clear that her resistance was staunch. There is no trace in Shakespeare of that covert desire which makes, for instance, Britten's *Rape of Lucretia* fraught. When Kathleen Ferrier or Janet Baker sings to Tarquin, 'In the forest of my dreams / You have always been the Tiger', there is a Keatsian sense of the rape as dream life taking its affective course. This tiger appeals to unconscious appetites in the

chastely housebound Lucretia; and, in one of the opera's finest moments, Tarquin hymns 'the linnet in [her] eyes' that 'Lifts with desire, / And the cherries of [her] lips . . . wet with wanting'. 'Can you deny', he asks, 'your blood's dumb pleading?' 'Yes, I deny', she says, but Britten's music points up the ambivalence of such affirmative negations. Shakespeare avoids them. Indeed, the motif of dream life is raised in his poem to extinguish, at Tarquin's arrival, the idea of desire. We are asked to 'Imagine her as one in dead of night', and one

> From forth dull sleep by dreadful fancy
>   waking,
> That thinks she hath beheld some ghastly
>   sprite,
> Whose grim aspèct sets every joint a shaking;
> What terrour 'tis! but she, in worser taking,
>   From sleep disturbed, heedfully doth view
>   The sight which makes supposed terrour
>   true.   (lines 449–55)

Lucrece awakes to find a dream truth, but there is no doubting its nightmarish tenor. Moreover, Tarquin's appeal to the 'blood's dumb pleading' is, in Shakespeare, set among words and images only too familiar by this stage of the poem. 'The colour in thy face', he declares,

---

[30] Joseph Edmondson, *A Complete Body of Heraldry*, 2 vols. (London, 1780), vol. 2, Qq2ʳ; *The Fairie Queene*, for example, I.v.9.6, I.xi.46.3, II.x.24.7.

[31] Erotic thoughts flush Porphyro's brow 'like a full-blown rose' (in draft 'more rosy than the rose') at lines 136–7, they contribute to Madeline's annunciation via 'warm gules' and 'Rose-bloom' (again the app. crit. shows 'rose' being rationed at lines 217–22), and they issue in the 'rose' which 'Blendeth . . . with' or 'Marrieth' the 'violet' at lines 320–2. For 'gules' as roseate, and 'derived from . . . the Arabic word *gule*, a red rose', see William Berry, *An Introduction to Heraldry* (London, 1810), p. 55, and *Encyclopoedia Heraldica, or Complete Dictionary of Heraldry*, 4 vols. (London, 1828–40), vol. 1, Ee2ᵛ, and for 'gules' as 'vermeil' (so that Madeline is finally subdued to the scutcheon), see James Dallaway, *Inquiries into the Origin and Progress of the Science of Heraldry in England* (Gloucester, 1793), p. 405.

(That even for anger makes the lily pale,
And the red rose blush at her own disgrace)
Shall plead for me, and tell my loving tale:
Under that colour am I come to scale
　　Thy never-conquer'd fort; the fault is thine.

(lines 477–82)

There is no music, whether from the English Chamber Orchestra under Britten or Madeline's 'lute', to enforce this claim. 'Colour', 'the lily pale', 'the red rose', and Tarquin's martial imagery ominously recall his misreading Lucrece' blazon (lines 50–84), and the false 'disputation' which made him think that blushing 'beauty pleadeth' (lines 183–280). Now, as then, he 'construes' blushes 'in their worst sense' and proceeds.

In the rape itself, Lucrece is withheld. Ravishment, Shakespeare implies, is the act of one, begotten on itself like jealousy. In the interpreted foreground which is this poem, the question with which Renaissance commentators on the story busied themselves, 'Did Lucrece enjoy the rape?',[32] is not answered because it has no room to crystallize. Tarquin fills the scope of our attention, and, remarkably, the images culturally fabricated for Lucrece are transferred to him. Instead of hers, his female soul is spotted; his is the virgin-like 'consecrated wall' smashed down (lines 719–28). This makes him his own worst enemy. He ravishes himself. Even so, Lucrece is convinced of her pollution. In an important echo of the narrator's description of Tarquin, she finds her soul's house

　　　　sack'd, her quiet interrupted,
Her mansion batter'd by the enemy;
Her sacred temple spotted, spoil'd, corrupted,
Grossly engirt with daring infamy.

(lines 1170–3)

Robbed of honour, Lucrece laments. Indeed, drawing on the conventions of the Complaint, and thus invoking a form through which women poets emerged into English,[33] a mode in which women's powerlessness was typically transmuted into eloquence, Shakespeare allows his heroine to lament at lengths which might be felt to distort a poem called *The Rape of Lucrece*. But those words, emphasizing Tarquin's action, appear on no title-page until 1616.[34] The title printed during Shakespeare's lifetime coincides with the heroine in ways which make acutely suggestive the drift of her plaint. 'Make me not', she appeals to 'night',

　　　　object to the tell-tale day!
The light will shew charàcter'd in my brow,
The story of sweet chastity's decay,
The impious breach of holy wedlock vow:
Yea, the illiterate that know not how
　　To 'cipher what is writ in learned books,
　　Will quote my loathsome trespass in my
looks.　　　　　　　　　　　(lines 806–12)

The 'object' which would be opaquely illegible in Keats becomes in Shakespeare 'something presented to the sight' for reading, and Lucrece, previously ignorant of the self's 'glassy' essence, begins to construe herself as *Lucrece*. A definite shift in her stance is apparent. Indeed, when deciding how to clear herself, Lucrece explicitly images herself as text. She will summon her kinsmen, she announces, knife herself, and bravely declare: 'How Tarquin must be us'd, read it in me' (line 1195). Whether or not Shakespeare approves

---

[32] For an instructive summary, see Ian Donaldson, *The Rapes of Lucretia: A Myth and its Transformations* (Oxford, 1982), esp. chapter 2.

[33] Note the recent work on Cambridge University Library MS Ff.1.6: Rossell Hope Robbins, 'The Findern Anthology', *PMLA*, 59 (1954), 610–42; Richard Beadle and A. E. B. Owen, Introduction to the facsimile edition of *The Findern Manuscript Cambridge University Library MS Ff.1.6* (London, 1978); Kate Harris, 'The Origins and Make-up of Cambridge University Library MS Ff.1.6', *Transactions of the Cambridge Bibliographical Society*, 8 (1983), 299–333; and, most directly, Elizabeth Hanson-Smith, 'A Woman's View of Courtly Love: The Findern Anthology Cambridge University Library MS Ff.1.6', *Journal of Women's Studies in Literature*, 1 (1979), 179–94.

[34] The standard edited form reproduces Q1's head and running-title and echoes Harrison's entry in the Stationers' Register, 'the Ravyshement of Lucrece'.

the suicide, he seems concerned to show in *Lucrece* an initiation by violence into reading.

Certainly, after the rape, she becomes as obsessively concerned with life's and language's dissembling interpretable surfaces as the philosophical rhetoricians – Puttenham, for instance, in the closing chapters of *The Arte of English Poesie*.[35] Writing to Collatine, her pen hovers uneasily over the page, seeking words neither 'curious-good' nor 'blunt and ill'. What Collatine will deduce from the note becomes of pressing concern, since in its natural artfulness, she knows, he will construe her. Her sorrow needs communication, but not its cause, and the letter becomes a paradox in which '"woes are tedious, though . . . words are brief"' (lines 1296–1302). Even the groom commanded to take the note is caught up in interpretative scrutiny. Blushing at the greatness of his charge, he is read as reading Lucrece' shame, and she blushes in return (lines 1331–58). Shakespeare and Embarrassment. The scene is an awkward re-run of Tarquin's first encounter, in which the rush of blood was read only on his side. Lucrece then had no desire to 'moralize', but the rape makes her, if anything, morbidly prompt to 'pick' messages from 'parling looks'.

Ill fame, meanwhile, haunts her. Having displaced covert lust as a motive from the ravishment, Shakespeare chose to stress the idea that Lucrece succumbed because Tarquin threatened to kill a churl and put him in bed beside her. 'If thou deny', he declares,

> some worthless slave of thine I'll slay,
> To kill thine honour with thy life's decay;
> And in thy dead arms do I mean to place
> him,
> Swearing I slew him, seeing thee embrace
> him.
>
> So thy surviving husband shall remain
> The scornful mark of every open eye;
> Thy kinsmen hang their heads at this disdain,
> Thy issue blurr'd with nameless bastardy:
> And thou, the author of their obloquy,

> Shall have thy trespass cited up in rhimes
> And sung by children in succeeding times.
>
> (lines 515–25)

Among Tarquin's hundreds of words, these are the ones which stick; Lucrece recalls them just before her suicide. What frightens her is 'infamy' (line 1638), and a blurring of those 'lines to time' – both 'issue, offspring' and 'self discoursed' – marked in the Hampstead *Sonnets*.[36] Lucrece imagines herself misconstructed as a fable, storied in false 'rhimes' and dishonoured by what she 'authorised'. Everything inward and organic is discounted at this point. Instead we find what Keats underscored – fame, storying, a desire for praise – made cruelly explicit, and formative of behaviour.

The problems raised by Tarquin pursue Lucrece into her account of the painted cloth. The most extended act of reading in the poem, this is also the one most completely bound up with inherited obloquy. For the fabric stories the fall of Troy, and its betrayal by Sinon, the Greek spy remembered as a hypocrite. In him we find depicted what a lasting slur can mean, and through Lucrece' efforts he becomes an image of Tarquin. But not without close reading. Stanza by stanza, Shakespeare elaborates the enigmas of appearance. With Ajax and Ulysses, for instance, 'The face of either 'cipher'd either's heart; / Their face their manners most expressly told' (lines 1396–7). Yet the latter, when scrutinized, is, despite his 'mild glance', 'sly'. Nestor may be honest, but the painting arrests his lifted hand, which 'beguil[es] attention, charm[s] the sight' (line 1404) in ways that now prompt caution. Like Chapman in the ecphrasis of Hero's scarf,[37] Shakespeare makes his artefact an icon of

---

35 On Puttenham, and Renaissance semiotic suspicion in general, see Frank Whigham, *Ambition and Privilege: The Social Tropes of Elizabethan Courtesy Theory* (Berkeley, 1984), esp. chapters 2 and 4.

36 Sonnet 18.

37 *Hero and Leander* (London, 1598), Sestiad IV, at H2ᵛ–H4ʳ.

moral ambivalence. Indeed, like Chapman in the final stanza of that interpretative puzzle, *Ovid's Banquet of Sense*, he exploits a prevalent mistrust of foreshortening and shadowing[38] to provoke textual suspicion:

> For much imaginary work was there;
> Conceit deceitful, so compact, so kind,
> That for Achilles' image stood his spear,
> Grip'd in an armed hand; himself, behind,
> Was left unseen, save to the eye of mind:
>   A hand, a foot, a face, a leg, a head,
>   Stood for the whole to be imagined.

Reading, Lucrece finds a reflex of her grief in Hecuba and Priam, in Troilus and in Hector. Gaining authority, she supplements the 'painted woes' with speech, and 'sad tales doth tell' – in a verse underlined in the Keats text – 'To pencil'd pensiveness and colour'd sorrow' (lines 1492, 1496–7). Yet Sinon, whose 'enchanting story' (line 1521) betrayed Ilion as Tarquin's deluded her, poses a challenge to her 'advised' acumen. Like Ulysses 'mild' and plausibly 'ciphered', he seems at first miscalculated by the painter. Only when Lucrece remembers Tarquin can she comprehend Sinon: '"It cannot be"', she says, construing that 'painted' surface, '"But such a face should bear a wicked mind"' (lines 1539–40).

Keats learned something similar in 1818. 'A year ago', he wrote to George, 'I could not understand in the slightest degree Raphael's cartoons – now I begin to read them a little.'[39] Yet the qualities he learned 'to read' in those tapestry designs[40] were evidently different from the lurid, articulate, and shadowed effects encountered by Lucrece. 'And how did I learn to do so?', Keats went on:

By seeing something done in quite an opposite spirit – I mean a picture of Guido's in which all the Saints . . . had each of them both in countenance and gesture all the canting, solemn melo dramatic mawkishness of Mackenzie's father Nicholas.

Granted, the ecphrastic setting of Madeline's chamber includes 'dusk curtains' and a 'carpet' with 'Broad golden fringe' (lines 281–5). But these objects are, like the candied fruit, felt out inwardly, unfigured save in mass and line. Nothing could be less like Lucrece' 'tear[ing] the senseless Sinon with her nails' (1564), enwoofing herself with the storied surface, than the affective enmeshing of curtained bed and fringed carpet and Madeline's closed eyelids and Porphyro's musing 'entoil'd in woofed phantasies' (in stanza 32 of the later poem). Nor can one imagine Keats lingering to decode the 'arras, rich with horseman, hawk, and hound' (line 358) which lies behind the lovers as they elope. The vague richness of Keats's influential drapery[41] has all the dense obliquity of the scutcheon in his window. It tells us something about the lovers' status, as the hunt reminds us of their need for haste, but the fabric does not intrude into the foreground to engage, be read by, and read with, the characters.

Lucrece' tearing Sinon is a dramatic motif that leads away from drama. To read Middleton's *The Ghost of Lucrece* is to realize just how untheatrical Shakespeare has chosen to be, and to sense why this 'graver labour' stands outside the mainstream of his development. When Keats wrote to Taylor in 1819, 'I wish to diffuse the colouring of S[t] Agnes eve throughout a Poem in which Character and Sentiment would be the figures to such drapery', he was pointing, through that distinction between human nature and the textual arras (extrapolated from the lovers' elopement), a way towards his 'writing of a few fine Plays – my greatest ambition – when I do feel ambitious.'[42] By reducing the distinction, Shakespeare excluded the free, unstable qualities which would make his poem

---

[38] For a suggestive account of this mistrust, see Lucy Gent, *Picture and Poetry, 1560–1620: Relations between Literature and the Visual Arts in the English Renaissance* (Leamington Spa, 1981).

[39] *Letters*, ed. Rollins, vol. 2, p. 19.

[40] Now in the Victoria and Albert Museum, the fragmentary NT cycle was lent by the Prince Regent to the British Institution, piecemeal, during 1816–19.

[41] Ford, *Keats and the Victorians*, pp. 36, 87.

[42] *Letters*, ed. Rollins, vol. 2, p. 234.

potential theatre. True, Lucrece stabs herself in the closing phase of the story, but her action has none of the emotive shock we feel when, for instance, the Countess of Salisbury whips out her daggers in *Edward III* and invites the King to swear to kill if he wants her adulterous love (2.2). Equally, when Heywood in his Red Bull *Rape of Lucrece* has Collatine ask,

Why how is't with you *Lucrece*, tell me sweete?
Why do'st thou hide thy face? and with thy hand
Darken those eyes that were my Sonnes of joy,
To make my pleasures florish in the Spring?[43]

the shoddiness of the poetry cannot wreck that moment of human truth which asks 'Why do'st thou hide thy face?' This, Shakespeare decides not to be interested in. Instead he describes a heroine who, to earn herself an honourable 'place i' th' story', subdues her nature and narrates what we know.

Philomel had been otherwise. Locked in the woodland hut by Tereus, she wove a tapestry to communicate her situation to her sister, and between them they ravaged the rapist by feeding him his children in that bloody banquet which Shakespeare appropriated for the end of *Titus Andronicus*. Philomel may use a sedentary art to further her revenge, but she does not lapse into passivity. Lucrece, a placid spinner among her maids in 'The Argument', neglects even that labour in the poem itself. Instead of inactivity, and rather than filling Ithaca and Rome full of moths or mots – in Valeria's scornful image (1.3.84–6) – Philomel uses female craft to challenge masculine violence. She does not, like Lucrece, scratch at the face of evil, but, like Clarissa writing to Anna Howe of the plots to punish Lovelace, she creatively transcends her plight and seizes the initiative. Lucrece invokes Philomel at her most passive, warbling her betrayal in the depths of a grove. Moreover, she fastens on that apocryphal addition which makes the nightingale lean against the thorn, inciting herself to song by the pain of what she has suffered. The prick, as so many Renaissance wits observed, is something that the bird does

not flinch from, and in Lucrece' developing an idea of self-slaughter from this emblem (above, page 111) we find her accepting a masochism which the legend known to Shakespeare questioned. One should read *Lucrece* with a poem such as Gascoigne's 'Complaynt of Phylomene' – where the nightingale merges with Nemesis – in mind. The painted cloth, not in Livy and inserted by Shakespeare with a purpose, reminds us how dispassionately fabled is Lucrece' self-destruction.

Even so, she changes. Our experience of the text may be statically self-explicative, but tragedy here makes room for metamorphosis, with something of the spirit of *Titus Andronicus*, by cultivating the temporal. Hence the present tense in which the narrative unfolds, and the meditation on Time which rings like a passacaglia through the closing phases of the poem, from the rape itself to Old Lucretia's lament. 'The perfect' may be, for the reasons Susanne K. Langer offers, 'the characteristic tense of story',[44] but Shakespeare needs a present to grow through and recoil from. For what Lucrece learns to value in this much-storied realm is intimate with storying itself. As in *Julius Caesar*, we observe identity formulating itself to be construed. Living in the present, characters such as Brutus and Lucrece continuously look back on themselves, from the vantage-point of fame, hoping to find themselves perfect. They prepare for death with such lines as 'Brutus' tongue / Hath almost ended his life's history' (5.5.39–40), or appeal for vengeance by retreating from the moment into a seeing the self as past. 'For she that was thy Lucrece – now attend me; / Be suddenly revenged on my foe' (lines 1682–3).

Again, and finally, Keats can help. To extraordinary effect, his narrative slips in and out of

---

[43] London, 1608, quoting from the expanded 1638 text, ed. Allan Holaday, Illinois Studies in Language and Literature, 34 (Urbana, 1950), p. 120.
[44] *Feeling and Form: A Theory of Art Developed from 'Philosophy in a New Key'* (London, 1953), p. 264.

SHAKESPEARE SURVEY

its conventional perfect to play an ending game with time:

> The arras, rich with horseman, hawk, and
>   hound,
> Flutter'd in the besieging wind's uproar;
> And the long carpets rose along the gusty floor.
>
> They glide, like phantoms, into the wide hall;
> Like phantoms, to the iron porch, they glide;
> Where lay the Porter, in uneasy sprawl,
> With a huge empty flaggon by his side:
> The wakeful bloodhound rose, and shook his
>   hide,
> But his sagacious eye an inmate owns:
> By one, and one, the bolts full easy slide –
> The chains lie silent on the footworn stones: –
> The key turns, and the door upon its hinges
>   groans.
>
> And they are gone: aye, ages long ago
> These lovers fled away into the storm.
>   (lines 358–71)

In Keats, temporal recoil carries the characters out of fiction. Haunting breaks with the perfect of 'arras' and gusted 'carpets', and in gliding through the hall the lovers seem immediate yet distant, like things less tangible than art can render and more the residue of lives once lived. That Porter may come squarely before us 'in uneasy sprawl', yet 'lay the Porter' fixes him in the past tense of the 'story'. He belongs with the fabric, is figured in drapery together with the dog that 'rose' and sank like carpeting (lines 360, 365–6). It is the poem's last door that springs decisively into the present. Poised at the liminal, its key 'turns' and hinges 'groan'. Across that threshold the lovers step, and all at once the tenses fold. 'They are', Keats writes, but 'they are' also 'gone', and nothing more can be told of them. Through the storm, across the southern moors,[45] they vanish into the not-story we read as life. While Lucrece turns the tenses back to begin the process of storying herself, Keats's couple escape our scrutiny.

If their poem ends where life begins, those left behind in the fable are pointedly deprived of life:

>   Angela the old
> Died palsy-twitch'd, with meagre face
>   deform;
> The Beadsman, after thousand aves told,
> For aye unsought for slept among his ashes
>   cold.   (lines 375–8)

The contrast with *Lucrece* could scarcely be more conclusive. There death almost becomes what it cannot be, 'an event of life', since the heroine's existence continues after the suicide. Indeed, the self-inflicted wound of lines 1723–4 is conspicuously a prologue to the slow fabling of blood, as currents of black and crimson gore surround Lucrece' corpse and are set off by a 'watery rigol': a heraldry of death, 'moralized' by the poet (lines 1737–50). Nor does the tale end with this gory effusion, 'bubbling' like the 'fountain' which flows from raped Lavinia's lips.[46] Cleopatra in defeat had offered herself and her women, with some irony, as 'scutcheons and . . . signs of conquest' to 'Hang in what place [Octavius] please' (5.2.131–2). The dead Lucrece becomes such an icon of triumph, for her corpse is carried through the streets and deployed against the royal house, fomenting rebellion. Like Julius Caesar's in the tragedy, read as a lecture to the Roman mob, Lucrece' 'bleeding body' contrives, book-like, 'to publish Tarquin's foul offence' (lines 1850–2). Its argument is written in history. Fame and honour ripple from the death, through Livy and Ovid into the poem Shakespeare writes. That narrative self-consciousness which leads Keats to mark the limits of artifice prompts Shakespeare to encode the historicity of his text. If suicide is the end of the heroine's woes, it is so by virtue of its securing a storied fame, and our reading, as she did the tapestry, and Keats her, *Lucrece*.

---

45 Replacing 'dartmoor blak' and 'the bleak Dartmoor' in draft (line 351), phrases which put the pair too clearly on the map and allow reading to pursue them.
46 Compare with *Lucrece*, lines 1734–5 and 1737–41, *Titus Andronicus*, 2.4.18–19 and 22–5.

THE RESOURCES OF CHARACTERIZATION IN *OTHELLO*

PETER HOLLAND

At the beginning of the last act of Ben Jonson's *The Alchemist*, Lovewit, returning to his house from the country now that the plague has abated, is met by a crowd of his neighbours. The neighbours are eager to tell him all about the peculiar events that have gone on in the house during his absence. As with great excitement and more than a little credulity – as one might expect in the play that finds credulousness to be a universal feature of the city – the six neighbours trip over each other breathlessly with yet more fragments of gossip and corroborating detail, their comments grow together until they become a chorus of Londoners:

[LOVEWIT] Has there beene such resort, say you?
NEI. 1 Daily, sir.
NEI. 2 And nightly, too. NEI. 3 I, some as braue as lords.
NEI. 4 Ladies, and gentlewomen. NEI. 5 Citizens wiues.
NEI. 1 And knights. NEI. 6 In coches. NEI. 2 Yes, & oyster-women.
NEI. 1 Beside other gallants. NEI. 3 Sailors wiues. NEI. 4 *Tabacco*-men.
NEI. 4 Another *Pimlico*.[1]

The anonymous group of undifferentiated and undifferentiable voices can only vaguely be defined, even corporately, as a group. They are plainly of a lower social class than Lovewit himself; they keep addressing him as 'sir'. One of them, Neighbour 3, is a tradesman, 'a smith, and't please your worship' (line 43). But they are hardly individualized; their char-acters are dissolved into their choric function, a credulous chorus and they can claim no greater identity than that.

All that is, except one, Neighbour 6. As Lovewit questions them about the where-abouts of Jeremy the butler, Neighbour 6 chips in with his gory fears: 'Pray god, he be not made away!' (line 31). Like many of us, Neighbour 6 is only too ready to contemplate the most macabre possibility. But he has a reason for his fear: 'About / Some three weeks since, I heard a dolefull cry' (lines 33–4). Lovewit questions him about it: 'Didst thou heare / A cry, saist thou?' 'Yes, sir, like unto a man / That had been strangled an houre, and could not speake' (lines 35–7). It is a delic-iously comic moment. But I have suppressed, momentarily, the line that marks Neighbour 6 out, that changes his status so completely: 'About / Some three weeks since, I heard a dolefull cry, / As I sate up, amending my wives stockings' (lines 32–4). With entirely characteristic Jonsonian brilliance, that single line transforms Neighbour 6. Suddenly and with no preparation, the character loses the anonymity of the crowd and has a history, a personality, a differentiated self-hood. Out of the single line we can start to sketch him: poor, with a domineering wife who gets him to do

---

[1] Ben Jonson, *The Works*, eds. C. H. Herford and P. and E. Simpson, 11 vols. (Oxford, 1925–52), vol. 5 (1937), 5.1.1–6.

the tasks that are rightly or conventionally hers, he sits up till 2 a.m. (the time Neighbour 2 says he heard the cry) working at his domestic chores and in the quiet of the middle of the night his mind begins to run riot and his thoughts become bloodthirsty. Any bit-part actor, any hireling in the King's Men who was given Neighbour 6, would surely recognize straight away that he had been given something very different from his fellows.

I am inordinately fond of Neighbour 6, but the way he appears out from the crowd defines the change in the nature of characterization consequent on the beginnings here of an increased definition, a visibility of individuality. As that particular individuality flourishes for a moment here, so that separateness from the crowd is particular, individual, different. Neighbour 6 is both a part of the group and a unique member of it, perhaps significantly the only member to proclaim in his language his uniqueness. It is not, crucially for my argument, that Neighbour 6 is a character and the other neighbours are not – that would be an unhelpful distinction since it would necessitate remarkably factitious lines of demarcation between certain modes of speaking role, allowed the status of characters, and others who sink back into a mass of something else, unlabelled and unimportant. Instead, the gap that his one defining line opens out is sufficient to change the type of character he is, change the actor's and the audience's response to him, and ought to change in consequence the critical tools appropriate to our description and analysis of him.

As I have read more widely in the critical tradition of the analysis of Shakespearian characterization, I have become more and more troubled by the inability of the methods used, and of the presuppositions implicit in the writing, to cope with the problem posed by Jonson's Neighbour 6, let alone the far more complex and sophisticated problems that seem to me to be posed in Shakespeare himself. In so many senses there is little difference between the critical language tried out falteringly in the eighteenth century and typified for us by, say, Maurice Morgann's *Essay on the Dramatic Character of Sir John Falstaff* (London, 1777) and such recent analyses as those collected in *Shakespeare Survey 34* (1981), devoted to papers from the International Shakespeare Conference on 'Characterization in Shakespeare', or the essays on Shakespeare's styles collected in honour of Kenneth Muir.[2] The critical language has of course become immeasurably subtler and many of the recent essays display a sensitivity and perceptiveness that I unashamedly envy. Yet I hope my arrogance will be excused if I rather glibly declare that while the terms have changed the scope of the analysis has not. Too much has been left out.

I can best arrange my anxieties under six heads:

(i) There seem to be too few characters in the traditional model. It is obvious that Hamlet deserves far far more attention than Second Gentleman and the dominance of the major roles in the creation of the performance is entirely right and proper. But the methods appropriate to the analysis of the major rarely fit the minor, and the extrapolated synoptic generalizations about Shakespeare inadequately express or consider the range of roles performed. We are left with an apparent ability to analyse most of the lines spoken, but unable to analyse most of the characters in any one play, assuming somehow that the few characters we can analyse will adequately represent the others.

(ii) There has been little concern to identify the way in which distinctive qualities in characterization emerge at different stages in Shakespeare's career, that his view, in effect, is not static but changing. There have been, under this heading as under the first, isolated exceptions: Anne Barton's fine essay on 'Language and Speaker in Shakespeare's Last Plays'

---

[2] P. Edwards, I.-S. Ewbank and G. K. Hunter, eds., *Shakespeare's Styles* (Cambridge, 1980).

develops, with satisfying results, the perception that 'for whatever reason, Shakespeare at the end of his writing life chose to subordinate character to action in ways that seem to give Aristotle's conviction of the necessary primacy of μυθος a new twist'.[3] But it is nonetheless true that far too little attention has been paid to this chronological change.

(iii) The relationship of actor to character is seen within a static perspective governed critically early and late by what actors might see as a ravening Stanislavskian maw. Broadly naturalist, heavily psychologized, and occasionally but all too rarely social (in for example the work of Robert Weimann[4]), the method of characterization is recuperated within developing senses of the actor's self. It is assumed that there is a wholeness of interpenetration of actor and role, consequentially powerfully engaged as a model of performance with an assumed emotional reaction on the part of the actor – and hence of the audience in relation to that actor. Even when actors attempt to describe their mode of working, there is usually an unquestioned psychologism, a particular relation to the actor's own psyche very near the surface, throughout the tradition of British and American Shakespeare performance.

Michael Pennington, for instance, describing his preparatory work on Hamlet, generalizes that 'the player is working in a specially subjective way, and the production is likely to be reflecting his own basic personality. It would be surprising to find him reaching very far from his theatrical self'.[5] Though I would want to quiz quite closely the implications of the word 'theatrical' here, Pennington is still describing a mode of interconnection of actor and character that, for all its possible appropriateness to Hamlet, will not work for many characters outside an obvious few. Must an actor approach, say, Claudius 'in a specially subjective way'? Indeed it could be argued that Hamlet *necessitates* and Claudius *denies* that premise of actor subjectivity. Stanislavskian dictates, such as finding the good in the bad,

the bad in the good, are a subjectivized normalization of characterization, accommodating character within limited socio-psychological ranges of behaviour. They still provide the basis for most actors' work in classic drama.

(iv) The relationship of character to audience is trapped within a similarly unitary vision. At times, indeed, it has seemed that the consideration of the audience at all has been completely absent, that character study is still based on an assumption that the theatrical must be suppressed in favour of the fictional, and that Shakespeare only wrote plays through the misfortune of having been born too early to have written novels. The novelistic stress on character is still dominantly visible in a recent work as intelligent and influential as John Bayley's *Shakespeare and Tragedy* (London, 1981).

The study of the relationship of character to audience will have complex parameters depending on such factors as the position of actor on stage, with its own specific consequences in, for example, the degree of directness of audience address. Yet this relationship is rarely considered critically. The relationship of audience to particular actors or roles, the role of clown for example, is similarly potent and largely uncharted. Again there are exceptions: Weimann's work on locus/platea distinctions in the tradition of popular theatre has enormous and as yet largely unrealized consequences for the study of dramatic character.[6] Other work has meant that we can

---

[3] In *Shakespeare's Styles*, 131–50, p. 137.

[4] Robert Weimann, 'Society and the Individual in Shakespeare's Conception of Character', *Shakespeare Survey 34* (1981), 23–31.

[5] 'Hamlet', in *Players of Shakespeare*, ed. P. Brockbank (Cambridge, 1985), 115–28, p. 122.

[6] R. Weimann, *Shakespeare and the Popular Tradition in the Theatre* (Baltimore, 1978); see, for example, pp. 224–37. See also M. E. Mooney, '"Edgar I nothing am": *Figurenposition* in *King Lear*', *Shakespeare Survey 38* (1985), 153–66.

now accept that Hamlet establishes a peculiarly close and direct rapport with the audience from his very first lines, and we can see that as manifesting an attitude towards the action, a commentary status which deserves enquiry. But it is not related to other parallel modes of communication with the audience so that its specific resources can be checked and corroborated. It seems to me, for instance, that in this case the closeness of comparability with the interaction of clown and audience is highly significant and will allow the ways in which we are starting to observe the place of comic method in the development of Hamlet's character to emerge with a wholly different bias.

(v) In the analysis of character we have not yet built on the highly stimulating work done in the last few years on Shakespeare's methods and art of construction. We could by now have developed the implications of such comments as Anne Barton's, which I quoted on the relation of character to action, to pin-point a remarkable variety of modes of relationship between character and narrative – a relationship in which we could afford to borrow with due circumspection from the development of narrative theory over the past twenty years. Actantial analysis, which can trace as one of its antecedents Vladimir Propp's work on Russian folk-tale (subsequently reformulated by A.-J. Greimas),[7] can also see a root in Etienne Souriau's book *Les Deux Cents Milles Situations Dramatiques* (Paris, 1950). But the analysis of dramatic situation has not profited from formalist actantial analysis. I am not proposing for a moment that we should develop diagrammatic formulations of Shakespearian narrative that identify which character is the villain, donor, helper, dispatcher, hero, and false hero of Greimas's model, or the lion, sun, earth, Mars, scale, and moon of Souriau's, but rather that a flexible perception of the balance between character and action will allow the actantial forces to be observed

surfacing at particular moments with significant results.

I am suggesting specifically the use of pre-structuralist and indeed structuralist work of actantial analysis rather than any post-structuralist and deconstructionist modes. It is repeatedly significant to me that the attempts to dissolve subjectivity, as a concept in the analysis of character in narrative fiction in so much recent analysis, have been oddly unhelpful for the analysis of character in drama. It always seems to me consequent on the physical presence of the body, the body of the actor, that the separation of subject from corporeality is impossible in dramatic analysis. Those odd, by which I mean occasional as well as eccentric, recent attempts to dissolve the concept of the subject in the analysis of dramatic character have always been heavily tinged with the experience of reading rather than the theatre. The coherence of character is marked by the integrity and coherence of the unity of the physical existence of the actor, whether that actor plays one or fifteen roles in a particular play. The relation of that coherence to extra-dramatic principles of the coherence of the subject in the social construction of normality in behavioural individuality is consistently subordinated to the fact of the unitary presence foregrounded in the actor.

(vi) While some of the very best work on Shakespearian characterization recently has focused on relationships between language and character, even a work as provocative and subtle as Giorgio Melchiori's piece on 'The Rhetoric of Character Construction: *Othello*'[8] treats the creation of dramatic idiolects out of specific rhetorical tropes as if the relationship of a character to its language were undeviatingly single. Obviously this can overlap with

---

7 See for example Vladimir Propp, *Morphologie du conte* (Paris, 1965) and A.-J. Greimas, *Sémantique structurale* (Paris, 1966).
8 *Shakespeare Survey 34* (1981), 61–72.

my last point. But it does come as a refreshing comment to read Nicholas Brooke's remark on the First Murderer's lines in *Macbeth*: 'The west yet glimmers with some streaks of day. / Now spurs the lated traveller apace / To gain the timely inn' (3.3.5–7) – that these lines 'belong absolutely to the play and are absolutely alien to the speaker'.[9] The discrepancy, repeated and significantly so amongst minor characters, is also part of the dissociation of line from character that we can find surfacing in the traditional core group of characters usually analysed.

My six points are of course neither exhaustive nor discrete. They interact with each other in various configurations time and again. Similarly their interaction is not of a fixed mode but instead varies between different characters in the same play, consistently within individual roles and, with potent effects, inconsistently, within a scene, a speech, or a line, across the expanse of a play. But the drift of my critique should by now be clear. We have not yet begun to take on the true extent of the infinite variety of Shakespearian characterization. We have not yet charted the parameters of that problem in a manner that convinces me that we can represent its breadth of vision and its potential. Until we have the bases for such analysis comprehensively and systematically available, we are producing character analysis that is limiting and constrictive rather than enlarging and inclusive.

Obviously it will not be possible here to suggest fully what that set of axes might be like or even to chart some of the parameters for any of the axes. My generalizations here suggest investigations well beyond the scope of a single article; all I shall do is sketch some of the possibilities in relation to the resources of characterization in a single play, *Othello*. With a proper openness of response to the wider problem of character we should however be able to see, for instance, how the relation of character to function operates and learn for our critical practice the sort of lesson that actors often understand better than critics.

At its most reduced, character is a mute piece of set-dressing, filling the stage with people and using those people to define status and circumstance. Kings are accompanied by attendant lords, few of whom are given anything to say but whose presence is part of the definition of the court surrounding the king. Most actors begin their careers as this sort of human wallpaper. There was a tendency in the productions of Shakespeare which Stanislavsky staged for the Moscow Art Theatre with Vladimir Nemirovich-Danchenko, to build on the work of the Meiningen company until every member of a large and largely silent crowd had an individual identity and history. That was an act of humane generosity as well as theatrical theory, but it strikes me as essentially opposed to Elizabethan practice. Yet the precise definition of these groups of anonymous characters is something over which Shakespeare appears to have been concerned, and even in the variants between the Quarto text of 1622 and Folio text of 1623 for *Othello* there seem to be suggestions of significant change.

The precise source of these Q and F variants is obviously unclear. Not until there is substantial change in the words spoken by a character could I feel confident about the possibility of ascribing the variants to Shakespeare. But my checking of Q/F variants in a number of other plays has shown that the sort of variants in the identification of a character (in speech-prefixes and stage-directions) that I shall be describing for *Othello* is surprisingly uncommon. Since we cannot deny their authorial status and since, as I shall be suggesting, some of these variants are potentially significant I am prepared to claim that they are at least as likely to be authorial as to reflect

---

[9] *Shakespeare's Styles*, 67–77, p. 69.

non-authorial playhouse influence. Their most likely source seems to me to have been the fruitful interaction between playwright and company in the process of rehearsal and repertory performance.

It does for instance make a difference whether in Act 1 Scene 2 Brabanzio and Roderigo, arriving to find Othello, are accompanied by 'others with lights and weapons' as in Q or with 'Officers, and Torches' as in F. In Q they arrive with those members of Brabanzio's household woken by Iago in the first scene, with 'all my kindred' that Brabanzio wants raised (1.1.169) and those he has found at 'every house . . . / I may command at most' (1.1.182–3). It makes the effect of their arrival in 1.3 into a street brawl with rival groups of attendants trying to take Othello off to prison or to prevent the kidnap. In F, Brabanzio has had time to collect officers on the way, 'some speciall Officers of night' (1.1.184; 'night' derives from Q; F has 'might'). This makes the threat of prison much more official and contrasts his officers with those who arrived with Cassio as messengers from the Duke, two forms of social authority, the Duke and the law, set against each other and anticipating the double demands on state business made in the next scene.

There are similar distinctions to be made according to whether Othello enters to stop the night riot in Cyprus accompanied by Gentlemen as in Q or attendants as in F. The Gentlemen might well include some of those who wait with Montano for news of incoming ships in 2.1 – at least those who are not actually rioting; the 'attendants' suggest a different group entirely. It may indicate a difference in social status and social relationship that is very much a part of the play's inquiry. The more precisely we are aware of social status, as G. K. Hunter has reminded us,[10] the more such moments are illuminated. It may have mattered far more, originally, than it does to us, whether the messages that reach the Senate in 1.3 are carried by a sailor and a messenger or

by two messengers, whether the line 'A messenger from the galleys' is spoken by the sailor himself (as in Q) or by one of the Duke's officers (as in F), or whether the news of Iago's ship's arrival in 2.1 is brought by a messenger or another of the gentlemen who accompany Montano in this scene. In each and every case there are small, but nonetheless noticeable, consequences dependent on which character it is, what social group he belongs to, and what his relationship is to the other characters around him on stage in the scene. This too must be a part of character analysis.

We can sense this kind of change more strongly in the difference between Othello's proclamation, which constitutes the single-speech scene 2.2, being spoken by a Herald (F) or read by a Gentleman (Q). This first is an official statement spoken by an officer of Othello's quasi-court; it requires automatically and unalterably a strong, direct, and impersonal delivery, the Herald as mouthpiece through which Othello's pleasure is made known. The Quarto version with a Gentleman reading it could be the same. The Herald could be a Gentleman, I suppose, or the Gentleman speech-prefix may indicate that Q's proclaimer belongs to a different social group. But it could also be played by the Gentleman as a commentary on it, someone reading the proclamation to himself as well as to the audience, with perhaps the last line, 'Heaven bless the isle of Cyprus and our noble general, Othello', separated from the official language into a genuine benediction or even an ironic one. Either way there are possibilities in Q's version that are not available in F's.

Much more significant is the change between Q and F in the use of the First Senator in the Senate scene. F gives him eight more lines, enabling him to offer carefully considered reasons for his belief that the Turkish

---

[10] G. K. Hunter, 'Flatcaps and Bluecoats: Visual Signals on the Elizabethan Stage', *Essays and Studies*, NS 33 (1980), 16–47 (especially pp. 25–37).

fleet is heading towards Cyprus rather than Rhodes (1.3.25–31), allowing him to cut across the messenger's speech to show that the true information matches his perception of Turkish strategy ('Ay, so I thought'), and making him question the messenger to elicit further information ('How many, as you guess?', 1.3.37). It means that by the time Brabanzio and Othello arrive at the Senate, the First Senator has spoken considerably more than the Duke, spoken wisely and accurately and seemed to participate in the operation of the Venetian state with great dignity and assuredness. It is this dignified and responsible figure who is plainly marked throughout the rest of the scene as being on Othello's side from his first greeting, 'Here comes Brabanzio and the valiant Moor' (1.3.47), to his specific invitation, not the Duke's, for Othello to defend himself against these charges:

> But Othello, speak,
> Did you by indirect and forcèd courses
> Subdue and poison this young maid's
>   affections,
> Or came it by request and such fair question
> As soul to soul affordeth?   (1.3.110–14)

Even Othello's willingness to leave immediately on the state's business is differently managed. Q's dialogue runs:

> Du.   . . . you must hence to night,
> Desd. To night my Lord?
> Du.   This night.
> Oth.   With all my heart.
>   (1.3.277–8)

F's allows the First Senator yet another intervention and deletes Desdemona's line:

> Sen. You must away to night.
> Othe.   With all my heart.

This actually removes the instruction from the Duke to the Senator and makes Othello's immediate agreement directed towards his friend and supporter in the Senate, the man who will later advise him 'Adieu, brave Moor.

Use Desdemona well' (1.3.291). I do not believe that any actor would be terribly thrilled by the prospect of playing First Senator in either text but the increased status and significance of the role in F mean that there are substantial consequential changes in the relationship between Othello and Venetian authority as exemplified in the Senate. The changes, to my mind unequivocally deliberate and consistent, alter subtly how Othello is treated, where authority is vested, how the state operates, and whether it can cope with the problems posed by the stranger, the alien Othello.

Character here is functional, outward-looking. The significance of the First Senator is not essentially in what his role reveals about himself, nor even what sort of people are senators in Venice. Instead the actor's task, in playing First Senator, is to use him unselfishly – almost selflessly – as a mediation between Ducal Senate and Othello, to make him indicate those facets of the state and its General that he alone can mediate. This absence of intrinsic significance, an actantial purpose without self-hood, is the principal denominator of the majority of characters in the play.

None of these roles is really very significant. They all belong to the broad group of anonymous actors whose presence we hardly even deign to notice. But they belong in the same group from which come those moments of shattering import in other plays, when minor characters determine to take part in the action or when those previously mute speak. There is nothing of this in *Othello*, but only from the perspective of such work here can we see what happens when the human wallpaper demands the right to take part in the play's centre. This technique, the sudden transition of actor from one type of role, one type of character, to another is present from Aeschylus onwards. On two familiar occasions in the *Oresteia*, for instance, Aeschylus plays on the novelty of the availability of a third actor, the innovation of Sophocles that the older dramatist learnt from.

When Agamemnon and Clytemnestra, in the first play of the trilogy, leave the stage along the sea-red, blood-red carpet, the audience must have assumed that what would follow would be a choric ode. Nothing in their experience could have prepared them for the cry that bursts from an actor, the actor playing Cassandra, mute till now and assumed to be mute throughout, but suddenly and trans-formingly changed from mute to actor, screaming from the pain of her vision of what Apollo has done to her: 'otototoi popoi da / Apollo Apollo'.[11] In the second play of the trilogy something remarkably similar occurs as Orestes, wrestling with the crisis of whether to kill Clytemnestra or not, turns to his friend Pylades and asks 'Pylades! What shall I do?' The audience does not expect him to receive an answer, but the previously mute actor speaks 'Remember Apollo and all that you swore' (p. 79). Not only does the mute speak but the mute speaks for the god, acting oracularly as Apollo's mouth-piece, reminding Orestes that his duty to Apollo is greater than his bond to his mother. Pylades does not speak again.

This virtuosity, moments of enormous theatrical power created by the use of a new device – having three actors available – is not possible in Shakespeare. But there is an obvious moment in *King Lear* which builds on a remarkably similar transition of character from one state to another, when one of the mute servants who have aided and abetted Cornwall in the seizing and blinding of Gloucester is compelled to intervene, unable to remain passive and acquiescent in his master's actions. The first servant changes from being human wallpaper, claims his part in the action, demands that we see that Cornwall's men are not to be identified with Cornwall. As he cuts across his lord's line:

> Hold your hand, my lord.
> I have served you ever since I was a child,
> But better service have I never done you
> Than now to bid you hold;
>
> (Q: 14.70–3; F: 3.7.70–3)

so Regan's furious comment, 'A peasant stand up thus!' (line 78), indicates something of the transition accomplished, the change from mute to speaker, the denial of generalized inhumanity in favour of a real concern. The caring is extended at the end of the scene, in Q at least, by the servants who will 'fetch some flax and whites of eggs / To apply to his bleeding face' (14.104–5). The first servant's intervention has, of course, strong structural parallels, parallels that tie character to actantial function and dramatic situation, with Kent's refusal to acquiesce in Lear's treatment of Cordelia. The first servant's lines that I have quoted fit just as well the situation in which Kent found himself, if without Kent's magnificent anger. Kent's breaking into the ceremonial ritual of Lear's love-test has meta-morphosed into the first servant's breaking into the hideous violence of Cornwall. The functional interconnection of the moments (which could be developed) places *its* strain on the creation of character for both Kent and the servant. It is a moment at which the director's responsibility, as much as the actors', is to point up the link, to make the audience observe the situational parallel and the substi-tution of one attendant's humane concern by another, lesser character's similar refusal to remain silent. There is nothing as shattering or as consoling in the treatment of the minor characters in *Othello*.

The only other minor character in *Othello* on whom I would like to comment poses a very different problem indeed: the Clown. No one has much good to say about Othello's Clown: critics usually ignore him completely, pro-ductions usually cut him. He is eminently forgettable even though he has two scenes (3.1.3–29 and 3.4.1–22) late enough in the play and extensive enough to warrant some thought. We can see, of course, that there are

---

[11] Aeschylus, *The Oresteia*, translated by Tony Harrison (London, 1981), p. 31.

extremely complex and resonant implications in the Clown's discussion of music and sex. The weight given to Iago's lines on Othello and Desdemona 'O, you are well tuned now, / But I'll set down the pegs that make this music, / As honest as I am' (2.1.200–2) carries heavily on into the dialogue on syphilis, tails, wind-music, and silent music that the Clown provides in 3.1.[12] There is incidentally yet another Q and F variant here in which the Clown's wit is directed either at the First Musician or at a Boy (F and Q respectively). He also ends his first scene mocking the affectation of Cassio's language: 'If she will stir hither, I shall seem to notify unto her' (lines 27–8). The Clown's quibbles in his second scene, with their punning on lying, have a similar resonance when Othello will soon fall into his epileptic fit, punning on the same word in similar ways, and when a soldier's lines, Iago's rather than Cassio's (though Iago's about Cassio), have already begun to work their evil.

But our evaluation of the function of the scene disguises the status of the Clown who speaks them. Clown is not just another character but a character of a very different type. He may be Othello's servant but he is also the Clown of the company and identified as such by the speech-prefixes. He has then a clear social role within the play's fiction and an even stronger theatrical role through the play's relation to the theatre company. Though he probably did not thank Shakespeare for the part, it was presumably designed for Armin. No one else would have been able to take roles called Clown at that time. Like Feste he jests with the ladies, enjoys quibbles and catechisms and music. The part has, in other words, many of the characteristics that we have learnt to associate with the parts Shakespeare wrote for Armin.[13] Clown is then not a signifier of a role in the play, but a role in the King's Men, a role in the theatre company. The scenes have, therefore, an external, theatrical basis that is in a conventionalized tension with their fictional form. They are the routines of the company's

Clown, their comedian, claiming his usual place in another play the company is putting on. Armin is, after all, the only member apart from Burbage of whose role in the first performance of *Othello* we can be reasonably sure. There is, then, a certain visibility of the actor here over the character, a connection from type of role to player, that evidently had an immediacy of perceptibility for the original audience that it does not have for us. Its place along the axis of *audience* to character is substantially different from that of every other character in the play: the Clown is the way he is because he *is* Armin, the company's Clown. Othello is the way he is with help from the abilities of Burbage, but without being so indissolubly linked to him. It makes no sense at all to begin looking at the character of the Clown by identifying him as Othello's servant and wondering why on earth Othello employs such a peculiar and unlikely door-keeper. He wanders into the play because Armin is needed – and also, I suspect, because Armin demanded some sort of part however small, possibly even a part he could embroider slightly in performance, even though Armin was never such a dangerous ad-libber as Will Kemp. The mixing of the Clown and tragedy is so unhomogeneous here, unlike, say, the gravediggers in *Hamlet* a few years previously, that the theatrical origins of the scene are all the more glaringly visible, both to us and to its audience. The Clown's function within this, or indeed almost any comparable play, cannot be defined by reference to the traditional

---

12 See also L. J. Ross, 'Shakespeare's "Dull Clown" and Symbolic Music', *Shakespeare Quarterly*, 17 (1968), 107–28.

13 On Armin see M. C. Bradbrook, *Shakespeare the Craftsman* (London, 1969), chapter 4; Gareth Lloyd Evans, 'Shakespeare's Fools: the Shadow and the Substance of Drama', in *Shakespearian Comedy*, eds. M. Bradbury and D. Palmer, Stratford-upon-Avon Studies, 14 (London and New York, 1972), pp. 142–59; David Wiles, *Shakespeare's Clown* (Cambridge, 1987), chapter 10.

individualist parameters of character analysis.

There is one further implication in the Clown that I want to mention. The Clown is the first of the characters I have glanced at in the play to be played by an actor-sharer in the King's Men rather than a hireling. We know little enough about the internal organization of the company, and the massive labours expended recently on trying to puzzle out the ways in which plays were cast have done little more than make us draw back from the worst excesses of earlier critics' work. But it does seem likely to me that the actor-sharers were a recognizably distinct group, automatically claiming the largest roles and probably largely free from the dreary necessities of doubling, vexed issue though that has now become. My point is that the hierarchy of control within the organization of the King's Men has substantial effects on character, not only hierarchically, but also typologically. It is not only that the senior actor-sharers, other than the Clown, take roles that are larger, more dominant, and, in a sense, more noticeable, but also that their roles may be qualitatively different, belonging to different modes of characterization, different qualities of intrinsic significance, different ranges of selfhood and consciousness. A typology of Shakespearian characterization would, I suspect, have to hypothesize a correlation between the sharer/hireling division in the company and differing points along the axes I have been implying.

There will of course also be divisions between boys and adults, between those who play women's parts and those who do not. So far, there has been remarkably little sustained and thoughtful consideration of the effects of boy actresses on the creation of female roles in English Renaissance drama; too little for us to be able to assess yet what effects they may have had on the development and formation of gender roles within the drama or the mode of interaction, and the distinctions in that interaction, between the actor and the character and

the audience, the triangle of theatrical relationship. The status of Shakespeare as sharer in the company, bound to them and producing on average two plays a year for them, must have had profound effects on the range of characterization he developed. It is another still undervalued feature of the problem.

It is time now to face up to the single largest problem for the analysis of character in *Othello*: the figure of Iago. It is not after all that there has been any shortage of attempts from many different angles to provide an answer. Indeed the history of Iago criticism has often seemed to me a remarkable example, in another mode, of what Richard Levin in his mocking attack on thematic criticism dubbed the 'my theme can lick your theme' school.[14] Each critic triumphantly brandishes aloft the new key that will unlock all the mysteries once and for all. But the result, self-defeatingly, has usually been to lock the character away into a different cell of the critic's own devising and the effect is as separating and limiting, as opposed as ever to the variety of possibility in the role.

In part, the mechanics of the attempts have tended to be associative. In the title for this article I deliberately used the word 'resources' of characterization rather than 'sources' in order to indicate a *potentiality* in the available materials rather than an identifiable single antecedent or group of antecedents. If we identify the basis of Iago's character as, for instance, the inheritance of the figure of Vice from the tradition of sixteenth-century morality drama, we can find in the model one rich vein of possibility. It will in some senses *account* for the wicked humour in the role, our sense of the trickster, the stage-manager of intrigue, manipulatively pushing the characters around the stage. We can see immediately the analogy with Edmund, in *Lear*, spotting Edgar arriving 'like the catastrophe

14 R. Levin, *New Readings vs Old Plays* (Chicago, 1979), p. 28.

of the old comedy' (Q: 2.129–30; F: 1.2.131). This energetic humorous attractiveness of Vice will have consequential effects on our perception of the operation of morality in the play. That tendency is so brilliantly explored in a play like *Mankinde*, for there, the immorality of Vice enables it to disguise itself into a supposedly harmless amorality, a joyful cynicism at the expense of those for whom morality is of great significance, and is in turn transformed into the cold harshness of the pain of Mankinde's humiliation. It is a moral and dramatic trajectory that has strong similarities with the audience's dynamic in its response to *Othello*. The Vice figure finds in its dramatic antecedents the very notion of morality as play-genre and socio-religious problematic that is its dramatic field of operations. Vice as *source* suggests a character *resource* of a certain staginess, a conscious theatricality that is then available for the actor to use. It enforces a particular mode of close connection with the audience, a deliberate sharing of the malign joy of the corruption of Othello's joy, a position downstage mediating the action through this shared observation of the trick. It creates a remarkably strong dissociation of character from the mechanics of the social world of the play, replacing it with a sustained pose of authoritative and knowledgeable observation. Vice has overlapping links with the choric presenter, the disengaged watcher.

The terms of this approach have of course been varied. It has been suggested that the rich vein of satanic language in the play, the depiction of Iago as more than Vice and more like Devil, can too see its antecedents dramatically, finding its roots in the devils of the cycle drama.[15] But the creative results of the diabolic analogy or direct satanic representation have often been for critics to push the play into an emblematic struggle of absolute good and absolute evil. This has an immense and rebounding effect on, for instance, the characterization of Desdemona: the more diabolic Iago is, the more 'enskied and sainted'

(*Measure*, 1.4.33) Desdemona becomes. She has, then, to be played as similarly abstracted and exemplary, with Othello caught dramatically between his play's versions of the good and evil angels. Stanley Edgar Hyman, in his fascinating study of approaches to Iago,[16] separates these two modes, Vice and Devil, into different chapters, the Vice mode belonging to what he calls 'genre criticism' – Iago as 'stage villain' – and the Devil mode as 'theological criticism' – Iago as 'Satan'. But the two more properly connect at the level of source and resource, in both cases an essentially similar dramatic root rather than a root in contemporary theological debate.

There is a deep incompatibility between such approaches and such equally enticing explanations as, in all their variant forms, the psychologistic readings. These reach, of course, some sort of apotheosis in the full-scale pseudo-psychoanalytic studies, creating the whole history of the character as case-study and discovering in Iago, most notoriously, latent homosexual attachments to Othello, Cassio, and even Roderigo. Yet, while critical antipathy has tended to dub such analyses extraneous and novelistic, they have obviously offered resonant possibilities for actors throughout this century, and there are traces of a perception of its potential in pre-Freudian performances by Edwin Booth and others. It did not need Freud to teach actors such a method, any more than it needed Stanislavsky. My concern is not qualitative judgement and I firmly believe that there are plenty of indications, even in Elizabethan psychological theory, to enable us to contemplate such an approach as available and comprehensible in its stopping up of certain channels of emotional desire and its scooping out of new ducts to carry its powerful affects into action. But the

---

15 Leah Scragg, 'Iago – Vice or Devil?', *Shakespeare Survey* 21 (1968), 53–65.
16 S. E. Hyman, *Iago: Some Approaches to the Illusion of his Motivation* (New York, 1970).

effect of such a method on the interaction of audience and character – and hence actor and character – is substantially at variance.

The Vice encourages the audience towards an adoption of his perspective, teaches the audience or persuades them to adopt his point of view as a monocular vision of human behaviour. It is a participatory mode. The psychologistic is distancing in its relationship, prescriptively separate from and observed by the audience, as complete an inclusion of the character into the drama as the other is separate and dissociating. They suggest, for instance, opposing degrees of directness of audience address and contact.

It may well be that the mode of Jacobean performance of such realist roles is more closely analogous to a quasi-Brechtian *presentation* of the character than to a pseudo-Stanislavskian *representation*, but the effect of that is to create a link between actor and audience (rather than between actor and character). Such a model, rather than seeing the identification of actor and character as identifiably whole, marks out the continual separation of the actor from the role to such an extent that the audience is encouraged to share the actor's observation of the character, located now as separably external to the mind that presents it, a separation in effect of character's consciousness from actor's consciousness. This form of sharing connects actor and audience almost at the expense of character. Crucially, by contrast with the Vice mode, the psychologistic mode replaces the character into the play, denying the dissociation of actor from character or from play.

Analogously, though in a delightfully contrary way, Empson's astonishing analysis of the implications of the word 'honest'[17] turns the word into an index of social structure. When the word is seen as being used patronizingly, in a way which 'carried an obscure social insult'(p. 219), then the play's use of the word, which 'amounts to a criticism of the word itself', is both a representation of the difficulty of the association of honesty with double-dealing and, at the same time, an analysis of the social organization that builds so extensively and confidently on the socially superior use of the word without being able to control its soft vulnerability to Iago's actions. The relationship established in the play between honest and Iago is then a means of the character's acting as index of social thought and class insult. Iago as honest soldier, the reliable man who is not officer material in the way that Cassio's gentlemanly manner makes the lieutenancy so naturally his, becomes oddly less intrinsically interesting for Iago himself than for what the character's social position reveals about others and about the society that created him. What such a view of the character necessitates theatrically is a strong creation of the Venetian social system, its closed ranks of aristocratic control, turning Iago, just as much as Othello, into the outsider. The social creation of character creates in its turn an ambivalent engagement and disengagement of character to a play, an indexical functionality explicable in broadly realist terms – associative with play in its own social location, but dissociative in its indexical mode.

Oddly, then, Empson's approach, the richest and most resourceful of all attempts to engage singly and reductively with Iago, has the paradoxical effect of enciphering the character, reducing him to this indexicality, a pointer to something else, where the Vice mode, while similarly placing Iago as pointer also identifies intrinsic and consequential interest and significance in the identity of the pointer itself. Empson's view is passive in its function, the Vice approach equally active.

The variety of the approaches to Iago which I have sketched, the multiple resources which each claims, and the hierarchized dominance which each annexes, have not countenanced the various points on the axes actor–audience,

---

17 W. Empson, *The Structure of Complex Words* (London and New York, 1951), pp. 218–49.

actor–character, and character–audience, to which each belongs. We can of course out of our own critical prejudices align ourselves with each one to a greater or lesser extent. We can see the way each claims single control over individual lines in the play and we can see, as Hyman does with some success, how each climactic moment is an interaction of these oppositional resources, so that, as he suggests, Iago's line 'I am your own forever' is:

simultaneously a pinnacle of duplicity for the stage villain, Satan's revelation of Othello's eternal damnation, William Shakespeare's oath of fealty to his own imaginative creation, the repressed homosexual's marriage vow, and the Machiavel's veiled boast that he is not servant but master.   (p. 139)

But are these contradictory dramatic and theatrical relationships that I perceive as endemic in the contradictory approaches in any sense simultaneously playable and perceptible, or is the modern audience's normal desire for a simplifying model of performance control entirely correct? In many respects, the conditions of Jacobean performance make the contradictions I am exploring here more easily available within a single mode of performance technique than such obviously incompatible psychologized or individualistic models as have tended to accrete around Othello. I cannot see the same lines, the same actions, and the same gestures being potentially indicative of nobility and gullibility in the same performance, but the Iago possibilities can co-exist, if not moment by moment then certainly distributed across the play.

The multiple and opposing ways in which an actor playing Iago is able to play out his, and the character's, relationship to the audience reach their most acute state of tension not in the interactive dialogue with the other characters but in the interactive monologues with the audience. In a recent article Raymond Williams began, with only limited success, the massive task of suggesting how we might systematize the modes of dramatic monologue, creating a typology of dramatic language like the one I have suggested we need for dramatic character.[18] Iago's language partakes of all the types he defines, slipping and sliding between them with a virtuosity unparalleled in the rest of the play, indeed in the rest of Shakespeare. The traditional concept of the sort of relationship between speech and character that soliloquy is supposed to represent, the spoken thoughts of a realized character, the overheard internal speech, simplifies inordinately the dazzling variety of resources of speech Shakespeare gives to Iago. It is a rhetoric to whose multiple theatricalities we have been inadequately responsive. Character shifts with the possibilities available in the forms of its speech. The actor must transform himself from, say, anguished internal doubt for 'I do suspect the lusty Moor / Hath leapt into my seat, the thought whereof / Doth, like a poisonous mineral, gnaw my inwards' (2.1.294–6), to perhaps a direct, amused mockery for 'And what's he then that says I play a villain?' (2.3.327) – though the earlier example is, of course, just as open to such a mode as this is. There are very different resources of characterization operative here.

It may seem odd that I have reached the end of an article on *Othello* without any consideration of Othello himself. One comment I will make, however. Emrys Jones has noted how Othello's reality is tightly bound up with performance, that he 'acquires full reality only in the presence of a theatre audience'.[19] Othello exhibits the passion, elemental and powerful, in which the audience takes delight. It is a provocative and, I believe, accurate comment. The assumption has been that the creation of character occurs on stage and is communicated to the audience. Jones makes it an interactive quality, depending not simply on complicity from the audience, but rather on

---

[18] Raymond Williams, *Writing in Society* (London, 1983), pp. 31–64.
[19] Emrys Jones, *Scenic Form in Shakespeare* (Oxford, 1971), p. 132.

their emotional hunger, their demand for the theatre to satisfy their emotions. The significance of this in placing the onus of the creation of character so firmly with the audience is huge.

When the Duke in *Measure for Measure* tells Angelo 'There is a kind of character in thy life / That to th'observer doth thy history / Fully unfold' (1.1.27–9) he had no idea yet of the extent of the character whose history the play would proceed to unfold to the observers. My interest is in extending this unfolding history to those characters and those forms of characterization whose history has not yet been unfolded. Even Jonson's Neighbour 6 has a history.

OVID AND THE MATURE TRAGEDIES: METAMORPHOSIS IN *OTHELLO* AND *KING LEAR*

JONATHAN BATE

The orthodox account of the relationship between Shakespeare and his favourite classical poet, Ovid, proposes that it was explicit early in his career when his schoolboy reading of the *Metamorphoses* was fresh in his mind (thus *Titus Andronicus*, *Venus and Adonis*, and *Lucrece* are his most overtly Ovidian works), implicit in the metamorphic art of the comedies (*A Midsummer Night's Dream* especially), and profoundly reawakened in the late romances.[1] Put like this, there is an obvious gap which has occasioned surprisingly little critical attention: are we to suppose that an influence the importance of which was second to none early and late in Shakespeare's career was non-existent or dormant in the middle of it?[2] This essay, which represents work in progress towards a full-scale revaluation of the question of Shakespeare and Ovid, uses *Othello* and *King Lear* as test cases in an attempt to read the mature tragedies in Ovidian terms.

One reason for the neglect of the tragedies' Ovidianism is the fact that the *Metamorphoses* tend to bring to mind the golden age, with its associations of the forest, the springtime, leisure, youth, and love. But Ovid described the age of iron too, and the language in which he does so may suggest to us the world of Shakespeare's tragedies. I quote from Arthur Golding's 1567 translation (these lines, incidentally, are immediately preceded by a Timon-like reference to the divisive power of 'yellow golde' dug from the ground):

Men live by ravine and by stelth: the wandring
    guest doth stand
In daunger of his host: the host in daunger of
    his guest:
And fathers of their sonne in laws: yea seldome
    time doth rest
Betweene borne brothers such accord and love
    as ought to bee,
The goodman seekes the goodwives death, and
    his againe seekes shee.
The stepdames fell their husbands sonnes with
    poyson do assayle.
To see their fathers live so long the children
    doe bewayle.
All godlynesse lyes under foote. And Ladie
    Astrey last

---

[1] Strong recent work contributing to this orthodoxy includes Leonard Barkan, *The Gods Made Flesh: Metamorphosis and the Pursuit of Paganism* (New Haven, 1986), William Carroll, *The Metamorphoses of Shakespearean Comedy* (Princeton, 1985), and David Armitage, 'The Dismemberment of Orpheus: Mythic Elements in Shakespeare's Romances', *Shakespeare Survey 39* (1986), 123–33.

[2] A few of the local parallels which I consider have been noted by other scholars – see, for example, Barry Nass, '"Of one that loved not wisely, but too well": *Othello* and the *Heroides*', *ELN*, 19 (1981–2), 102–4, and S.P. Zitner, 'Iago as Melampus', *Shakespeare Quarterly*, 23 (1972), 263–4 – but such notings have not been developed into a sustained reading. The only wide-ranging work I know which bears on the *Metamorphoses* and the mature tragedies is Reuben Brower, *Hero and Saint: Shakespeare and the Graeco-Roman Heroic Tradition* (Oxford, 1971), though this is concerned with Homer and Virgil more than Ovid.

Of heavenly vertues from this earth in slaughter
  drownèd past.[3]

This famous passage is the source of the tag
'Terras Astraea reliquit', which in *Titus Andronicus* Shakespeare quotes in the original
Latin.[4] The age of iron, like the time of
tragedy, is characterized by the breaking of
sacred bonds – the bonds between host and
guest, as in *Macbeth*, and above all those within
the family. The divisions between kin
described here are analogous to those of which
Gloucester complains in the second scene of
Lear; children tiring of seeing their fathers live
so long are especially relevant to *Lear* (remember Edmund's 'I begin to find an idle and fond
bondage in the oppression of aged tyranny' in
the forged letter). A sense of the relation
between tragedy and the later of Ovid's four
ages is reinforced by Thomas Heywood's
popular *Age* plays (published 1611, 1613,
1632): the *Golden* and *Silver Ages* are concerned
with the loves of the gods, while the *Brazen
Age* includes such stories as 'The Tragedy of
Meleager' and 'The Tragedy of *Jason* and
Medea', and the two parts of *The Iron Age* tell
the tragic story of Troy.

Shakespeare's turn from comedy to tragedy
may be conceived as a movement from the
golden age to the iron. That turn was by no
means sudden, as we have been shown by the
many critics who have written in recent years
of the darker, potentially tragic elements in the
comedies. Like Ovid's tales, Shakespeare's
comedies never lose sight of the painfulness
and the potential for the grotesque wrought by
love's changes. If part of the Ovidianism of the
comedies is their potential for violence and
tragedy, it would seem logical to expect
Ovidianism to be developed in the tragedies.
A single group of allusions will suffice to
make the connection.

Lorenzo and Jessica's 'In such a night . . .'
exchanges at the beginning of the final act of
The Merchant of Venice sound to innocent ears
like lyrical evocations of great lovers past. Yet
to the mythologically literate members of

Shakespeare's audience, the allusions would be
shot through with irony appropriate to the
sharpness that underlies the relationship
between Lorenzo and Jessica. It is hardly auspicious that at this moment of union and
harmony the lovers compare themselves to
Troilus and Cressida, Pyramus and Thisbe,
and Dido and Aeneas. Troilus and Cressida
speak for themselves; the tragedy of Pyramus
and Thisbe may be a farce in *A Midsummer
Night's Dream*, but it is an important analogue
for *Romeo and Juliet*; Dido and Aeneas will be
cardinal for *Antony and Cleopatra*. Furthermore, 'Dido with a willow in her hand' closely
echoes an image in the lament of another
woman deserted by her lover, Ariadne left on
Naxos by the promiscuous Theseus in Ovid's
Heroides.[5]

But most sinister of all is 'In such a night /
Medea gathered the enchanted herbs / That did
renew old Aeson' (5.1.12–14). At first glance
this might seem to be an image of regener-
ation, perhaps a suggestion that old Shylock
will come to accept his daughter's marriage.
But what was Medea's motivation for the
rejuvenation of Aeson? In book seven of the
Metamorphoses – and it is unquestionable that
Shakespeare was thinking of the *Metamorphoses*
here, for the words 'enchanted herbs' and
'renew' are lifted from Arthur Golding's translation of the passage[6] – we learn that it was part
of a peculiarly disgusting plot to take vengeance on the family of Pelias for the wrong

---

[3] *Shakespeare's Ovid: Being Arthur Golding's Translation of
the Metamorphoses*, ed. W. H. D. Rouse (London, 1904,
reprinted Carbondale, Ill., 1961, and New York, 1966),
1.162–70. Subsequent quotations are from this edition.

[4] *Titus Andronicus*, 4.3.4.

[5] *The Merchant of Venice*, 5.1.10; compare Ovid, *Heroides*,
10.39–42. I do not see why Chaucer's *Legend of Good
Women* is given prominence in discussions of this scene
(see, for example, the footnotes in John Russell Brown's
new Arden edition (London, 1955)) – Medea's rejuvenation of Aeson, for instance, is in Ovid but not
Chaucer.

[6] Golding, 7.204, 381: 'chaunted herbes', 'renew'.

done by him to Jason's family: having rejuvenated Aeson by boiling him in a cauldron with those magic herbs, she gave the daughters of Pelias the opportunity to submit their father to the same process, but this time left out the key ingredients and thus killed Pelias. Shakespeare knew the Medea section of the *Metamorphoses* particularly well, in both the original and Golding's translation (it is from here that he would eventually make his most extended Ovidian borrowing, Prospero's 'Ye elves of hills . . . '); by activating it here, he is contaminating a superficially lyrical interlude with a precursor text that is marked by bodily dismemberment akin to Shylock demanding his pound of flesh, and indeed *Titus Andronicus*, along with a grotesque recipe for the cauldron of a woman endowed with dark supernatural powers – this same passage will provide ingredients for the weird sisters.

In the foregoing analysis two different kinds of connection have been suggested: *allusions* and *affinities*. The mythological references in the final act of *The Merchant of Venice* are allusions, while the similarity between the age of iron and the tragic universe are affinities. The two kinds of association may, but do not necessarily, co-exist: an allusion may signal a more far-reaching correspondence, but it may be merely incidental or ornamental; an affinity may be made apparent on the surface of the text, but it may operate at the level of the imagination. Paradoxically, the most profound affinities may be the least demonstrable precisely because they go deeper than the explicit local parallel.

Titus Andronicus, which for all its crudities is paradigmatic of Shakespearian tragedy, provides a ready example of the co-existence of allusion and affinity. Allusion to Ovid's myth of Philomel functions as both a plot mechanism and a central point of reference for the characters. A copy of the *Metamorphoses* is actually brought onto the stage and Lavinia 'quotes the leaves' (4.1.50), telling her own story through Philomel's; the wood in which she is raped is 'Patterned by that the poet here [i.e. in *Metamorphoses*, 6] describes' (4.1.56). But the relationship goes further than this overt allusion: in the same scene, Lavinia's little brother, who has been studying the *Metamorphoses*, says that he has learnt that:

> Extremity of griefs would make men mad,
> And I have read that Hecuba of Troy
> Ran mad for sorrow. (4.1.19–21)

Specifically, he would have read in the *Metamorphoses* that Hecuba was wrought upon by grief until she was eventually transformed into a dog; more generally, he would have found in the *Metamorphoses* a vast repertory of tales in which extremity of suffering brings about transformation. Shakespeare and his audience inherited a tradition centuries long in which Ovid's literal transformations were interpreted as metaphors for the internal changes effected by emotional and behavioural extremity. In the words of Georgius Sabinus (Georg Schüler) in the prefatory material to his widely used 1555 edition:

Titulus inscribitur Metamorphosis, hoc est, transformatio. Finguntur enim hic conuerti ex hominibus in belluas, qui in hominis figura belluae immanitatem gerunt: quales sunt ebriosi, libidinosi, violenti & similes, quorum appetitus rectae rationi minime obtemperat.
[The title is Metamorphosis, that is, transformation. For here are represented those who have changed from men into beasts, who bear the barbarity of the beast in the figure of man: such are the drunken, the libidinous, the violent and similar, whose appetite submits minimally to right reason.][7]

Whilst the boy's allusion to Hecuba is significant, especially if we think forward to *Hamlet*, there is a broader affinity between Ovid's pattern of physical metamorphoses brought about by 'extremity' of suffering or desire and Shakespeare's tragic pattern of similarly induced, but internal, metamorphoses.

---

[7] *Metamorphosis seu fabulae poeticae* (Wittenburg, 1555; reprinted Frankfurt, 1589), sig.) (8ᵛ (my translation).

'Extremity of griefs would make men mad': the idea is relevant not only to Hecuba in the *Metamorphoses* and Titus and Lavinia in the play, but also to the various kinds of madness suffered by Hamlet, Othello, and Lear.

My contention, then, is that the *allusions* to Ovid became less frequent in the mature Shakespeare, as he no longer felt it necessary to display his literacy, but that the metamorphic *affinities* remained. *Othello* pivots on the metamorphosis of the hero at the hands of Iago. 'These Moors are changeable', Iago informs Roderigo early on (1.3.346); 'The Moor already changes with my poison', he says in the interlude between the two central encounters in the temptation scene (3.3.329). The deceitful language with which he convinces Othello that Desdemona has been unfaithful acts as a verbal equivalent to the poisonous shirt of Nessus with which Deïanira is deceived into destroying another great martial hero, Hercules, after he has been unfaithful. I make this connection – which I think of as affinity, not allusion – because the shirt of Nessus has similar properties to the handkerchief: it is a charmed object that is supposed to subdue the partner entirely to the love of the person who gives it (compare *Othello*, 3.4.58–60), but in fact becomes the mechanism through which the lovers are destroyed.

The play's recurring images of monstrous birth and bestial transformation are also Ovidian. Sabinus read the *Metamorphoses* in terms of the animal in man; the play uses similar language of bestiality. In Sabinus' list of destructively metamorphic vices ('ebriosi, libidinosi, violenti'), drunkenness may seem the mildest, but Cassio knows that after he has been inveigled into drunkenness 'what remains is bestial' and that in getting drunk we 'with joy, pleasure, revel, and applause transform ourselves into beasts' (2.3.258, 285–6). Iago's devilish skill is to transform the civilized Cassio into one of the 'ebriosi' and the noble Othello into one of the 'violenti' by persuading him that his wife is among the 'libidinosi'. His

success in doing so owes much to the way in which he plays perniciously on the prejudice that merely through being a Moor Othello is already close to being a beast: 'you'll have your daughter covered with a Barbary horse, you'll have your nephews neigh to you, you'll have coursers for cousins and jennets for germans' (1.1.113–15). In the temptation scene he infects Othello with the same kind of language: 'Exchange me for a goat', 'I had rather be a toad' (3.3.184, 274). By the end of the scene, the transformation has been effected and Othello is threatening to behave like a beast: 'I'll tear her all to pieces' (3.3.436).

Shakespeare, then, persistently plays on the Ovidian idea of raw emotion, much of it engendered by sexuality, reducing man to the level of the beast. When Othello demands that Iago give him 'ocular proof' of Desdemona's infidelity, he says that if he does not, Iago 'hadst been better have been born a dog / Than answer my waked wrath' (3.3.367–8). This is based on a passage in the play's source, '"If you do not make me see with my own eyes what you have told me, be assured, I shall make you realize that it would have been better for you had you been born dumb"',[8] but the change from the vague 'been born dumb' to the specific 'born a dog' produces one of a number of associations between Iago and a dog which may have an Ovidian provenance. The pattern of images culminates in Lodovico's 'O Spartan dog' (5.2.371). Why 'Spartan'? The New Cambridge editor notes that 'Spartan dogs were, according to Seneca's *Hippolytus* (trans. J. Studley, 1581), "eager of prey"',[9] an association that would tie in with Lodovico's ensuing line, 'More fell than anguish, hunger, or the sea'. But Iago is not merely eager of prey; he is treacherous. When Shakespeare had

---

8 Cinthio, *Gli Hecatommithi*, trans. Geoffrey Bullough, in his *Narrative and Dramatic Sources of Shakespeare*, vol. 7 (London, 1973), p. 246.
9 *Othello*, ed. Norman Sanders, New Cambridge Shakespeare (Cambridge, 1984), p. 186.

wanted a dog a few years earlier in *The Merry Wives of Windsor*, he had remembered Actaeon 'With Ringwood at [his] heels' in Golding's Ovid (*Wives*, 2.1.114, compare Golding, 3.270). At the head of the list of Actaeon's dogs was Melampus, described by Ovid as 'Spartana gente' (*Metamorphoses*, 3.206–8) – 'Blackfoote of *Spart*', as Golding has it (3.245–7).[10] I do not want to overstretch the idea of Iago as Blackfoot, though it might be recalled that earlier in the scene Othello has said with reference to Iago's devilry (and thus blackness), 'look down towards his feet' (5.2.292). But I do think that 'Spartan dog' is supposed to suggest the foremost of Actaeon's dogs who destroy their own master – George Sandys referred in his commentary on book three of the *Metamorphoses* to servants who become traitors and 'inflict on their masters the fate of Actaeon'.[11]

If Iago is one of Actaeon's dogs, is Othello then an Actaeon? Is there more than a conventional reference to cuckoldry in Othello's feeling that he is sprouting horns: 'I have a pain upon my forehead here', 'A hornèd man's a monster and a beast' (3.3.288, 4.1.60)? After all, in *The Merry Wives*, another play about jealousy, the figure of Actaeon is of considerable importance – the joke on Falstaff is that in donning the buck's head of Herne the Hunter, he thinks he resembles a god disguised as a beast so as to have a woman, but he in fact becomes an Actaeon, persecuted in punishment for his own illicit desire. Characters in the *Metamorphoses* feel an intensely physical process at work when their arms begin to become the branches of trees or they start growing animal appendages; this may account for the highly tactile quality of Othello's 'I have a pain upon my forehead here.' Images of metamorphosis and the tearing of the body are common factors in the fates of Othello and Actaeon, but apart from this and the Iago/Melampus link I can see no correspondence beyond the broad sense in which Actaeon stands for all who are destroyed by sexuality.

If we are looking for an Ovidian myth that has more tonal affinity with *Othello*, we would do better to turn to an exemplary tale of love, such as Ceyx and Alcyone in book eleven of the *Metamorphoses*. Arthur Golding makes them into the ideal married couple: 'In Ceyx and Alcyone appeeres most constant love, / Such as betweene the man and wyfe too bee it dooth behove' (Epistle, 232–3). David Armitage has pointed out that the marine language of this tale was important for Shakespeare's late romances.[12] In particular, he singles out the image of the waves seeming to mount as high as the clouds: 'fluctibus erigitur caelumque aequare videtur / pontus et inductas aspergine tangere nubes' (11.497–8), 'The surges mounting up aloft did seeme too mate the skye, / And with theyr sprinckling for too wet the clowdes that hang on hye' (Golding, 11.573–4). Shakespeare's use of this image is not confined to Armitage's instances, for one of the most memorable is in *Othello*, when the Second Gentleman describes the storm which caused the segregation of the Turkish fleet:

> The chidden billow seems to pelt the clouds,
> The wind-shaked surge, with high and
> monstrous mane
> Seems to cast water on the burning Bear
> And quench the guards of th'ever-fixèd Pole.
>
> (2.1.12–15)

The image itself is a conventional one, which Shakespeare probably first encountered not in Ovid, but in the rhetorical handbook of Susen-

---

[10] Ovid's Actaeon is almost certainly the source for Theseus' 'My hounds are bred out of the Spartan kind' (*Midsummer Night's Dream*, 4.1.118), *pace* Harold Brooks's claims for Seneca's *Hippolytus* in his new Arden edition (London, 1979), p. 94.

[11] George Sandys, *Ovids Metamorphosis Englished, Mythologiz'd, and Represented in Figures* (Oxford, 1632). Although it post-dates Shakespeare, Sandys's commentary may be used as evidence since it synthesizes interpretations, such as those of Comes and Sabinus, that would have been familiar to the more educated among Shakespeare's audience.

[12] 'The Dismemberment of Orpheus', p. 128.

brotus, used in schools, where 'ad sidera fluctus' ('the waves to the stars') is illustrative of hyperbole.[13] But the elaboration of it is Ovidian in its specificity: the water is truly wet, which it is not in the conventional figure. And the context is Ovidian too, with the motifs of lovers' separation, of sea-voyage and storm (Shakespeare departs from his source here, for in Cinthio the Moor and Disdemona go in the same ship and the sea is 'of the utmost tranquillity'[14]).

The affinity with Ceyx and Alcyone is strengthened by the ensuing image of Desdemona's beauty restoring the sea to calmness:

> Tempests themselves, high seas, and howling
>   winds . . .
> As having sense of beauty do omit
> Their mortal natures, letting go safely by
> The divine Desdemona.   (2.1.69, 72–4)

Here she is like Alcyone, who becomes the Halcyon during whose days 'the sea is calme and still, / And every man may too and fro sayle saufly at his will' (Golding, 11.859–60). Given this identification, Golding's characterization of Alcyone's husband becomes suggestive, for the following could as well have been written of Othello as of Ceyx: 'His viage also dooth declare how vainly men are led / Too utter perill through fond toyes and fansies in their head' (Epistle, 236–7). The difference is that Othello puts too much faith in Iago, whereas for Golding, Ceyx puts too much faith in an oracle. Similarly, Othello's metamorphosis is wrought by Iago, whereas Ceyx's is by the gods. Ovid's psychological realism is retained while his supernatural agencies are removed.

These identifications should not be overstressed. Ceyx and Alcyone are drowned, while Othello and Desdemona survive the storm only to be destroyed when they reach dry land. Equally, the story of Ceyx and Alcyone does not end with tragedy; the lovers' transformation into birds effects release and reunion. It is a matter less of plot parallels than of the way in which Shakespeare has, I believe,

learnt certain emotional and verbal effects from Ovid. An argument about plot parallels might be developed with respect to Cephalus and Procris. One of the most uncompromisingly tragic tales in the *Metamorphoses*, this story turns on the way in which jealousy, fear of infidelity, credulity, and misinterpretation precipitate the destruction of an initially joyous marriage. But if there is an influence on the plot of *Othello*, it is probably indirect, mediated through an updated version of the Cephalus and Procris story in George Pettie's *A Petite Pallace of Pettie his Pleasure*.[15]

Ovid has a wonderful way of fixing the moment of death. The final words in Cephalus' narration of his wife's tragic end are:

> labitur, et parvae fugiunt cum sanguine vires,
> dumque aliquid spectare potest, me spectat et
>   in me
> infelicem animam nostroque exhalat in ore;
> sed vultu meliore mori secura videtur.
>   (7.859–62)

>   and with hir bloud
> Hir little strength did fade. Howbeit as long as
>   that she coud
> See ought, she stared in my face, and gasping
>   still on me,
> Even in my mouth she breathed forth hir
>   wretched ghost. But she
> Did seeme with better cheare to die for that hir
>   conscience was
> Discharged quight and cleare of doubtes.
>   (Golding, 7.1112–17)

Golding's cumbersome fourteeners lose much of Ovid's simplicity and concentration, and, as so often, introduce an inappropriate moraliz-

---

[13] See T. W. Baldwin, *William Shakspere's Small Latine and Lesse Greeke*, 2 vols. (Urbana, 1944), vol. 2, p. 148.

[14] Bullough, vol. 7, p. 243.

[15] Bullough (vol. 7, pp. 205–6) cites Pettie as a possible source, but does not explore the Ovidian connection. It is revealing that for Pettie the story is exemplary of 'that hatefull helhounde Jealousy' – *A Petite Pallace of Pettie his Pleasure* (1576), ed. Herbert Hartman (Oxford, 1938), p. 186.

ing tone. It is the original Latin, with its clear focus on a pale figure, a kiss and a look, that makes us think of the death of Desdemona or Cordelia. What may be most profoundly Ovidian about *Othello* are certain touches in the final scene.

When Othello addresses the sleeping Desdemona at the beginning of the scene, he speaks as if she is already dead. His images suggest that she has been metamorphosed into an object. Her skin is 'smooth as monumental alabaster' (5.2.5): it is not that she is in her tomb, but that in Ovidian fashion she has become her tomb, her own monument. After the explicitly mythological, though not Ovidian, image of Prometheus, Othello continues:

> When I have plucked thy rose
> I cannot give it vital growth again.
> It needs must wither. I'll smell thee on the tree.
> (5.2.13–15)

It is again as if she is no longer a person but an object in nature; the arresting of 'vital growth' is precisely the process that takes place at the moment of Ovidian metamorphosis.

Having metaphorically addressed Desdemona as a tree in his elegy to her, Othello introduces a further arboreal simile in his elegy on himself:

> of one whose subdued eyes,
> Albeit unusèd to the melting mood,
> Drops tears as fast as the Arabian trees
> Their medicinable gum.   (5.2.357–60)

The New Cambridge editor says that 'The reference is to the myrrh tree and probably comes from a conflation of two passages in Pliny's *Naturalis Historia*.'[16] I do not see why it is necessary to go to two sources in Pliny when in book ten of the *Metamorphoses*, the primary source for Shakespeare's first narrative poem, we find the following description of the demise of Myrrha:

> Her bones did intoo timber turne, whereof the marie was

> The pith, and into watrish sappe the blood of her did passe.
> Her armes were turnd too greater boughes, her fingars into twig,
> Her skin was hardned into bark . . .

> Although that shee
> Toogither with her former shape her senses all did loose,
> Yit weepeth shee, and from her tree warme droppes doo softly woose:
> The which her teares are had in pryce and honour. And the Myrrhe
> That issueth from her gummy bark dooth beare the name of her,
> And shall doo whyle the world dooth last.
> (Golding, 10.566–9, 572–7)

Shakespeare must have known this passage, since it immediately precedes the story of Venus and Adonis; indeed, Adonis is born from this very tree. The collocation of 'tears', 'gum', and the verb 'drop' strongly suggests that Golding shaped Othello's image, especially as a few lines earlier Myrrha has been described 'straying in the broade / Datebearing feeldes of Arabye' (10.547–8). Sandys's later commentary also notes the tradition that the myrrh tree grew only in Arabia.[17]

But the source is less important than the effect. What would Shakespeare's original audience have made of Othello's image? I believe that the more educated among them would have remembered Ovid's aetiological explanation of the oozing of the myrrh tree: the gum represents the repentant tears of Myrrha. It does not necessarily follow from this that Othello would have been seen as Myrrha, the exemplar of incest; but it does, I think, follow that the image would have been interpreted in terms of repentance and release from past error. After the shifts and changes of the passions, the tree finally offers something fixed and solid.

---

[16] Sanders, p. 186.
[17] Sandys, p. 364.

The difference between the last moments of Myrrha and those of Othello is that she is released by the gods while he releases himself through suicide. My Ovidian reading of Othello's last words will now take a sideways step: the richest classical source of last words and suicides is not the *Metamorphoses*, but the *Heroides*, Ovid's book of elegies in the form of imaginary letters from heroines to their husbands or lovers. Shakespeare's dealings with Ovid's other works than the *Metamorphoses* are another surprising gap in the critical literature (despite the fact that the *Fasti* are the primary source for *Lucrece*). The *Heroides* were a very popular school text; there would have been particular interest in them around the turn of the century, following the great success of Michael Drayton's imitations of them, *England's Heroicall Epistles* (first published in 1597, augmented and reprinted in 1598, 1599, 1602, and 1605). Let us suppose, then, that Shakespeare reread or recollected the *Heroides* at this time. Their relevance to Othello's last speech lies not only in their elegiac content, but also in their epistolary form:

> I pray you, in your letters,
> When you shall these unlucky deeds relate,
> Speak of me as I am. Nothing extenuate,
> Nor set down aught in malice.   (5.2.349–52)

The *Heroides* are the exemplary letters concerning 'unlucky deeds'; Ovid's deserted heroines speak of themselves as they are, nothing extenuate, nor set down aught in malice.

Consider, for example, *Heroides*, 2, 'Phyllis to Demophoon'. This story is the usual one of a woman deceived by a man, not the *Othello* one of a man deceived by a man into falsely believing that he has been deceived by a woman. Othello is no Phyllis – she in fact has affinities with Desdemona, in that even on her deathbed she refuses to denounce the lover who has wronged her ('invita nunc es amante nocens' (2.10), 'even now your lover is reluctant to pronounce you guilty'). The parallel here is not of character or situation but of tone

and emotion; the two suffering women share a language of simplicity and direct statement. What Shakespeare learnt above all from the *Heroides* was a way of writing about grief and a language that he could give to characters on the point of death.

Thus Phyllis asks, 'Dic mihi, quid feci, nisi non sapienter amavi?' (2.27), 'Tell me, what have I done, except not wisely love?' Whether or not we see this as the actual source of Othello's 'one that loved not wisely', the two characters share a desperate desire to justify themselves. In addition, Phyllis and Othello both lament how they have been beguiled by the words of others; both her letter and his speech juxtapose past martial deeds with present catastrophic love; each concludes abruptly with an image of death by one's own hand. For all the manifest differences between them, the letter and the speech end with a similar kind of dramatization. Phyllis closes with the words that she wishes to be inscribed on her tomb: 'PHYLLIDA DEMOPHOON LETO DEDIT HOSPES AMANTEM; / ILLE NECIS CAUSAM PRAEBUIT, IPSA MANUM.' The language here is extraordinarily compressed – to render it in English, George Turberville had to expand twelve words into twenty-three:

> Demophoon that guilefull guest,
>   made Phyllis stoppe her breath:
> His was the cause, and hers the hande
>   that brought her to the death.[18]

The translation loses not only Ovid's compression, but also the drama in the way that 'ipsa manum', 'her own the hand', is held back to the very end. Ovid's original offers a rhetorical stroke precisely analogous to Othello's dramatic 'And smote him thus.'

---

[18] George Turberville, *The Heroycall Epistles of the Learned Poet Publius Ovidius Naso, in Englishe Verse* (London, 1567), from *Heroides*, 2.147–8. I attach no special significance to 'the cause', since I have found no evidence that Shakespeare used Turberville as he did Golding (he would have had little trouble understanding the *Heroides* in their original Latin).

How do these affinities affect our interpretation of Othello's last speech? Do they have any bearing on the debate about whether Othello is deluding himself or, in Eliot's famous phrase, '*cheering himself up*'? I think they do, because they reveal that Othello and Phyllis are doing the same thing, namely, composing a suicide note. A suicide note is an act of self-justification which may involve self-delusion, but it is also the most intense expression of the self. It articulates the sense of one's self for which one is willing to die and by which one wishes to be remembered. Phyllis composes her own epitaph, Othello his own funeral oration. Someone who writes a suicide note and then does not commit suicide may justifiably be accused of spurious self-dramatization; the integrity of Othello is that he acts upon his words immediately. He stands – or rather falls – by what he has said, and for that he can only be admired. Similarly, the audience of the *Heroides* know from their prior acquaintance with the myths that such heroines as Phyllis will act upon their words and go to their deaths. It is this integrity that gives them exemplary, that is to say mythological, status. I have no doubt that for an Elizabethan audience, schooled in Ovidian mythology, Othello would have taken on similar status.

I have frequently used words like 'analogy', 'affinity', 'suggests', and 'similar'. I therefore run the risk of being accused of Fluellenism: Fluellen 'proves' that Henry V is another Alexander the Great because the former was born in Monmouth, the latter in Macedon, there is a river in each place, 'and there is salmons in both'. In Richard Levin's words, Fluellenism 'can be used to equate any two objects in the universe, by searching through all the facts about them and seizing upon those that represent similarities, regardless of their importance, while ignoring all the rest'.[19] It would be a simple matter for the Fluellenist to 'prove', say, the influence of the *Metamorphoses* on *King Lear*.

If it is accepted that Shakespeare converts literal Ovidian metamorphoses into metaphors, the play's recurrent canine imagery, its sense of people being reduced to the level of dogs, could be derived from Ovid's story of Hecuba (which, as we know from *Hamlet*, is an archetypal tragic set-piece). A representative passage could be singled out:

> But shee was dumb for sorrow.
> The anguish of her hart forclosde as well her
>   speech as eeke
> Her teares devowring them within. Shee stood
>   astonyed leeke
> As if shee had beene stone. One whyle the
>   ground shee staard upon.
> Another whyle a gastly looke shee kest too
>   heaven. Anon
> Shee looked on the face of him that lay before
>   her killd.   (Golding, 13.645–50)

The power of silence, the notion of extremity of emotion impeding utterance, the stress upon the heart, the corrosive quality of tears, the image of being turned to stone, the look to the heavens, the final concentration on the face of the dead child (her youngest-born): each element may be referred to *Lear*. Alternatively, Lear holding the body of his child and cursing the heavens may be related to Niobe in book six of the *Metamorphoses*; after all, it is Niobe who most famously literalizes the image implicit in Lear's 'O, you are men of stones' (5.3.232).[20] Or again, Lear's character could be illuminated by means of reference to Narcissus. 'So great a blindnesse in my heart through doting love doth raigne' (Golding, 3.461): does not Lear's blindness arise from Narcissus-like self-love? As the Fool recognizes, Lear becomes his own shadow – pre-

---

[19] *New Readings vs. Old Plays: Recent Trends in the Reinterpretation of English Renaissance Drama* (Chicago, 1979), p. 97.

[20] Quotations from *Lear* are from the Folio version (*The Tragedy of King Lear: The Folio Text*) unless otherwise stated; references to the Quarto version (*The History of King Lear: The Quarto Text*) are prefaced by 'Q'.

cisely the fate of Narcissus. More locally, when Lear swears by 'The mysteries of Hecate and the night' (1.1.110), it might be recalled that in Golding, Jason swears to Medea 'By triple *Hecates* holie rites' (7.136). And so one could go on.

The problem with this approach is that such *topoi* are common in the Renaissance. Many of them may have been learnt by Renaissance writers from Ovid more than from any other source; many of them are used by Shakespeare with a freshness, a precision, and a dramatic power that seem closer to Ovid than any other source. Consider, for example, the moment when Lear identifies with the elements because the storm is less unkind to him than his daughters. I know of no passage closer to this in manner and tone than the following in the *Heroides*:

> hiemis mihi gratia prosit!
> adspice, ut eversas concitet Eurus aquas!
> quod tibi malueram, sine me debere procellis;
> iustior est animo ventus et unda tuo.
> . . . duritia robora vincis.   (7.41–4, 52)

[Let the storm be my grace! Look, how Eurus tosses the rolling waters! What I had preferred to owe to you, let me owe to the stormy blasts; wind and wave are juster than your heart . . . in hardness you exceed the oak.]

But I cannot prove that the storm in *Lear* is actually derived from Ovid or that a Renaissance audience would have associated it specifically with Ovid. All one can say is that the spirit of the Roman poet has been caught in a way that licenses our applying Francis Meres's famous remark about the soul of Ovid living in Shakespeare to works other than 'his *Venus and Adonis*, his *Lucrece*, his sugred *Sonnets*'.[21]

Yet there is perhaps some harder evidence in the text of *Lear*. Fluellenism consists of the ingenious critic perceiving connections that others have not perceived (he is always likely to perceive them because once he has found one he hunts hard for others in order to support his case). It is a different matter if we make connections that the text asks us to make. Metamorphosis takes place when identity breaks down; it is the process we see Lear undergoing from Act 1 Scene 4 onwards. In that scene, he begins to lose a sense of his own self ('Does any here know me? This is not Lear', 1.4.208), then by the time he exits the image of metamorphosis is explicit:

> Thou shalt find
> That I'll resume the shape which thou dost
> think
> I have cast off for ever.   (1.4.288–90)

To the educated Elizabethan, Ovid's book of changes was the central point of reference for the notion of transformation – one need think only of how extensively Spenser draws on Ovid in the 'Mutabilitie' cantos and how Pythagoras' discourse on change in the final book of the *Metamorphoses* informs many of Shakespeare's sonnets. Given this centrality, I do not see how audiences could have avoided calling the *Metamorphoses* to mind in response to Lear's image of shape-shifting. And given the Renaissance reading of Ovidian metamorphosis as metaphor for monstrous human behaviour, Albany's castigations of Goneril, such as 'Thou chang'd and self-covered thing, for shame / Bemonster not thy feature' (Q: 16.61–2), would have evoked a similar response.

The theatre provides special opportunities for the exploration of shape-changing, since in becoming a character an actor undergoes a kind of metamorphosis. Shakespeare frequently draws attention to and compounds this process by having his characters become actors and don disguises. Thus Lear's involuntary psychological metamorphosis is accompanied by Edgar's controlled, if forced, transformation into Poor Tom:

> I will preserve myself, and am bethought
> To take the basest and most poorest shape

---

21 Francis Meres, *Palladis Tamia* (London, 1598); excerpt reprinted in *Elizabethan Critical Essays*, ed. G. Gregory Smith, 2 vols. (Oxford, 1904), vol. 2, 308–24, p. 317.

That ever penury in contempt of man
Brought near to beast.   (2.2.169–72)

With Gloucester, Edgar works through a series of roles or metamorphoses, including an imaginary one that transforms him into a fiend with eyes like full moons, a thousand noses, 'Horns whelked and wavèd like the enragèd sea' (4.5.71). Although the idea of a fiend tempting one to commit suicide is Christian, the description is more mythological. This is Shakespeare's only use of the word 'whelked'; given the context, it is likely that he remembered it from Golding's translation of some lines in the *Metamorphoses* concerning the Libyan god Ammon: '*Joves* ymage which the Lybian folke by name of *Hammon* serve, / Is made with crooked welked hornes that inward still doe terve' (5.416–17). The verbal parallel suggests the association in Shakespeare's mind; the finished image does not overtly allude to Ammon, but does summon up a monstrous pagan creature of supernatural power like Ammon.

Ovid is much preoccupied with monsters in books four and five of the *Metamorphoses*: the reference to Ammon comes shortly after the story of Perseus, which may itself lie behind another image of monstrousness in *Lear*,

Ingratitude, thou marble-hearted fiend,
More hideous when thou show'st thee in a child
Than the sea-monster.   (1.4.237–9)

Critics have had some difficulty identifying this sea-monster.[22] I would say that the image conflates two of the monsters slain by Perseus: 'marble-hearted' and 'hideous' come from the grotesque Gorgon's head which turns to stone, and the sea-monster itself is that from which Perseus saves Andromeda.

Such mythological allusions create an Ovidian context for the play's imagery of people becoming as beasts or behaving like monsters. Probably the most telling allusion of this sort is Lear's powerful and painful comparison of women to centaurs: Ovid was the *locus classicus* for centaurs. Their 'duplex

natura' (*Metamorphoses*, 12.503) was the perfect image for man's double nature as both beast and rational creature; as 'semihomines' (12.536) and 'biformes' (9.121), they are arrested in a perpetual state of semi-metamorphosis, an emblem of the process which is Ovid's theme.[23] All this also makes them an ideal emblem in *King Lear* (Shakespeare's fullest exploration of dual nature) of humanity's approximation to the bestial.

Lear obviously has his daughters in mind when he makes his comparison: does this implicitly make him into the father of the centaurs? The mythologically literate Elizabethan would have known that the centaurs were begotten by Ixion and a cloud-form sent by Jupiter in the shape of Juno, whom Ixion aspired to love. As a punishment for his presumption, Ixion was bound on an ever-turning wheel in the underworld. When Lear contrasts the heavenly state of Cordelia ('Thou art a soul in bliss') with a sense of his own punishment ('I am bound / Upon a wheel of fire', 4.6.39–40), the fate of Ixion is evoked. This moment is a characteristically Renaissance combination of the Christian and the classical: the fire suggests medieval images of Hell and Purgatory, the idea of being bound on a wheel suggests the figure of Ixion.[24] What was Ixion's punishment taken to symbolize?

---

22 H. H. Furness's New Variorum edition (Philadelphia, 1880, p. 86) proposes the hippopotamus, the whale, a monster at Troy, and a picture said to be portrayed in the porch of the temple of Minerva at Sais. The most convincing of these possibilities is the monster from which Hercules rescues Hesione at Troy, alluded to as 'the sea-monster' in *The Merchant of Venice* (3.2.57) – here again, the source is Ovid (*Metamorphoses*, 11: 'a monster of the Sea', Golding, 11.237).

23 For a characteristic Renaissance view of the centaur embodying man's dual nature (from the wisdom of Chiron to the destructive drunkenness of the battle with the Lapithae), see Natalis Comes, *Mythologiae* (1551; reprinted Venice, 1567), p. 215ᵛ.

24 Who is, incidentally, alluded to in Harsnett's *Declaration of Egregious Popish Impostures*, to which the vocabulary of *Lear* owes much (see Kenneth Muir's new Arden edition (London, 1952), p. 255).

Sabinus refers it 'ad homines in Republica irrequietos', 'to men restless in matters of state'.[25] Lear is thus paying the price for tampering with the running of the state by dividing his kingdom. Sabinus also offers a psychological reading of the punishments in Ovid's underworld: 'Genera suppliciorum allegorice ad animi perturbationes relata' (p. 137). Sandys expands upon this: 'all these forementioned punishments are allegorically referred to the perturbations of the minde . . . *Ixions* wheele, to the desperate remembrance of perpetrated crimes, which circularly pursue, and afflict the guilty.'[26] Not only is the 'perturbation of the minde' a wonderful phrase for Lear's state at this point, but the specific interpretation of Ixion's punishment is appropriate to both the awakening scene, where so much turns on Cordelia's forgiving response to Lear's 'desperate remembrance' of his own errors, and the last part of the play in general, where we see perpetrated crimes circularly pursuing and afflicting the guilty. Ixion's wheel is a powerful symbol for this process of crime catching up on the perpetrator: Edmund recognizes at the end that 'The wheel is come full circle' (5.3.165). The image picks up on the Fool's 'Let go thy hold when a great wheel runs down a hill, lest it break thy neck with following; but the great one that goes upward, let him draw thee after' (2.2.245–8). There is an interesting variant here in that this is an image of going up and down rather than round in a circle: the wheel has perhaps been displaced from Ixion and applied to the figure who is adjacent to him in Ovid's underworld, Sisyphus 'that drave against the hill / A rolling stone that from the top came tumbling downeward still' (Golding, 4.569–70).

O. B. Hardison argues in an elegant article[27] that the myth of Ixion is actually an important source for *King Lear*. He establishes a considerable number of correspondences between the play and Renaissance interpretations of the myth: Ixion was read as a symbol of the desire for pomp without responsibilities and as a type of ingratitude, the thunderbolt that hurls him to hell was interpreted as a symbol of both sudden disillusionment and providential justice, the centaurs were seen in some interpretations as both Ixion's offspring, representative of lust, and his hundred unruly retainers (this reading derives from the false etymology *centum armati*; it is an especially striking correspondence given that Lear's followers are not numbered one hundred in any of the play's direct sources).

Hardison's argument is attractive – it would make the myth of Ixion into the 'pattern' of *King Lear* as that of Philomel is the pattern for *Titus Andronicus* – but it depends on the synthesis of several mythographic sources. Even if it is accepted that Shakespeare made this synthesis, it seems unlikely that he would have expected his audience to do so. I think it is more probable that the allusive pattern is focused on Ovid, as it is in *Titus*, where the references to Philomel are accompanied by allusions to other metamorphoses, such as those of Hecuba and Io. The centaur and Ixion allusions come too late in *Lear* for the audience to read the whole play in terms of a sustained correspondence. I believe that, rather than impose a retrospective pattern of single analogy, they combine with the language of transformation, bestiality, and monstrousness, to release the potential that is already there for the *Metamorphoses* to be brought to bear upon the play. They perhaps offer confirmation of earlier glancing intuitions that Lear might be a Narcissus or a Niobe. They certainly validate the claim that Ovid presides over not only the magical changes wrought by love in Shakespearian comedy, but also the dehumanization wrought by extremity of emotion in the mature tragedies.

[25] Sabinus, p. 137.
[26] Sandys, p. 163.
[27] 'Myth and History in *King Lear*', *Shakespeare Quarterly*, 26 (1975), 227–42.

THE PASSING OF KING LEAR

IAN J. KIRBY

Generations of scholars have grappled with the problems posed by the ending of Shakespeare's *King Lear*: not one of the solutions proposed to date has commanded general and lasting assent. As Bridget Lyons put it:

Lear's words just before his death have always eluded the attempts of critics to label what he sees, does or feels at the moment that he utters them.[1]

Such critical attempts have been varied in the extreme: for G. R. Hibbard, they range from the 'sentimental wishful thinking' of writers such as Paul N. Siegel to the 'reductive nihilistic rant' of Jan Kott.[2] Reactions to these attempts have been equally varied: what to one scholar is sublime is ridiculous to another. As a result, one senses the tendency, at the present time, to feel that this is perhaps one of the Shakespearian mysteries we are not intended to solve: that we should be content to say of Lear, as the churlish priest said of Ophelia, that his end was doubtful. It is therefore clear that any further attempt to provide a solution to the enigma must, if it is to have the slightest hope of carrying conviction, be based on foundations laid with the very greatest care. I shall thus begin by inviting assent to a certain number of premises essential to my later arguments.

The first of these can be most briefly expressed in the words of Terence Spencer at a medieval symposium a decade ago: 'Shakespeare was a medieval.' Contrary to the views of certain critics who in the recent past have tried to minimize, or ignore, such features in Shakespeare's work, it must be strongly affirmed that in his plays he used beliefs, ideas, attitudes, themes which are more familiar to the medieval than the modern mind; and it therefore follows that if in a given context we adduce an interpretation based on a medieval rather than modern viewpoint, such an interpretation must be considered on its merits, and

---

[1] 'The Subplot as Simplification in *King Lear*', in *Some Facets of 'King Lear': Essays in Prismatic Criticism*, eds. R. L. Colie and F. T. Flahiff (Toronto and Buffalo, 1974), p. 23.

[2] See, respectively, '*King Lear*: A Retrospect, 1939–79', in *Shakespeare Survey 33* (1980), 1–12; *Shakespearean Tragedy and the Elizabethan Compromise* (New York, 1957); and *Shakespeare our Contemporary* (New York 1964). Among the many articles relating to the ending of the play which are not specifically cited in the present paper are Nicholas Brooke's 'The Ending of *King Lear*', in *Shakespeare 1564–1964*, ed. E. A. Bloom (Providence, 1964), pp. 71–87; O. J. Campbell's 'The Salvation of Lear', *Journal of English Literary History*, 15 (1948), 93–109; H. L. Hennedy's '*King Lear*: Recognizing the Ending', *Studies in Philology*, 71 (1974), 371–84; and J. Stampfer's 'The Catharsis of *King Lear*' and J. K. Walton's 'Lear's Last Speech', both in *Shakespeare Survey 13* (1960), 1–10 and 11–19 respectively. Surveys of critical approaches to the problems are also found in L. S. Champion, '*King Lear*': *An Annotated Bibliography*, 2 vols. (New York and London, 1980); J. T. Spikes, 'Bradleyism at Mid-Century: The Death of King Lear', *Southern Quarterly*, 5 (1966), 223–36; and E. W. Talbert, '*King Lear*', in *Critical Approaches to Six Major English Works*, eds. R. M. Lumiansky and Herschel Baker (Philadelphia, 1968), pp. 167–208.

not dismissed on the spurious grounds that in Shakespeare was the light of the Renaissance, and no medieval darkness at all.

This last phrase foreshadows my second premise. Whether Shakespeare was a 'born-again Christian', as one or two critics have tried to demonstrate with very limited success, or merely assented to the so-called 'Established' views of his time, he nevertheless wrote within what now tends to be called the Judeo-Christian tradition. On many occasions in his plays he used beliefs, ideas, attitudes that are rooted in the religious views of his time; and it therefore follows that if in a given context we adduce a Christian rather than pagan or secular, an eternal rather than temporal, interpretation, such an interpretation must, again, be judged on its merits.[3]

My third premise is, in essence, a combination of the first two. On many occasions in his plays, Shakespeare used beliefs, attitudes, ideas, themes which are familiar in medieval Christian thought. To take an exceedingly obvious example: Horatio's farewell to Hamlet takes the form of a prayer that his eternal destiny may be the bliss of Heaven:

> Good night, sweet prince,
> And flights of angels sing thee to thy rest.
> (5.2.312–13)

It is to Hell that Hamlet is determined to send Claudius and for this reason renounces his best opportunity to execute vengeance on him:

> A villain kills my father, and for that
> I, his sole son, do this same villain send
> To heaven . . .
> No . . .
> Up, sword, and know thou a more horrid hint
>   . . .
> And that his soul may be as damned and black
> As hell whereto it goes.   (3.3.76–8, 87–8, 94–5)

But it is equally clear that the immediate destiny of King Hamlet was neither Heaven nor Hell but a prison-house where he is, as he says:

> confined to fast in fires
> Till the foul crimes done in my days of nature
> Are burnt and purged away.   (1.5.11–13)

The penultimate word of this excerpt makes it abundantly clear that it is from the purgatory of pre-Reformation Christian belief that King Hamlet comes to walk the battlements of Elsinore. Examples could easily be multiplied of the use of medieval Christian ideas in Shakespeare's plays: and it is thus clear that if we should adduce such ideas in relation to the interpretation of specific passages, such a critical approach must, again, be judged on its merits. To dot the 'i's and cross the 't's: it is not necessary that the critic be a Christian himself for him to admit a Christian interpretation of a given passage; it is not necessary for us to prove that Shakespeare was a convinced Christian before we can claim that he gave a Christian slant to a given passage; all that is necessary is to show that certain ideas were current in his day, and preferably that he or his contemporaries used them in other contexts. This may sound obvious; but it has not always seemed so to those who have written on the ending of *King Lear*.

Premise number four: words, words, words. The last of the above quotations illustrates a commonplace of criticism, that Shakespeare was a master-craftsman with words, and that on occasion he used a single word to demonstrate clearly his visualization of a particular situation. An understanding of the precise value of each individual word of Shakespeare's text is as essential as ever it was

---

[3] This premise is not invalidated by Shakespeare's decision to use the Classical pantheon in *King Lear* rather than the Judeo-Christian setting of the Chronicle play of *King Leir* (see for example W. R. Elton, '*King Lear' and the Gods* (San Marino, 1966), chapter 4), for it has long since been demonstrated that biblical reference and allusion are by no means absent from his play. And as Elton accepts (his chapter 5), certain of his characters approximate in their behaviour to certain of the Christian virtues. On this, see also R. B. Heilman, *This Great Stage: Image and Structure in 'King Lear'* (Baton Rouge, 1948), particularly chapter 10.

to sound criticism; and this must take into account differences in the semantic value of words in Shakespeare's time and our own. I have not observed, for instance, that any critic has commented on the meaning of one significant word in the final statement of the play, which begins: 'The weight of this sad time we must obey' (5.3.299).[4] It is true that one recent editor has come up with the remarkable suggestion that the choice of the word 'weight' may imply that the speaker already has the dead body of Lear in his arms! But in my view it is more significant that the word 'sad' does not necessarily mean, in this context, what one might naturally assume. The use of the word in its present-day sense by Kent at 5.3.265 ('your sad steps') may blind us to the fact that Shakespeare frequently used it in the older sense 'serious', 'solemn'; and the use of 'weight' accords at least as well with this meaning of the word. That this is a solemn moment in the play is beyond doubt; how far it is also 'sad' is open to question.

From words to actions. If Shakespeare was a master-craftsman with words, he was also very much a man of the theatre, adapting his text to the exigencies of the place of performance, and frequently indicating how the words of his text were to be backed up by action on the part of the players. Hamlet's dislike of fools who spoke or did more than was set down for them, and of leading actors who might be tempted to 'out-Herod Herod' is well known (3.2.1–35): to quote another of his comments which seems to reflect his creator's opinion, the players should 'suit the action to the word, the word to the action'. We are therefore obliged to consider, in any context, how the individual scene can be realized on stage, and if possible how Shakespeare himself envisioned it. For while the literary critic may on occasion modestly admit defeat in his attempt to determine what Shakespeare intended, directors of his plays cannot permit themselves the same licence: they must of necessity take a view, which may or may not be consonant with that of Shakespeare. The

final line and a half of Lear's last speech has in the wisdom of different critics been interpreted in terms of extreme despair and extreme joy; the director has to make a choice. My final premise, then, is that in any examination of the ending of *King Lear* the possible range of actions, and any help Shakespeare may give us in his text, must be given full consideration.

From premises to motifs. Over the years, much critical thought has been devoted to a number of issues raised by *King Lear*. One such issue relates to the structure of the play. It has long since been noted that the basic framework of the play has this in common with such works as *Macbeth* and *Richard III*, that in its treatment of British history we move from a situation of stability through a period of instability and back to stability again; on the other hand, the device whereby the sub-plot reflects the main plot in many respects is highly distinctive, emphasizing as it does the personal aspects of the double tragedy. More recently it has been pointed out that in *King Lear* Shakespeare frequently frustrates the expectations of his audience: and in fact this functions now for evil, now for good – such instances as Edgar's congratulating himself that things cannot get any worse just before he meets his blinded father, and the complete change in the character of Albany, come readily to mind. Such reversals come thick and fast as the play draws to its close: the unexpectedness of the defeat of Lear and his daughter; the reversal of Edmund's fortunes; the so-called 'false ending'; and, supremely, Lear's final entrance. But on one point the critics have been far from unanimous: for one critic, every up-turn in the second part of the play is followed by a down-turn; for another, the opposite is true.[5] Bradley, commenting on the final scene, takes

---

[4] Unless otherwise stated, quotations from *Lear* are from *The Tragedy of King Lear: The Folio Text*.
[5] See, for instance, Carol Marks, '"Speak what we feel": The End of *King Lear*', *English Language Notes*, 5 (1968), 163–71, and J. H. Summers, *Dreams of Love and Power* (Oxford, 1984), p. 99.

the former view: 'It is', he says, 'as if Shakespeare said to us: "Did you think weakness and innocence have any chance here? Were you beginning to dream that? I will show you it is not so."'[6] Many have followed Bradley. But is Lear's final entrance, with Cordelia in his arms, indeed the final reversal?

The second motif I shall touch on is the problem of the justice of the gods as portrayed in *King Lear*. There is apparently a contradiction in the play. On the one hand, we have Albany's:

> This shows you are above,
> You justicers, that these our nether crimes
> So speedily can venge,   (4.2.46–8)

in relation to Cornwall's death, and the darker comment of Edgar at the end of the play:

> The gods are just, and of our pleasant vices
> Make instruments to plague us.
> The dark and vicious place where thee he got
> Cost him his eyes.   (5.3.161–4)

By contrast, there is Gloucester's 'O cruel! O you gods' (3.7.68), and Albany's 'The gods defend her! – Bear him hence a while' (5.3.231), followed at once by that most memorable of all stage directions: '*Enter Lear with Cordelia in his armes.*' Critical reaction to the problem has varied greatly; but in the last decade or so scholars have been far more inclined to underline the occasions in the play when the justice of the gods is less than apparent.

This problem is closely bound up with another, that of crime and punishment in the play. At first glance it may seem that the evil characters get off lightly – that the quick and relatively easy deaths they die compare most favourably with the hell, or rather purgatory, on earth that Lear, Gloucester, and to a smaller extent Kent go through. But in his essay in *Shakespeare 1564–1964*[7] Kenneth Myrick emphasized the difference between twentieth- and seventeenth-century thinking on this issue. Most of our contemporaries, whatever their religious outlook, tend to regard a quick

death as being much more desirable than a long-drawn-out one – witness that well-known medievalist C. S. Lewis, who in his *Screwtape Letters* (London, 1942) compared favourably the death of his protagonist in an air raid with that of an elderly rich man struck down by an incurable disease and condemned to the gradual realization of his mortality. More typical of earlier thinking on the subject are the words of the Litany: 'from battle and murder, and from sudden death. Good Lord, deliver us'.[8] The sudden death which seems so relatively agreeable to many moderns was in most cases the greatest of tragedies for those who believed that their eternal destiny was conditioned by their actions during life and their spiritual state at the moment of death. Thus, the Ghost in *Hamlet* makes it plain that in killing him Claudius had not merely committed fratricide but had condemned him to an appalling purgatorial experience of indeterminate duration (1.5.9–22): to quote his own words, he was:

> Cut off even in the blossoms of my sin,
> Unhouseled, dis-appointed, unaneled,
> No reck'ning made, but sent to my account
> With all my imperfections on my head.
>   (1.5.76–9)

And since the lightest pain of purgatory was thought to be greater than the worst punishment human cruelty could devise, the second aspect of Claudius' action was demonstrably worse than the first.

Now, if we apply this thinking to *King Lear*, we see at once that the above passage applies with peculiar force to Cornwall, Oswald, Goneril, Regan, and in some measure Edmund. As Myrick (p. 67) pointed out, 'One

---

[6] A. C. Bradley, *Shakespearean Tragedy*, 2nd edn. (London, 1905), p. 271 (henceforward Bradley).

[7] 'Christian Pessimism in *King Lear*', *Shakespeare 1564–1964*, pp. 56–70 (henceforward Myrick).

[8] *The Book of Common Prayer 1559: The Elizabethan Prayer Book*, ed. John E. Booty (Charlottesville, Va., 1976), p. 69.

by one, the five villainous characters in *Lear* are destroyed in the exact circumstances in which the Elizabethan had been trained to see and dread the judgement of an angry God' – that is, when they are about to commit, or have recently committed, a fault; when everything seems to be going well for them; with great suddenness. Cornwall has just blinded Gloucester; Oswald is preparing to kill Gloucester; Regan seeks the death of her father, and has ordered the killing of Gloucester; Goneril has poisoned her sister; Edmund has ordered the execution of Lear and Cordelia.

Myrick's point seems to me incontrovertible: but I should like to add a further justification of it which has wider implications.

My fourth premise was the importance of individual words; and it seems to me very noteworthy that Cornwall and Oswald, and Goneril and Regan, are linked in their deaths by words of special significance. Cornwall's final speech ends with the words:

> Regan, I bleed apace.
> Untimely comes this hurt. Give me your arm,
> (3.7.95–6)

while Oswald's last words are 'O untimely death! Death!' (4.5.249). Now, the use of 'untimely' in both cases can certainly be seen in terms of temporal misfortune: as Myrick (p. 66) says, everything is going well for Cornwall, who seems to have nothing to lose by his cruelty, and for Oswald, who has much to gain from his intended action. But if we go beyond temporal to eternal considerations, it is clear that their deaths are untimely in the extreme. Shakespeare, in fact, has used a single word to imply, almost in passing, that the crimes they have committed, or are about to commit, carry an eternal as well as temporal punishment – they are, indeed, cut off amid the blossoms of their sin.

As to Goneril and Regan: the circumstance of their deaths is reported three times in the final scene, and one of these reports is apparently inaccurate. We are first told, by a Gentleman with a bloody knife, that Goneril has poisoned her sister and committed suicide. This account is echoed in Edmund's words:

> The one the other poisoned for my sake,
> And after slew herself.   (5.3.216–17)

But a mere fifty lines later Kent, speaking to the heedless Lear, says:

> Your eldest daughters have fordone
>   themselves,
> And desperately are dead.   (5.3.267–8)

Largely, this has gone unremarked: such comments as have been made mostly assume a slip on Shakespeare's part in the heat of composition. However, it seems to me far more important that Shakespeare has deliberately linked these two in this final statement concerning their end, and that what he is saying is that Goneril and Regan have brought about their own destruction, and have died in despair.[9] The word 'desperately' has, then, a comparable function to 'untimely' in the previous example; Goneril and Regan die in a state of despair,[10] and what that means is well illustrated in Shakespeare's own lifetime by Spenser's *Faerie Queene*, where in Book One the Red Cross Knight's most dangerous enemy is not the dragon but Despair personified (see Canto ix). Again, therefore, Shakespeare has in a single word rounded off his statement concerning the temporal and eternal destiny of two of his characters.

This practice of Shakespeare's is not, however, limited to the evil characters. Goneril and Regan die in despair; Gloucester seeks death because he is in a state of despair – as Edgar says:

---

[9] The first quarto reads 'foredoome', emended in the second quarto to 'fore-doom'd'. If the emendation is correct, it suggests that Shakespeare originally meant Kent to say that Goneril and Regan have condemned themselves in advance and have died in despair. This reading, of course, avoids the apparent contradiction.

[10] Compare and contrast G. K. Hunter's note to 5.3.290 in his New Penguin edition of *King Lear* (Harmondsworth, 1972), p. 310.

Why I do trifle thus with his despair
Is done to cure it.   (4.5.33–4)

After his apparently miraculous deliverance from death, Gloucester is content to bear his affliction, though he welcomes Oswald's attempt to end it for him (4.5.229–30). The circumstances of his death are related by Edgar in the final scene, where we learn that it is in fact Edgar himself who is the immediate cause of his father's passing. Edgar relates how he:

became his guide,
Led him, begged for him, saved him from
despair   (5.3.182–3)

and then told him the whole story of his share in his father's purgatorial experience, but (he continues)

his flawed heart –
Alack, too weak the conflict to support –
'Twixt two extremes of passion, joy and grief,
Burst.   (5.3.188–91)

That is, in contemporary terminology, the conflict of the overwhelming emotions of sorrow for his son's sufferings, and joy at their reunion, brings on a heart attack that kills him. However, if this is our last word, it is not Shakespeare's, for Edgar's speech in fact ends:

but his flawed heart . . .
'Twixt two extremes of passion, joy and grief,
Burst smilingly.   (5.3.188, 190–1)

Another single word; a comparable function. Gloucester dies in joy, knowing his beloved son Edgar to be alive.

So far, we have seen that the final words spoken by, or about, five of the principal characters are of particular importance in the assessment of Shakespeare's final statements about them; it will thus be appropriate, in due course, to take note of the import of other 'last words'. But we can also maintain that in the case of these five characters 'The gods are just' (5.3.161) in respect of their passing: of the evil characters, two die an untimely death both temporally and eternally, two die in the despair which also adumbrates damnation;

conversely, Gloucester passes through the temporal purgatorial experience called for by his 'sins' to end his life at a moment when hope has not only banished despair, but has itself been emptied in delight.

What of the others? The case of Edmund, which is but a trifle here, is plain on the temporal level; he is justly killed for his own treachery, as he himself implicitly acknowledges.[11] On the post-temporal level his case is not as clear as those of the other evil characters. His death is doubtful: but I am inclined to think that because he is unable to complete the penitential sequence of contrition, confession, and satisfaction – Cordelia dies because he delays – it is dubious whether his 'deathbed confession' is sufficient to enable him to escape the eternal consequences of his actions.

Thus we are left with Kent, Cordelia, and Lear himself. Kent, because it is clear that in the final scene of the play he is living the last hours of his life.[12] Questions of crime and punishment are irrelevant to him; but he has shared in the sufferings of his master, and in the final scene his quasi-purgatorial experience reaches its climax when Lear, in his agony over Cordelia, lumps him with the 'murderers, traitors all' (5.3.244) who have brought about her death. His unremitting faithfulness to his master is, however, rewarded on the temporal level in Lear's belated recognition of him, in the eulogy of Edgar ("Tis noble Kent, your friend', 5.3.243), underscoring as it does his earlier reception by Cordelia:

O thou good Kent, how shall I live and work
To match thy goodness?   (4.6.1–2)

and, supremely, in Albany's offer that he and

---

11 Instant confession on such occasions is not limited to Edmund and Laertes; for another example, Horner the Armourer, see *The First Part of the Contention* (*2 Henry VI*), 2.3.98.

12 In the quarto version Edgar describes Kent as having suffered a heart attack (24.212–15); in both versions Kent comes to bid his king and master aye good night (Q: 24.230–1; F: 5.3.209–10).

Edgar should rule jointly in the realm. However, Kent's own last words make it clear that his ultimate reward is not an earthly one: it is, rather, reunion with his beloved master beyond the grave:

> I have a journey, sir, shortly to go:
> My master calls me; I must not say no.
>
> (5.3.297–8)

His sufferings and his reward thus compare with, and contrast with, those of Edgar. For one, there is an earthly kingdom; for the other, the kingdom that awaits those who have been faithful unto death.

And Cordelia? Critics from Samuel Johnson onwards have, understandably, preferred to say little about the tragedy of her passing; and it is well known that a bastardized form of the play, with a 'happy ending', held the stage for a century and a half. Judged by purely temporal criteria, her death is an abomination: it compares in its violence and suddenness with that which overtakes Cornwall, Oswald, Goneril, and Regan; the 'consolation' aspects of the deaths of Gloucester and Kent, as set out above, are absent, or at least not conspicuously present; and there are no 'last words' to guide us. True, Shakespeare's main concern in the final moments of the play is with the effect Cordelia's death has on Lear; but to suggest that this is sufficient justification for the death Shakespeare gives her is unthinkable. There must, I believe, be another answer to the problem. But since I do not think that Cordelia's death can be understood apart from Lear's passing, I shall not anticipate my conclusions here, but move on to the fourth and last of my themes, which has already been adumbrated in this preceding section: the portrayal of good and evil in *King Lear*.

The main point I wish to make here is that among Shakespeare's plays *King Lear* is unusual in the extreme in its treatment of the good. In his earlier plays, Shakespeare tends towards a merely temporal view of good and evil. Thus, in the history plays the virtue of the English is often contrasted with the villainy of their opponents (Shakespeare's treatment of Joan of Arc is especially notorious); the virtues of the first of the Tudors are in total contrast to the vices of his predecessor. The love of Romeo and Juliet is contrasted with the hate of their respective families; in the substantially later *Measure for Measure*, the lust of Angelo is unable to overcome the virtue of Isabella. And so on. Furthermore, from his earliest years Shakespeare created convincing embodiments of evil: Aaron, Richard III, and Iago are just three of the names that come readily to mind. However, when we look for their counterparts, we find that extreme evil is not in general balanced by extreme good; rather, the good are relatively neutral and even on occasion colourless. Shakespeare does his best for the future Henry VII, but fails to make him convincing; Cassio is an honest man, and Desdemona an honest wife, but little more; we sympathize, and later rejoice, with Macduff; we sorrow with Ophelia, and admire Horatio. But the good qualities of these characters are all relatively subdued.

What happens in *King Lear*? Edmund has been described as a more likeable Iago; Goneril and Regan call both Tamora and Lady Macbeth to mind; the evil in Cornwall parallels that in Aaron and Richard III. But to whom can Cordelia be likened, outside this play? I submit that one of the things Shakespeare set out to do in *King Lear* was to establish an absolute contrast between the quintessence of good and the extremes of evil, and that he achieves as nowhere else the positive portrayal of good. He does so partly through the force of contrast: the simple goodness of Cornwall's surviving servants as portrayed in the quarto version, and of the old man in Act 4 Scene 1, who is prepared to perform a last service for his master at the risk of death, shine out the more clearly against the appalling act of cruelty we have just witnessed. But he also builds up, in different ways, the characters we recognize as good so that at the end of the play they are infinitely more than such figures as Henry Richmond, Malcolm, or even Horatio. Words and actions alike have their part to play in this process. Albany moves from a theoretically commendable 'great love' of his unworthy spouse to a clear recognition of the essential evil in her nature, and thence to an acceptance and fulfilment of his chief responsibility, the restoration of good order in the state. Kent's honesty in the first scene of the play, and his faithfulness subsequently, are the essence of his goodness, which is underlined no less than three times by Cordelia at the moment of their reunion; and his own simple and moving words, 'Kind and dear princess' (4.6.26), are certainly the most effective witness to the total contrast between Cordelia and her sisters.

But this is not all. While much of the goodness depicted functions on a temporal level, it is impossible to ignore the other dimension. The faults committed in this play – Gloucester's adultery, Lear's pride, Cornwall's wrath, the murderous intentions of Goneril and Regan which are the ultimate consequence of their lack of duty to their father – operate simultaneously on the temporal and spiritual levels, the latter calling to mind the Ten Commandments and the Seven Deadly Sins. The virtues shown by the 'good' characters have a similar ambivalence, and this is particularly well demonstrated in the case of Edgar. In the Dover cliff scene, Shakespeare considered it necessary to underline one aspect of the events – as Gloucester prepares for death, Edgar says:

> Why I do trifle thus with his despair
> Is done to cure it.   (4.5.32–3)

Critics who concern themselves only with the temporal aspects of this play have been offended by the sequence of Edgar's actions. What we need to realize, however, is that Edgar does far more than save his father from death at this point: when he recalls the circumstances of Gloucester's passing: 'Led him, begged for him, saved him from despair'

(5.3.183), we are certainly meant to regard the last four words as the climax of the statement; in Act 4, Edgar saves his father both from physical and from spiritual death. Gloucester passes from despair to hope, a hope which is ultimately realized. And hope is also the keynote of Edgar's response to his own sufferings. This is explicit both in his words and his actions:

> The low'st and most dejected thing of
>   fortune,
> Stands still in esperance, lives not in fear,
>   (4.1.3–4)

reflects his approach to his situation in the latter part of the play; it is hope that drives him on in his challenge to Edmund, whom he takes on, not sure, though hoping, of the good success he achieves. And, as Gloucester's resignation turns towards a barely expressed hope that he may once again see his son:

>   O dear son Edgar,
> The food of thy abusèd father's wrath –
> Might I but live to see thee in my touch
> I'd say I had eyes again   (4.1.21–4)

– a hope that is ultimately rewarded, so Edgar's hope is fulfilled, for:

>   All friends shall taste
> The wages of their virtue, and all foes
> The cup of their deservings.   (5.3.278–80)

If, then, the goodness of Kent takes the form of faithfulness above all, and that of Edgar is essentially motivated by hope, what of Cordelia? Shakespeare's own words suffice:

>   O dear father,
> It is thy business that I go about . . .
> No blown ambition doth our arms incite,
> But love, dear love, and our aged father's
>   right.   (4.3.23–4, 27–8)

Faithfulness, hope, love, these three. And yet: Edgar is restored to his rights, with boot and such addition as his honour has more than merited; Kent approaches the end of his life in the knowledge that evil is destroyed and in the anticipation that death means reunion with his master; Cordelia is hanged.

There is, then, an apparent discrepancy common to the themes we have considered. Evil, on the verge of triumph at the beginning of the final scene of the play, is destroyed before its end, together with its perpetrators; good is largely triumphant, with stability restored to Britain and the virtuous in part restored to their rights. So far, the justice of the gods is vindicated. But they do not save Cordelia, or Lear. Gloucester dies of joy, knowing Edgar to be alive, but it seems that the death of Cordelia leads inevitably to the death of Lear. One thing is clear: if there is any solution to this paradox, it can only be found in the last moments of the play, and in the passing of King Lear.

Criticism ancient and modern alike has concentrated on Lear's final speech in its attempts to determine exactly what happens at the end of the play; and most of the conclusions reached, particularly in the last twenty-five years or so, are in accordance with one of two views. The first sees both Lear and Cordelia as involved in the destruction which envelops good and evil alike. The despair into which Lear falls is maintained right up to the moment of death: and his last words as recorded in the folio text are to be interpreted as his final certainty that there is indeed 'no life' in Cordelia. Lear dies of despair, knowing Cordelia to be dead.

If what I have said so far be accepted, it is not difficult to refute such an interpretation. What we are being asked to accept is that Lear's sufferings, unlike those of Gloucester, are for nothing; that unlike Gloucester, unlike Kent, but like Goneril and Regan, Cornwall and Oswald, he dies not in a state of grace but in the opposite, and that the purgatorial experience, which in Gloucester has led to hope ultimately justified, leads Lear only to destruction.

The second viewpoint, far more common, and indeed adopted by most editors and critics

alike, is best known from Bradley's analysis of the ending:

though he is killed by an agony of pain, the agony in which he actually dies is one not of pain but of ecstasy . . . He is sure, at last, that she *lives*.

(p. 291)

Kenneth Muir expresses the point even more succinctly: his note on the passage, following Bradley, reads: 'Lear dies of joy, believing Cordelia to be alive'.[13]

In my opinion, the one service that has been done to *Lear* criticism by those who hold the first of these views has been to highlight the limitations of the second. As they rightly say, what we are being asked to accept is that, while Gloucester dies knowing the truth, Lear dies deceived by appearances. The parallel between the main plot and the sub-plot, including the temporal purgatorial experiences of Lear and Gloucester, which has been maintained throughout the play so far is then, if we are to believe Bradley and those who have followed him, broken in the terminal experience of their respective lives, and to no apparent purpose. It seems clear that neither of these views should be adopted if there is a defensible alternative. For me, Bradley was closer to the truth in his immediately following comment:

To us, perhaps, the knowledge that he [Lear] is deceived may bring a culmination of pain: but, if it brings *only* that, I believe we are false to Shakespeare, and it seems almost beyond question that any actor is false to the text who does not attempt to express, in Lear's last accents and gestures and look, an unbearable *joy*.

(p. 291)

The final moments of Lear's life are dealt with in fifty-five lines; sixteen more separate his death from the end of the play. Lear's first speech includes two apparently final statements about Cordelia: 'She's gone for ever'; 'She's dead as earth' (5.3.234, 236). But in the exchanges that follow, Lear is clearly trying to

---

13 Kenneth Muir, ed., *King Lear*, new Arden Shakespeare (London, 1972), p. 205, note to line 309.

convince himself that somehow, miraculously:

> This feather stirs. She lives. If it be so,
> It is a chance which does redeem all sorrows
> That ever I have felt.   (5.3.240–2)

This alternation between hope and despair, signalled by the stage direction '*Enter Lear with Cordelia in his armes*' (TLN 3216; 5.3.232.2),[14] is the motive force of this penultimate section of the play. For Lear, nothing else matters: not noble Kent, his friend; not the death of his elder daughters; not the restoration of his royal authority. His attention is hardly diverted from the one stark fact which no looking-glass, no feather, can controvert, and which he, and we, come finally to recognize: Cordelia is dead.

> And my poor fool is hanged. No, no, no life?
> Why should a dog, a horse, a rat have life,
> And thou no breath at all? Thou'lt come no
>   more,
> Never, never, never, never, never.   (5.3.281–4)

The certainty of her death; the final, violent, reaction against the apparent injustice of the gods; the valley of the shadow of despair: Lear's penultimate moments are comparable with the last moments of Goneril and Regan. The next line makes it clear that he is gasping for breath; and it is pleasant to suppose, though Shakespeare does not make it plain, that the last simple earthly service, the loosening of the button at his neck, is performed by Kent. The final words Shakespeare gives him are crucial. In the quarto text, the words 'Thank you, sir' are followed simply by a fourfold 'O', generally interpreted as no more than the last gasp of a dying man (Q: 24.304). In the folio, by contrast, are fourteen enigmatic words:

> Do you see this? Look on her. Look, her lips.
> Look there, look there.   (5.3.286–7)

The relationship between the quarto and folio texts of the play has been the subject of much discussion in recent years. In the present context, P. W. K. Stone, who considers the folio a revision by a hand other than Shakespeare's, comments:

> It is difficult to see these lines as anything more than an attempt on the reviser's part to provide Lear's speech with a more dramatic ending . . . The reviser . . . unable to supply anything original, reverts weakly to an idea that has already been exploited to moving effect (V.iii.265–7 and 271–2), *viz.* that Lear fancies Cordelia may still be alive.[15]

His general position has, however, been rejected by several critics, including Steven Urkowitz and Gary Taylor,[16] who regard Shakespeare himself as having been responsible for the folio text; and Thomas Clayton largely rejects Stone's strictures on the folio ending, commenting thus on Lear's last speech as it appears there:

> The relations between the passage, its antecedents in the immediate context, and the whole play help to give it a range and power as well as subtlety mostly lacking in the ending of the earlier version: the passage is imaginative and dramatic in itself, and full of significance and histrionic potentialities.[17]

To this it may be added that the quarto text of Lear's last speech is almost certainly imperfect: even as printed in the Oxford Shakespeare (24.300–4) there is one hypermetric line, and in certain others the blank verse halts badly. By

---

14 The addition 'dead' to this stage direction, adopted by many editors, is unfortunate: as G. W. Williams reminds us, we need to recover the uncertainty experienced by the original audience ('Petitionary Prayer in *King Lear*', in *The South Atlantic Quarterly*, 85 (1986), 360–73, p. 361). See also C. F. Williamson, 'The Hanging of Cordelia', *Review of English Studies*, NS 34 (1983), 414–18.

15 *The Textual History of* King Lear (London, 1980), p. 247.

16 *Shakespeare's Revision of 'King Lear'* (Princeton, 1980); and '*King Lear*: The Date and Authorship of the Folio Version', in *The Division of the Kingdoms: Shakespeare's Two Versions of 'King Lear'*, eds Gary Taylor and Michael Warren (Oxford, 1983), pp. 351–468.

17 '"Is this the promis'd end?" Revision in the Role of the King', in *The Division of the Kingdoms*, 121–41, p. 135.

contrast, there is nothing self-evidently wrong with the folio text. In consequence, I would judge it unsafe to base any argument on the quarto reading, and concur, with Clayton, in the almost unanimous critical standpoint, that the folio text reflects Shakespeare's own decision regarding the words which accompany the passing of King Lear. But what do we see? Why should we look at her lips? Look where? Look where?

If Lear's last speech has been the subject of innumerable comments, the final sixteen lines of the play have received little attention. Yet to me they seem vital to our understanding of what happens at the last moment of Lear's life.

These lines fall into two structural units. The first is an exchange between Edgar and Kent; the second is the final statement by Albany, his offer to Edgar and Kent to assume responsibility for the 'gored state', and their respective responses.[18] In the former unit, the audience's attention, which in Lear's final speech had been concentrated on Lear and Cordelia to the exclusion of all else, becomes divided between Edgar, who has rushed forward to attend to Lear, and Kent, who this time stands aloof. This division, it seems to me, is not arbitrary: Shakespeare establishes a specific contrast between Edgar and Kent which functions on two levels. First, with regard to the temporal fact of Lear's passing. Kent, whose faithfulness to his master during his lifetime knew no bounds, stands aside; Edgar, whose comparable service to his father saved Gloucester from death at the wrong time, acts now when the time for action is past – much like the enthusiastic young doctor or nurse who drags a terminally ill patient back from death only to condemn him to months or years of further suffering. The misguided enthusiasm of youth; the mature wisdom of age. Good in combination, of course, as Albany recognizes when he offers them joint sovereignty in the kingdom. The second level of contrast relates to the implications of Lear's death for each of them: Edgar tries to detain

Lear in this world, but Kent is no longer concerned primarily with time, but with eternity. His first words show this. 'Break, heart, I prithee break' (5.3.288) is not an expression of heartbreak, of despair: it is essentially a prayer – a prayer that his life may end at the moment which is for him supremely right.[19] He had come to bid his king and master aye good night: now, only death can reunite them. And the sense in which we are to understand this is clearly set forth in Kent's next words:

> Vex not his ghost. O, let him pass. He hates him
> That would upon the rack of this tough world
> Stretch him out longer.　　　(5.3.289–91)

That is, Edgar should not attempt to detain Lear in this world, but allow his spirit to pass from this world to the next, through nature to eternity. And Kent's final words, as important as some we have already examined, underscore the imminence of their reunion:

> I have a journey, sir, shortly to go:
> My master calls me; I must not say no.
> 　　　　　　　　(5.3.297–8)

To dot the 'i's and cross the 't's once more: Kent is dying, but his death will lead to reunion with his master, not in the grave, but in life after life.

Shakespeare, then, points us in two directions at once, in the last sixteen lines of *King Lear*. We look at Edgar, and see the restoration of temporal order: his youthful enthusiasm, though sometimes misguided, will blend well with Albany's hard-won wisdom. We look at Kent, and see one who stands between time and eternity, and who already begins to see the second.

---

[18] I accept, without being entirely convinced about it, the Folio attribution of the last speech of the play to Edgar.

[19] These words, given in the quarto text to Lear, are often taken as referring to Lear's heart rather than Kent's own. On balance, however, I accept Bradley's view (p. 309).

It is time to recall the premises with which I began. From ancient times, certain experiences have been associated with those who are 'fey'; others have been reported by those who have witnessed the moment of death. To take a few instances from medieval and earlier literature: King Saul receives no comfort from the spirit of Samuel, called back from eternity on the eve of Saul's death; Olaf Haraldsson, King of Norway, has a vision of the world spread out before him on the eve of his final battle; a rather different but also highly symbolic vision is included in the treatment of the last days of Arthur in Laȝamon's *Brut*. That the mantle of Elijah falls on Elisha is conditional upon Elisha's witnessing the passing of Elijah; and one of the commonest topoi in saints' lives and other medieval works is the account of those present at the passing of saints and good men, accompanied by flights of angels to sing them to their rest.[20]

Experiences of a comparable kind are by no means absent from Shakespeare's plays. Visions of the dead are common: Brutus is visited by Caesar, and will see him again at Philippi; Banquo appears to Macbeth; and in the night before Bosworth Field a sequence of Richard's victims call down despair and death on him and bring comfort to Richmond. Horatio sees nothing at the moment of Hamlet's death, but his prayer is based solidly on medieval tradition. Kent envisions his reunion with his master.

What then of Lear? I have tried to show that it is both unthinkable and illogical that he dies in despair: he passes, indeed, through despair, as Gloucester does, but the last fourteen words he utters constitute, in my view, the final reversal in Shakespeare's statement about him. But I have also implied that for Lear to die in joy, believing Cordelia to be alive, is almost as unthinkable and certainly just as illogical. However, there is a third possibility, mentioned or hinted at in the past, which in the last quarter-century has tended to be dismissed by some critics as 'sentimental wishful thinking' and treated by others with the contempt they

consider it deserves. Yet it seems eminently logical to affirm that when we have eliminated what appears impossible, that which remains, however unpalatable it may be to such critics, is likely to be the truth.

In his final moments, Lear's attention is clearly diverted from both his despair at Cordelia's death and his own gasps for breath and towards the body of Cordelia. One or two commentators have suggested or implied that he is still fiddling about with a looking-glass or feather, but the time for that is past. Whatever he sees, it is so overwhelming that he is provoked into the final burst of energy that kills him. It brings him once more towards Cordelia and fixes his, and our, attention on her lips. So much is clear; the rest is not. What is it that he sees, does, and feels at the moment of his passing?

If we reject, as I believe we must, a merely temporal significance in this event, we are faced with the recognition that Shakespeare here adumbrates two of the commonest moment-of-death experiences, attested both in literature and in the reports of those who have been present at the death of a loved one. The first I have already mentioned: in earlier literature, notably the saints' lives, the soul leaves the body at or soon after physical death – and

---

[20] See, respectively: 1 Samuel 28; Saint Olaf's saga, chapter 213 (Snorri Sturluson, *Heimskringla*, trans. Samuel Laing, Everyman's Library, vol. 722 (1914; London, 1964) and see chapter 226; Laȝamon, *Brut*, eds. G. L. Brook and R. F. Leslie, Early English Text Society, no. 277, vol. 2 (London, 1978), pp. 734–7; 2 Kings 2. Of the many early examples of the last-mentioned topos which might be cited, there are Bede's accounts of the deaths of Eorcengota, Fursa, and the Abbess Hild (*Bede's Ecclesiastical History of the English People*, eds. Bertram Colgrave and R. A. B. Mynors (Oxford, 1969), pp. 238, 270, and 412); while from the end of the medieval period we have Malory's account of the death of Lancelot – after he has been 'howselyd and enelyd', a vision is granted to the bishop in which he saw 'syr Launcelot . . . with mo angellis than ever I sawe men in one day. And I sawe the angellys heve up syr Launcelot unto heven, and the yates of heven opened ayenst hym' (*Malory: Works*, ed. Eugène Vinaver, 2nd edn. (Oxford, 1977), p. 724).

of course through the mouth, as depicted in both medieval and renaissance art[21] – and is received by either angelic or demonic powers. As Shakespeare might have written, and with greater justice, 'Goodnight, sweet princess, and flights of angels sing thee to thy rest.' The second experience: at the moment of death, or somewhat earlier, the dying person sees one or more of those he has known and loved during his life. As I have shown, this type of experience is partly reflected elsewhere in Shakespeare's plays, though it is more often hate than love which provokes such happenings; and it is obviously this experience which Kent either has, or envisions, at the moment he utters his last words.

I thus conclude that there is one portrayal of Lear's passing which fits the evidence. As Bradley said, though for the wrong reason, Lear's last words express an unbearable joy. His antepenultimate movement draws him to Cordelia's body: he bends towards her once more, but this time not because he thinks he sees at her lips signs of life – Stone was right in regarding such an ending as bathetic.[22] His penultimate movement draws him into an upright position, from which he collapses in what Edgar perceives as a faint; his words 'Look there, look there' are not, in consequence, directed to Cordelia's body but to her spirit which, as the spirit of Caesar did for Brutus, stays for her father. 'My daughter calls me: I will not say no.' Lear and Cordelia pass, together, from life into life.[23]

In the past, many critics have rejected the suggestion that there may be more than a temporal element in *King Lear*. George Sampson, indeed, opens the single paragraph he devotes to the play with the statement:

The power of *King Lear* . . . is so stupendous that we are astonished to remember that it makes no use of the supernatural.[24]

This is, indeed, to look at the play with one eye closed! What we should rather do is to look at that final scene and perceive, on the one hand, the temporal tragedy symbolized by the corpses of Lear and Cordelia – removed, be it noted, before the play ends – and on the other the solitary figure of Kent, standing between time and eternity. And if we look at both, as Shakespeare most certainly intended us to do, we may, without being condemned for sentimental wishful thinking, express the passing of King Lear in terms in which logic, justice, and sentiment concur. Lear dies of joy, not because he believes Cordelia to be alive, but because he knows that their last parting has come and has gone, and that he will never need to say goodbye to his beloved daughter again.

---

[21] This paper was originally prepared for the conference entitled 'Zeit, Tod und Ewigkeit in der Renaissance Literatur', held in Mattsee, Austria, in May 1986. By a happy coincidence, Dr James Hogg's paper 'A Morbid Preoccupation with Mortality' was accompanied by a selection of illustrations from the Carthusian MS British Library Additional 37049, one of which, from fol. 29r, depicts precisely this kind of happening. Such examples are of course legion. It is also noteworthy that W. R. Elton admits the possibility of this interpretation (*'King Lear' and the Gods*, p. 258, note 210), in relation to Cordelia.

[22] It is on this issue, principally, that I part company with C. F. Williamson, whose article (cited at note 14 above) convincingly demonstrates that Lear had every reason to entertain the belief that Cordelia might have survived the 'hanging'. Lear's actions and reactions in this scene are, consequently, not deluded but eminently sane.

[23] This is, of course, the answer to the problem set forth earlier. Kent's ultimate reward is not, as we have seen, on the temporal plane; neither is Cordelia's. But there is an important parallel to be noted with Edgar as well. Edgar's loving care of his father brought Gloucester back from despair and both temporal and eternal death; Cordelia brought her father back to sanity and an understanding of the depths of her love for him. It remains only to be emphasized that there is one class of human beings for whom the moment of death is immaterial – those who have lived in such a way that they have no cause to fear it. Marlowe's Faustus dies in terror because he has sold his soul to the devil; Shakespeare's King Hamlet suffers the pains of purgatory to eradicate the foul crimes done in his days of nature; Cordelia's is the love that conquers all things.

[24] *The Concise Cambridge History of English Literature* (Cambridge, 1941), p. 266.

SHAKESPEARE PERFORMANCES IN LONDON AND STRATFORD-UPON-AVON, 1986–7

STANLEY WELLS

In a year of exceptional financial crisis for the Royal Shakespeare Company, relieved at last (though only temporarily) by the promise of massive sponsorship from the Royal Insurance Company, a year during which the government made clear that funding for the arts would depend increasingly upon the private sector – including people who pay for tickets – theatregoers were offered a good selection of Shakespeare's more popular histories, comedies, and tragedies, the only comparative rarity – *Titus Andronicus* – playing in a smaller auditorium, the Swan. And in spite of financial stringencies, the year saw performances, given in the provinces, at the Old Vic, and overseas, by a newly formed group, the English Shakespeare Company, in which the considerable but diverse talents of Michael Bogdanov and Michael Pennington unite in the effort 'to produce and to tour large-scale classical drama'.

The new company's first production presented Parts One and Two of *Henry IV* along with *Henry V* as a cycle, and I saw all three plays at the Old Vic during a single day. Such theatrical endurance tests, though popular, are of doubtful validity. Of course, this one provided an opportunity to enjoy within a short space of time an extraordinary diversity of dramatic writing linked by a narrative thread. It also brought audiences together in a curious sort of bonding with their fellow theatregoers and the performers, with both of whom they experienced an unnaturally close relationship

for a concentrated period of time. There is a self-gratulatory air about such audiences, speaking of their experience as a marathon while they queue for lavatories and sit on staircases to eat improvised meals during the relatively short breaks between performances. In the auditorium, heads droop on to neighbouring shoulders as the day wears on, and at the end of it all is a sense of celebration of the successful survival of a self-inflicted ordeal.

Michael Bogdanov's production revealed the artificiality of regarding these three plays as a cycle even by the means it used to weld them together. Absence of *Richard II* both left a gap in the historical narrative and encouraged an emphasis on the development of Prince Hal into Henry V; but the two Parts of *Henry IV* notoriously fail to provide the materials for a clearly developing study.

Bogdanov opened genially with a song in which the whole company joined, sketching a context for the story of 'a king who was mighty, but wild as a boy' and inviting us to 'list to the ballad of Harry Leroy'. Both the popular mode of the ballad and the simplistic reduction of the narrative reflected Bogdanov's missionary zeal as one who would mediate Shakespeare to his notions of what constitutes a popular audience. Costumes (designed by Stephanie Howard) were eclectic and mainly of the twentieth century. Simple settings (by Chris Dyer) suggested locations by the use of minimal properties, hangings, scaffolding, and a movable bridge which provided an upper acting area. Action was steadily paced, speech consistently clear, the meaning well digested and forcefully conveyed. Production devices identified groupings among the characters and set one group against another. The English court was characterized by formality – symmetrical groupings, frock coats and scarlet uniforms, standard English pronunciation. Snatches of classical music – a Bach organ toccata, a Handel coronation anthem – and sometimes the striking of Big Ben introduced their scenes. The rebels generally wore khaki and denims, spoke in an assortment of local accents (not consistently well sustained), swigged from bottles with their feet on tables, and displayed a tendency to take their shirts off – Douglas even on the battlefield. Their scenes were introduced by urgent, strident, modern music.

Shakespeare's set pieces were given their full value. In Part One, the big tavern scene was admirably built up, with on-stage spectators directing the responses of their counterparts in the auditorium, reacting with delight to Hal's and Falstaff's fecundity in the coining of epithets. Welsh speeches were amply written in for the benefit of Lady Mortimer, and a visible group of instrumentalists provided the music that Glyndŵr speaks of conjuring up. It was all part of a very proper realization and enjoyment of the text's theatrical values, extending at points to the invention of episodes: Bardolph entered playing 'Silver threads among the gold' on his trombone, followed by John Woodvine's purple-suited Falstaff. Meditatively, Falstaff slowly cracked six eggs, one after the other, into a tankard, filled it to the brim from a vodka bottle, swirled the tankard around, and drank, all to Bardolph's continuous, maudlin accompaniment. The audience applauded. (Presumably it was after this that Falstaff developed his distaste for 'pullet sperm' in his 'brewage'.) In Part Two, Pistol especially provided the opportunity for another series of tableaux; at times I was reminded of children's-paper versions of Shakespeare that print the full text alongside garish, comic-strip illustrations of the action.

The element of simplification in the production style carried over into Michael Pennington's characterization of the Prince. Pennington is a well graced actor, easy of movement, finely built, honey-tongued. In the earlier scenes of Part One he subdued his princeliness to Hal's wilder side. He was affectionate with Falstaff, rather drunk in the first tavern scene, fraternal with Charles Lawson's aggressively Irish Poins, derisively rude (against the implications of the text) to the Sheriff and the Carrier (portrayed, characteristically, as modern policemen) who come to complain of the robbery. Called before the King his father, he was at first detached and sullenly rebellious, gabbling his first expressions of penitence as an empty formality. Only when the King spoke of Hotspur was Hal stung to a sense of responsibility; then he rapidly took on the characteristics of the court party. The closing scenes were rearranged, presumably in order to make more plausible Hal's return to the tavern in Part Two. The King was present to hear Sir John's claim to have killed Percy, and silently showed that he believed it, to Hal's evident distress. The play ended with Sir John's resolution to 'live cleanly, as a nobleman should do'; and when we first saw him in Part Two he wore medals.

A simplified pattern was thus imposed on an already schematic play, and if Pennington's performance lacked subtlety, this may have been through acquiescence in his director's concept. Part Two is more resistant to schematization, but the contrast between court and rebels continues, and though Patrick O'Connell played the King sympathetically, the rebel cause was implicitly endorsed. In Bogdanov's semiotics the swigging of beer from bottles contrasts favourably with the serving of short drinks in glasses. So, in Gaultree Forest, a uniformed Prince John offered wine to the tweedy, cardiganned rebel lords; after he had betrayed them they were shot on stage to the

5 *The History of Henry the Fourth* (*1 Henry IV*). English Shakespeare Company on tour, 1986–87. Prince Harry (Michael Pennington, centre) and Poins (Charles Lawson, right) challenge the account of the events at Gad's Hill given by Sir John (John Woodvine, left) in Act 2 Scene 4

jubilant strains of 'The King shall rejoice'. Hal, entering to the dying King, looked ready for a game of tennis; but the subsequent reconciliation became the play's emotional centre, marked by a closeness of physical contact as well as emotional rapport that made Falstaff's rejection inevitable; when it came, the sense of pain was confined to Falstaff; police brutality in both the carting of Doll Tearsheet and the committal of Sir John to the Fleet suggested that Hal had become head of a police state.

Bogdanov's wooing of the audience sometimes seems at odds with his overall antiestablishmentism. There was condescension in his over-jokey portrayal of the Gloucestershire recruits, and an element of audience flattery in his presentation of the English attitude to war in *Henry V*: the playing of 'Jerusalem' during the embarkation for France might be regarded as satire, but the simultaneous display of a banner inscribed 'Fuck the Frogs' drew delighted applause in which it was difficult not to detect an element of jingoistic self-satisfaction. Later, when Exeter deliberately walked over a cloth on which ladies of the French court were picnicking (drinking champagne from glasses, of course), his rudeness seemed implicitly endorsed as a proper way of treating foreigners.

Pennington's King was not strongly characterized except by the actor's natural grace. His performance was consistently intelligent, but a lack of inwardness, of emotional penetration, made it difficult to discern any strong interpretative bent. He wore battledress like his soldiers, and was comradely but always the officer, whether standing on a tank for 'Once more unto the breach', delivered to soldiers crouched behind piles of sandbags, or wooing the Princess. His men might behave brutally – as Pistol did with Le Fer, cutting his throat on hearing of Henry's order to kill the prisoners – but Henry himself remained aloof. There were original, inventive touches: on 'There's for thy labour', dispatching Mountjoy with a defiant message to the Dauphin, he presented him with a tennis ball. And it was ingenious to treat Grandpré's lines beginning 'The horsemen sit like fixèd candlesticks' as a poem that he was composing on a typewriter, taking the paper out on 'Description cannot suit itself in words'.

As one who prefers classical to popular music, and wine in glasses to beer in bottles (let alone cans), I tend to feel got at by Bogdanov's productions; and I acknowledge, of course, that I may be the kind of person at whom he wishes to get. While I admire his concentration on theatrical values, his determination to illuminate all areas of the text, and his company's intelligent understanding and projection of Shakespeare's language, I am sometimes repelled by reductive over-simplifications and vulgarities. There was much theatrical life in *The Henrys*, but I was left with a feeling that I had been talked down to.

By contrast, Bill Alexander's thoughtful production of *The Merchant of Venice*, which opened at Stratford-upon-Avon in April, though it emphasized racial, religious, and psychological issues, showed that contemporary relevance can be achieved without resort to modern dress or to radical textual adaptation. As in much of this director's work, visual effects were often reminiscent of the Victorian and Edwardian theatre. Kit Surrey's set was heavily Venetian, offering no sense of Belmont as a world elsewhere. A bridge of sighs spanned the stage throughout; the stage platform suggested a landing stage, with poles for gondolas to each side. Only shifts of lighting from a chalked Star of David to an icon of the Madonna on the back wall, accompanied by the appearance of stage properties, provided visual evidence that we were in Belmont.

From the sounds of the Kyrie Eleison with which the production opened, matched by off-stage Jewish chanting, religious issues were stressed. Shylock's Jewishness was vividly illustrated, even to the insertion of a Hebrew prayer and sacrificial ritual as Shylock prepared to cut into Antonio's flesh; this too was matched by anguished chanting of Latin prayers from the Christians. But there was no suggestion that Christianity implied moral superiority. The spitting that Shylock complains of in his opening scene became a symbol of anti-semitic behaviour. Three Venetian urchins elaborated the action, baiting Shylock, crying 'Jew, Jew, Jew' after him and Tubal, mimicking and mocking their victims; and this kind of behaviour extended upwards to Salerio and Solanio, to Graziano, even to Bassanio and Antonio; among the male characters, only the Duke was free from it in the courtroom scene.

These emphases rendered Shylock, initially at least, exceptionally sympathetic, an impression increased by the natural charm in Antony Sher's detailed, fluent performance, as eloquent in the language of the body as of the tongue. Submissive in adversity, he was yet immensely exciting in the self-justifying parable of Jacob and the sheep, vigorously and rhythmically slapping one fist into the palm of his other hand as he illustrated 'the work of generation'. His first reaction to the suggestion of the bond was playful, as if he entered into it with the hope of humouring, even of pleasing, the Christians rather than with the expectation that its provisions would become a reality. It was Jessica's defection to the Christian party,

6   *The Merchant of Venice*. Royal Shakespeare Theatre, 1987. Shylock (Antony Sher) is tormented by Salerio
(Michael Cadman, left) and Solanio (Gregory Doran) in Act 3 Scene 1

and his own subsequent grief, that caused him
to see the bond as an opportunity for revenge.
His initial reaction was intensely sympathetic
as he rushed in, deeply distressed, pursued by
urchins, poked at with sticks, mocked by
Salerio and Solanio, and with blood on his
injured brow. The repetitions of 'Let him look
to his bond' became increasingly impassioned,
as if to indicate that this was the point at which
he began to take the bond seriously, and the
eloquent climax of the 'I am a Jew' speech
came with the word 'Revenge'. The point was
hammered home at the end of the scene, the
more emphatic for coming just before the
interval: Shylock sat at the corner of the stage,
prayed (in Hebrew), and rocked backwards
and forwards muttering obsessively of
revenge as the house lights went up. From
being a representative of a wronged race he
had become a vindictive individual; but even in

court he still made a plea for sympathy which
was also a bitter attack on Christian practices
as, on the words 'You have among you many a
purchased slave', he dragged forward a cower-
ing young black to illustrate his point.

The production's interpretative emphasis on
religious and racial issues extended to psychological ones in the romance plot, where again
the director manipulated our reactions, con-
veying extra-textual significances mainly
through interpretative business and emotional
nuance. He opened the play with what was
virtually a tableau: John Carlisle as Antonio,
not caught in mid-conversation as the text
suggests, but standing centre-stage, staring
glumly into the middle distance, only later to
be approached by Solanio and Salerio. Here
was the merchant of Venice, and it was soon to
be made clear that his melancholy stemmed
from frustrated sexual desire for Nicholas

163

7 *The Merchant of Venice*. Royal Shakespeare Theatre, 1987. Shylock (Antony Sher) prepares to
take his revenge in the trial scene, Act 4 Scene 1

Farrell's Bassanio. Antonio reeled as Bassanio spoke in praise of Portia, and kissed him with despairing passion but little response as they parted. Antonio was obviously to be understood as a depressive homosexual, and Bassanio's reciprocation of his affection did not preclude the thought that their relationship might have been physical as well as emotional; but Bassanio was enthusiastic in his pursuit of Portia, squaring up to the caskets on which his fate depended as if to a feat of supreme athleticism. The director appeared to be trying to create here the kind of tension more commonly associated with the courtroom scene, as if to point to a parallel between the importance for Bassanio of making the right decision about the casket and the importance for Shylock of achieving his revenge. Bassanio's enthusiasm might have been interpreted as a sign of his need for Portia's money, but Portia, too, was clearly desperately anxious for him to succeed, and they conveyed their anxiety with broadly exaggerated comic gestures, assisted by the full resources of the Belmont Choral Society. But Bassanio's passion for Portia did not diminish his concern for Antonio, and he displayed deep distress on hearing of Antonio's losses, a climactic emotion which the director reinforced by causing Lorenzo to mirror it silently.

In the courtroom, Antonio's depression became suicidal. Portia had no idea until the very last moment of how she could save Antonio, nor did he wish her to do so. When Bassanio declared 'The Jew shall have my flesh, my blood, bones, and all / Ere thou shalt lose for me one drop of blood', Antonio cast him violently aside in the fierce intensity of his wish to sustain his role of a 'tainted wether of the flock' to the point of martyrdom; and he continued to offer his body to the knife even after Shylock's defeat.

The social and psychological seriousness with which this production invested a text that owes much to the conventions of romance made the play more disturbing than usual,

reducing its comic and lyrical potential, and this was reflected in Deborah Findlay's interpretation of Portia. Elaborate dresses and ostentatious jewellery displayed her wealth; her racialist attitude to her unsuccessful suitors was disturbing rather than amusing. This was not a fairy-tale Portia conquering through charm and generosity of spirit, but it was a well-executed carrying through of a less than wholly attractive interpretation of the role which was in tune with the production. Even the high poetic romance of Lorenzo's love duet with Jessica was undercut, partly because the lovers began it far apart, standing at opposite sides of the stage as if on capstans looking out to sea, and partly because of a touch of self-mockery in Paul Spence's likeable Lorenzo. Graziano's closing couplet was played with a strong, even crude emphasis on the lovers' sexuality. The play ended, as it had begun, with an expressive tableau in the neo-Victorian style. Antonio remained on stage, Jessica returned to retrieve the crucifix that Gobbo had earlier given her as a present from Lorenzo; Antonio, who had picked it up, dangled it before her as if to question the values and practices of those for whom it was a symbol.

Since Antony Sher played Richard III – also with Bill Alexander as director – he has been consciously a star actor, one of whom great things are expected and who seems determined to make something special out of every role he plays. The production of *The Merchant of Venice* was strong enough to contain him; and he wisely sought no tragic climax to the role. The same cannot be said of his performance in *Twelfth Night*, which joined the Stratford repertoire in July. This is essentially a company play, one that demands strong performances in many roles, and one that will not fulfil its true potential unless the balance is right. Though I have never seen a performance that did not afford considerable pleasure, it remains theatrically elusive, requiring the transmuting alchemy that Peter Hall brought to it in 1958, and John Barton in 1969, to turn the text into more than the sum of its parts.

Much about Bill Alexander's production felt right. Kit Surrey's firmly Adriatic set – this *is* Illyria, lady – a jumble of archways, alleys, stairways, windows, and benches, all glittering white against a permanently blue sky – allowed scenes to flow into one another with easy continuity. It sacrificed the sense of two distinct households, Orsino's and Olivia's, but was unspecific enough to allow our imaginations to supply the required shifts in location; and the ethnic costumes and customs provided a useful compromise between fantasy and reality. But Bill Alexander's use of the set was over-confining, at least in Malvolio's letter scene. Usually Sir Toby, Sir Andrew, and Fabian are placed on the main stage behind Malvolio, sometimes hiding behind box trees, sometimes emerging into view with greater or lesser danger to the success of their trick; much of the scene's comedy derives from the tension between Malvolio's self-absorption and the danger that they will burst into it with their outraged reactions to his presumptions. Placing them in windows where they had little freedom of movement upset the balance of the scene, throwing too much emphasis on Malvolio's fantasies, too little on the tricksters who had stimulated them.

Nevertheless, there were good things in the production. We were immediately touched by Viola's situation as she entered carrying her brother's clothes, still choking back sobs for his loss. Olivia's entry with her black-clad train, headed by Malvolio as an obsequiously zealous director of mourning, on her way to pay tribute to her brother's memory at a shrine let into a wall, helpfully established the resemblance between her situation and Viola's. The poetic heart of the play was touched during the wordless interplay of emotion between Orsino and Viola as Bruce Alexander's mellifluously unaccompanied singing of Feste's 'Come away, death' moved Orsino with thoughts of his despairing love for Olivia and also relaxed the disguised Viola to a point at which, only just holding back a caress, she came close to revealing her love for Orsino. This was beautifully conceived and executed. Harriet Walter was a gently appealing, elegant, wistful Viola, lacking in comic drive and disconcertingly mannered of speech, but touching in both the hopes and the actuality of reunion. And Deborah Findlay, while leaving us in no doubt that her Olivia could sway a household, palpitatingly conveyed her disturbed desire for Cesario. Roger Allam played a younger, handsomer Sir Toby than usual; he has an easy command of the stage, but it seemed odd to make Sir Toby the sexiest character in the play, and this Sir Toby drunk was too like Sir Toby sober, except that he belched louder and longer and played tricks with the smoke from his cheroot.

These actorish tricks exemplify what I missed most in this production: a sense of personality expressing itself in action, of a group of fully realized characters all working in unison towards the fulfilment of the plot. The character who came closest to my ideal was Sir Andrew Aguecheek in David Bradley's totally coherent, self-consistent portrayal. Bemused, bedraggled, and bewildered, unremittingly conscientious in his efforts to keep pace with his more sophisticated companions, he was touchingly uncomprehending in his failure to do so. Merely to contemplate him was to induce sympathetic laughter; yet Sir Andrew himself never laughed. The pursuit of pleasure is a serious business; and he was sadly exploited by Sir Toby.

The comic wholeness of this performance put it in direct contrast with Antony Sher's Malvolio, which allowed the effort to be both funny and original to take precedence over the establishing of a credible character who believed in himself. Whereas Sher's Shylock served the play, remaining within the framework of the directorial concept, his Malvolio burst out of the frame, achieving brilliance at the expense of the play's overall balance.

8 *Twelfth Night*. Royal Shakespeare Theatre, 1987. Viola (Harriet Walter) and Orsino (Donald Sumpter) listening to the song 'Come away, death' in Act 2 Scene 4

Comic business in the earlier scenes seemed no more than a succession of effortful points, whether Malvolio was popping up unexpectedly close to Olivia in response to her call, appearing in a hairnet and beardnet (but otherwise fully dressed) in the scene of midnight revelry, walking with knees bent to conceal his yellow stockings, turning his pockets and hat inside out to show that they too were yellow, or exposing himself to Olivia's shocked attendants in gleeful self-satisfaction. The effort to be funny was all-too-apparent, but it was the effort of a hard-working actor rather than the revelation of a deeply imagined character.

The later part of the performance was based on a theory: that Malvolio is driven out of his wits as a result of the tricks played on him. In the prison scene he emerged through a trap, tethered to a stake, visibly suffering; the darkness surrounding him was mimed by Feste, who tormented him with exploding caps. A half-naked Sir Toby and Maria were visible at a window, more absorbed in their love-making than in the outcome of their trick. And at the end Malvolio was distressingly insane, a broken man who flailed out like an enraged bear at the whole pack of those whom he saw as his tormentors, and, completely crazed, danced and sang snatches of Feste's song from the end of the prison scene. There would have been no point at all in entreating this Malvolio to a peace.

The staging of this episode was indebted, I suspect, to Ralph Berry's article '*Twelfth Night*: The Experience of the Audience', which compares it to a bear-baiting: 'The audience become spectators, Malvolio the bear.'[1]

---

[1] *Shakespeare Survey 34* (1981), 111–19, p. 118.

9   *Twelfth Night*. Royal Shakespeare Theatre, 1987. Malvolio (Antony Sher) displays his yellow-lined pockets to Olivia (Deborah Findlay) in Act 3 Scene 4

Though Ralph Berry rightly draws attention to the disturbing aspects of Malvolio's discomfiture, Malvolio can be bear-like without being mad; indeed, to make him mad destroys the point of the opposition between him and Feste. Feste's wisdom lies in his admission of folly; Malvolio's folly lies in his belief in his own wisdom. To relieve him of responsibility at the end by making him mad is to sentimentalize him in the manner that Shylock has been sentimentalized by actors who have tried to turn *The Merchant of Venice* into the tragedy of Shylock. If Malvolio has a tragedy it is not that he goes mad, but that he remains irremediably sane.

Both *The Merchant of Venice* and *Twelfth Night* were given virtually complete. I was prejudiced against Jonathan Miller's production of *The Taming of the Shrew* (which opened at Stratford in September) as soon as I

heard that – like Miller's earlier productions on both stage and television – it was to omit the Induction. I disapproved not simply because the Induction contains most of the best writing in the play and one of the most memorable of Shakespeare's lesser characters, but also because the trick of transmutation played upon Sly seems to me a necessary prologue to the process by which Petruccio 'tames' Katherine – a prologue whose omission robs the play of its most brilliantly imaginative dimension – and also because the style in which the shrew action is written is deliberately fitted to its status as a play-within-the-play.

The decision seemed particularly perverse in view of the heavily stylized manner in which much of the action was presented. A *commedia* ambience was suggested by the street scene of Stefanos Lazaridis's ingenious set, and by the presence at the start, and at intervals thereafter,

10   *The Taming of the Shrew*. Royal Shakespeare Theatre, 1987. Petruccio (Brian Cox, right), accompanied by Grumio (Barrie Rutter, to the left of and behind Cox), finally arrives to marry Katherine (Fiona Shaw, centre) in Act 3 Scene 2

of a partially masked on-stage band dressed in *commedia* costume and playing Stephen Oliver's Renaissance-style music with the somewhat lugubrious air of musicians who feel that this sort of thing should really be left to actors. There were some bright touches of comedy, especially in Griffith Jones's sweetly crazed Nathaniel, repeating everything his master said like an echo-chamber, but the director seemed to have concentrated his attention on a psychological interpretation of the Petruccio-Katherine relationship, very much in line with Bernard Shaw's view of the play as a realistic comedy. Fiona Shaw presented Kate as a woman unbalanced through feelings of inferiority to her sister, whom she mocked behind her back at her first entrance, and later assaulted with physical brutality. Brian Cox precisely embodied Shaw's view of Petruccio as a man who 'shews his character by pricking up his ears at the news that there is a fortune to be got by any man who will take an ugly and ill-tempered woman off her father's hands, and hurrying off to strike the bargain before somebody else picks it up',[2] except that, catch-

---

[2] *Shaw on Shakespeare*, ed. Edwin Wilson (1961, reprinted Harmondsworth, 1969), p. 197 (from an article originally printed in the *Saturday Review*, 6 November 1897).

ing sight of her face in repose at the climax of the first wooing scene, he made us believe that he admired her beauty; and the warmth of her response to his hearty kiss demonstrated that she was well on the way to acceptance.

This was fine, and caused no problems with Petruccio, played throughout with great integrity and admirably understated comedy. But Fiona Shaw was required to convey in Kate an extra-textual degree of neurosis and did so with a battery of bodily and facial signs – hand through hair, fingers to cheek, mouth gaping wide open, head thrust forward in astonishment, impatient tappings of the foot, exasperated puffs of breath – that approached caricature. Her entrance in the last scene was clumsily masked, at least from my seat in the stalls, by those sitting at the table stretched across the front of the stage; in the submission, spoken from the side, she destroyed the verse rhythms in favour of an emotional intensity that Petruccio found deeply moving. The audience burst into applause as he kissed her – whether as a tribute to the performers or in romantic enjoyment of the match was not clear. (Nor was it possible to determine whether more men applauded than women.) The play's ending was subdued, emphasizing Lucentio's and Hortensio's discontent with their wives' behaviour.

Productions of Shakespeare's tragedies during 1987 have varied in style from the heavily interpreted to the minimalist. Adrian Noble's 1986 Stratford-upon-Avon production of *Macbeth* – like Trevor Nunn's productions of 1974 and 1976 – concentrated on the psycho-drama of the Macbeths at the expense of the play's concern with public affairs. This was achieved with few textual adjustments except in the closing scenes, which kept the focus firmly on Macbeth himself, sacrificing much of the alternative perspective afforded by the rebels.

Bob Crowley's set, a black box built around a rostrum on which seven tattered banners fluttered at the play's opening, was claustrophobically atmospheric. Acting styles tended to the colloquial and familiar, humanizing the dialogue and evading rhetoric. Alfred Burke's Duncan was no symbol of saintliness, but an admired leader of men; the witches were shambling, impoverished, ordinary women. Sinead Cusack's young, beautiful, and vulnerable Lady Macbeth, scarcely credible as an invoker of spirits, was moving in disintegration. Jonathan Pryce played her husband as a little man, both physically and morally, dependent for strength on his relationship with his wife, constantly, nervously explaining himself, both to her and to the audience. The interpretation was anti-Bradleian in its denial of Macbeth's poetic imagination; emotional resonance was avoided, 'If it were done' was expounded rather than felt, and 'To be thus is nothing', too, was a self-justification. Only with 'Come, seeling night' did Pryce, normally light-toned, open up into sonorousness to convey a sense of imaginative mystery which briefly brought Lady Macbeth under his spell, but instantly he punctured the effect with comic gibbering, as if it had all been an act to frighten her.

Though this interpretation was moralistic in its refusal to allow Macbeth any grandeur of imagination and in its down-playing of his physical heroism, it permitted some sympathy for the Macbeths, or at least suggested a psychological explanation for their evil, in its emphasis on children and on the protagonists' childlessness. The theme was sounded in the opening scene, when the witches, scavenging on the battlefield, raised a cloak to reveal a young boy beside the recumbent figure of a wounded soldier; the boy walked off, the soldier remained to become the 'bloody man' of the following scene. Macbeth slapped his wife after she had taunted him with cowardice; their subsequent tussle had an intense erotic charge; 'I have given suck' aroused anguished memories in both of them, and after 'Bring forth men children only' they grew so amorous as to suggest that fresh procreation was imminent. Appearing for the first time as King and Queen, splendid in black and gold, they found the young Fleance (whom Macbeth had previously treated with affection) cheekily seated in the throne, unconscious of their presence; after an uncomfortable pause, Macbeth jokily dropped his crown over Fleance's head, and, when the court's laughter had subsided, addressed him, instead of Banquo, as 'our chief guest'. Pretty children, later revealed as Macduff's, took the role of the apparitions in what was no longer the cauldron scene: it appeared to be taking place in a nursery with tinkling music to accompany the children's speeches; Macbeth himself spoke the third prophecy, as if repeating the lines from the whispered promptings of the child on his lap. The show of eight kings followed by Banquo existed only in Macbeth's mind, and the children played blind-man's buff around him as he reacted to it in horror.

This emphasis on children served a psychological interpretation, deepening our sense of Macbeth's humanity and our awareness of the values that he rejects. But it was not achieved without strain. Perhaps the director hoped to overcome the unreality and the potential absurdity of the apparitions by internalizing them as dream figures, emanations of Macbeth's conscience; but the scene was trivialized, partly because of a disparity between the children's enchanting appearance and the solemnity of what they said, and also because Macbeth's reactions seemed in excess of what had stimulated them. But it did permit an emphasis upon the emotion that this Macbeth conveyed above all others: fear. It was evident on his first encounter with the witches, when, having expressed comic surprise at their appearance – 'What are these, so withered and so wild in their attire?' aroused laughter – he collapsed in a dead faint on their prophecy that he would 'be king hereafter'. It was there in the dagger soliloquy (far more strongly in London than in Stratford) and in his reaction to

Banquo's ghost (which only he saw), and above all in the final scenes, when the walls of the set closed in upon him and he appeared like a clown, his shirt hanging out of his baggy trousers, an absurd figure who slammed porridge in the face of the messenger who carried bad news, overturning table and chairs in his hysteria. The emotional climax of the role came with his reaction to the news of his wife's death: 'Tomorrow and tomorrow . . . ' was run on after 'There would have been a time for such a word' (to the detriment of the sense of the rest of the speech), and Macbeth broke down in naked grief and abject terror. The black room had virtually become the inside of his own head; spears cracked into its walls like death blows, Macduff burst (somewhat melodramatically) through the floorboards in a puff of smoke, and Macbeth died ignominiously, on stage.

Like Adrian Noble's *Macbeth*, Terry Hands's *Julius Caesar* (which opened the Stratford season) employed little stage furniture, as if to throw emphasis on the play's inner drama. It was in the same line as a number of this director's productions of other plays, such as *Coriolanus* (1977) and *Othello* (1985), in its use of a pared-down, visually simple production style, with a tendency to stylization, to the use of generalized symbols, and to underpopulation of the stage. The vast set was the stage and walls of the theatre itself, lined with thousands of bricks. There were brilliantly pictorial lighting effects, the storm was spectacular in its flashes of lightning and sharp cracks of thunder (but distracted attention from what was being said), and follow-spots were constantly used to highlight faces. The principal visual symbol was a large statue of Caesar which dominated the opening scenes; after Caesar's death, the shadow of this statue and, at other times, of a Roman eagle was projected on to the back wall. This reinforced the play's concern with the consequences as well as the causes of the assassination, as did the presence of Caesar's reanimated corpse stalk-

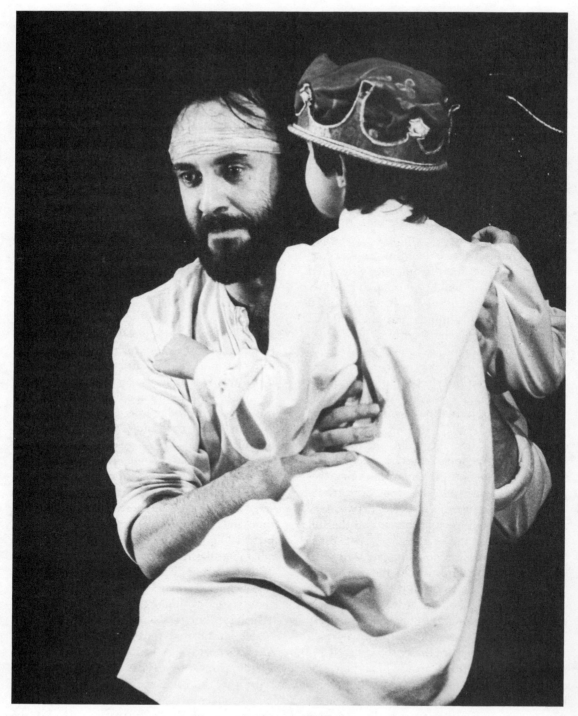

11 *Macbeth*. Royal Shakespeare Theatre, 1986, and Barbican Theatre, 1987. Macbeth (Jonathan Pryce) holds one of the children representing the apparitions in Act 4 Scene 1

12 *Julius Caesar*. Royal Shakespeare Theatre, 1987. Caesar (David Waller) at the beginning of the assassination scene, Act 3 Scene 1. (Joseph O'Conor later took over the role)

ing the field of battle. Otherwise the stage was bare of furnishings except for the quarrel scene, where we had a large, graceful tent, a brazier, and a few stools and chairs. Virtually, the characters existed in a void, with no social setting. Costumes were drained of colour – almost entirely black and white – and more or less uniform in design. Action, too, was often stylized. At the opening of the assassination scene Caesar entered first, alone, to be followed by the other characters filing on from both sides of the stage and then parading forward, goose-stepping behind him. The moment of assassination had an almost balletic quality, and was accompanied by music. Later, too, as Brutus addressed the citizens of Rome, his fellow conspirators stood in stylized poses behind him.

This threw a heavy burden of responsibility on the performers, who tended to adopt a stagily rhetorical style, with large gestures and full vocalization; it suited Caesar's self-dramatization, and Joseph O'Conor filled in the outlines of the role with warm humanity.[3] Roger Allam, as Brutus, had a similar quality – a sympathetic presence, natural earnestness, a well modulated voice with easy command of the verse, though even he resorted at times to rant, especially in the quarrel. His Brutus managed at once to be noble and self-deceived, a man who had turned his rhetoric on himself and was guiltily aware of the speciousness of his reasoning. In Sean Baker's Cassius, technique was uppermost to the point of mannerism; the actor seemed to have found no point of human contact with the character.

The principal casualty of the director's sty-

---

[3] David Waller played the role in the earlier part of the season; I did not see his performance.

lization was the Forum scene, in which the audience, supplemented by a few pre-recorded shouts, was required to stand in for the people of Rome. This was taking minimalism too far. Though Nicholas Farrell was an incisive Antony, both he and Brutus, deprived of the reactions of their hearers, were reduced to the status of actors demonstrating their skills at an audition, and the play lost an important dimension. What sense of climax can Antony induce with 'Now let it work . . . ' (*Caesar*, 3.2.253) if we have not seen the inflamed plebeians rushing off to 'burn his body in the holy place, / And with the brands fire the traitors' houses' (*Caesar*, 3.2.247–8)?

This production had considerable pace. The decision to play it without an interval justified itself in making us conscious of the importance of Caesar in the overall sweep of the action. The play's structure was clearly laid before us, its rhetoric was vividly presented, characters were boldly sketched. What was missing was a sense of Rome – of a densely populated city whose inhabitants form an important section of the community of characters – and of fully realized human relationships.

There was no shortage of extras in David Hare's National Theatre production of *King Lear* (which opened in December 1986). He positioned them tidily over the wide open spaces of the Olivier stage like chessmen, but all too often they – and indeed all of the principals when they were not speaking – simply stood, impassively oblivious to what was going on around them. David Hare seemed to be treating the play (which he gave in a slightly abbreviated version of the traditional, conflated text) as a kind of staged oratorio. There was a background of three vast screens, scroll-like in form, billowing like sails, on to which a stormy, moonlit cloudscape was projected before the action began. Costumes were eclectic in style and period. Little effort was made to convey differences in social status, either through costumes or accents. The King of France wore an expensive-looking raincoat. Lear himself was unregally dressed, and there was no suggestion that he ruled through ceremony or ritual.

As in the RSC's recent productions of tragedies, stage furnishings were kept to an austere minimum, with a few significant exceptions. Servants carried on a large wooden map of Britain like a table jigsaw, cut into three parts, for the division of the kingdom and again at the end. Kent's stocks were mounted on a cart, and the mock-trial was played on a double-levelled structure suggesting the interior of a hovel. Symbolic production devices appeared from time to time. As Lear spoke 'Let me not stay a jot for dinner', an assortment of animal carcasses moulded in plaster descended from above to hang suspended in mid-air, along with a trapeze bearing a life-size image of a naked, two-headed hermaphrodite garlanded with leaves and suckling a baby which it was about to stab. When Edgar declared his intention to disguise himself, seven bedlam beggars trotted on and gibbered beside him for a few seconds before trotting off again; no more was heard or seen of them. The statue, however, returned during the war scenes, human corpses replacing the animal carcasses; images of corpses were also spreadeagled over the siege engines and other instruments of war. These devices seemed like half-hearted attempts to suggest on the one hand a social context for the action, and on the other a symbolic significance for it. Neither was followed through.

The absence of social setting along with a production style that discouraged emotional interaction – Anna Massey's powerful Goneril and all the onlookers remained impassive even during Lear's curse – made it difficult for the actors to establish character. We had a colourlessly lachrymose Cordelia, a didactic, unentertaining Fool who spoke all his songs, a glamorous but shallow Edmund, and a silly-ass Edgar who became paraplegic as Poor Tom and did nothing to establish an essential reality underlying the character's shifting personae.

13 *King Lear*. Olivier Theatre, 1986. King Lear (Anthony Hopkins) rages against Goneril (Anna Massey) in Act 1 Scene 4

Perhaps the director was aiming at a Brechtian absence of involvement. Certainly more lines and actions than usual provoked laughter, among them Lear's 'But I'll not chide thee', Gloucester's ''Tis the time's plague, when madmen lead the blind', his fall and his question 'have I fallen or no?', several of Lear's speeches to blind Gloucester, Goneril's sexual straddling of the wounded Edmund, even Albany's 'That's but a trifle here'. Michael Bryant's unlyrical but clear and forceful Gloucester showed little suffering in the horrifically staged blinding scene, but was moving in his penitent recollection 'If Edgar live . . . '

If the production had an interpretative emphasis it appeared to be on Lear's failure as a father. There was a sense of familial contempt in his treatment of his elder daughters; he stuck his tongue out at Goneril at the end of the curse, but then kissed her passionately on 'I'll resume the shape which thou dost think / I have cast off for ever'. In a partly comic display of choler before 'reason not the need' he nearly came to blows with Regan, and on 'No, you unnatural hags' assaulted her. This was particularly striking in a production in which physical contact was rare, and hints of incest in the relationship with Goneril were inescapable, but there was none of the consistent exploration of a psychological subtext such as characterized Adrian Noble's *Macbeth*. Anthony Hopkins's Lear, grizzled, shaven-headed, plebeian, impressive in anger, touching in his grief for the dead Cordelia, had a warmth deriving from the actor's ability to convey intimacy even in the cold, open spaces of the Olivier Theatre, but the character's disintegration was inadequately conveyed, there seemed no reason why this Lear should say 'Does any here know me?' since there had been no sense of growing dislocation in his dismissive, comic attitude to the Fool during the preceding episode, and too often lines were spoken as if learned by rote, one sentence following fractionally too quickly after another for us to believe that they came from the man himself.

I never see a performance in the Olivier Theatre without being made conscious of the demands made by the building. Most actors seem to feel a need to extend themselves vocally, sometimes to the point of strain. The size of the stage discourages intimacy; the fan-shaped spread of the seating requires sets that are open at the sides, and acting that radiates in different directions simultaneously. The high open space above the stage level creates a void unless positive use is made of it (which may help to explain those suspended corpses in David Hare's *King Lear*). It is not easy to create a sense of communication between the stage and the nether reaches of the auditorium.

Such a theatre space has decisive effects on the style in which plays are presented within it. Sir Peter Hall's ample experience of its exigencies no doubt contributed to make his 1987 production of *Antony and Cleopatra* the most successful of his Shakespeare productions at the National, even though there were still signs of strain in his theatrical realization of this demanding play. As has been his custom at the National, Sir Peter used a full text. I cannot in all honesty say that my attention was uniformly gripped throughout the long evening, but I should hesitate before blaming this on the production. *Antony and Cleopatra* has its longueurs; it appears to have been printed from a pre-performance script, and it would not be surprising if Shakespeare and his fellows tightened it up at rehearsal.

It was appropriate that a Jacobean reconstruction of the classical world should be projected in the visual terms of Renaissance art.

Alison Chitty designed a great, bronzed, crescent-shaped structure that could define a manageable acting area, but was capable also of rearranging itself to suggest changes of location, and of retreating altogether when the full stage area was needed. It was tall enough to occupy some of the void over the stage and to provide an upper level for Cleopatra's monument, and it incorporated a massive central doorway. Colour-coded costumes – browns and red for Egypt, a cold blue for Rome – suggested Veronese or Titian. The second part of the play opened with a clamorous realization of the stage direction calling for the noise of a sea-fight, and the battle scenes encompassed the audience, with processional entries down the aisles and trumpet blasts from the raised extremities of the stage, uncomfortably close to some of the spectators. The event was theatrical in the grand style that the auditorium demands; it shared something of the stylization observed elsewhere in its avoidance of naturalism in setting and furnishings, but was humanized by a mode of production that gave the actors every opportunity to exploit to the full that interest in the idiosyncrasies, the rich irrationality of human behaviour that Shakespeare indulges in his late Plutarchan plays.

Political realities were not neglected. Social status was more sharply differentiated than in *King Lear*; we were aware of royal abundance, of events with momentous, international consequences. But, from the moment that the central doors opened to reveal Cleopatra riding on Antony's shoulders as a prelude to a scene of riotously heated sensuality, we never forgot that these events were controlled by desperately mortal human beings. Anthony Hopkins, indeed, was more convincingly the 'old ruffian' than the noble warrior. In his bluff humanity he contrasted strongly with Tim Pigott-Smith's neurotically frigid Octavius, frightened of physical contact with all but his sister. The contrast was most apparent during the song on Pompey's galley, when Antony

14   *Antony and Cleopatra*. Olivier Theatre, 1987. Cleopatra (Judi Dench) and Antony (Anthony Hopkins) in
Act 1 Scene 1

taunted Octavius into comradelinesss, pulling him to the ground, tugging at his boots, holding him down and tickling him. There was no difficulty in believing that this Antony could inspire loyalty among his troops, but he did not rise to the heights of 'Where souls do couch on flowers' – a passage that stays in my mind with a strange, unearthly beauty from Olivier's performance as long ago as 1951, spoken, as I remember, with arms outstretched in an idealized vision of an Elysian future with the woman he believed to be dead. Rather similarly, though Michael Bryant as Enobarbus was able to draw on all his long experience of the Olivier Theatre to give a wonderful, unbuttoned ease to his description of Cleopatra in the barge, growing increasingly absorbed in the reality of his

memories until he had almost physically to shake himself free of the enchantment, he made little of the mystery of his death.

It was Judi Dench, as Cleopatra, who brought greatness to the production in a feat of classical acting by which she extended herself into every aspect of the role, from the sordid to the sublime, while never losing the sense of a unifying self that could encompass Cleopatra's 'infinite variety'. From her first appearance, this was clearly a woman of volatile passions, physically restless, richly sensual yet with a shrewd, instinctive intelligence that probed suspiciously, vulnerably, behind the appearances with which she was presented. As we should expect from this actress, the comedy of the role was realized with perfect timing and brilliant transitions; as she questioned the

15 *Titus Andronicus*. Swan Theatre, 1987. Titus (Brian Cox) is borne in by his captives (from the left) Aaron
(Peter Polycarpou), Chiron (Richard McCabe), Demetrius (Piers Ibbotson), and Alarbus (Stephen Eliot) in Act 1
Scene 1; Tamora (Estelle Kohler), who is at the end of the chain held by Titus, stands directly behind him. The sons of
Titus are positioned behind the ladder upon which he sits, and enter beating their swords on it; they are (from left to
right) Mutius (Sean Pertwee, behind Aaron), Martius (Linus Roache), Quintus (Ian Bailey), and Lucius
(Derek Hutchinson, behind Alarbus)

messenger about Octavia, her self-confidence grew until, at 'I do think she's thirty', the smile froze on her face and, gathering her skirts, she swirled abruptly round and almost left the stage. But the poetry of the role, too, was fully realized, climactically when, her restlessness subdued, she spoke 'I dreamt there was an Emperor Antony . . . ' with rapt, hushed lyricism to a Dolabella who stood in the auditorium aisle with his back to us, so that she was addressing us as well as him. At moments such as these an audience, even in the Olivier auditorium, can be united in a single emotion.

At the opposite extreme from the splendour of the National's *Antony and Cleopatra*, Deborah Warner's *Titus Andronicus*, in the

Swan Theatre at Stratford-upon-Avon, offered no theatrical glamour, none of the allurements of pageantry or of sumptuous costumes with which directors have sometimes sugared what they have obviously regarded as a bitter pill of a play. Her staging, which seemed based on the most austere interpretation of Elizabethan methods, could have been transferred with little difficulty into a reconstruction of the Globe, which too could have offered an upper level, a stage pit, and such basic properties as coffins, ropes, a ladder, and a dinner table. Yet the production resembled Peter Hall's of *Antony* in that it seemed exceptionally 'straight', one in which the director did not appear – like Bogdanov –

178

to be inviting us to see modern parallels to the action, or – like Alexander and Noble – to be probing a subtext for psychological resonances. The text was given, exceptionally, with no cuts – even Peter Brook's 1955 production that restored the play to theatrical respectability cut some 650 lines. The violence was not shirked; there was none of the escape into burlesque that has appealed to both critics and directors as an evasion of the play's grimmer aspects. Only the fact that Titus' chopped-off hand and his sons' severed heads were represented by stuffed cloth bags lessened the physical representation of horror; Peter Brook had the sons killed off-stage, but here we saw their murder, and the blood flowed. The director had worked on the premise that everything in the text was there for a purpose, that the dramatist knew what he was about. There was even a degree of pedantry in her determination to test the text at every point with relentless rigour; yet the result was overwhelmingly impressive.

Of course, the production's apparent simplicity was not uncalculated. The play presents a twin problem. How do you stage its horrors – murder, rape, mutilation, cannibalism – without driving the audience over the bounds of credulity into giggling hysteria? And how, on the other hand, do you cope with its self-conscious literariness – the Latin quotations, the extended similes, the long, rhetorical speeches uttered by characters who according to any normal standards of behaviour should be capable of nothing but shocked speechlessness or hysterical incoherence? Deborah Warner's approach to these problems revealed the hand of an immensely skilful, even cunning, director. The rhetoric was plumbed for its deep sources, which were then brought to the surface so that even the most artificial verbal structures became expressive of emotion. Marcus' description of Lavinia immediately after her rape may read like a heartless verbal exercise by a bright boy from the local grammar school; spoken in

Donald Sumpter's hushed tones it became a deeply moving attempt to master the facts, and thus to overcome the emotional shock, of a previously unimagined horror. We had the sense of a suspension of time, as if the speech represented an articulation, necessarily extended in expression, of a sequence of thoughts and emotions that might have taken no more than a second or two to flash through the character's mind, like a bad dream.

Inappropriate laughter was avoided by the exploitation of all the genuine comedy latent in the text – along with a little that Shakespeare had not thought of. Brian Cox established Titus as a credible, human character by making him a bit of a card – an odd, shambling hero, very much a law unto himself. In the opening scene he started to paw Tamora, then slapped his cheek as if to remind himself of his unburied sons. He defensively isolated the second line of:

> Romans, of five and twenty valiant sons –
> Half of the number that King Priam had

as if to counter accusations of excessive breeding. And he stuffed his fingers into his ears, pretending not to hear his brother and sons pleading for Mutius' burial. Estelle Kohler, as Tamora, and her two sons played her bombastic accusation of Bassianus as if it were a burlesque playlet put on for their victims' entertainment; Demetrius' sudden stabbing of Bassianus seemed all the more horrific as a result. Acknowledgement of the comedy in the situation when Titus, Lucius, and Marcus squabble over who shall have the honour of losing a hand in the hope of saving Titus' sons intensified the pain of the moment when Titus outwits the others by getting Aaron to mutilate him while they have gone to fetch an axe.

This method reached a climax in the extraordinary, emblematic 'fly' scene when Titus, driven to madness, berates his brother for having killed 'a poor, harmless fly'. Marcus, seeking an excuse, claims that he did so only because 'it was a black ill-favoured fly, / Like

16   *Titus Andronicus*. Swan Theatre, 1987. Titus (Brian Cox) speaks to the mutilated Lavinia (Sonia Ritter) in Act 3 Scene 1

to the Empress' Moor'; Brian Cox made a marvellous moment of the transition, represented in the text only by 'O, O, O', from the tragicomic absurdity of his initial reaction, through dawning acceptance of the validity of Marcus' excuse, to the ferocity of frustrated despair with which he cast himself on the table, repeatedly stabbing at his enemy's surrogate. This was masterly acting.

In the last scene, the director permitted herself a wordless interpolation: servants whistled a merry tune as they carried on the furniture for the Thyestean banquet. It was what Romeo calls a 'lightning before death', a sudden shift of perspective of an authentically Shakespearian kind, like the introduction of the Clown in the closing episodes of *Antony and Cleopatra* (and, indeed, of *Titus*). I should never have imagined that the subsequent stretch of action, in which Titus kills his own daughter (sickeningly) to rescue her from her

shame, and then, within the space of three lines, kills Tamora and is himself killed by her husband, who is then killed by Titus' son, could have been so chilling in its effect. The chorus of servants played its part, squatting in ranks to each side of the stage before the pie was served ('Welcome, all', said Titus to the inhabitants of the pie, with a last touch of macabre humour), stretching forward in horror at the death of Lavinia, bending as Titus stabbed Tamora, gasping as Saturninus killed Titus, and finally rushing off through the audience as Lucius killed the Emperor. This choric action both directed and channelled off the audience's reactions.

The Swan Theatre seems to concentrate the attention of players in minor as well as major roles. Saturninus might profitably have been more colourfully played, and it seemed perverse to give the role of Aaron to an actor who looks Greek instead of the raven-black Moor of the text, but Richard McCabe was a giggling, psychotic Chiron, Sonia Ritter a quiveringly traumatized Lavinia, Estelle Kohler a stingingly waspish Tamora. Brian Cox searchingly explored the role of Titus in a performance of unremitting concentration and impassioned integrity. He found the shape of the role in a manner that defined the movement of the play, achieving ever-increasing intensity of suffering up to the mirthless laughter with which he preceded the line 'Why, I have not another tear to shed', and playing the rest of the role on an upward curve as Titus found release in the action needed to effect his revenge, marvellously gleeful with his comrades in the scene with the arrows, desperately cunning in his assumed madness.

Like any strong production, this one impelled its audience to revalue the play. *Titus Andronicus* stood in greater need of revaluation than most of its author's works, and this production gave it what it needed at this point in its history. It emerged as a far more deeply serious play than its popular reputation would suggest, a play that is profoundly concerned with both the personal and the social consequences of violence rather than one that cheaply exploits their theatrical effectiveness. I was impressed as never before by the art of its structuring: its twin climaxes of violence, one directed at Titus, the other directed by him; by the force of the counteraction, led by Lucius; and by the part played within the whole by details of language, such as the recurrent, increasingly horrific emphasis on 'hand' and 'hands' (between them, the words occur some seventy times). This production increased my respect, too, for the play's first audiences; groundlings who made this play popular, if they experienced it in full, were not merely seeking cheap thrills. It did not emerge as an unflawed masterpiece in this revelatory production, but subsequent directors will have far less excuse than before for evading its problems by textual adaptation or by evasive theatricalism.

PROFESSIONAL SHAKESPEARE PRODUCTIONS IN THE BRITISH ISLES, JANUARY–DECEMBER 1986

compiled by

N. RATHBONE

The list includes some amateur productions and adaptations. Information is taken from programmes, supplemented by reviews, held in the Birmingham Shakespeare Library. Details have been verified wherever possible, but the nature of the material prevents corroboration in every case.

ANTONY AND CLEOPATRA

Theatre Clwyd, Mold; Theatre Royal, Haymarket: 26 May 1986–
Directors: Toby Robertson and Christopher Selbie
Designer: Simon Higlett
Cleopatra: Vanessa Redgrave
Antony: Timothy Dalton
See *Shakespeare Survey 40* (1988), pp. 181–3. Played in repertory with *The Taming of the Shrew*.

AS YOU LIKE IT

Royal Exchange Company, Manchester: 9 Jan.–15 Feb.; and tour 7 April–17 May 1986
Director: Nicholas Hytner
Designer: Di Seymour
Rosalind: Janet McTeer
See *Shakespeare Survey 40* (1988), p. 174.

RSC at The Barbican, London, in rep: 12 Dec. 1985–
Director: Adrian Noble
Designer: Bob Crowley
Rosalind: Juliet Stevenson

See *Shakespeare Survey 39* (1987), pp. 199–203, for a review of this production's Stratford run.

TAG Theatre Company, Citizens' Theatre, Glasgow, at the Edinburgh Festival; and tour: 18 Aug.–10 Oct. 1986
Director: Ian Brown
Designer: Stewart Laing
An adaptation for seven actors, incorporating music and dance.

THE COMEDY OF ERRORS

Wolsey Theatre, Ipswich: 29 Jan. 1986–
Director: Antony Tuckey
Designer: David Knapman
Music: Martin Waddington

Lyric Players Theatre, Belfast: 22 Jan.–15 Feb. 1986
Director: Patrick Sandford

Tavistock Repertory Company at The Tower, Cannonbury, Islington: 11–18 Oct. 1986; and Rokoko Theatre, Prague Sept. 1986

Theatre Set Up based in Enfield: tour 12 June–6 Sept. 1986
Directors: Wendy MacPhee, Frank Jarvis
Costumes: Joan Field
Open air performances in National Trust and other venues. Simply staged, fast moving, and well thought out.

CORIOLANUS

Kick Theatre Company at The Almeida, Islington, 17 Sept.–11 Oct. 1986; and tour

Director: Deborah Warner
Performed in a ring of boxes, with a cast of twelve. Simple costumes in whites, browns, and greys. Uncut text. Reviews praised the direction.

HAMLET

The National Theatre workshop production at the Cottesloe, London; and tour Nov. 1985–March 1986
Director: Cicely Berry
Designer: Chris Dyer
Hamlet: Tim McInnery
A slightly cut text, performed with minimal props, in casual clothes, emphasizing the language. Reviews found Hamlet neurotic and unsympathetic, and the pace of the production rather slow, though with useful insights into the text.

Octagon Theatre, Bolton: 29 Jan.–22 Feb. 1986
Director: John Adams
Designer: Mick Beamish
Hamlet: Douglas Hodge
The set might be part of war-torn Beirut and the production emphasized political uncertainties and violence. Fortinbras was seen as a potential threat, and his assumption of power became a coup.

The Young Vic, London: 22 May–21 June 1986
Director: Ian Thompson
Designer: Jackie Pilford
Hamlet: Madeline Bellamy
A cut text, played on a minimal set. Reviews generally found this a slow, disappointing production, which gained nothing from casting a female Hamlet.

Actors' Touring Company: June–Dec. 1986
Director: Mark Brinkman
Designer: Angie Dove
Hamlet: Simon Binns
Ophelia: Irene McDougall
Polonius: Paddy Fletcher

Claudius/Ghost: Clive Kneller
Cut text, played in modern dress. Played as a fast-paced thriller, emphasizing the sexual aspects of the play. The Ghost, dressed as a blind man, frequently appeared as an observer. The acting was consistently of a high standard, and reviews were mixed, but generally favourable.

Rollercoaster Theatre Company at the Duke of Wellington, London: Aug. 1986
Director: Robert Chevara
Hamlet: Rikki Beadle-Blair
A traditional presentation, but with a black actor playing Hamlet.

Oxford Playhouse Company, Oxford: 29 Sept.–11 Oct. 1986; and tour including Edinburgh, Elsinore, and Israel 3 Aug. 1986–
Director: Richard Williams
Designer: Nadine Baylis
Hamlet: David Threlfall (David Acton in Wolverhampton)
Polonius: Richard Kay
A cut version, which omitted the instructions to the players, played on a stark, black set, in a mannered, eighteenth-century Court. There was a chorus of black-cloaked, white-faced, tricorn-hatted courtiers, and no tangible ghost, in a production which emphasized Hamlet's madness. Polonius was given unusual authority and competence.

London Shakespeare Group at Croydon Warehouse Theatre, Croydon: 14–18 Oct. 1986; and tour of Japan 10 Nov.–13 Dec.
Director: John Fraser
Designers: John Fraser, Stephanie Howard
Hamlet: Rob Edwards
Ophelia: Amanda Waring

Hamlet Improvised, Marginal Bard Productions at The Village Theatre and Café Theatre, Cricklewood: 16 Nov.–21 Dec. 1986
Director: Kevin Carr
Spontaneous Shakespeare based on audience suggestion. Different actors improvised every week.

HENRY IV

Albion Theatre Company, British tour April–
June 1986; American tour July 10–
Directors: Peter Geddis, Andrew Killim
(Adapted by Andrew Killim for a cast of five.)
Henry IV and Falstaff: Mike Shannon
Hal: Steve Morley
A fast, naturalistic production, with some con-
fusion caused by doubling.

HENRY IV PTS 1 AND 2, HENRY V

English Shakespeare Company at the Theatre
Royal, Plymouth: première of an 11 city tour
on 3 Nov. 1986; Old Vic, London: 16 March
1986–; and tour of France and Germany 1986,
Toronto and New York 1987.
Directors: Michael Pennington, Michael
Bogdanov
Designers: Chris Dyer, Stephanie Howard
Hal: Michael Pennington
Falstaff: John Woodvine
Henry IV: Patrick O'Connell
The first presentation of the cycle since 1975.
See pages 159–62 of this volume.

HENRY V

National Youth Theatre at Regent's Park
Open Air Theatre: Sept. 1986
Director: Michael Croft
Henry V: Hakeem Kae-Kazim

HENRY VIII

The Norwich Players at The Maddermarket
Theatre, Norwich: 7–15 Nov. 1986
Director: Ian Emmerson
Designer: John Warden
Music: Clive Anderson

JULIUS CAESAR

Vanessa Ford Productions, tour: autumn 1986
(with *King Lear*)
Director: David Wylde
Designer: David Collis

Mark Antony: Philip York
Brutus: James Cormac
Setting suggested sometimes Fascist Italy,
sometimes Stalinist Russia. Weapons ranged
from swords to sub-machine guns. Heavily
cut text.

Young Vic at The Cut, London: 13 Nov.–20
Dec. 1986
Director: David Thacker
Designer: Fran Thompson
Brutus: Corin Redgrave
A bare, wooden set; black and grey Puritan
costumes.

KING LEAR

Nottingham Playhouse: 3–26 April 1986
Director: Andrew Hay
Designer: Ruari Marchison
Lear: Russell Dixon

Vanessa Ford Productions: tour autumn 1986
(with *Julius Caesar*)
Director: Peter Dews
Designer: David Collis
Lear: Nigel Davenport
Edmund: Jon Finch
Fool: John Warner
Setting used black drapes with minimal props;
costumes were brown uniforms of no par-
ticular period. A rather static production.

New Victoria Theatre, Newcastle under
Lyme: 5 Nov. 1986–
Director: Peter Cheeseman
Designer: Peter King
Lear: Clive Swift

The National Theatre at The Olivier Theatre,
London: 11 Dec. 1986–11 Nov. 1987
Director: David Hare
Designer: Hayden Griffin
Lear: Anthony Hopkins
See pages 174–6 in this volume.

MACBETH

Everyman Theatre, Liverpool: 30 Jan.–1
March 1986

Director: Glen Walford
Designer: Claire Lyth
Macbeth: Ralph Brown
Lady Macbeth: Karen Mann
A fast-moving *Macbeth*, with punk witches, emphasizing supernatural effects and blood, but minimizing poetry.

New Horseshoes Theatre Company at the Basingstoke Haymarket, Basingstoke: 13–29 March 1986
Director: Ian Mullins
Designer: Stephen Howell
Macbeth: Keith Drinkel
Lady Macbeth: Maev Alexander

Compass Theatre Company, Sheffield, at the Edinburgh Festival; and tour April–Oct. 1986, Feb.–June 1987
Director: Neil Sissons
Macbeth: Nick Chadwin
Lady Macbeth: Jilly Bond
Included the use of mime and masks. Six performers and minimal props concentrating on the language.

Elsie and Norm's Macbeth, by John Christopher Wood, Birmingham Repertory and Bristol Express Theatre Company, at Birmingham: 6–29 March; and tour April–Nov. 1986
Jan Shand and John Grex (John Wood) – a take-off of *Macbeth* for two players, set in a suburban living room.

Northcott Theatre, Exeter: 8–26 April 1986
Director: George Roman
Designer: Sean Cavanagh
Macbeth: Pip Miller
Lady Macbeth: Nina Holloway
An all-purpose set on several levels, with five main acting areas, heavily daubed in red. Seductive witches. Modern dress production, using commando uniforms.

Footsbarn Theatre Company, world première in Adelaide, Australia: March 1986; U.K. tour 14 Oct.–9 Nov. 1986; Footsbarn also toured France and Germany

Sets, staging, props: David Hayter, Spencer Mead, Bruno Hocquard
Footsbarn act as a co-operative, with no director or named actors in particular parts. The production, developed in Australia, drew on primitive tribal culture. Mime, dance, half masks, headdresses and bodypaint, drum and pipe music were used. An unusually protracted Porter's scene gave very effective comic relief.

Torch Theatre, Milford Haven: 23 Oct.–15 Nov. 1986
Director: Les Miller
Designer: Terry Brown
Macbeth: Rob Dixon
Lady Macbeth: Joanna Foster

Royal Lyceum, Edinburgh: 7–29 Nov. 1986
Director: Jules Wright
Designer: Colin MacNeil
Macbeth: Jonathan Hyde
Lady Macbeth: Judy Covington
A grey-green box set was used, with full height slat doors at the back, which opened to reveal Malcolm's army. The storm effects in Scene 1 and the banquet slightly overpowered the dialogue.

RSC at the Main House, Stratford: première 6 Nov. 1986–
Director: Adrian Noble
Designer: Bob Crowley
Macbeth: Jonathan Pryce
Lady Macbeth: Sinead Cusack
See pages 170–1 of this volume

Nightshriek, by Trisha Ward (a revised version of *Rocbeth*, a musical), at the Shaw Theatre, London: to 6 Sept. 1986
Director: Edward Wilson
Designer: Brian Lee

THE MERCHANT OF VENICE

Haymarket Studio, Leicester; and Almeida, Islington: 16 Jan.–29 April 1986
Director: Michael Joyce

Designer: Stephanie Howard
Shylock/Lorenzo: David Fielder
Seven players doubled up in a light, humorous production. Costumes were Edwardian; Antonio was given a suggestion of homosexuality. The clowns were heavily cut.

Actors' Co-op at Stranmillis College Theatre, Belfast: March 1986
Director/Antonio: Paddy Scully
Shylock: Niall Cusack
Modern dress production.

RSC, Natwest regional tour: 6 Oct. 1986–7 Feb. 1987 (with *Much Ado About Nothing*)
Director: Roger Mitchell
Designer: Di Seymour
Shylock: Nigel Terry

THE MERRY WIVES OF WINDSOR

RSC at The Barbican, London, in rep: 23 Jan.–25 Sept. 1986
Director: Bill Alexander
Designer: William Dudley
See *Shakespeare Survey 39* (1987), pp. 197–9, for a review of this production's Stratford run.

A MIDSUMMER NIGHT'S DREAM

Cheek by Jowl at the Donmar Warehouse, London: 17 March–5 April 1986; and tour
Director: Declan Donnellan
Designer: Nick Ormerod
Oberon/Theseus: Martin Turner
Titania/Hippolyta: Anne White
A modern setting production, using nostalgic twenties songs, with the Mechanicals as an amateur dramatic group, Flute and Quince played by women, and Bottom as a curate.

Contact Theatre, Manchester: 24 April–17 May 1986
Director: Anthony Clark
Designer: Kate Burnett
Music: Mark Vibrans
Oberon/Theseus: Malcolm Hebden
Titania/Hippolyta: Jenny Howe

A production in the round, with costumes and setting influenced by Picasso's circus pictures, emphasizing the surreal and psychological aspects of the play.

The Young Vic at The Cut, London: 1 May–7 June 1986; also workshops
Directors: David Thacker, Jeremy Bell
Designers: Shelagh Keegan, Jessica Bowles
Hippolyta/Titania: Estelle Kohler
Theseus/Oberon: Clive Arrindell
Simple artificial grass set and costumes in plain colours. A punk Puck, in a production which treated the play as sexual farce.

The Norwich Players at The Maddermarket Theatre, Norwich: June 1986
Director: Dave Harris
Designer: John Warden
Song settings: Nicci Parslow
A black and silver late Victorian art nouveau setting, placing the action in the Indian army.

Royal Lyceum, Edinburgh: 27 June 1986–
Director: Ian Wooldridge
Designer: Gregory Smith
Oberon/Theseus: Neil Cunningham
Titania/Hippolyta: Vivien Dixon
Bottom: Roland Oliver
A woodland setting, with costumes influenced by the East. The production emphasized the poetry.

Regent's Park Open Air Theatre, London: June 1986
Directors: David Conville and Emma Freud
Designer: Simon Higlett
Music: Gary Yershon
Bottom: Bernard Breslaw
A revival of Toby Robertson's 1985 production, staged by a group of strolling players, dressed in late Victorian costume, with rather punk fairies. The production emphasized pantomime, slapstick elements in the play.

Aba Duba Company at The Canal Café Theatre, London: 1–20 July 1986

Bottom's Dream; or, The Midsummer Nightmare.
An adaptation by Ailine Waites and Robin
Hunter.

RSC at the Main House, Stratford: première
3 July 1986–
Director: Bill Alexander
Designer: William Dudley
Titania/Hippolyta: Janet McTeer
Oberon: Gerard Murphy
See *Shakespeare Survey 40* (1988), pp. 173–4.

Everyman Theatre, Cheltenham: 18 Sept.–11
Oct. 1986
Director: Phyllida Lloyd
Designers: Peter Appleton, Chris Crosswell
Score: Gary Yershon: acoustic music
Puck: Madeline Church
A high-tech production, using an acoustic set
of 'sound sculptures' made of suspended metal
rods, on which the cast 'play'. Costumes were
white, nuclear age suits, with green linings,
and dark glasses. The play-in-a-play was pre-
sented as though by Coward.

St. Georges Theatre, London: 21 Oct. 1986–
Director: George Murcell
Music: Philip Thorby
Oberon/Theseus: Michael Sadler
Titania/Hippolyta: Leigh Funnell

MUCH ADO ABOUT NOTHING

London Theatre of the Imagination, tour 7–21
April 1986; also workshops
Benedick: Clive Kneller
Beatrice: Julia Munrow
London Theatre of the Imagination is a co-
operative, and has no director.
Eight actors, doubling up, in a fast, though
uneven production.

RSC, Natwest regional tour: 6 Oct. 1986–
7 Feb. 1987 (with *Merchant of Venice*)
Director: Ron Daniels
Designer: Di Seymour
Beatrice: Fiona Shaw
Benedick: Nigel Terry

OTHELLO

RSC at The Barbican, London, in rep: 2 Jan.–
Director: Terry Hands
Designer: Ralph Koltai
Othello: Ben Kingsley
Iago: David Suchet
See *Shakespeare Survey 39* (1987), pp. 205–6,
for a review of this production's Stratford run.

The Tower Shakespeare Company at the
People's Palace Theatre (Queen Mary
College), London: 7–31 Oct. 1986
Directors: Rosalind King, Nigel Alexander
Othello: Wali Ajo
Uncut version of the text.

RICHARD II

RSC at the Main House, Stratford: première 4
Sept. 1986–
Director: Barry Kyle
Designer: William Dudley
Richard II: Jeremy Irons
See *Shakespeare Survey 40* (1988), pp. 180–1.

ROMEO AND JULIET

The Young Vic at The Cut, London: 6 Feb.–22
March 1986
Director: David Thacker
Designer: Anthony Dean
Costumes: Christine Rowland
Romeo: Vincenzo Ricotta
Juliet: Suzan Sylvester

Cheek by Jowl at Regent's Park Open Air
Theatre, London: 2 June 1986–
Director: Declan Donnellan
Designer: Nick Ormerod
Romeo: Ralph Fiennes
Juliet: Sarah Woodward
Late Victorian/Edwardian costumes. Mercu-
tio was presented as homosexual. Some
reviews praised the production's irony, others
criticized the production as lacking romance.

RSC at the Main House, Stratford: première
31 March–

Director: Michael Bogdanov
Designer: Chris Dyer
Romeo: Sean Bean
Juliet: Niamh Cusack
See *Shakespeare Survey 40* (1988), pp. 178–80.

Ludlow Festival 24 June–5 July 1986
Director: Chris Hayes
Designer: Sean Cavanagh
Costumes: Sarah Greenwood
Music: Stanley Glasser
Romeo: Richard Garnett
Juliet: Abigail Cruttenden

Nutshell Productions (not a student pro-
duction) at New College, Oxford: 25 July–16
Aug. 1986
Directors: Alan Leigh, Tim Price
Designer: Alan Leigh
Romeo: Alan Leigh/Tim Price
Juliet: Sarah Finch

Caer Actors' Company, tour of Wales: 2–15
Aug. 1986
Director: Ruth Martin
Designer: Tracy Spottiswoode
Romeo: Paul Garnault
Juliet: Tracy Spottiswoode
Open air production, performed in historic
Welsh sites.

The Lyric, Hammersmith, Studio, London: 13
Aug.–6 Sept. 1986
Director/Romeo: Kenneth Branagh
Designer: Kate Burnett
Juliet: Samantha Bond
The setting comprised a scaffold and platform
between two staircases. Juliet was costumed in
1950s dress, men in red or yellow shirts, black
trousers and boots. A vigorous, naturally
spoken, rather uneven production.

Moving Being at St Stephens, Cardiff: Oct.
1986
Director: Geoff Moore
Romeo: Timothy Lyn
Juliet: Gwenith Owen
Modern-dress version. Reviewers found it
excellent in parts, though rather gimmicky.

TAMING OF THE SHREW

RSC, Natwest regional tour: 4 Dec. 1985–25
Jan. 1986
Director: Di Trevis
Designer: Pamela Howard
See *Shakespeare Survey 40* (1988), pp. 169–73.

The Medieval Players, Brentford Watermans
Arts Centre, Brentford: 13–15 March 1986
Performed on a bare stage, with few props,
and with a man as Kate.

Theatre Clwyd, Mold; Haymarket, London:
17 April–June 1986
Directors: Toby Robertson, Christopher
Selbie
Designer: Simon Higlett
Kate: Vanessa Redgrave
Petruchio: Timothy Dalton
See *Shakespeare Survey 40* (1988), p. 173.

THE TEMPEST

TNT Theatre Co-operative tour: Jan. and Feb.
1986; also toured abroad
Directors: Paul Stebbings, Alastair Cording
Tempest Now. A collaboration of actors and
classical musicians, with Simon Drake, a professional illusionist. A contemporary reflection
of *The Tempest*, focused on American involvement in Latin America.

Chichester Festival Theatre: The Sandpit, 9
Sept. 1986; the Main House, 3–4 Oct.
Director: Matthew Francis
Designer: Howard Burden
Music: Mia Soteriou
Prospero: Gordon Gostelow
Played in the round on a sand-strewn floor,
with ladders and rigging at the sides.

Northumberland Theatre Company, tour: 11
Sept.–1 Nov. 1986
Director: Ronan Patterson
Designer: Fran Thompson
Prospero: Edmund Dehn
Caliban/Ferdinand: Paul Alder
Played with six actors on a scaffold set.

Caliban was represented as a beautiful black youth. The production included an extended dance scene.

Moving Being at St. Stephens, Cardiff: 27 Nov. 1986–5 Jan. 1987
Director: Ceri Sherlock

TROILUS AND CRESSIDA

RSC at The Barbican, London, in rep: 1 May–25 Sept. 1986
Director: Howard Davies
Designer: Ralph Koltai
Costumes: Liz da Costa
Troilus: Anton Lesser
Cressida: Juliet Stevenson
See *Shakespeare Survey 39* (1987), pp. 203–5, for a review of this production's Stratford run.

TWELFTH NIGHT

Mercury Theatre, Colchester: 16 April–3 May 1986
Director: Michael Winter
Designer: Helen Scott
Lighting: Jim Bowman
Malvolio: Frank Barrie
Feste: Robert Warner
Sir Toby Belch: Robert Turnstall
A geometric, stark but beautifully lit setting. Seventeenth-century costume.

Kent Repertory Company, Hever Castle: 9–19 July 1986
Director/Designer: Richard Palmer
Malvolio: Robert Taylor
A traditional, open air production in early Stuart costume.

Elizabethan Theatre Productions, Leamington Spa; Whitefriars, Coventry; Warwick Castle: 2 July–9 Aug. 1986; production and workshops
Director: Barry Russell
Designer: John Bell
Malvolio: Christopher Campbell

Cheek by Jowl at Donmar Warehouse, London: 12 Jan.–14 Feb, and tour, Aug.–Nov. 1986
Director: Declan Donnellan
Designer: Nick Ormerod
Malvolio: Hugh Ross
Mainly black and white 1930s costume, with Aguecheek as a Texas cowboy. A very fast, musical production which emphasized the homosexual possibilities of the text intelligently.

London, National Youth Theatre at the Shaw Theatre, London: 16 Sept. 1986–
Director: Bill Buffery

Duke's Theatre, Lancaster: 8 Oct.–1 Nov. 1986; short regional tour and workshops
Director: Jonathan Petherbridge
Designer: Pip Nash
Malvolio: Bev Willis
The setting used sand, driftwood, a willow, a wrought iron gate, a toy boat, a seagull, and Father Time. Victorian costumes. The production was played for psychological realism.

Haymarket Theatre, Leicester: 1 Oct. 1986
Director: Nancy Meckler
Designer: Leslie Gilda, costumes, Dermot Hayes, set
Malvolio: Christopher Ravenscroft
The setting was a decayed segment of a many-galleried Elizabethan playhouse; costumes were a Victorian recreation of the Elizabethan period. The production was rather sombre, with low-key comic scenes.

TWO NOBLE KINSMEN; SHAKESPEARE AND FLETCHER

RSC at the Swan, Stratford: première 26 April 1986–
Director: Barry Kyle
Designer: Bob Crowley
Palamon: Gerard Murphy
Arcite: Hugh Quarshie
Gaoler's daughter: Imogen Stubbs
See *Shakespeare Survey 40* (1988), pp. 175–7.

THE WINTER'S TALE

Bradford Playhouse, Bradford: Feb. 1986
Director: Brian Otto
Leontes: Tony Priestley
Included dances based on early English styles, to contemporary music recorded on early English instruments.

The Young Company (students from the Polytechnic) at Birmingham Repertory Theatre: 3–22 March 1986
Director: Clive Perry
Designer: Chris Morley
Leontes: Peter Woodward
Reviews noted a lack of contrast between the Court/winter and rustic/summer scenes.

RSC at the Main House, Stratford: première 25 April 1986–
Director: Terry Hands
Designer: Gerard Howland
Leontes: Jeremy Irons
See *Shakespeare Survey 40* (1988), pp. 177–8.

Sherman Theatre, Cardiff: 8 Oct. 1986–
Director: Gareth Armstrong
Designer: Peter Mumford
Leontes: David Collings
Sicilia was mainly black and white, with a reflecting black wall which doubled the number of courtiers. Bohemia was verdant green. Mamillius becomes the teller of the tale, re-appearing as Time.

Miscellaneous

SHAKESPEARE: THE WORKS (LOGGERHEADS)

Nola Rae and John Mowatt, the London Mime Theatre, on tour 1986
Director/Designer: Matthew Ridout

Romeo and Juliet, mime satirizing balletic presentations; *King Lear and his Fool*; *Double, double, toil and trouble*, Anne Hathaway inspires *Macbeth*; *Hamlet*, Nola Rae hand-mime.

ACTING SHAKESPEARE

Ian McKellen at the National Theatre Studio, London: 31 Aug. 1986; following American and European tour.
Extracts from the plays.

SHAKESPEARE THROUGH THE LOOKING-GLASS, by Graham Ashe

Vanessa Ford Production, Theatre Royal Presentations at The Barbican Theatre, Plymouth: 8 Sept. 1986; and tour
Director: David Wylde
Designer: David Collis
Extracts from the plays.

Disputed plays

EDMUND IRONSIDE

Bridge Lane Theatre, London: 8 April–3 May 1986
Director: Tim Heath
Designer: Narelle Sissons
Costumes: Sara Van Loock
Music: Martyn Brabbins
Producer: Diana West
Edmund: Toby Ostrom
Uncut text, the first modern production.

See-Change Theatre Company at the Selly Oak Centre, Birmingham: summer 1986
Director: David McCormack
Designer: Fiona Henderson
Very basic costumes and considerable doubling up made the plot difficult to follow, but it was interesting to see this supposedly early Shakespeare on the stage.

THE YEAR'S CONTRIBUTIONS TO SHAKESPEARE STUDIES

1. CRITICAL STUDIES
reviewed by R. S. WHITE

OLD TIMERS

On anybody's list of great Shakespearians of the mid-twentieth century there would surely figure three names above all: C. L. Barber, Northrop Frye, and G. Wilson Knight.

C. L. Barber did not live to complete *The Whole Journey: Shakespeare's Power of Development* (Berkeley and Los Angeles: University of California Press, 1986), and it fell to Richard P. Wheeler to prepare with painstaking care the manuscript documents for publication. It is tragic that Barber did not see the result, for it is his own 'whole journey' traced through the entire Shakespearian canon. He was loved and respected as a teacher and critic, and one can see the underlying reason for this in the nostalgic attractiveness of his assumptions concerning 'Shakespeare's ideal of a gracious, organic society' (p. 124) and its violation in plays like *Richard III* and *Titus Andronicus*. Barber retrieves an image of Shakespeare as generous, 'richly sociable', and empathetic, and whether or not these qualities lay in the dramatist, they belonged to the critic. He accounts for Shakespeare in predominantly psychological terms. Shakespeare's experiences of witnessing the worldly failure of a lovable father, and being cherished by a strong mother, who was inadvertently betrayed by the weakness of her husband, are seen to feed into patterns in the plays which are regarded as an evolving canon. The pattern is implicit in *The Comedy of Errors* as the intact family is refound, but in 'the whole journey' different aspects become prominent at different times. The history plays 'avert father and son conflict' by presenting the mother as ' not redemptive but menacing', an equal threat to father and son, a process of which Falstaff is the paradoxical result. Eventual confrontation and conflict between father and son dominate the tragedies, and *Hamlet* presents the outcome in its most complex form as the father is split into benevolent (dead), natural father and threatening, evil stepfather. In the Sonnets (which Barber appears to date later than most critics) Shakespeare manifests his own identity as that of 'cherishing parent', and in the last plays 'the generous, masterful mother, giving new unity to the long-dispersed family', is placed centrally. Not only familial but social factors are seen to be relevant to Shakespeare's development: 'the polarity between his own middle-class heritage and his court-centred art' (p. 66). The book, full of richly detailed exposition, constantly opens up stimulating lines of thought. Barber seems aware, at least tacitly, of the attacks by new literary theorists on claims for 'objectivity' in literary criticism, but he wholeheartedly embraces the possibilities opened by an unashamedly personal engagement with the texts, an act of re-creation. It may turn out eventually, when the dust has settled, that great critics remain great because of their confident acceptance that if the reader has as important a presence as a text in the act of interpretation, then a full revelation of the reader's understandings may lead others along new, shareable pathways.

Northrop Frye on Shakespeare (New Haven and London: Yale University Press, 1986) comes as quite a surprise. It is basically an edited version of transcripts of Frye's lectures to undergraduates, and the result retains the qualities of an oral medium. Where his books are portentous in tone, culturally omnivorous, sometimes distant from the detail of specific texts, these chapters are quite the opposite. They are breezy and informal, obviously immensely entertaining and enlightening to their auditors, and centred on the plays. The learning is still there, but half-hidden behind a joke or aside. It is, one must admit, rather strange, after wading through Frye's scholarly contributions, to find his distinction between Old and New Comedy condensed into a lucid page (in the chapter on *A Midsummer Night's Dream*), and his theory of myths of comedy and tragedy presented in a paragraph here and there (in chapters on *King Lear* and *Measure for Measure*), as if there were nothing at all difficult to grasp about them. There are times when the cultural anthropologist comes to the fore, as in his graphs of 'the Lear world', and occasionally there are characteristically Christian, even bib-lical readings, but by and large there is a refreshing concentration on dramatic moments. While displaying respect for Bradley, Frye in his Introduction reveals his own distinctive concentration, not on char-acter, but on situation: 'Obviously [Shake-speare] starts with the total situation and lets the characters unfold from it, like leaves on a branch, part of the branch but responsive to every tremor of wind that blows over them' (p. 4). We could hardly have a better descrip-tion of Frye's own enterprise in his more

theoretical works. He may take a play here and there, as if inspecting leaves, but it is the tree, the total cultural 'situation', that really pre-occupies him. At times in this book he seems to oversimplify the intricacies of the dramatic text, but it is refreshing to see behind the formidable reputation to a very engaging per-sonality who clearly has the capacity to enthuse and inspire students engaged in the study of Shakespeare.

For a tremor of wind in the world of criti-cism at the passing in 1985 of Wilson Knight, 'the most important Shakespeare critic since Coleridge', we need to go as far afield as a Melbourne journal, *Scripsi*,[1] and as far back in time as 1954, as John Jones 'revisits' his pro-gramme broadcast for BBC Three. He argues for Knight's enormous achievement, and laments the institutionalized neglect which threatens this great critic as much in death as in life.

NEW HISTORICISTS

There is evidence that new historicism is beginning its inevitable route towards Shake-speare. The reason given by one of its pro-ponents, Jonathan Crewe, should cheer up those who may have been dismayed by the 'foregrounding' of popular literature, the irreverent challenges to 'the Canon'. Crewe detects an 'impulse on the part of many pro-fessional critics to recentre themselves on Shakespeare as the figure of supreme cultural authority, explicitly reclaimed as such'.[2]

Some writers associated with new histori-cism have begun with an area of specialization in the Renaissance and have edged towards Shakespeare: Stephen Greenblatt (Raleigh),

---

[1] John Jones, 'Shakespeare and Wilson Knight (Revisited)', *Scripsi*, 4 (University of Melbourne, July 1986), 51–8.
[2] Jonathan Crewe, *Hidden Designs: The Critical Profession and Renaissance Literature* (New York and London: Methuen, 1986), p. 130.

Jonathan Goldberg (literature under James I), David Norbrook (politics and poetry), Jonathan Dollimore, and Alan Sinfield. Some of their assumptions derive from the work of Herbert Butterfield, who stressed not the continuity of history but its discontinuities, and some from Marxist readings of history. When speaking of poetry, they unrepentantly emphasize the writer's political context (rather than 'historical background'), search for implicit 'ideologies' in texts and in later commentators upon the texts, and refuse to accept the primacy of individual inspiration or 'universality' in the writer's products. They also deny the possibility of 'objective' historical recovery since the historian's own assumptions are valid objects for enquiry, although the alternative is not 'subjectivity' but a form of radical scepticism which in many ways places texts in an unfamiliar, even alien light.[3]

Leonard Tennenhouse's *Power on Display: The Politics of Shakespeare's Genres* (New York and London: Methuen, 1986) begins interestingly, but seems to exhaust its ideas halfway through. It is somehow symptomatic that, after initially giving a good case for dissolving generic boundaries, the author even in his chapter divisions slips dutifully into the slots, as comedy, history, tragedy, and romance follow in familiar pageant. The earlier sections where examples are given of the politicization of desire in the 1590s are fascinating in their own right. As Elizabeth's potential relationships were attacked by powerful nobles like Sidney, so she proscribed liaisons of her subjects. The 'transfer of patriarchal power to a woman' (p. 68) is neatly traced through the *Arcadia* and Shakespeare's comedies. The approach, emphasizing 'the instrumentality of female desire' which ends up restoring power to the male at the end of the play, explains why, in Shakespeare's comic mode, 'the social order becomes more flexible and inclusive' (p. 62). Strangely, for a book on power which in places is an exercise in new historicism, the histories are treated most perfunctorily,

perhaps because Tennenhouse's interest is really in specifically patriarchal power and the politics of sex rather than in politics of the state. He is good on 'disguised ruler' plays, and his rebellion against the confines of genre lies in placing *Hamlet* among the histories. But as the book goes on it becomes wearisome in making Shakespeare so consistently and unreservedly supportive of authority, ignoring elements that are recalcitrant in Shakespeare's presentation, except where these are accommodated as diplomatic concessions by the monarch. Even a new historicist (especially a new historicist?) should recognize areas in which Shakespeare, as well as acting as a conduit for received, authoritarian patterns, is representing adversarial positions as well. The same author has written elsewhere on '*Coriolanus*: History and the Crisis of Semantic Order',[4] where political and psychological readings are merged. The ending of *Coriolanus* does not bring regret, illumination, resolution, or a new political order, because what Coriolanus represents has much earlier been displaced by new political forces in the Tribunes. The new historicist element comes in an equation between the tensions in Rome and those seen in Jacobean England between the King and the populace.

A modest contribution to new historicism is Robin Headlam Wells's short *Shakespeare, Politics, and the State*, a volume in the series Context and Commentary (London: Macmillan, 1986). The book is really a case-book of Renaissance statements on subjects such as 'Forms of Government', 'The Just Ruler', 'Rebellion', and 'Natural Law', while a commentary makes suggestions as to the relevance

---

3 For a general account of new historicism, see Edward Pechter, 'The New Historicism and its Discontents: Politicizing Renaissance Drama', *PMLA*, 102 (1987), 292–303.

4 In *Drama in the Renaissance: Comparative and Critical Essays*, reprinted from *Comparative Drama*, eds Clifford Davidson, C. J. Gianakaris, and John H. Stroupe (New York: AMS Press, 1986), pp. 217–35.

of these ideas in Shakespeare's plays. The enterprise is helpful in drawing attention to the variety of answers available to Renaissance writers on controversial subjects (thereby exploding the notion of a uniform 'Elizabethan world picture'), but in a volume dealing specifically with context we should be given more contextualization of the passages themselves. It should be stated more insistently that political theorists were (and still are) not disinterested spectators, but advocates of particular factional policies. The more they claim access to 'truth' the more we should suspect them of hiding their more self-interested premises, whether these be royalist or otherwise.

The business of uncovering such hidden assumptions is the subject of Jonathan Crewe's *Hidden Designs: The Critical Profession and Renaissance Literature* (London: Methuen, 1986). Despite its brevity, it is a difficult, elliptical book. Like other new historicists, Crewe did not begin with Shakespeare (rather, Puttenham), and the bulk of his book is a 'deconstruction' of works by Sidney and Spenser and of the Renaissance theatre. When he speaks of Shakespeare it is in terms of that writer's 'canonical logic', not a blind response to inner creative needs, but a development with reference to particular times and circumstances. *A Midsummer Night's Dream* is chosen as the exemplar of a play which mitigates Shakespeare's earlier 'excessive (despotic) will to resolve' (p. 134). Given the elaborateness of the critical apparatus, however, the analysis of the radical inconclusiveness of *A Midsummer Night's Dream* does not seem particularly original or weighty. Crewe seems to be less confident of the applicability of his ideas to Shakespeare, as compared with Puttenham and Sidney, and it may be unfair to take his Shakespearian forays out of context as more than examples of a larger topic.

David Norbrook, in conducting a fascinating investigation into the sources of *Macbeth*, strongly challenges 'Shakespeare's alleged independence from political ideol-ogy'.[5] Holinshed had been forced to draw upon Scottish historians, and in particular Buchanan, who reflects the constitutional views that in his country regicide may sometimes be condoned and that inherited kingship is not automatically the best system. As in Holinshed, so in Shakespeare, the attempt to evade or cover up these radical interpretations leads to some buried contradictions and vestiges of 'subtextual pressures'. Norbrook writes:

Many of the anomalies and contradictions in *Macbeth* can be explained not as manifestations of Shakespeare's desire to remain totally neutral but as difficulties inherent in the source material. In Holinshed there is a constant tension between some of the views held by Boece or Buchanan and the editor's controlling voice. (p. 96)

While giving us a conservative Shakespeare who never faces the problem of a monarch's accountability, Norbrook acknowledges the existence of other points of view in the play, and to this extent leaves us to make up our own minds about interpreting it. He is writing, as he admits, about historiographical problems rather than dramatic aspects, but interesting new insights into the play emerge from the detailed scholarship.

English Literary Renaissance has devoted a whole number to 'Studies in Renaissance Historicism', and volume 16 (Winter, 1986) begins with surveys of the new historicism by Louis Montrose and Jean E. Howard. Karen Newman's article 'Renaissance Family Politics and Shakespeare's *The Taming of the Shrew*' draws upon historical examples and Freud's theories of bisexuality to argue that the play deals with contradictions in patriarchy at a time when 'rebellious women' were a preoccupation. Kate's controversial homily on wifely

5 '*Macbeth* and the Politics of Historiography', in *Politics of Discourse: The Literature and History of Seventeenth Century England*, eds. Kevin Sharpe and Steven Zwicker (Los Angeles: University of California Press, 1987), pp. 78–116.

experience displays the social contradictions in the woman's role. While in content denying her own independence, Kate is transgressing in a linguistically powerful way the assumption of woman as silent object. She has the last, strong words, even though these words deny her strength. Carolyn E. Brown finds fascinating evidence of erotic flagellation ('the English vice' in the public school system) in the religious orders of Shakespeare's day in her attempt to connect religion, pain, and perverted sexuality in *Measure for Measure*. She pounces rather too earnestly on every word in the play that might hold a double meaning, and upon suggestive collocations such as: 'See our pleasure herein executed'. No character emerges unscathed from this relentless examination of 'subconscious motives', and one feels that the dangers of 'Old Historicism', an imposition of only marginally relevant historical detail, have not been avoided. Meanwhile, the most important essay in the volume, while not mentioning Shakespeare, has important implications for his work. Philip J. Finkelpearl's essay on censorship of the Jacobean stage establishes a rigorous methodology for examining a subject which is increasingly being seen as central. If the embedded politics of Shakespeare's drama are to be properly investigated, then the political constraints upon him, and the way these changed during his career, require strict attention. Finkelpearl's article is neatly complemented by Janet Clare's '"Greater Themes for Insurrection's Arguing": Political Censorship of the Elizabethan and Jacobean Stage', in *Review of English Studies*, NS 38 (May 1987), 169–83. This essay deals mainly with the history plays written by Shakespeare before 1600, and has some interesting comments about why in *Coriolanus* rebellion, while not condoned, is presented as justifiable.

Heather Dubrow, in an interesting article,[6] reminds us that the problems faced by new historicism – the trustworthiness of historical narrative and its capacity for mythmaking –

were faced by Renaissance historiographers themselves. Raleigh and Bodin, for example, realized that 'facts' cannot always be ascertained, and that their colleagues and ancestors were often 'pandering to their employers' in providing interpretations under the mask of 'facts'. Dubrow believes that in *The Rape of Lucrece* Shakespeare is exploring such debates carried on by contemporary historians. The undercutting of the apparently straightforward 'Argument', the questions hanging over causality, the concern for presenting different interpretations of the story, and even the uncertainty about genre (complaint or epic?) all attest to the writer as one aware of and involved in the complex problems surrounding history and poetry as modes of presenting the past.

The journal *Literature and History* is a British organ for new historicism. In the 1986 volume (12), Richard Dutton attempts to avoid modern appropriations of *King Lear* by exploring 'some of the similarities between Shakespeare's *King Lear* and Anthony Munday's Lord Mayor's Show for 1605, *The Triumphs of Reunited Britannia* – the latter a text which conspicuously has failed to transcend the context of its own age' (139–51, p. 140). A more vigorous onslaught on modern critics and reviewers comes in Richard Wilson's '"A Mingled Yarn": Shakespeare and the Cloth Workers', *Literature and History* (164–80). Wilson argues that modern, bourgeois abhorrence of populism and yearning for compromise is anachronistic in interpreting sixteenth century texts. 'Shakespeare's crowd-scenes belong . . . to the period of the emergence of the urban mob as a force in English politics. Though interpreted as if they demonstrated universal imperatives of law and order, no part of Shakespeare's writing is more entangled in the exigencies of his time and class' (p. 167). In another forceful article, '"Is This a Holiday?":

---

[6] 'The Rape of Clio: Attitudes to History in Shakespeare's *Lucrece*', *English Literary History*, 16 (1986), 425–61.

Shakespeare's Roman Carnival' (*English Literary History*, 54 (1987), 31–44), Wilson returns to the Shakespearian crowd. He argues here, through the example of *Julius Caesar*, that the public authorization of carnival and festivity was, in Shakespeare's day, a method of containing rebellious social impulses, and, as such, became the focus for competing ideologies to struggle for. In Umberto Eco's cryptic sentence, 'If carnival were always . . . emancipatory, it would be impossible to explain why power uses circuses' (quoted p. 36). Julia Lupton returns to power, the central subject for the new historicist, in a more familiar context, examining the presence of Machiavellian notions of fear and theatricality in *Hamlet*, in 'Truant Dispositions: *Hamlet* and Machiavelli'.[7]

The real thrust of new historicism, and the point that is also most contentious and can make its opponents very cross, is that 'history' can never be presented 'neutrally', and that every act of historical recovery or description is underpinned, often unconsciously, by interpretation and ideology. The same debates are going on, for example, in economics (where the argument runs that 'economic science' cannot exist without prior attention to 'economic philosophy'), and even in philosophy. Ina Schabert in 'Shakespeare als Politischer Philosoph: Sein Werk und die Schule von Leo Strauss',[8] grasps this nettle firmly by examining the implications of Strauss's work for Shakespeare criticism. Strauss was among the first to assert the priority of 'political philosophy', with its concentration on relativity and underlying assumptions, over 'political science', with its claim of objectivity. The analysis centres on the presentation of power in *The Tempest*, with wide reference to other plays, and includes a useful review of the writing on Shakespeare's political stance, as judged by writers either influenced by Strauss or with ideas similar to his.

Coppélia Kahn makes a case that new historicism shares ground with another new approach, feminist criticism, in that both methodologies focus on questions of power, gender, and identity, and on analysing underlying ideologies.[9] Her rather unexpected case-study is *Timon of Athens*, where the respective problems concern, it is argued, the Jacobean system of patronage, and maternal power. The issue of *Shakespeare Quarterly* in which Kahn's essay appears is devoted to feminist criticism, and Lisa Jardine examines, in both historical and feminist contexts, the 'learned woman' in Shakespeare, especially Helena and Portia.[10] A 'confused cultural response' emerges in the plays and in other Elizabethan documents. One version shows the woman as powerfully chaste and loyal, the other as threateningly unruly and disorderly. The endings of the plays limit her power. The analysis has clear significance for Kate in *The Shrew*, so perhaps 'learning' in the woman is not the crucial factor. Karen Newman's approach to Portia overlaps with those of Kahn and Jardine, although her concentration is upon the governing analogy between commerce and love in *The Merchant of Venice*.[11]

At first sight it is surprising that *Shakespeare's English and Roman History Plays: A Marxist Approach* by Paul N. Siegel (London and Toronto: Associated University Presses, 1986) is a sympathetic resurrection of Tillyard's 'Elizabethan world picture' which is nowadays largely discounted. Siegel argues that 'Tillyard's statement that the idea of cosmic order is "one of the genuine ruling

[7] *Journal of Medieval and Renaissance Studies*, 17 (1987), 59–82.
[8] *Deutsche Shakespeare-Gesellschaft West Jahrbuch 1986*, ed. Werner Habicht (Heidelberg: Quelle and Meyer, 1986); Schabert, 7–25.
[9] '"Magic of Bounty": *Timon of Athens*, Jacobean Patronage, and Maternal Power', *Shakespeare Quarterly*, 38 (1987), 34–57.
[10] 'Cultural Confusion and Shakespeare's Learned Heroines: "These are old paradoxes"', 1–18.
[11] 'Portia's Ring: Unruly Women and Structures of Exchange in *The Merchant of Venice*', 19–33.

ideas of the age, and perhaps the most characteristic" remains valid despite the attacks of his opponents' (p. 47). There is a profound difference, however, between Tillyard and Siegel over how we should evaluate 'the Tudor Myth'. While on every page Tillyard conveys the impression of his own personal commitment to values of hierarchy, tradition, and authority, Siegel more warily looks behind the 'myth' to find that 'The ruling ideas of an age are the ideas of its ruling class', and he interprets the world order as a useful rationalization of the social position of the new aristocracy. Shakespeare depicts the conflicts within the nobility, and the social changes, in his plays about English and Roman history. Whereas Tillyard accepts the idea that historical events are to be explained by God's plan, the Marxist recognizes that people, through their actions and the consequences, make history. 'Providence' exists, but it is the result of the deeds of men acting according to their class-views and economic necessity. Siegel does not argue that Shakespeare necessarily disbelieved in the Christian explanation, or that he understood the underlying economic bases upon which his characters act. However, Shakespeare's real interest is seen to lie in the actual deeds of men rather than in mystical causation, even if these men claim divine sanction. He is, if anything, a great observer, and the dramatic worlds he presents give to the Marxist critic enough evidence of social and economic conflict to justify his own position. The whole argument really returns us, not to Tillyard, but to Hazlitt, and it is a shame that Siegel does not draw upon, for example, Hazlitt's essay on *Coriolanus* rather than preoccupying himself with modern royalists. He is not afraid to draw modern parallels. A pungent section nails Richard III as a representative of the bourgeoisie of today, intent on status, 'business', money, and an individualism that maintains 'the principle that the entire world may be destroyed as long as he achieves his will' (p. 85).

Ideology and history are subjects which the dramatist Edward Bond insists are important for our understanding of Shakespeare. Christy L. Brown brings to academic notice the critique of Shakespeare's cultural hegemony carried out in *Bingo*.[12] Bond used as his source the 'Welcombe' contract made by Shakespeare to protect his property interests in the event of enclosure of fields in 1614, and the argument of *Bingo* is that this gesture marks a class-bias in Shakespeare that has consequences for the plays. Since Bond's approach to Shakespeare is now being assessed as of interest to Shakespearian critics (a fact which may not please him) I ought to come clean and admit that I was the 'confused teacher of Shakespeare' who appears in *The Rational Theatre*.[13] The fact that I should not now use the words attributed to me as a hapless academic is partly due to an increasing respect for the ideas of Bond and, more particularly, his mentor Brecht.

GENERAL TOPICS

A book which is certainly important and original deals with one of the most familiar subjects. Ann and John O. Thompson's *Shakespeare: Meaning and Metaphor* (Brighton: Harvester Press, 1987) brings to bear on what we normally call 'imagery studies' a set of sternly disciplined methodologies borrowed from linguistics and philosophy. It is by turns engrossing and arid. The application of Lakoff and Johnson's *Metaphors We Live By* (Chicago, 1980), a study of metaphors used almost unconsciously in everyday life, to time metaphors in *Troilus and Cressida* produces some fascinating insights into the conceptual density and range of elaboration built into Shakespeare's use of metaphor. Kittay and Lehrer's 'semantic field theory' (1978 and 1981) gives a

---

[12] 'Edward Bond's *Bingo*: Shakespeare and the Ideology of Genius', *Iowa State Journal of Research*, 60 (1985), 343–54.
[13] *Plays: Two* (London: Methuen, 1978).

new and helpful rigour to the critic attempting to analyse 'Animal Metaphors in *King Lear*'. We find the familiar terminology of tenors and vehicles replaced by donor fields and recipient fields, and the results, in terms of analytical precision, are valuable. J. J. Ross's theories of analogy and 'differentiation' (in *Portraying Analogy* (Cambridge, 1981)) are found to do justice to the complexity of a Shakespearian Sonnet at 'the micro-level linguistic sensitivity' (p. 159). On the other end of the comprehensibility scale lies the theory of synecdoche advanced by the writers of *Rhétorique générale* (who write under the name Group μ).[14] Here the complexity of the linguistic theory for its own sake may hold the purist's attention, but there is something faintly unnecessary about using its whole weight to fathom out the presentation of 'Metaphors of the Human Body and its Parts in *Hamlet*'. It is this theory that the writers have chosen to apply in article form, in a study of synecdoche in *Othello*,[15] with a little more lucidity. Reading the book as a whole is an experience akin to a fall from innocence. Literary critics can never again be arrogant enough to claim 'imagery studies' as an exclusive property of their own, without humble submission to the exacting and challenging findings of linguists in their explorations of metaphor. There is also, fortunately, a sense in which the most confident sections of the book are full of 'literary' perceptions, finely tuned observations of the varying functions of Shakespeare's metaphorical language. There appear to be too many misprints for a book which presumably had not one but two expert proofreaders. As a postscript to this field, I modestly note a collection of essays which deal with a particular linguistic theory (that hearers create meaning), *The Art of Listening*,[16] where in one essay I apply the theory to the example of conversation in several of Shakespeare's plays. Conversation, like metaphor, is a subject that seems to have attracted little direct attention from critics, which in itself seems very odd

since his plays are almost entirely conversational in mode.

Not everybody will share the estimation of Charles Warren in dealing with the contribution of T. S. Eliot to Shakespearian criticism:

Eliot is keeping Shakespeare alive for us. And we are in the end brought face to face with a great Shakespeare critic. Here is an interesting mind on the broadest scale, the equal of Coleridge and Johnson, offering a developed and highly individual view of Shakespeare.[17]

Even Warren's own careful presentation would seem to bear out the fact that Eliot owed many of his ideas to Wilson Knight and other *Criterion* writers, and to imply that his insistence upon judgement as more important than interpretation led him into many perversities. It is rather saddening that even today examiners dutifully present Eliot's quirky statements about Shakespeare and seventeenth-century poetry and drama to students, when in fact the kinds of opinions they present belong to the 1920s, and do not often stand up to close scrutiny. None the less, Warren at least convinces us that there is more Shakespearian criticism than one would expect among Eliot's prose works, and that his poems such as 'Marina' and 'Coriolan' can be viewed as oblique commentaries upon the plays which inspired them. The book is scrupulously detailed, with an Appendix on '*Criterion* Writing by Others than Eliot on Shakespeare and Related Subjects' and a full Bibliography, both of which are very useful. It could be quite

---

[14] Group μ, *Rhétorique générale* (Paris: Larousse, 1970), translated by Paul B. Burrell and Edgar M. Slotkin as *A General Rhetoric* (Baltimore and London, 1981).

[15] '"To Look So Low as Where They Are": Hand and Heart Synecdoches in *Othello*', *Southern Review*, 19 (University of Adelaide, 1986), 53–66.

[16] Edited by Graham McGregor and R. S. White (London and Sydney: Croom Helm, 1986). The essay is entitled 'Shakespeare and the Listener', pages 124–51.

[17] Charles Warren, *T. S. Eliot on Shakespeare* (Ann Arbor, Michigan: U.M.I. Research Press, 1987), p. 105.

revealing if an equally thorough and appreciative scholar would carry out the same kind of assessment of the contribution to Shakespearian criticism of Eliot's contemporary who has been neglected in this context, W. H. Auden.

Sidney Homan's book, *Shakespeare's Theater of Presence: Language, Spectacle, and the Audience* (London and Toronto: Associated University Presses, 1986), presents an argument informed by the experience of one who has had to wrestle with the plays in performance. The title, superficially one that attempts to catch everything in its net, is in fact a close description of the book's preoccupations. At the centre lies an exploration of the interrelationship, fluctuating from play to play, between the audience, what it sees (spectacle), and what it hears (language). Part One analyses the way the audience is pulled into the action, 'journeying into the play, hazarding our everyday concept of reality for this fictive . . . journey' (p. 45). It points to disjunctions between language, spectacle, and 'reality' in *The Comedy of Errors*, *The Winter's Tale*, and most interestingly in *Troilus and Cressida*, where the discrepancies lead to a 'failed enactment', an 'aesthetics of failure' (but not, it should be stressed, a failed play). Part Two dwells on spectacle, finding in *Julius Caesar* a male capacity for 'optical distortion', habits of misinterpretation and reinterpretation of observed actions, and detecting in *Macbeth* a stand made by the characters against paradox – 'mania for certainty, for what is clear and absolute' (p. 106) – in a world where certainty and security are impossible. The conflicts here lie between sight and otherworldly vision, between external reality and mental isolation. The book then moves on to 'Language, Private and Public', and presents Richard III as a skilled wordsmith who devalues language, and Henry V as one who seeks to forge a public language that does not outdistance the reality which speech seeks to represent. Finally, in a section which attempts to pull the threads together, *King Lear* is seen as a play in which language proves inadequate or tends towards silence. The eyes can be deceived as to 'what is', and yet the enterprise as a whole celebrates the 'life' beyond the theatre.

Homan can be illuminating in his readings of individual plays, but the book shares a tendency with many others that seem to emanate from the American Shakespeare industry. Professional and competent as they are, such books, by adopting a 'synthetic' argument, give the impression of moving the plays around like chess figures into unexpected configurations without actually surprising or engaging the reader at the level of ideas. It may be a tendency encouraged by the competitive nature of the American academy which favours certain formulas, endorses the presentation of familiar ideas in ingenious disguises, and perhaps positively discourages radical examination of leading assumptions. One wonders how many new packets can be designed to sell an old product, and the metaphor of marketing as a central consideration is the one that indeed springs to mind.

Beginning boldly with the statement 'Ours is not a heroic age', James C. Bulman in *The Heroic Idiom of Shakespearean Tragedy* (London and Toronto: Associated University Presses, 1985) seeks to counter modern scepticism about heroic achievement by examining the heroic 'idioms' which Shakespeare drew upon in his own culture. At the basis of his argument lies the belief, which surely commands a lot of agreement now, that art is representational, not in its 'truth to life', but in its complex relationship to its models, whether literary or otherwise. Shakespeare comes to shed the Marlovian idiom of heroism to discover, in the depiction of Hal, 'a new heroism of self-awareness' (p. 71), although this is itself an 'updating', an ironic treatment of the traditional conqueror play. Developing his own ability to 'incorporate and reshape prior art', Shakespeare in *Troilus and Cressida* wrestles with the paradoxical 'need to embrace and reject heroic conventions' (p. 17). Bulman is best on these plays, where he argues that Shakespeare asserts as strong a scepticism about heroism as a validation of it. Here, though, we might detect an inadvertent paradox in the author himself: in trying to get away from modern scepticism, Bulman discovers that it was Shakespeare who laid the foundations for our anti-heroic attitudes. (There is nothing wrong with this, but Bulman could have acknowledged it more clearly.) There are weak sections. In dealing with the Henriad, Bulman pays little more than lip-service to Falstaff's version of 'honour', surely more subversive of heroism than anything in Hal's theatricality, and he does not question as radically as Shakespeare does the concept of heroism itself. Instead, there is an alert differentiation between the different styles and representations of heroism in each king. The book is surprisingly thin on *King Lear*, where the terms of the argument seem restrictive and irrelevant.

The Cambridge Companion to Shakespeare Studies, edited by Stanley Wells (Cambridge: Cambridge University Press, 1986), is a wholly new version of the *New Companion* formerly edited by Kenneth Muir and Samuel Schoenbaum (Cambridge: Cambridge University Press, 1971). There are some essays which bring the story up to date, notably Robert Hapgood's 'Shakespeare on Film and Television' (the theme of *Shakespeare Survey 39*) and Terence Hawkes's 'Shakespeare and New Critical Approaches'. The latter is very partial, emphasizing some second-rate critics, peppered with illogicalities, and – surely with curious premeditation – omitting all reference to the work of Terry Eagleton. Some subjects are treated more as catalogues than discursive essays (Lawrence Danson on twentieth-century criticism of the Comedies, David Daniell on the traditions of comedy, and, more forgivably, Dieter Mehl on 'Shakespeare reference books'). Harry Levin provides the only real *essay*, 'Critical Approaches to Shakespeare from 1660–1904', a remarkable *tour de force* covering a great span of time with stylish

mastery. G. K. Hunter ('Shakespeare and the Traditions of Tragedy', 123–41), demonstrates that the price of fame is to be impelled into more and more general topics which are treated with some bewilderment. This critic is at his best when dealing with specific moments in particular texts. Inga-Stina Ewbank provides a quietly learned account of 'Shakespeare and the Arts of Language' (49–66). An inspection of her notes and bibliography, as well as her own practice, reveals the equal contribution women have made to the study of Shakespeare – which makes the fact that she is the only woman in this collection rather unfortunate. Edward Berry's conclusion on 'The Histories', that the genre 'requires new questions and new critical models', is already being proved correct.

Winifred Maynard, in a thorough and scholarly book, *Elizabethan Lyric Poetry and its Music* (Oxford: Clarendon Press, 1986), has a long chapter on Shakespeare's use of song. The book is useful for its sound presentation of facts, and deserves the status of a reference book, but the critical comments are so tentative and wishy-washy that they do not provide much of interest.

GENRE

After a year in which new literary theory dominated Shakespeare studies, we have seen a return to traditional approaches organized by the categories of genre bequeathed to us by the editors of the First Folio. This may be coincidence, or it may indicate a retrenchment by publishers while they await responses to their more adventurous initiatives.

Comedy is back in the lead. The most comprehensive and expansive book, *Shakespeare and the Uses of Comedy* by J. A. Bryant (Lexington: University Press of Kentucky, 1986), begins in the way most calculated to make the modernists tear their hair out: 'The subject of this book is Shakespeare's exploration of the human situation through the mode of dramatic comedy.' Have we not been told insistently that the 'situation' in which writers and readers and audiences live is specific to a time, a place, economic constraints, and political assumptions, that all a critic can mean by 'human' is his or her own, culture-specific expectations? The reviewer keen to be fair-minded must cry 'Return, Alpheus, the dread voice is past / That shrunk thy streams', and look at how books measure up to their own claims. Bryant's 'Exploration of the Human Comedy' is a genial survey of the issues raised by each comedy treated as a unique work. Even within its modest limits there are some contentious areas. The genre itself, for example, becomes loose and baggy when it can include *Troilus and Cressida* and, although embracing the last plays, exclude *Pericles* (because it is a 'romance'). *Troilus* is included largely because it has signs of being a satire on romantic love, although one would want a sharper, franker rebuttal of the argument that the particular kind of satire deployed is enemy rather than friend to comedy, an altogether more fundamental matter than the early comedies' fond mockery of lovers' poses. None the less, Bryant does a service to *Troilus* by playing down the savage and pessimistic qualities which other critics have perhaps overstated. He notes Hector's generosity (even regretting for a moment that Cressida did not meet him), Cressida's situational vulnerability that surely makes her less culpable, and even more unusually, Achilles' better motives. Bryant is hostile to Troilus' behaviour in love, which does seem to exhibit a doctrinal reliance upon market forces, and not a little hypocrisy. On some of the *cruces* of comedy criticism, Bryant has points of view. He is interesting on Kate's 'serenity' at the end of *The Shrew*, and on the way the world of the play has persistently denied her social freedom. Kate has, he argues, liberated Petruchio 'from the prison of masculine vanity'. It is hard to find the 'real forest' in *As You Like It* which is argued for on several occasions. The author tactfully, and without pressuring us, reminds us of his earlier thesis that the last plays present a series of

allegories (or analogies) for a reconciliation between the ancient cultures of Judaism and Christianity. It is good to see *The Merry Wives of Windsor* treated respectfully, though the analysis conventionally focuses on Falstaff's 'scapegoat' role. Behind the whole enterprise of the book lies C. L. Barber's sense of 'the going-on power of life' revealed through the comedies, for survival, renewal, and continuity are its themes.

Barber's influence can also be strongly detected in Robert Ornstein's *Shakespeare's Comedies: From Roman Farce to Romantic Comedy* (Newark, Delaware: University of Delaware Press, 1986). Again, it is fascinating to see which plays a critic includes or excludes from the category of comedy. Here we have no *Troilus and Cressida*, and no *Merry Wives* ('a skillful perfunctory exercise in comedy by a Shakespeare . . . bored by his assignment'); *All's Well* is here, but not much of *Measure for Measure*; three of the last plays, but again no *Pericles* (excluded because of problems of authorship). Some comedies receive less sympathy than others. *The Shrew* is 'uninspired work', 'competent and malicious hackwork', while *Love's Labour's Lost* is little more than a 'courtly dance', in fact 'a bit tiresome'. Ornstein creates the impression that (as he says of *As You Like It*) 'decency is the norm of life', and he shies away from 'unpleasant' problems, and these two words reveal the underlying structure of values in the book. Perhaps we should be more grateful than critical of such a tone in these casuistical days, and Ornstein does at least acknowledge the presence of 'sad' (but presumably not unpleasant) strains in the mature comedies. It is, however, not a book with a lot to get our teeth into, and follows an established pattern of the general survey, moving from Shakespeare's 'apprenticeship' through 'maturity' to his 'farewell to the stage'. Such a tempting mythology will probably be overcome only when somebody digs up a statement by Shakespeare on re-reading an early comedy, such as that of Swift when he re-read *The Tale of a Tub*:

'Good God! What a genius I had when I wrote that book.'

Shakespeare's Comedies and Poems by H. H. Anniah Gowda (New Delhi: Sterling Publishers, 1986) is even more weightless, though it wisely claims to be little more than an appreciative introduction to the delights of Shakespeare. There is some interesting material on parallels between Shakespeare's plays and Indian texts, and this should encourage western readers not to be too parochial.

Comedy from Shakespeare to Sheridan: Change and Continuity in the English and European Dramatic Tradition[18] does have tougher concentration on theoretical issues than the books above, and we should expect no less from a set of essays in honour of Eugene Waith. Alvin Kernan in a brief but suggestive essay cleverly links an examination of Shakespeare's courtly audience with contemporary political tensions. Rose Zimbardo follows this 'reception theory' approach with an exercise in reader-response criticism. She locates the beginning of modern concentration upon character in the decade 1680–90, contrasting earlier comments which indicate that 'what the early seventeenth century admired in Shakespeare was his ability to feign a world' and his dramatic variety. For example, in adapting *The Tempest*, Dryden and Davenant did not 'understand meaning . . . to rest in a single strong character who is torn by inner turmoil' (p. 222). The wheel may be turning slowly full circle, and a non-hierarchical, issue-dominated, and essentially theatrical approach to Shakespeare is rapidly gaining currency again. Jean E. Howard, drawing explicitly on the reader-response criticism of Iser, and theories of gestalt, shows that problems of closure in the comedies are real, and create 'a troubling and open-ended theatrical experience for the audience'. She presents some sensible conclusions (but not closures) about the end of *The Shrew* and concentrates on the most troubling of all the comedies, *Measure for Measure* and *The Merchant of Venice*. Other essays on Shakespeare are not so interesting. G. K. Hunter does not quite convince us that he has managed to locate with precision the 'inner structures' of manifestations of comedy lying along a spectrum between farce and romance. He is more confident when he turns to texts by Shakespeare and others. Kenneth Muir is rather bland in examining the 'element of testing' in comedy from Shakespeare through Calderon, Molière, and Marivaux. R. A. Foakes, in a dry and schematic essay, 'Tragicomedy and Comic Form', has a tendency to make one feel that literary evolution can be predicted from factors outside the individual writer, who is seen to be at the mercy of genre and other formal factors. Marjorie Garber would subtitle *As You Like It* 'The Education of Orlando', arguing that the real function of Rosalind's disguise is to enable her to teach Orlando about himself and about the nature of love, a rather pale explanation of the play's vitality.

I find it hard to accept a generic linking of *All's Well*, *Measure for Measure* and *Troilus and Cressida* as anything more than a critical red herring tossed into the pool by Boas, and there is little in Vivian Thomas's *The Moral Universe of Shakespeare's Problem Plays* (London and Sydney: Croom Helm, 1987) to shake this belief. If genre is important, then the first two plays are comic in structure, although pushing comedy to a limit, while the third is in form (and genre is a formal concern) a tragedy. If, as is common, the 'problem' is seen as one of audience response, then a host of plays join the ranks – *Coriolanus*, *Julius Caesar*, *Antony and Cleopatra*, *Henry V*, and *The Tempest*; while if we take the 'problem' to be one of indefinite tone, then *Timon of Athens*, *Hamlet*, and *Cymbeline* can be added. It is about time we did away with this unhelpful and arbitrary term. This reservation about the grouping of plays does not, however, detract from the contribution of Vivian Thomas's book itself. It is

---

[18] Edited by A. R. Braunmuller and J. C. Bulman (Newark: University of Delaware Press, 1986).

admirable in its careful and sober comparison of texts and sources, especially in the case of *Troilus and Cressida* where a factual analysis does shed light on the presentation of the most ambiguous characters in Shakespeare's play: Achilles, Cressida, and Thersites. In the analytical body of the book we find a sound, if unsurprising, commentary on 'The Fractured Universe' of *Troilus and Cressida*, where questions of value (and devaluation) and identity are persistently raised. 'Estimation' is seen to be at the heart of *All's Well*, and this time its fulcrum is social status opposed to inner virtue. Thomas goes further than even the most unsympathetic critics in his condemnation of Bertram's 'disgusting' behaviour ('nasty little egotist'), but in seeking to explain the power of the play in performance, he perhaps overstresses the controlled ambiguity of the ending and neglects the existence of some of the finest and most rounded women characters in Shakespeare.

Adrian Poole may have had to exercise his mind for some time to get the proportions of his title right. The result is *Tragedy: Shakespeare and the Greek Example* (Oxford: Blackwell, 1987). In this visually beautiful book, the central subject is Greek tragedy, juxtaposed with brief accounts of Shakespearian tragedy. *Macbeth* is seen in an Aeschylean light of 'the initiate fear' or what Wordsworth calls 'anxiety of hope'. *Hamlet* is compared with *Oedipus Tyrannus* as a tragedy in which the protagonist obsessively pursues 'questions' about his own psychic origins. In two chapters devoted to the Greeks exclusively, Euripides is placed among 'the black comedians of tragedy' who root us in a world where suffering is unavoidable and raw even when it appears in a comic light, and Sophocles, who transports his tragic characters to 'a world elsewhere', away from 'the real business of living', to 'high-risk places, where the prospects of survival and return are minimal'. Finally, *King Lear* is set beside the 'family' tragedies of Sophocles and Euripides respectively:

In all three plays discussed here, *Oedipus at Colonus*, *King Lear* and the *Bacchae*, two of the great differences in which everyone has a part – between parent and child and male and female – are fused together, in the bonds between Oedipus and Antigone, Lear and Cordelia, Agave and Pentheus. (p. 234)

Most of the book's concentration is upon the Greeks, whose tragedies are read 'both through and against Shakespeare' (Preface). Mr Poole adopts something of a 'high-risk' style himself, writing in a mode reminiscent of John Bayley and John Jones. Rather than adopting a coolly detached and analytical stance, he attempts to enter the spirit of his demanding subjects:

Tragedy's medicine for misery consists not in a kind of forgetting but in a kind of remembering, a commemoration of suffering through which human grief is at one and the same time relived and relieved. (p. 239)

When it works it is a style which I confess I admire, since it stresses the interaction of the aesthetic mode and the world of experience. Not very popular these days, but here it works effectively.

In *Captive Victors: Shakespeare's Narrative Poems and Sonnets* (Ithaca and London: Cornell University Press, 1987) Heather Dubrow tries, with only middling success, to create a new genre out of the non-dramatic poetry. The links are found to lie at the levels of a general theme indicated by the paradoxical title (weakness is turned into strength in the cases of Adonis, Lucrece, and the Sonnet narrator), and a common poetic strategy of 'seesawing between sympathy and judgment'. The best essay is the one dealing with *The Rape of Lucrece*, and given the paucity of good criticism on this difficult poem, it is a welcome contribution. Dubrow is strong on the role of the 'passive victim' in this poem, and what it tells us about tyrannical behaviour.[19] She takes

---

[19] The general emphasis is comparable with my own brief account of the poem in *Innocent Victims: Poetic Injustice in Shakespearean Tragedy* (London: Athlone Press, 1986).

the psychological state of Lucrece seriously, finding surprising similarities of treatment between Shakespeare and modern works such as *Rape Victimology*. This is fresh analysis of a poem which all too often is treated patronizingly as a mere exercise in rhetoric. The other sections cannot be praised so highly. By concentrating on the level of sympathies in *Venus and Adonis*, Dubrow risks letting her own irritation with Venus make her too eager to turn Adonis into a victim figure. A lot of the wit is lost, and also the pathos of an immortal goddess whose *raison d'être* is Love confronted with the brevity of mortality. To see her consistently as a 'self-centred' and selfish human being seems to miss a lot of the poem's point. There are interesting insights into the Sonnets, when 'the isolation of Shakespeare's speaker', the absence of a projected listener, are contrasted with the dramatic sociability of Astrophil and the wider, past-tense context evoked in the *Amoretti*. Our attention is thus focused on the temperament of the speaker, 'a living oxymoron' who demonstrates 'the psychological cost of equivocating' between praise and blame. The speaker is seen shifting position within a Sonnet, emerging as 'a powerful rhetorician and a powerless victim' at the same time. Throughout, power and victimization are the subjects of this readable, if sometimes longwinded, book.

Dieter Mehl's *Shakespeare's Tragedies: An Introduction* (Cambridge: Cambridge University Press, 1986) is a translation of a book originally published in 1983 as a guide for German students. It deserves a recommendation to English-speaking students since, despite the modesty of its 'introductory' scope, it provides consistent and trustworthy commentary on all the tragedies. Mehl is unrepentant in placing his emphasis on the 'unfashionable' subject of dramatic character, but he is aware of the plays as dramatic patterns. Sometimes too much so, for some chapters (*King Lear*, for example) stay too close to the level of the narrative to allow for individual interpretation. The chapter on *Hamlet* is the best, and one wonders if Germanic scholars have some secret inwardness with this play denied to others. The general intention of the book, 'to encourage the kind of active collaboration of readers (and audiences) that seems . . . the chief end of criticism', is refreshingly candid, and for many readers it will be achieved.

PLAYS

Only one book this year looks in detail at a single play, and its relative brevity puts it into the category of an extended essay. James L. Calderwood continues his own 'whole journey' through the Shakespearian canon as seen from a metadramatic point of view in *If It Were Done: 'Macbeth' and Tragic Action* (Amherst: University of Massachusetts Press, 1986). Referring to his previous book, Calderwood initially sees *Macbeth* as a 'Counter-Hamlet'. Whereas *Hamlet* is a reactive play where imagination is an impediment to action, *Macbeth* rushes us into a future, o'erleaping the present with its hero's imaginings. Hamlet spends much of his time remembering the past, Macbeth anticipating the future. Calderwood uses the prophetic or 'potentive' mood of *Macbeth* as justification for exercising his own leaps beyond the play, as if '*Macbeth* is not yet done, . . . its ending is an unending'. 'Feint' is a favourite word for Calderwood in dealing with this play, and it could, in its various senses, indicate the general critical strategy. He constantly flashes out daring ideas suggested by the text but not wholly inscribed in it, and subsequently half-retracts them as 'parodies' to make a point. For example, many critics (drawing perhaps most directly upon Orson Welles's screen version) detect a sexuality in the play which is barely articulated but seems significant. Calderwood revels unforgettably in the subject, picking up Lady Macbeth's 'imagined unsexings of herself' and Macbeth's 'unlikely comparison of himself to

Tarquin', and playing with the multiple associations of words such as 'want' (as verb and noun), 'do', and 'done' to suggest the frustrations of action. Similarly, in dealing with what he regards as the other central subject, violence, Calderwood feels free to move from the literal to the metaphorical in detecting a stratum of cannibalism. (As a service to my Scottish ancestry, I should prefer the writer to confine his expression of 'the fact that savagery is so deeply ingrained in Scots culture' (p. 72) to Shakespeare's point of view in this play rather than asserting it as a 'fact'.) One of Calderwood's conclusions about the nature and direction of violence in the play could well have been amplified, since it helps to account for the strong feeling that Macbeth, rather than being an ambitious man, is caught up helplessly in historical processes:

The impression given is that violence arises not from anything Duncan himself has done but from the mere fact of kingship itself, the royal difference.
(p. 80)

Generally speaking, Calderwood's 'feints' in this brief but penetrating book return us to the play with a sharpened perspective, although at times he is so clever that it is not clear whether he believes his own argument or not (for example, in his dealing with 'the Oedipal picture' on pages 54–5).

By accident, rather than design, a couple of articles develop some of Calderwood's lines of thought, although the sobriety of style befitting academic journals contrasts with his sparkle. In 'Macbeth's War on Time'[20] Donald W. Foster takes as his point of departure a questioning of the orthodoxy that the ending of the play shows order and the promise of a secure future, arguing instead that the play constantly stresses unending repetition and a troubled future. Nor can there be a 'return' to order when 'We are given no hint in Shakespeare that Duncan's reign was ever anything but bloody and chaotic.' An examination of the many references to time in Macbeth reveals

that, although all kings may wage a war against literal time, attempting like Macbeth to create their own futures, yet they are inevitably defeated by 'It was' – in Nietzsche's words, 'The will cannot will backwards' (quoted p. 324). On the other hand, the lies of the poetic artificer take revenge on figurative time:

Kings may like to think themselves the harbingers of the life to come, but when the hurly burly's done, when kings and subjects are dead and rotten, it is the verbal jugglers, the poets and playwrights, who 'give them all breath, / These clamorous harbingers of blood and death' (5.6.9–10).
(p. 341)

Foster's essay is timely and energetic, and deserves serious attention. Time is also the subject of Luisa Guj's 'Macbeth and the Seeds of Time',[21] although the nature of this article makes it a contribution to the history of ideas rather than literary criticism. Guj examines time in Macbeth in the light of Italian Renaissance scholars' comments, and especially those of Vincenzo Cartari. Rather different again in approach is David Willbern's 'Phantasmagoric Macbeth'[22] which begins ominously with 'Imagining Macbeth is a bloody labor'. It then plunges us into a world of regicide, infanticide, violent birth (through Caesarean section), and hallucination. All is observed through psychoanalytic theory, and the play is read as Shakespeare's observation of an historical moment when fictions of supernatural agency (Fate or witches) were being challenged by notions of individual pathology as an explanation for such states as 'obsession' and 'hysteria'. Rajiva Verma's project[23] of tracing contrasts between Macbeth and Antony and Cleopatra looks initially unlikely, but in fact it illuminates both plays, and makes the point that the latter play

[20] English Literary Renaissance, 16 (1986), 319–42.
[21] Shakespeare Studies, 18 (1986), 175–88.
[22] English Literary Renaissance, 16 (1986), 520–49.
[23] 'Winners and Losers: A Study of Macbeth and Antony and Cleopatra', Modern Language Review, 81 (1986), 838–52.

can be linked with the late romances rather than the tragedies. The conclusion about the two plays is that 'It almost seems as if, in the fullness of his being, Shakespeare were "playing" here with opposites, showing himself capable of empathy with radically opposed states of mind and opposite kinds of aesthetic experience.'

Hamlet is, as usual, well served by essayists. *Hamlet Studies*, 7 (1985) from New Delhi is gradually catching up with its schedule. Vernon Garth Miles argues that what makes Hamlet attractive to the twentieth century is his 'Search for Philosophic Integration'. Although 'caught at the crossroads of the sixteenth and seventeenth centuries, in the broad junction of humanistic optimism and Protestant determinism', at least he attempts to reconcile opposing absolutes. The idea that 'Hamlet's readiness does not signify resolution so much as it does resignation' (p. 36) is suggestive. Craig A. Bernthal specifically dwells on 'The readiness is all', and the preceding process of 'getting ready'. 'Readiness' to Bernthal is 'a state of heightened awareness and calmness' (p. 39) which is partly created through the eventual relinquishment of the search for a self. Paul Gaudet's '"He is justly served": The Ordering of Experience in *Hamlet*' (52–68) is a contribution to the developing study of 'audience response' (formally initiated by E. A. J. Honigmann)[24] and traces the sequential ordering ('*succession* and *synthesis*') of dramatic moments. The present reviewer has contributed to the volume an essay on the dramatic function of wit, comedy, and humour in *Hamlet*, seeing them as various forms of psychological response to political pressure in the world of the play ('The Spirit of Yorick, Or the Tragic Sense of Humour in *Hamlet*' (7–23).

Cherrell Guilfoyle in *Drama in the Renaissance*,[25] noting that Ophelia's name links her with ideas of succour and salvation, examines the Mary Magdalen-like doubleness of the character's significance to Hamlet. She is asso-

ciated in his mind with atonement and also female wantonness. I am too sentimental to accept that Hamlet's last reference to her, 'Be buried quick with her, and so will I', is his final rejection of her, despite Granville-Barker's authority for the reading. S. Nagarajan returns to the subject that hypnotically draws the attention of critics, 'The Nature of the Tragic Self in *Hamlet*',[26] arguing that in many of Shakespeare's plays 'the tragic hero is characterized initially by self-ignorance and the loss of identity, but later attains to a regrouping of the self and the establishment of a new identity' (p. 126). It is difficult to see why this interesting essay stresses *Hamlet* in the title, since almost equal attention is given to *Macbeth* and *King Lear*, and the terms of reference are taken from Angelo and Troilus. An equally alluring subject is signalled in David Frost's title, 'Constructing Hamlet's Mind'.[27] Taking Duncan's 'There's no art / To find the mind's construction in the face' as his point of departure, Frost speaks of 'The requirement that an audience infer a character's whole structure of disposition and motivation from cumulative hints and signs' (p. 5). The argument rambles from point to point and ends with an uncritical plea for 'empathy', but there are interesting suggestions along the way. In a lengthy study in Italian, Michele Marrapodi[28] uses infor-

---

24 *Shakespeare. Seven Tragedies. The Dramatist's Manipulation of Response* (London: Macmillan, 1976).

25 '"Ower Swete Sokor": The Role of Ophelia in *Hamlet*', in *Drama in the Renaissance: Comparative and Critical Essays*, eds. Clifford Davidson, C. J. Gianakaris, and John H. Stroupe (New York: AMS Press, 1986), 163–77.

26 *Shakespeare: Jadavpur University Essays and Studies*, ed. Debabrata Mukherjee, 5 (1986), 125–33. In the same journal Supriya Chaudhuri writes on '*Hamlet* and the Concept of Nobility' (19–36), and there are other interesting essays on 'Calvinist Psychology in *Macbeth*' and on the jesters, Kempe and Armin, among the other contributions.

27 *Sydney Studies in English*, 12 (1986–7), 3–20.

28 'Hamlet the Dane', *Nuovi Annali della Facoltà di Magistero dell'Università di Messina*, 4 (1986), 473–542.

mation about Elizabethan conventions and emblems to conclude that Hamlet is a sympathetically presented character standing for the ideal Renaissance prince debating within himself the moral issue of revenge, and searching for a 'well commeddled' balance of opposite royal virtues. He is finally seen as having been involved in 'una vendetta sanguinaria' (p. 542), a phrase which somehow captures better than English can, the mafia-like atmosphere of Claudius' court. Jill L. Levenson compares *Oedipus the King* and *Hamlet*.[29] Both plays involve the tragic protagonist in acts of solving riddles and enigmas, mainly through remembrance and retrieving the past. The essay is crisply informative, although less alert to linguistic subtlety than the book which cries out for comparison, that by Adrian Poole (reviewed above).

Finally, for those who prefer their criticism to be vintage rather than *nouveau*, there is a casebook edited by Joseph G. Price, *Hamlet: Critical Essays* (New York and London: Garland Publishing, 1986). To create an exemplary casebook of criticism of *Hamlet* is surely doomed, and although there is plenty of material here (516 pages of it) there is an overriding problem that all the pieces are snippets taken from lengthy studies, some of which do not focus centrally on *Hamlet*. One really needs a sense of the particular writer's overall argument in order to get the best out of the excerpts. There is an air of a scissors and paste job, and it might be preferable to direct students to a handful of sound books and articles that can be read as a whole. As a suggestion, if we are to be given Fielding, Goethe, Dickens, and Joyce, why not the great Australian novelist, Joseph Furphy, whose *Such is Life* contains lengthy and original discussion of *Hamlet* and Shakespearian tragedy in general? Whilst on the subject of casebooks, volume 4 has now arrived of the ambitious project, *Shakespearean Criticism: Excerpts from the Criticism of William Shakespeare's Plays and Poetry, from the First Published Appraisals to Current Evaluations*, edited by Mark W. Scott (Detroit: Gale Research Company, 1987). *Othello* is the centrepiece, surrounded by *Cymbeline*, *The Merchant*, and *Titus*. 'Current' seems to mean up to 1983 for this variorum-like enterprise.

King Lear, as we might expect, runs *Hamlet* a close second as the single play attracting most critical attention. An equivalent, perhaps, of *Hamlet Studies* is a book which, in its stress on the classroom as a test of ideas, could only have come from the USA: *Approaches to Teaching Shakespeare's 'King Lear'*, edited by Robert H. Ray (New York: Modern Language Association of America, 1986). Different writers indicate the ways in which they present the play to students, ranging from approaches based on theme and theatre to Jean Klene's 'An Approach through Visual Stimuli and Student Writing'. Michael Warren attempts to curb flights of fancy with the stern warning in 'Teaching with a Proper Text' that scholarship is reassessing the nature of the text(s) of *Lear*. The booklet as a whole creates the impression of a dizzying plurality that leaves a disconcerting sense that the play has slipped out of the many nets cast for it.

After reading so much dull and unoriginal criticism in journals, I found it a refreshing surprise to find 'Lear's Map' by Frederick T. Flahiff in *Cahiers Élisabéthains*, 30 (1986), 17–34. Flahiff discovers a 'mad pliancy' about references to place in Lear, ranging from vague contours, names that do and do not refer to places (Kent, Cornwall, etc.), to the 'bothersome particularity of the scene (ironically, an imagined creation) on "Dover Cliff"'. The spatial dislocations have analogues in the human world, leading into 'the shapelessness of war . . . the replacing of spatial by human relationships' (p. 19). The essay itself is, no

---

[29] 'Aletheia: Oedipus, Hamlet', in *Greek Tragedy and its Legacy*, essays presented to D. J. Conacher, eds. Martin Cropp, Elaine Fantham, and S. E. Scully (Toronto, 1986), pp. 281–93.

doubt deliberately, at times shapeless or frag-
mented, and 'the matter of Noah' is yanked
rather than coaxed into the argument, but it
starts the mind working in ways that other
articles positively prevent. Just as interesting in
different ways is Peter S. Anderson's 'The
Fragile World of *Lear*' in *Drama in the Renaissance: Comparative and Critical Essays*
(pp. 178–91). Approaching the play *via* Mon-
taigne, Anderson presents the world of *King
Lear* as 'a critique of justice, reason, nature,
social structure – perhaps Shakespeare's
deepest glance into the abyss' (p. 185). As a
'universal moral court' the play proposes 'that
only the guilty can get justice (one must be a
criminal in *Lear*'s court to be well served)' and
for the innocent 'there can be no justice'. John
Coates[30] reads *King Lear* as a 'spiritual
journey', albeit largely a pagan one, in which
'Poor Tom' is Lear's guide out of self-
centredness and out of 'a religious view which
has become untenable, under the attack of a
withering scepticism and naturalistic egotism'.
While he avoids barren questions concerning
the Christian element and the pessimism or
optimism of the play, it is not convincing to
sublimate Cordelia's death into spiritual significance without ignoring the secular shock,
anger, and moral outrage expressed by Lear
and (presumably) felt by audiences.

Judith H. Anderson deals delicately with the
existence of allegory in *Lear*.[31] While finding
no particular allegorical basis in the play, she
suggests that *Lear* shares many features with
sophisticated, problematical allegories, and
especially *The Faerie Queene*. By noticing in
the opening scene ideas found in the Cave of
Mammon episode, and by seeing that Lear's
'Come, let's away to prison' speech contains a
rich verbal memory of Spenser's hermit in
Book VI, counterpointed with Melibee's
interiorized landscape, we find our understanding of the play amplified. The reading has
the great advantage of returning *Lear* to its
literary context and its contemporary reader-
ship. It is a great shame that Shakespeare's use
of Spenser has been so scantily, and usually
badly, dealt with by critics. It may be a consequence of specialization, where few scholars
have expertise in both writers, or, more likely,
of an ill-defined feeling that Spenser looks back
to medieval times while Shakespeare looks
forward to our own. The whole subject cries
out for full investigation by somebody exercising the tact demonstrated by Anderson.
Further on the subject of sources, Jean MacIn-
tyre examines Shakespeare's echoes of Marlowe's *Doctor Faustus*,[32] particularly drawing
attention to the bloodletting scene and its
possible connection with Edmund's self-
wounding in *Lear*. The tempting possibilities
of a Faustian Edmund are handled with dis-
cretion. The general conclusion is that Shakespeare borrowed from *Faustus* only after 1600,
though he borrowed from other works by
Marlowe during the 1590s.

Martin Orkin in a courageous and welcome
article, 'Othello and the "plain face of
Racism"'[33], presents evidence from the play
that Shakespeare does not encourage us to
share the racial prejudice prevalent in his own
time, and that he consciously shows Iago
exploiting racist impulse, trying to persuade
Othello to accept a 'discourse of racism'. More
disturbingly, Orkin shows that a play which
'continues to oppose racism' has given rise to
criticism and performances (such as Olivier's)
which support racist doctrine and practice.
This is particularly so among many white
South Africans who, by focusing obsessively
on the figure of Othello himself rather than
recognizing Iago's strategy, evade or distort
the general perspective of the play. I fear that
many Anglo-American critics may not be

---

30 ‘"Poor Tom" and the Spiritual Journey in *King Lear*,
   Durham University Journal, 76, NS 48 (1986), 7–14.
31 'The Conspiracy of Realism: Impasse and Vision in
   King Lear', *Studies in Philology*, 84 (1987), 1–23.
32 '*Doctor Faustus* and the Later Shakespeare', *Cahiers
   Élisabéthains*, 29 (1986), 27–38.
33 *Shakespeare Quarterly*, 38 (1987), 166–88.

innocent of such conscious or unconscious 'readerly intentions', deceived perhaps by the perverse eloquence of F. R. Leavis and others. It does seem important to insist that in watching a Shakespeare play we are expected to recognize a moral dimension which, in accordance with Renaissance doctrine, may 'teach' humane lessons.

Steven Baker finds it of immense significance that 'precisely in the middle of *Othello*' Desdemona attempts to bind Othello's head with a handkerchief.[34] This tableau, we are encouraged to believe, evokes the blindfolded man, suggesting to the audience the traditional image of Blind Love. It looks like making a mountain out of a mole-hill, but then I suppose we ought to remember that Othello himself does the same, and from a handkerchief at that. In another article that seems initially just as unlikely, Balz Engler gives an unexpectedly physiological analysis of Cassio's 'For he was great of heart' (5.2.371).[35] Recognizing the problem in the apparently causal 'for', the writer suggests that the phrase, both in Elizabethan language and in Shakespeare's other uses, is properly understood as 'passionate, having strong emotions' and that it suggests 'beside himself' or even 'desperate'. This neatly explains why Cassio links Othello's great heart with suicidal intent, a problem which is not solved by the reading 'magnanimous', and certainly not evaded by Peter Alexander's quarantining semi-colon:

> This did I fear, but thought he had no weapon;
> For he was great of heart.

The less-than-major tragedies are not neglected. Rudolf Stamm conducts a close, almost word-by-word examination of the 'orchard scene' (2.2) in *Romeo and Juliet*.[36] He concludes that 'the laws of stillness and prudence' that dominate the scene are governed primarily by Romeo's control of his 'excessive impetuosity' and highlighted by Juliet's 'active part in the exchange'. 'Whereas Romeo tends to indulge in a dreamy kind of delightful fantasy, she

remains more controlled and practical'. While it is reassuring to have such detailed evidence for a reading that most would agree with, some uncharitable souls might feel that there is a tedious quality about the way it is presented. By contrast, the brevity of J. S. Carducci's 'Shakespeare's *Titus Andronicus*: An Experiment in Expression'[37] gestures towards a large subject. The writer demonstrates through apt quotation that the impossibility of using language to express pain and suffering is a central issue in the play. But if the subject is to be used to the full, one would expect more sophisticated amplification, probably in a meta-dramatic direction, and a more consistently comparative method. At least, however, she presents other critics with a fertile area for amplification.

Naomichi Yamada, like Stamm, conducts an almost line-by-line analysis of a chosen play, *Julius Caesar*.[38] This time the overt purpose is to conduct a source study, to identify and assess what Shakespeare owes to Plutarch and what he has invented. The conclusions, however, are of considerable interest to critics, and deserve to gain currency since they challenge some orthodoxies with thorough evidence. The most unusual conclusion, and one which I find welcome, is that the Roman populace, far from being fickle, are steadfast in loving and supporting Caesar throughout, while at the same time disliking tyrants. As a whole, the play shows two patterns of tragedy. It is a revenge tragedy,

---

[34] 'Sight and a Sight in *Othello*', *Iowa State Journal of Research*, 61 (1987), 301–9.

[35] 'Othello's Great Heart', *English Studies*, 68 (1987), 129–36.

[36] *A Yearbook of Studies in English Language and Literature, Weiner Beiträge zur Englischen Philologie*, ed. Otto Rauchbauer, 80 (1986), 237–48.

[37] *Cahiers Élisabéthains*, 31 (1987), 1–10.

[38] 'Two Tragedies in Harmony in *Julius Caesar* – Shakespeare's Reinterpretation of Plutarch', *Hitotsubashi Journal of Arts and Sciences*, 27 (Hitotsubashi University, Tokyo, 1986), 1–51.

showing the revenge of Caesar's death. It is also a tragedy of misconception, misconstruction, and misunderstanding, as 'men may construe things, after their fashion, / Clean from the purpose of the things themselves' (Cicero's words, 1.3.34–5). The two kinds of tragedy are incorporated to form a harmonious play.

Keiji Aoki's 'Commodity Theme and Irony in *King John*'[39] is yet another attack on the embattled suggestion that *King John* predated *The Troublesome Reign*, but since the argument is pursued not through textual detail but thematic exploration, it has interest for the critic. The 'Commodity Theme' is seen to be wider than just the Bastard's savage speech, and a generally convincing case is made for the widespread use of irony in *King John*'s dramatic structure (and, a lengthy and suggestive footnote tells us, in *Richard III*). The essay is eloquent on the Bastard's 'moral indignation' (p. 88).

Not all work on the History Plays is presented from an historicist's point of view. Annette Drew-Bear[40] concentrates on the text, with some help from rhetorical theory, in analysing 'embellished reports' in *1 Henry IV*. Falstaff is not the only one who lies. Hotspur and Worcester do also, in ways that show characters refusing to believe a truth that is politically unwelcome. False and embellished reports are part of 'the play's process of examining truth, falsehood, and belief in questionable reports', which is in turn related to Shakespeare's 'ability to see issues from different perspectives and to assume or explore a stance without a dogmatic commitment to it' (borrowing Rabkin's 'complementarity' and Driscoll's 'metastance'). Richard Adams gives a detailed reading of *2 Henry IV* as the reign of Rumour,[41] an abstract personification that begets others like Time. Rumour is like Falstaff in the capacities for self-dividing and creating a specious appearance of unity. By the end of the play Hal 'draws the sting' of Rumour, although it is not destroyed but reformed into a new abstraction, Fame,

holding 'a place of service in the new regime'.

The fortunes of the multitudinous Falstaff are leading him into fields which would surely draw a chuckle from the corpulent knight. Last year Socrates, this year the Gospels. Harold Bloom,[42] with an 'outrageous' but magisterial move, evokes the parable of Lazarus and Abraham, showing Shakespeare ironically reversing the New Testament story to let Lazarus, rejected by Abraham, into the heaven of Arthur's bosom. Beyond the story in Luke 16: 19ff., we find also the presences of Nietzsche, Socrates, and Freud summoned up to account for this profoundly original character. Joan Rees in 'Falstaff, St Paul, and the Hangman'[43] discovers that Hal's Pauline allusion ('redeem the time') is more than just verbal. It indicates that in rejecting Falstaff he is carrying out to the letter St Paul's words, having 'put off concerning the former conversation the old man, which is corrupt according to the deceitful lusts' (Ephesians 4: 22). The argument demands a Hal-centred approach, but even so, some may find the article a little harsh on Falstaff who, at the very least, entertains everybody in generous fashion. Finally (for the moment at least), Robin Headlam Wells and Alison Birkinshaw liken Falstaff to the 'Old Song' of the tavern, banished by St Paul's 'New Man' singing his new song.[44]

Paul Hammond, in a thoughtful study of *Measure for Measure*,[45] makes a case that the

39 *Review of English Literature*, 53 (Kyoto University, 1987), 77–106.

40 '"The Strangest Tale That Ever I Heard": Embellished Report in *1 Henry IV*', *Iowa State Journal of Research*, 61 (1987), 333–46.

41 'Rumour's Reign in *2 Henry IV*: The Scope of a Personification', *English Literary Renaissance*, 16 (1986), 467–95.

42 Harold Bloom, 'Falstaff', *Scripsi* (see note 1 above), 59–66.

43 *Review of English Studies*, NS 38 (1987), 14–22.

44 *Shakespeare Studies*, 18 (1986), pp. 103–116.

45 'The Argument of *Measure for Measure*', *English Literary Renaissance*, 16 (1986), 496–519.

play's 'withholding of solutions' is a deliberate strategy on the dramatist's part. It is designed to draw attention to the limitations of the comic form, to the inefficacies of language, and to the inadequacy of formal procedures of argument to solve complex human problems. The formal stabilities of language cannot be taken to infer moral reassurance, and close study of the Isabella–Angelo scenes and the finale show this. Less convincing is Maurice Hunt's 'Comfort in *Measure for Measure*',[46] a study dealing with the motif of *Pax vobiscum*, concluding that the giving of comfort 'becomes an overriding value' in the play. A value, yes, and we can be grateful for its existence, but it does not 'override' in any worldly sense the corruption and bungling in high quarters. The very inefficacy of positive values in Viennese society in this play is surely part of the play's bleak emphasis.

Useful essays on some comedies appear in *A Yearbook of Studies in English Language and Literature, 1985/6, Weiner Beiträge zur Englischen Philologie* (see note 36), a Festschrift for Siegfried Korninger, edited by Otto Rauchbauer. Stanley Wells provides a sensible comparison of the ways in which conventions of 'the reunions of characters who have endured a separation that they have not desired' operate in *The Comedy of Errors* and *Twelfth Night*. By linking the earliest comedy with the latest romantic comedy, Wells stresses motifs that endured in Shakespeare's comic patterns. Manfred Draudt, intending to demonstrate that *The Merchant of Venice* 'possesses a much greater degree of unity than has commonly been assumed', uses as evidence 'the unusually frequent references to "hazard" and "venture"', suggesting that the theme of fortune is central to the play's meaning.

It seems curious that, after several centuries of neglect, the subject of *billets doux* should have attracted the attention of two critics in one year.[47] There hardly seems anything auspicious in the *zeitgeist* of the 1980s to prepare us for such a coincidence. I fear, however, that the partial eclipse does not hold profound significance for the future of Shakespearian criticism. One article concentrates on the dramatic significance of love letters in *The Two Gentlemen of Verona*. The second, without contradicting the first, looks at the fate of the convention which began as a perfectly respectable romance device, only to be mercilessly parodied in *The Merry Wives* and *Twelfth Night*, and to reappear surprisingly with grotesque but tragic consequences in *Far From the Madding Crowd*. (Is Malvolio the prototype of Boldwood, as Lear is Henchard's?)

Matthew H. Wikander in a subtle and interesting essay, 'As Secret as Maidenhead: The Profession of the Boy-Actress in *Twelfth Night*', in *Comparative Drama*, 20 (Winter, 1986–7), 349–63, argues for a metadramatic analogy between Viola's predicaments, seen as rites of passage to adulthood, and the paradoxical nature of the 'boy-actress's' profession. Another who writes on *Twelfth Night* is Edmund Taft,[48] who, drawing upon De Rougemont's theories of love, sees Eros in this play as 'secretly opposed to life: by definition, it is boundless desire seeking its own annihilation' (p. 409). A less doom-laden view of love in the comedies is sketched by Sailendra Kumar Sen in 'Who Ever Lov'd that Lov'd Not at First Sight'.[49]

After a mighty revival, the Romances are falling again on barren ground. Only two articles deal with them, both on 'minor' representatives, and neither quite satisfactory. Stephen Dickey's suggestion that in *Pericles*

---

[46] *Studies in English Literature*, 27 (1987), 213–29.
[47] Frederick Kiefer, 'Love Letters in *The Two Gentlemen of Verona*', *Shakespeare Studies*, 18 (1986), 65–86; R. S. White, 'The Rise and Fall of an Elizabethan Fashion: Love Letters in Romance and Shakespearean Comedy', *Cahiers Élisabéthains*, 30 (1986), 35–48.
[48] 'Love and Death in *Twelfth Night*', *Iowa State Journal of Research: Shakespeare and His Contemporaries*, 5 (1986), 407–16.
[49] *Jadavpur University Essays and Studies* (see note 26 above), pp. 1–7.

both Gower and Pericles, after beginning as speakers of cliché and aphorism, gradually discover an effective dramatic speech (which includes silence)[50] may be convincing in its own terms. But to build an approach to this play in particular on the basis of fine linguistic discriminations does not seem quite appropriate to its mode of action and atmosphere of wonder. And when David Frost[51] provides us with a wholeheartedly ironist reading of *Cymbeline*, suggesting that its context was Shakespeare's desire to hit back at the critics of Romance by presenting his play as burlesque, he does not do justice to the admittedly curious, but also very mixed, tone of the play. There are moments of intimacy mixed with strange stasis and fascination (preeminently Giacomo observing the sleeping Innogen and the pastoral scenes) that have to be glossed over to arrive at such a reading. The answer to this play's puzzles will probably be found in the theatre in some inspired and sympathetic production.

---

[50] 'Language and Role in *Pericles*', *English Literary Renaissance*, 16 (1986), 19–38.
[51] '"Mouldy Tales": The Context of *Cymbeline*', *Essays and Studies* (1986), 19–38.

2. SHAKESPEARE'S LIFE, TIMES, AND STAGE
reviewed by RICHARD DUTTON

Yoshiko Kawachi's *Calendar of English Renaissance Drama, 1558–1642* is likely to find its way on to the reference shelves of most libraries.[1] It attempts to present, in tabular form and chronological order, as much essential information as possible about every known play, masque, or entertainment of consequence in the period, extant or lost, acted or not. (The only significant omissions would appear to be the less noteworthy provincial religious dramas and civic entertainments, which are being dutifully catalogued in the *Records of Early English Drama* series.) Each entry lists, in so far as the information can be determined, whether the work was performed or not, the date of first performance (subsequent recorded performances receive separate entries) or other early evidence of existence (such as date of licensing, entry in the Stationers' Register, or publication), the place of performance and principal persons before whom it was performed, the actors, the title, the type of the work (tragedy, pastoral, masque etc.), the author(s), date of the earliest editions and existence of any manuscripts, and a brief indication of the source of the information. This is all cross-referenced by works, authors, and acting companies. There are, inevitably, limitations. Where, as in many cases, matters of dating or authorship are disputed, the *Calendar* does no more than suggest limits or note queries, relying for the most part on standard authorities like the *Annals of English Drama*, Chambers, and Bentley; it does not refer us to the most recent discussions of such matters. More niggling faults are that the print of the tabular layout is small and cramped, so it is not easy to follow an entry across the page; and the year is only indicated where the New Year falls, not on successive pages. Nevertheless, it is extremely useful to have all this information in a single, convenient volume, and Mr Kawachi is to be commended for his labours.

What of the people who attended the performances listed in Kawachi's *Calendar*, or at least of those who paid good money to do so? Andrew Gurr's *Playgoing in Shakespeare's London* is a significant and timely contribution to the debate about the paying customers for whom English Renaissance drama was writ-

---

[1] New York and London: Garland Publishing, Inc. (Garland Reference Library of the Humanities, Vol. 661), 1986.

ten.[2] It is, in effect, a detailed expansion of the final chapter in the author's *The Shakespearean Stage, 1574–1642*,[3] based on a comprehensive survey both of persons known to have attended the commercial theatres of Tudor/ Stuart England and of contemporary comments about them and their tastes (the data are presented in two substantial appendices). Professor Gurr's present title, about which he admits some unease, comprehends both the persons who attended the theatres and the conditions they met with there; it attempts to avoid privileging either 'audience' or 'spectators' (since both were contemporary terms, with implications about the theatrical experience), and to echo Ann Jennalie Cook's *The Privileged Playgoers of Shakespeare's London, 1576–1642*,[4] a book with which in some respects he takes issue. His main aim is to resist the tendency evident in Cook, and previously in the works of Alfred Harbage, to reduce the 'audiences' of the period to broad demographic generalizations. He stresses, rather, the variety among the theatres and their repertoires and among those who attended them: 'Paul's boys differed from the Blackfriars boys. The Globe differed from the Red Bull. The Cockpit differed from the King's Men at the Blackfriars. None of these differences remained constant. The evidence needs sifting with particular care, and merges eventually into the history of changing play fashions' (p. 72). Gurr does indeed sift the evidence with great care, convincingly distinguishing between the different playhouses and the tastes for which they catered, with an economy and precision I have not encountered elsewhere. As anyone who followed the debate about Cook's book will know, this is not merely a matter of theatrical archaeology. Although Gurr does not elaborate the point himself, his thesis has implications for modern 'political' readings of Renaissance plays, which often invoke the supposed complexion of the original audiences and the socio-political status of the theatres. *Playgoing in Shakespeare's London* will lend

strength particularly to those who resist the tendency to reduce 'the Shakespearian stage' to a single archetype and those who emphasize the factional, or at least competitive, nature of Renaissance theatre. (Gurr has pursued this aspect of his thesis in a separate article. 'Intertextuality at Windsor' examines the repertoires of the Lord Chamberlain's and the Lord Admiral's Men in the mid–late 1590s and the ways in which they echo each other, in a rivalry we may construe as either commercial or factional or a mixture of both.[5]) If there is ever a second edition of this important book, a few distracting details might be amended. A point about the relative timings of play performances and church services (p. 33) is made so obliquely as to be puzzling; Cecil/Salisbury is described as Lord Treasurer in 1605 (p. 97), though he did not attain this post until 1608; and we are told (p. 160) that 'the early version of *Every Man In* . . . was set in Rome' (by implication, ancient Rome), when it is actually set in modern Florence.

In Kawachi's *Calendar*, *Sir Thomas More* is entered under 1595 as possibly performed then by an unknown acting company, which might have been the Lord Chamberlain's Men. It suggests that this would have been a revision of a play 'originally composed *c.* 1590–1593. 1600–106 also urged for revision'. Not too much of this would find favour, I suspect, with Scott McMillin, whose *The Elizabethan Theatre and 'The Book of Sir Thomas More'* approaches the play as a text for the playhouse rather than a stalking ground for palaeography and questions of authorship.[6] He regards it as dramatically coherent and theatrically competent in both its versions (allowing for the known lacunae in the original); by applying

---

[2] Cambridge: Cambridge University Press, 1987.
[3] 2nd edition, Cambridge: Cambridge University Press, 1980.
[4] Princeton: Princeton University Press, 1981.
[5] *Shakespeare Quarterly*, 38 (1987), 189–200.
[6] Ithaca and London: Cornell University Press, 1987.

criteria from theatrical history and practice, he chronicles a strong case for the first version having been written between the summers of 1592 and 1593 for Strange's Men performing at The Rose, and for the revision having been undertaken for the Admiral's/Prince Henry's Men at the Fortune in 1603/4 (shortly after Henslowe's comprehensive record comes to an end). He cannily avoids the question of whether Hand D's contribution is Shakespeare's, but suggests that it belongs to the original version of the play (that subjected to Tilney's censorship) rather than to the revision undertaken by Dekker and, perhaps, Heywood and Chettle; he vouches for its dramatic competence, mischievously dwelling on the possibility that its author might be the same person as Hand C, so often condescended to as a playhouse functionary, tidying up loose ends and bringing the text to some sort of order – essential roles in the theatre, but not what we ask of literary genius. McMillin's arguments are cogently put, with broad sideswipes like this at library-based scholars and their assumptions about literary, as distinct from theatrical, texts. But it has to be said that he only really tests one hypothesis in respect of each version of the play and never directly confronts, for example, Carol Chillington's argument for the revision having been undertaken for Worcester's Men,[7] which is endorsed and expanded in David Wiles's book, reviewed below.[8] He would not have had a chance to see Giorgio Melchiori's piece, 'The Booke of Sir Thomas More: A Chronology of Revision',[9] which examines the question of the revision in painstaking detail: 'One conclusion of the present enquiry . . . is that all the alterations to the original text of Sir Thomas More, including the writing of the additions and the intervention of the bookkeeper, took place within a very limited period of time . . . not later than 1593–94, fairly close to the composition of the original text' (p. 307) – Kawachi rather than McMillin, so to speak. This is a preliminary to the Revels edition of the play, of which Melchiori is to be a co-editor.

W. R. Streitberger has been studying Edmond Tilney (or Tyllney), the Master of the Revels who censored Sir Thomas More, for several years, and the main fruits of his researches have come together in Edmond Tyllney, Master of the Revels and Censor of Plays: A Descriptive Index to His Diplomatic Manual on Europe.[10] Although there is a biographical introduction and some discussion of Tilney's role as a censor, the main focus of the book is implied in its sub-title. In the 1590s and early 1600s Tilney worked assiduously on a confidential diplomatic work of reference, with carefully structured and indexed 'Topographical Descriptions, Regiments, and Policies' of the principal countries of Europe. It was intended for presentation to Queen Elizabeth and, on her death, was revised with a dedication to King James, though in the end it appears not to have been presented to either of them. 'Topographical Descriptions' would be of general interest to scholars in various fields, not least to students of Renaissance drama for whom it plainly demonstrates Tilney's knowledge of, and sensitivity to, the major political and religious controversies of his day. But the work runs to over a quarter of a million words, and Streitberger judges – correctly, I should say – that specific interest would hardly warrant the enormous cost of publication: 'Consequently I have settled on a descriptive index, designed to help scholars assess the significance of the work and to facilitate study of it.' Having recently been to the Folger Shakespeare Library, where one of the two manuscripts of 'Topographical Descriptions' now is, I can vouch for the usefulness of his labours.

[7] In 'Playwrights at Work: Henslowe's, Not Shakespeare's Book of Sir Thomas More', English Literary Renaissance, 10 (1980), 439–79.
[8] Shakespeare's Clown, pp. 80–1.
[9] Shakespeare Quarterly, 37 (1986), 291–308.
[10] New York: AMS Press, 1986.

On the question of censorship – particularly interesting in the light of Philip Finkelpearl's article on 'The Comedians' Liberty' reviewed here last year – Janet Clare now argues: 'Relative details of Elizabethan and Jacobean censorship suggest that in the early Jacobean period there was some relaxation of censorship as well as a shift in its concerns.'[11] Can this be related to the rather shadowy transition of functions from Tilney to his successor, Buc, in this period?

One detail of Tilney's biography that is not raised in Streitberger's book is a letter from Tilney to Sir William More, in which he refers to 'the most Arrogantist letter that Ever I recevid [from one Thomas Vincent] only for finding fault therewith, and yett have I recevid divers brave letters from the last Lord Chamberlayn When he and I were att odds'. In 'When Lord Cobham and Edmund Tilney were att odds',[12] Robert J. Fehrenbach argues that 'the last Lord Chamberlayn' referred to was William Brooke, Lord Cobham (in office 8 August 1596–5 March 1597) and that they were 'att odds' over Tilney's 'allowance' of Shakespeare's use of the Oldcastle name in *1 Henry IV* (Oldcastle being a previous Lord Cobham) for the character we now know as Falstaff. Streitberger was once of this opinion (in his unpublished doctoral dissertation), but argued in 'On Edmond Tyllney's Biography'[13] that the letter was much earlier and must refer to a previous Lord Chamberlain. Fehrenbach, however, now adduces quite reasonable evidence for assigning the letter to 1599 or 1600, in which case Cobham would be the man referred to, and the Shakespearian connection would be quite plausible if some way short of certain.

The question of the Oldcastle/Falstaff substitution was, of course, revived by Gary Taylor, one of the editors of the *Complete Oxford Shakespeare*. He has returned to the fray with 'William Shakespeare, Richard James, and the House of Cobham'.[14] He reviews here the dating and sequence of the presumed objections to the Oldcastle name in *1 Henry IV* (reiterating that it was never used on stage in *2 Henry IV* or *Merry Wives*), and also considers the 'Brook/Broom' substitution in *Merry Wives*. He looks afresh at the evidence provided by Dr Richard James, the antiquary who first pointed to William and Henry Brooke (7th and 8th Lords Cobham) as the objectors to the Oldcastle name, and finds it consistent with the facts in all particulars. He establishes that James wrote down his comments later than J. O. Halliwell-Phillipps (who unearthed them) supposed and at a time when James mixed in circles where accurate information about such matters might be current. John Jowett, meanwhile, argues that 'if Oldcastle is restored, so too should be Russell and Harvey' for the characters we usually know as Bardolph and Peto.[15] This is largely a study of the textual problems involved, but relevant here in that he also adduces evidence why these names, like Oldcastle, might have caused offence.

In a very different context, David Wiles re-opens the case for the role Oldcastle/Falstaff having first been created by the clown in Shakespeare's company, Will Kemp.[16] Kemp has often had a bad press, not least from those who believe that Hamlet's strictures about clowns speaking no more than is set down for them refer to him, and there is a widespread assumption that he was neither disciplined nor sophisticated enough as an actor to carry a role as sustained as Falstaff. Wiles's detailed and sympathetic study of the clown tradition,

---

11 '"Greater Themes for Insurrection's Arguing": Political Censorship of the Elizabethan and Jacobean Stage', *Review of English Studies*, NS 38 (1987), 169–83, at pp. 181–2.
12 *Shakespeare Studies*, 18 (1986), 87–101.
13 *Review of English Studies*, NS 29 (1978), 11–35.
14 *Review of English Studies*, NS 38 (1987), 334–54.
15 *Review of English Studies*, NS 38 (1987), 325–33, p. 325.
16 *Shakespeare's Clown: Actor and Text in the Elizabethan Playhouse* (Cambridge: Cambridge University Press, 1987).

which takes 'a holistic view of the Elizabethan theatrical experience', may well make people reconsider. He examines Kemp's career within the 'tension between a neo-classical aesthetic which could not accommodate the clown and a performing tradition in which the clown was central' (p. 43) and argues that 'Kemp was not wilfully turning his back on history when he decided to join Worcester's company. The company's repertoire was a radical one, both in political and artistic terms. An adequate part was provided for Kemp in each play, and the actor's talents were properly exploited' (p. 82). The book does contain a chapter on Kemp's successor in Shakespeare's company, Robert Armin, but there is no doubting where its heart lies. (Incidentally, this is the third book to be considered here – along with Gurr and McMillin – to build much of its case around the consistent repertoires and house-styles of particular acting companies, with detail and conviction that we would hardly have found even ten years ago. That such distinctions can be made, and are important, has rapidly become one of the modern ortho-doxies, though clearly there is still a lot of research to be done in this area.)

A much more traditional line of enquiry into Shakespeare's plays, though for many years out of fashion, is the question of the influence of the Bible on his writing. The last major contribution to this field, though naturally there have been secondary studies, was Rich-mond Noble's *Shakespeare's Biblical Knowledge and Use of the Book of Common Prayer*, published as long ago as 1935 (London). It is striking, therefore – and unfortunate, in respect of some inevitable duplication – that two books on the subject should appear in the same year. Naseeb Shaheen's *Biblical References in Shakespeare's Tragedies* is the more broadly based study, dealing with all the tragedies and containing two prefatory chapters dealing with 'The English Bible in Shakespeare's Day' and 'Shakespeare and the Anglican Liturgy' which students will find helpful.[17] Peter Mil-

ward's *Biblical Influences in Shakespeare's Great Tragedies* restricts itself to the quartet of plays canonized by Bradley, contains relatively little commentary, and is largely composed of 'a series of annotations, as it were supplementing the existing editions of the great tragedies, which are usually all too meagre in their recog-nition of Biblical echoes and allusions' (p. xiii).[18] Such 'annotations' form the main substance of Shaheen's book too, though he also weighs suspected Biblical and liturgical allusions against other known sources for the same passage, to illuminate where Shakespeare borrowed directly, adapted the source, or introduced the allusion himself. In this respect, as in others, Shaheen is more scrupulous (or narrow, depending on your point of view) about what actually constitutes a Biblical allu-sion. Where Milward speaks of having 'tried to keep my ear open for all kinds of Biblical echoes, allusions, references, parallels, images, ideas, and themes' (p. ix), Shaheen has a chapter carefully graduating 'Criteria for a Valid Reference'. So, for example, at *Hamlet* 1.1.128, 'It was about to speak, when the cock crew', Milward cites Matthew 26: 74–5, where Peter denies Christ 'and immediately the cock crew' etc., but Shaheen explicitly eschews this as one of several examples 'too tenuous and far-fetched to be accepted as valid and convincing biblical parallels' (p. 55). The contrast demonstrates the perils of all allusion studies. But either of these scholarly works should prove illuminating for most readers, if approached in the right spirit, and most illumi-nating of all (where they overlap) read in parallel.

A number of reissues or new editions of standard works, whose subjects border on the Shakespearian stage, deserve a mention.

---

[17] Newark, Delaware: University of Delaware Press; and London and Toronto: Associated University Presses, 1987.

[18] Bloomington and Indianapolis: Indiana University Press, 1987.

Allardyce Nicoll's *The World of Harlequin* (first published 1963) is reissued in a convenient, if not exactly cheap, paperback format.[19] Glynne Wickham's *The Medieval Theatre* (first published 1974) has reached a third edition; the early part of the text is lightly revised, but there is also a new final chapter, tracing the losing battle that 'Gothic' theatre fought with the forces of neo-classicism across Europe in the sixteenth and early seventeenth centuries.[20] The closing phase of that battle in France is the subject of Tom Lawrenson's *The French Stage and Playhouse in the Seventeenth Century: A Study in the Advent of the Italian Order.*[21] This is a completely revised and up-dated version of the author's *The French Stage in the Seventeenth Century* (1957), completed before his death in 1982, and now finally seen into print – in every way a fitting tribute – by his colleagues at Lancaster.

But the reissue of most pressing interest to Shakespearians will be that of S. Schoenbaum's *William Shakespeare: A Compact Documentary Life.*[22] This is, for the most part, a reprint of the 1977 edition, though Schoenbaum has revised sparingly to take notice, for example, of E. A. J. Honigmann's *Shakespeare: The 'Lost Years'* (Manchester: Manchester University Press, 1985)[23] in his account of the supposed Lancashire connection and silently to amend minor mistakes such as the site of John de Stratford's tomb (p. 9). He has, however, substantially expanded the Postscript to include discussion of an array of issues raised over the last ten years, including further evidence of John Shakespeare's business dealings, other aspects of the 'Lancashire connection', and the question of Shakespeare's signatures. He also makes good his inadvertent omission of all mention of 'The Phoenix and the Turtle'. There is still, however, no mention of the 'Brook/Broom' business in *Merry Wives* (see the Gary Taylor article mentioned above). Maurice J. O'Sullivan's 'Shakespeare's Other Lives' entertainingly expands upon S. Schoenbaum's *Shakespeare's Lives* (Oxford, 1970) to examine conscious fictions about Shakespeare, which may indirectly have coloured popular notions about him almost as much as supposedly factual biographies.[24]

Donald W. Foster brings a lot of good sense to bear on the question of Thomas Thorpe's epigraph (rather, he insists, than dedication) to the 1609 edition of the *Sonnets*. Basing his argument on extensive comparisons with other complimentary puffs and literary salutations from the period, he maintains that there is nothing that a contemporary reader would have found odd or puzzling. 'Begetter', for example, could only have been understood as 'author', and the whole mythology has been based on failing to acknowledge the obvious – that 'W.H.' is a misprint for 'W.S.' or 'W.SH.'. He demonstrates that the printer, Eld, could be a lazy proof-reader and that there are numerous parallel examples from the period.[25] Marion Colthorpe, similarly bent on demythologizing, pours scholarly cold water on the notion of Queen Elizabeth's having attended any special performance of *A Midsummer Night's Dream* staged in connection with some aristocratic wedding or other; she particularly casts doubt on Elizabeth's pres-

---

[19] Cambridge: Cambridge University Press, 1986.

[20] Cambridge: Cambridge University Press, 1987.

[21] New York: AMS Press, 1986.

[22] New York and Oxford: Oxford University Press, 1987.

[23] Last year in this review I mentioned Sidney Thomas's suggestion that a redundant stage direction proves that *The Troublesome Raigne* preceded *King John*, which would undermine an important element of the dating in *Shakespeare: The 'Lost Years'*. The Spring 1987 issue of *Shakespeare Quarterly* chews this over in its new and enterprising 'Exchange' section (pp. 124–30): Honigmann replies to Thomas; Paul Werstine also questions Thomas's case, though on other grounds; while Thomas defends his original explanation as 'the simplest and most plausible yet offered'. Let the readers decide.

[24] *Shakespeare Quarterly*, 38 (1987), 133–53.

[25] *PMLA*, 102 (1987), 42–54.

ence at the Thomas Berkely–Elizabeth Cary wedding of 1596, suggesting this was not celebrated with any special festivities.[26]

Three hundred and fifty years after his death, we finally have a scholarly biography of Ben Jonson, a remarkable delay given that we know so much more about him than about any other contemporary writer. Rosalind Miles's *Ben Jonson: His Life and Work* is a soberly traditional assembling of the factual record, comprehensive in that it does not overlook anything that ought to be there, and a great advance on the bare skeleton provided by Herford and Simpson in the *Complete Works*.[27] If my praise is less than fulsome it is because the book seems to me to fall some way short of the vitality and complexity of its subject. To make one example serve for many: the question of how and when *Sejanus* was staged in 1603 (given that the theatres seem to have been shut from the death of Elizabeth onwards) is relegated to a note, where the theory of a court performance is credited to Herford and Simpson, and Chambers, but not examined; the charge of 'popery and treason' advanced by Northampton is unequivocally associated with the play, though the wording in the Drummond *Conversations* is highly ambiguous; the search for 'the second pen' in the original version is compressed into the assertion that 'scholars are agreed' that Chapman is the likeliest candidate. Nothing here is inherently implausible, but we are shown nothing of the range of other possibilities, of the complexity of the evidence. And no kites are flown about why exactly the Privy Council might have been disturbed by the play (the fall of Essex? Raleigh?). The facts are assembled, but their most intriguing implications are not probed (an omission most evident in the account of Jonson's involvement in the Gunpowder Plot). On top of this, the text contains too many errors for comfort; for example: '1587' for '1687' (p. 8); 'Sidney's brother Robert who had succeeded to the title' (p. 87) – there was no *Sidney* title, until Robert himself became

Lord Lisle and later Earl of Leicester; 'Duchess [for Countess] of Bedford' (p. 91); 'After [1608] he wrote all his remaining plays for [the King's Men] except one' (p. 118) – this should be 'two' (*Epicoene, Bartholomew Fair*), or even 'three' (*A Tale of a Tub*), if we accept – as Dr Miles appears to, though again the issue is not discussed – that this was a new play in 1633. This is a useful book in the main, but not a totally satisfactory one, and I feel bound to mention that another (and more substantial) biography is on its way from the States, though I have not seen it yet.

Michael Justin Davis's *The Landscape of William Shakespeare* is a cut above the usual glossily illustrated survey of Shakespeare's England.[28] An intelligent text follows the contours of Shakespeare's life and career with the Chamberlain's/King's Men, including their tours, examining the local history and customs of the places with which he and they realistically may be associated. The choice of contemporary illustrations is generally helpful, though many of the modern photographs that mingle with them seem to have been taken with an eye to colour and atmosphere rather than complementing the text. For example, there are several places covered where the rooms in which the actors would probably have performed are still standing; it would have been enterprising to track these down rather than go for moody shots of rivers, forests etc. There are a few errors in the text: George Buc was not Edmond Tilney's nephew (p. 95), nor were Philip Sidney and Fulke Greville first cousins (p. 153); if Will Kemp was ever a student at Cambridge (p. 133), David Wiles knows nothing about it (see above); Queens' College, Cambridge, is mispunctuated throughout, and the captions to pictures on pp. 87 and 89 have been transposed. Nicholas Fogg's *Stratford Upon Avon:*

[26] *Notes and Queries*, 34 (1987), 205–7.
[27] London: Routledge and Kegan Paul, 1986.
[28] Exeter: Webb and Bower, 1987.

Portrait of a Town, similarly, is not to be mistaken for a tourist guide; it is a serious, though lively, piece of local history, tracing the pattern of life in the town down to Edwardian times.[29] Mr Fogg perhaps tells us nothing new about Shakespeare (though he tells us more about some of his Stratford associations and, in particular, about his son-in-law, Dr John Hall, than do many of the biographies), but the effect upon Stratford of its happening to be Shakespeare's birthplace is a persistent theme in his pages, perhaps best summed up in an anecdote of Constance Benson's: 'one of the porters, "meaning to be most appreciative and gracious", said to her, "We have a lot to thank you and Mr Benson for, you are making Stratford another Blackpool"' (p. 224).

Returning to the theatres Shakespeare used, rather than those he inspired, John H. Astington has been looking into 'Counterweights in Elizabethan Stage Machinery', arguing the case for their use in rising traps (particularly useful in scenes of diabolic conjuration); he finds evidence in records of a court performance (*The Knight of the Burning Rock*) as early as 1579 and examines the possibility of more widespread use thereafter.[30] Robert E. Burkhart, in 'The Dimensions of Middle Temple Hall', questions the over-neatness of some of the accepted figures for the dimensions of the hall where John Manningham saw *Twelfth Night* performed.[31] In 'Edward Alleyn's Early Years: His Life and Family', S. P. Cerasano, still presumably on the trail of Philip Henslowe (see the last two issues of this review), outlines what is known about his son-in-law and partner's life to 1606 *other than* his theatrical career and associations.[32] And William Ingram looks into the biography of another of the money-men behind the Elizabethan theatres, 'Robert Keysar, Playhouse Speculator', the goldsmith involved in the (second) Blackfriars and Whitefriars enterprises, suggesting that further enquiries along these lines might usefully throw more light on the personalities and circumstances behind the playhouses.[33]

We have our usual crop of proposed sources and textual explications. The most striking, if accepted, would be Gary Schmidgall's claim for *Primaleon, Prince of Greece* as a significant source for the main plot of *The Tempest*, which is generally held to be a rare instance of Shakespeare's unaided invention.[34] This anonymous Spanish chivalric romance was translated into English by Anthony Munday; Book 3, which is central to Schmidgall's argument, is not known to have been printed before 1619, but he makes a reasonable case for its having been available by 1610/11. Coming to *The Tempest* from a different angle, Margaret Hotine seeks to reinforce the idea of its relation to Jacobean thinking on contemporary themes, notably colonialism, magic (John Dee and the 'wizard' Earl of Northumberland), and the Gunpowder Plot.[35] Horst Breuer confronts a famous old crux, '"The Late Innovation" in *Hamlet*', arguing that it makes perfectly adequate sense within the play's own terms, without reference to external factors like the boys' companies or the Essex rebellion: '"Innovation" (which means "constitutional change" rather than "insurrection") refers to the play's main plot event itself: the death of the old ruler, and his ... supersession by his younger brother'.[36] In 'But Why Enobarbus?', R. MacG. Dawson examines Shakespeare's promotion of this character to a more central role than he has in the sources, and also the adoption of the cognomen Enobarbus (emphasizing the red hair and beard) over the family

---

[29] Chichester: Phillimore, 1986.
[30] *Theatre Notebook*, 41 (1987), 18–24.
[31] *Shakespeare Quarterly*, 37 (1986), 370–12.
[32] *Notes and Queries*, 34 (1987), 237–43.
[33] *Shakespeare Quarterly*, 37 (1986), 476–85.
[34] 'The Tempest and Primaleon: A New Source', *Shakespeare Quarterly*, 37 (1986), 423–39.
[35] 'Contemporary Themes in *The Tempest*', *Notes and Queries*, 34 (1987), 224–6.
[36] *Notes and Queries*, 34 (1987), 212–5.

name of Domitius, suggesting that it singles him out as a master-leaver and suicide, like the traditionally red-bearded Judas Iscariot.[37]

The breaking down of traditional distinctions between 'text' and 'context' or 'background' has made it increasingly difficult to draw the line on what are the proper concerns of a review section devoted to the 'Life, Times, and Stage'. The following items involve textual analysis and evaluation that would normally be classified as 'criticism', but they do so in ways that invoke either Shakespeare's 'Times' or his 'Stage'. So Richard Wilson, in '"A Mingled Yarn": Shakespeare and the Cloth Workers', invigoratingly relates 2 Henry VI to the cloth-workers' riots of 1592, to the appropriation of the Elizabethan theatre by the dominant class interests of the day, and to modern ideological appropriations of Shakespeare;[38] while in '"Is This a Holiday?": Shakespeare's Roman Carnival', he extends similar arguments to the forms of authority and disorder reflected in Julius Caesar, significantly the earliest play that we can with reasonable confidence assign to The Globe.[39] Both of these essays would probably be described as New Historicist or Cultural Materialist, not recognizing essential distinctions between 'plays', 'theatres', and 'history', but seeing all as examples of discourse within an ideology of power. Last year I mentioned here a couple of articles on these critical movements. I should also now mention Edward Pechter's 'The New Historicism and Its Discontents: Politicizing Renaissance Drama', which acknowledges 'the enormous interest and energy this kind of criticism has generated' and admires some particular instances, but views it sceptically as a branch of Marxist criticism with premises which its exponents do not always adhere to consistently and which we are not obliged to share.[40] Nevertheless, it is interesting to see how Cultural Materialism has joined forces with Feminism in two reappraisals of the time-honoured subject of boys playing the female roles on the Elizabethan stage. In 'The Act, the Role and the Actor: Boy Actors on the Elizabethan Stage', Kathleen McLuskie examines the historical and sexual dislocations created by our knowledge of the original playing conditions, concluding with how 'the reminder of the original boy actresses might alert the reader to the complex theatrical construction and the historical specificity of the Elizabethan drama, which might provide a salutary disruption of the authority of their images of womanhood'.[41] Phyllis Rackin, in 'Androgyny, Mimesis, and the Marriage of the Boy Heroine on the English Stage', sees the whole phenomenon as very specific to the period before the Puritan Revolution; she considers five plays – Lyly's Gallathea, Shakespeare's The Merchant of Venice, As You Like It, and Twelfth Night, and Jonson's Epicoene – as evidence of a developing theatrical tradition of transvestite boy heroines, in a time when there was still fluidity in the definition of sexual roles, before 'the masculinist ideology that shaped the modern world established its hegemony in the same period when the theatres were closed'.[42] Michael MacDonald's 'Ophelia's Maim'd Rites' might also be mentioned here, since its broader aim is to test the traditional historicist approach of 'text' and 'context' as evidenced by R. M. Frye's The Renaissance Hamlet: Issues and Responses in 1600 (Princeton: Princeton University Press, 1984): 'My narrower purpose is to show that contemporary attitudes to suicide were more ambivalent and mortuary customs more uncertain than Frye admits.' But ultimately this only confirms him in the time-honoured belief that 'cultural history can deepen our awareness of the complexity of Shakespeare's

---

37 Notes and Queries, 34 (1987), 216–17.
38 Literature and History, 12 (1986), 164–80.
39 ELH, 54 (1987), 31–44.
40 PMLA, 102 (1987), 292–302.
41 New Theatre Quarterly, 3 (1987), 120–30.
42 PMLA, 102 (1987), 29–41.

artistry'.[43] A candid New Historicist might have used the same evidence to suggest that we read 'cultural history', as we read the 'text', to make of it what we will.

Another example of a traditional critical approach retooled for the modern world occurs in Michael Bath's admirable 'Weeping Stags and Melancholy Lovers: The Iconography of *As You Like It*, II.i.', a wide-ranging study of the emblem of the weeping stag, which is not adduced as a kind of extended footnote to the 'univocal' text, but to help explore 'the play's articulation of received iconographic topoi, as it continually questions the problems of representation and illusion and the relation of language to received convention' (p. 32). This article is in the welcome first issue of *Emblematica: An Interdisciplinary Journal for Emblem Studies*, which all Renaissance scholars will want to keep an eye on. This issue also includes a useful bibliography of 'Facsimiles, Microform Reproductions, and Modern Editions of Emblem Books' by Alan R. Young.[44] There is evidence, too, that stage-orientated criticism may be moving into new modes. Harry Berger, Jr discusses, in 'Textual Dramaturgy: Representing the Limits of Theatre in *Richard II*', how 'a new reading of *Richard II* and the *Henriad* implicates a new approach to what may be called *textual dramaturgy* – that is, to indications of staging given by the Shakespeare text'.[45] Judd D. Hubert's 'The Textual Presence of Staging and Acting in *Measure for Measure*' exactly fits the model of *textual dramaturgy* promoted by Berger, though he does not use the term.[46]

We move now to the history of Shakespearian production and reception from the Restoration to the present day. Even here the critical methodologies do not always fit into the old moulds, as may be seen in Matthew H. Wikander's 'The Spotted Infant: Scenic Emblem and Exclusionist Politics in Restoration Adaptations of Shakespeare'.[47] Taking these adaptations more seriously than is often done, he adroitly blends questions of staging technique

and political ideology to demonstrate how they made 'a Shakespeare more politically conservative and more iconographically simplistic' (p. 342), a process he considers 'no less politically serious and artistically self-conscious' (p. 358), than the adaptations of *Coriolanus* by Brecht and *King Lear* by Ingmar Bergman. Bergman, incidentally, figures prominently in Ann Fridén's *Macbeth in the Swedish Theatre 1838–1986*, a conscientious and revealing study of a single Shakespeare play appropriated by another language and culture, where differences in ideological and theatrical approaches are inevitably more starkly foregrounded. The book traces different responses to *Macbeth* from the liberal struggle of 1838 to two productions in 1986 performed in the wake of the assassination of the Prime Minister, Olof Palme. But the main substance of the book is devoted to detailed analyses of three major twentieth-century productions: Knut Ström's expressionist one of 1928; Olof Molander's 1931 psychological monodrama, heavily influenced by Gordon Craig; and Bergman's 1948 exercise in surrealism.[48] Much of what Ann Fridén has to say about Bergman was first printed in *Shakespeare Survey 36* (1983).

Shakespeare in the nineteenth century is just as alien to many modern readers as is *Macbeth* in Sweden. Two new books, however, help us to make the cultural adjustments necessary to understand different aspects of what was going on. R. S. White's *Keats as a Reader of Shakespeare* is a sensitive and detailed examination, not only of *what* Keats read and admired in Shakespeare (most things, though preeminently *A Midsummer Night's Dream*, *The*

[43] *Shakespeare Quarterly*, 37 (1986), 309–17.
[44] Volume 1 (1986) was published by AMS Press, New York. Bath's article is on pp. 13–52, with illustrations; Young's bibliography is on pp. 109–56.
[45] *Theatre Journal*, 39 (1987), 135–55, p. 135.
[46] *New Literary History*, 18 (1987), 583–96.
[47] *Shakespeare Quarterly*, 37 (1986), 340–58.
[48] Malmö: Liber Förlag, 1986.

Tempest and *King Lear*), but *how* he read the works, what seized his imagination or focused his attention, and how this affected his own poetry and critical theories. White distinguishes Keats as a Romantic critic from Coleridge, aligning him more closely with Hazlitt in his delight in the sensuous particularity of Shakespearian language and his responses to the dramatic characters as quasi-autonomous beings. These are the qualities that Keats looked for even in productions of Shakespeare, praising Kean pre-eminently for his illumination of them above any question of the dramatic integrity, themes, or stagecraft of the plays. White's systematic analysis of the evidence makes this a significant advance on the two earlier major studies of Shakespeare and Keats, those by Middleton Murry and Caroline Spurgeon, linking Keats's intuitions as a reader with modern literary theory and reader-response criticism.[49]

Richard Foulkes has brought together a lively and varied collection of essays, *Shakespeare and the Victorian Stage*, illuminating numerous aspects of the dramatist's pervasive impact on the Victorian era.[50] The book is divided into six sections. 'Shakespeare in the Picture Frame' includes W. Moelwyn Merchant's brief survey of 'visual criticism' of Shakespeare in pre-Victorian illustrations of the plays, notably by John Runciman and William Blake, and in the scenic designs of Charles Kean and E. W. Godwin; James Fowler dissects David Scott's famous painting of a mythic event, *Queen Elizabeth Viewing the Performance of the 'Merry Wives of Windsor' in the Globe Theatre*; Richard Foulkes himself places Charles Kean's *Richard II* in the context of the Ethical Gothic and Pre-Raphaelite movements; Marion Jones examines the extent and nature of attempts at historical verisimilitude in Victorian theatrical costumes.[51] 'Shakespeare and the Lyceum Dynasty' has Michael R. Booth on the stylized pictorial qualities of Ellen Terry's performances; George Rowell on William Terriss (another pictorial actor and

one cut off in his prime) concentrating on his Romeo; Peter Thomson (in splendidly provocative mood) emphasizing the subversive, the neurotic, the morbid, and the mesmeric beneath the respectable surface of Sir Henry Irving; Cary M. Mazer (intriguingly adjacent to Thomson, though in a very different style) drawing parallels between acting and criminality in the career of Sir Henry's son, 'Harry' Irving.[52] 'Shakespeare Ancient and Modern' offers three analyses of the ways in which Victorian productions of Shakespeare made his concerns their own: J. S. Bratton reviews what she sees as their 'failure to come to grips with *King Lear*' (p. 131), the play as Shakespeare wrote it apparently unable to meet the taste of the age; Carol J. Carlisle gives a detailed account of Charles Macready's painstaking revival of *Cymbeline* on 21 January 1843, tracing his practical solutions to the play's many stylistic difficulties, against a consciousness of the play's nationalistic concerns; Ralph Berry is more specifically concerned with 'the imperial/patriotic' as 'a manifest presence' in Beerbohm Tree's productions generally, but with his versions of Shakespeare's Roman plays and *The Tempest* in particular.[53] 'Shakespeare as a Contemporary' considers Shakespeare's impact on

---

[49] London: The Athlone Press, 1987.
[50] Cambridge: Cambridge University Press, 1986.
[51] The essays are, in order: 'Artists and Stage Designers', 14–22; 'David Scott's *Queen Elizabeth Viewing the Performance of the 'Merry Wives of Windsor' in the Globe Theatre* (1840)', 23–38; 'Charles Kean's *King Richard II*: A Pre-Raphaelite Drama', 39–55; 'Stage Costume: Historical Verisimilitude and Stage Convention', 56–73.
[52] 'Pictorial Acting and Ellen Terry', 78–86; 'Mercutio as Romeo: William Terriss in *Romeo and Juliet*', 87–96; '"Weirdness that lifts and colours all": The Secret Self of Henry Irving', 97–105; 'The Criminal as Actor: H. B. Irving as Criminologist and Shakespearian', 106–119.
[53] 'The Lear of Private Life: Interpretations of *King Lear* in the Nineteenth Century', 124–37; 'Macready's Production of *Cymbeline*', 138–52; 'The Imperial Theme', 153–61.

several Victorian creative artists: Christopher Murray resurrects James Sheridan Knowles, once highly respected and now almost totally neglected, whom contemporaries frequently compared with the Elizabethans and occasionally with Shakespeare himself; Jane M. Stedman describes what amounted to a subgenre of Victorian drama, plays written in more-or-less conscious imitation of Shakespeare's fairy plays, *A Midsummer Night's Dream* and *The Tempest*; Arthur Jacobs looks at Sullivan, divorced from Gilbert but wedded to Shakespeare, who wrote scores for six productions and settings for five songs.[54] 'Shakespeare as a Foreign Dramatist' comprises Simon Williams's account of attempts in Germany, largely stemming from the promptings of Ludwig Tieck, to stage Shakespeare in a manner approximating to Elizabethan conditions; Christopher Smith's reconsideration of Shakespeare on the French stage ('always occup[ying] a place apart, as a corrective first to the routines of classicism, then to the rigours of realism', p. 238), taking as its starting point Sarah Bernhardt's decision – in this context, neither capricious nor absurd – to stage *Hamlet*, with herself in the lead; and Kenneth Richards on the London Shakespearian performances of the Italians, La Ristori, Salvini, and Rossi.[55] (This incisive piece was clearly written before the appearance of Marvin Carlson's *The Italian Shakespearians* (London: Folger Books, 1985), reviewed here last year.) Finally, 'Shakespeare in the Provinces' has Arnold Hare considering the Shakespearian repertoire of the Bath–Bristol stock companies based at the Theatre Royal, Bath, from 1805 till their disintegration in 1884; Jeremy Crump examining the genuine popular taste for Shakespeare among the various Chartist and working-men's movements in Leicester in the mid-century; and Kathleen Barker reviewing the career of Charles Dillon, a typical 'star' in the provinces in the 1850s and 60s.[56]

It is reasonable to surmise that the piece by J. S. Bratton, mentioned above, grew out of a large enterprise on which she was engaged. She and Julie Hankey are the general editors of an admirable new series, *Plays in Performance*, published by Bristol Classical Press, and they have led from the front by contributing the first two volumes – Bratton with *King Lear* and Hankey with *Othello*.[57] At first sight these could be mistaken for the start of yet another edition of Shakespeare, but closer inspection soon dispels that idea. The heart of these volumes is not the texts of the plays but the commentary, based on the entire theatrical history of these works, and describing – scene by scene, moment by moment, with pictures and photographs – how memorable productions and performers have handled them. Substantial introductions (twice as substantial, oddly, in the *Othello* as in the *Lear*) also describe the broad outlines of that theatrical history. The series will apparently be Shakespeare-centred, though 'other Jacobean dramas' are also promised, and it seems likely that students and teachers whose approach to plays is through performance will find them invaluable. My only real reservation about the format of the series relates to factors beyond the editors' control. For ease of reference, they reproduce the old Cambridge version of the plays *en face* to the commentary. This is generally reliable, appropriate in that it broadly reflects the view of Shakespeare's texts in the

---

54 'James Sheridan Knowles: The Victorian Shakespeare?', 164–79; 'Victorian Imitations of and Variations on *A Midsummer Night's Dream* and *The Tempest*', 180–95; 'Sullivan and Shakespeare', 196–205.

55 'The "Shakespeare-Stage" in Nineteenth-Century Germany', 210–22; 'Shakespeare on French Stages in the Nineteenth Century', 223–39; 'Shakespeare and the Italian Players in Victorian London', 240–54.

56 'Shakespeare in a Victorian Provincial Stock Company', 258–70; 'The Popular Audience for Shakespeare in Nineteenth-Century Leicester', 271–82; 'Charles Dillon: A Provincial Tragedian', 283–94.

57 *King Lear*, edited by J. S. Bratton; *Othello*, edited by Julie Hankey; both published by Bristol Classical Press, Bristol, 1987.

period from 1850 to 1950, from which a preponderance of theatrical examples are drawn (the *Lear* also has an appendix with key scenes from Nahum Tate's version, which held the stage for many years before that), and conveniently out of copyright. The worry must be that students will be tempted (with ever-shrinking finances) to use these as their *only* texts of Shakespeare, thus denying themselves all the benefits of textual explication that decent modern editions bring with them. It is to be hoped that teachers who, very properly, adopt this useful series will point out its limitations in this regard.

Christine Dymkowski's *Harley Granville Barker: A Preface to Modern Shakespeare* is unfortunate only in its timing.[58] When it went to press, her claim that 'no one has yet undertaken a detailed and systematic study of [Barker's] Shakespeare productions and criticism' (p. 11) was true in its entirety. Since then Dennis Kennedy's *Granville Barker and the Dream of Theatre* (Cambridge: Cambridge University Press, 1985) has appeared and stolen some of the thunder; it was reviewed here last year. The two books inevitably overlap in many particulars, especially in their detailed descriptions of Barker's historic productions of *A Midsummer Night's Dream*, *Twelfth Night*, *The Winter's Tale*, and his late (1940) and uncredited work on *King Lear*. But the structure and thrust of the two books is quite different. Kennedy looks at Barker's entire career in the theatre, including his own plays, and of this the Shakespearian productions were only a part, if an important one. Dr Dymkowski concentrates exclusively on Barker's Shakespearian endeavours, including not only the productions but also his extensive critical writings (which scarcely figure in Kennedy), demonstrating the connections between them. Her accounts of the Savoy seasons of 1912–14 and, especially, of Barker's collaboration with Lewis Casson in the Gielgud *Lear* are fuller than those of Kennedy, and significantly more heavily illustrated. Both employ similar

methodologies, reconstructing the productions mainly from the evidence of reviews and prompt-books, both have an eye to Barker's influence on subsequent developments in British theatre, especially the staging of Shakespeare, and both properly decry the misfortune that his talents were not more fully employed within the theatre in his later years. I would not like to recommend one book over the other, beyond pointing out their different points of focus, since both are excellent.

R. Chris Hassel, Jr's *Songs of Death: Performance, Interpretation, and the Text of 'Richard III'* is gratifyingly difficult to categorize.[59] It approaches *Richard III* from a variety of different directions – via performances, the sources, textual problems, issues such as providence and military strategy, the language, and the dramatic sequence – and synthesizes its insights in a way that makes this the most comprehensive and compelling study of the play that I know. The opening chapter is built around a comparison of the two performances of the play that should be accessible to most people – the Olivier film (1955) and the 1982 BBC videotape, with Ron Cook in the title role. The 'Epilogue' is a consideration of Bill Alexander's 1984–5 RSC production, in which Antony Sher was so memorable. (It was apparently staged after the bulk of the book was written, and adds a fittingly fresh perspective on which to end.) Between the two the play addresses intriguingly varied questions: What exactly are we to make of the conflict between Richard and Richmond? What problems are posed by the quarto and folio texts, and the differences between them? Where does Shakespeare stand in relation to his sources on the issue of divine providence? To each Hassel brings an impressive knowledge of what earlier critics and performers have thought,

[58] Washington: Folger Books; London and Toronto: Associated University Presses, 1986.
[59] Lincoln and London: University Press of Nebraska Press, 1987.

but invariably brings new light to bear with his own synthetic approach. Much of the book has appeared before in periodicals, but the whole is distinctly more than the sum of its parts.

Hassel's book seems a good context in which to mention Stanley Wells's piece on 'Shakespeare Scholarship and the Modern Theatre', in which he considers 'some ways in which scholarship and critics are at present interacting with the world of Shakespeare production'.[60] As the new Director of Birmingham's Shakespeare Institute, he will be ideally placed to further that interaction. One obvious and welcome context in which scholarship has recently affected production is in the RSC's new Swan Theatre. Laurie E. Maguire offers a useful review of 'The New Swan's First Season', describing its 'ambience of an Elizabethan playhouse within a loose approximation of the original' and discussing the use of the stage in the first four productions – *Two Noble Kinsmen*, *Every Man In His Humour*, *The Fair Maid of the West* and *The Rover*.[61]

Regular readers of *Shakespeare Survey* will know that issue *39* (1987) was largely devoted to 'Shakespeare on Film and Television'. Perhaps the sub-title should also have included radio, since two contributions suggest it is not yet a dead medium – Stuart Evans, specifically concerned with 'Shakespeare on Radio', and Anthony Davies reviewing the critical response to the way all three media have handled Shakespeare.[62] The late Orson Welles, fittingly, figures prominently in many of the contributions: two concentrate directly on perhaps his most memorable film adaptations of Shakespeare, Robert Hapgood on *Chimes at Midnight* and Lorne M. Buchman on *Othello*.[63] E. Pearlman compares him with Polanski and Kurosawa as a political interpreter of *Macbeth*, and he even figures (a surprise to this reader, at least) in Kenneth S. Rothwell's analysis of *King Lear* on screen, having played the title role on US television in 1953.[64] Details of all of these, and much else besides, appear in an extremely useful selective Shakespeare 'filmography',

compiled by Graham Holderness and Christopher McCullough.[65] Michèle Willems and Neil Taylor, finally, offer different reflections on the most comprehensive of all attempts to render Shakespeare on film or, at least, videotape, the BBC series, the latter specifically comparing the contributions of two directors, Jane Howell and Elijah Moshinsky.[66]

Michèle Willems is also the editor of *Shakespeare à la télévision*, a collection of interviews and essays largely stemming from the BBC enterprise.[67] The first half of the book is devoted to interviews and round-table discussions with participants in the series – one producer (Shaun Sutton), four directors (David Jones, Jack Gold, David Giles, Jane Howell), and one actor (Patrick Stewart – Claudius in *Hamlet*); these are all in English. The second half of the book is a collection of general and interpretative essays (in French, though English abstracts are also provided). For incorrigible Anglo-Saxons I reproduce the English titles from the abstracts, though the page numbers refer to the French text: Michèle Willems writes both discursively on televised Shakespeare, reviewing the BBC's record and raising some questions of audience response, and more specifically on the two history tetra-

---

[60] *The Bulletin of the John Rylands University Library of Manchester*, 69 (1986), 276–93, p. 279.

[61] *Theatre Notebook*, 41 (1987), 101–7.

[62] 'Shakespeare on Radio', 113–21; 'Shakespeare and the Media of Film, Radio and Television: A Retrospect', 1–11.

[63] '*Chimes at Midnight* from Stage to Screen: The Art of Adaptation', 39–52; 'Orson Welles's *Othello*: A Study of Time in Shakespeare's Tragedy', 53–65.

[64] '*Macbeth* on Film: Politics', 67–74; 'Representing *King Lear* on Screen: From Metatheatre to "Meta-Cinema"', 75–90.

[65] 'Shakespeare on Screen: A Selective Filmography', 13–37.

[66] 'Verbal-Visual, Verbal-Pictorial, or Textual-Televisual? Reflections on the BBC Shakespeare Series', 91–102; 'Two Types of Television Shakespeare', 103–111.

[67] Rouen: Publications de l'Université de Rouen, 1987.

logies within the series.[68] J.-P. Petit offers two comparative studies, one of two *Lears*, the Jonathan Miller/Michael Hordern (1982) and the Michael Elliot/Laurence Olivier (1983), and the other of two *Othellos*, the Orson Welles (1951) and the John Dexter/Laurence Olivier/Stuart Burge (1964/65).[69] François Laroque offers a defence of Elijah Moshinsky's *A Midsummer Night's Dream* (1981), which was not well received in all quarters; Raymond Willems argues that Jonathan Miller's *Othello* (1981) is 'a remarkably coherent, but sadly restrictive interpretation'; and Jean-Pierre Maquerlot generalizes in proposing the drama telefilm (the mode of the BBC series – specifically composed for television) as 'a hitherto neglected subject in semiotics, which stands at the crossroads of three different modes of dramatic presentation: the theatrical, the cinematographic and the televisual'.[70] Since television is overwhelmingly the principal point of access to performed Shakespeare in *all* cultures, these are matters we should not ignore.

---

[68] 'Shakespeare on Television', 7–22; 'The Two Tetralogies on Television: Historical Documentaries or Reflections on History?', 157–75.

[69] 'Two Memorable Television Productions of *King Lear*', 135–42; 'A Note on Two Filmed Versions of *Othello*', 143–50.

[70] 'Elijah Moshinsky's *A Midsummer Night's Dream* Reconsidered: A Plea for its Aesthetic and Educative Aspects', 121–34; 'Jonathan Miller's *Othello*', 151–6; 'The Drama Telefilm', 107–20.

3. EDITIONS AND TEXTUAL STUDIES
reviewed by MacDonald P. Jackson

'Editing might . . . be provisionally defined as a total waste of time which periodically reconstructs our image of the past.' Gary Taylor ends the first paragraph of his introduction to the Oxford Shakespeare's *Textual Companion* with this quip about the double-bind in which editors are caught: those who evade ridicule as pedantic drudges fussing over trivia expose themselves to charges of recklessness, presumption, and cultural vandalism.[1]

Nobody is likely to dismiss the Oxford editors' prodigious labours as inconsequential drudgery. They have produced two separate volumes of *Complete Works*, one in old spelling and one modernized, that are spectacularly unlike any other. Reviewers wishing to convict them of 'hurlyburly innovation' that threatens a national monument as the Percies threatened King Henry the Fourth's state must somehow demolish Taylor's general defence of the editors' procedures, rebut the evidence supporting hypotheses about the textual histories of individual plays, and challenge the arguments with which the four editors have justified their choices of variants and their emendations. 'No edition of Shakespeare can or should be definitive', writes Taylor. 'Of the variety of possible and desirable undefinitive editions one asks only that they define their own aims and limitations: that they be self-conscious, coherent, and explicit about the ways in which they mediate between writer and reader' (*TC*, pp. 3–4). The new Oxford *Complete Works*, in each of its orthographical guises, triumphantly fulfils these requirements. Taylor's general introduction to the *Textual Companion* is a vivid description of the materials available to editors of Shakespeare

---

[1] William Shakespeare, *The Complete Works* and *The Complete Works: Original-Spelling Edition*, eds. Stanley Wells, Gary Taylor, John Jowett, and William Montgomery (Oxford: Clarendon Press, 1986); Stanley Wells and Gary Taylor, with John Jowett and William Montgomery, *William Shakespeare: A Textual Companion* (Oxford: Clarendon Press, 1987). Page references preceded by '*TC*' are to the *Textual Companion*. My line references are to the modern-spelling volume of *Complete Works*.

and a cogent exposition and vindication of the Oxford editors' principles. Over a century ago the old Cambridge Shakespeare provided the first full collation of early quartos and Folios of Shakespeare's poems and plays, together with a record of scholars' conjectures and emendations. The new Oxford *Complete Works* represents a different kind of advance on its predecessors: it is a product of the most sustained attempt yet to *use* the whole range of textual evidence by thinking hard about all the relevant data and the problems these data pose. It invigorates by its constant display of logical rigour, open-mindedness, and intellectual energy.

The gradual realization in the first half of the twentieth century that a group of 'good' Shakespearian quartos, probably printed from the author's own drafts, could be distinguished from a group of 'bad' ones, based on manuscripts pirated from memory by actors who had performed minor roles in the plays, vindicated Heminges and Condell's claim that the First Folio superseded certain 'stolen and surreptitious' editions, but encouraged a tendency to undervalue the authority of the Folio's variations from good quarto texts. Confident that the 1600 Quarto of *2 Henry IV* and the 1604/5 Quarto of *Hamlet*, for example, had been set from scripts penned by Shakespeare himself, editors based their own texts firmly upon them, dismissing most Folio divergences as the vulgarizations, sophistications, and tinkerings of compositors, scribes, and anonymous theatre folk, and attributing all Folio omissions to accident or to theatrical cutting undertaken without authorial sanction. Shakespeare, like God, had performed his act of creation, seen that it was good, and rested: thereafter corruption had set in. When, as in the case of *King Lear*, the Folio afforded a version clearly better than that of the by no means contemptible 1608 Quarto, the flourishing theory of memorial reconstruction could be pressed into service to explain the Quarto's inferiority. Alice Walker, from

whom Wells and his team took over as editors of the Oxford *Complete Works*, diagnosed 'memorial contamination' even in the excellent 1622 Quarto of *Othello*. And once the memorially corrupt bad quartos themselves had been identified, they were largely ignored except in so far as they corrected obvious misprints in the better texts or offered clues to details of staging.

The Oxford editors, taking the view that the Globe and Blackfriars were places in which Shakespeare's intentions were realized rather than betrayed, find in many Q/F variants clear indications that the dramatist reconsidered and reworked his scripts in co-operation with his fellow actors. Plays are textually the least stable of all literary works, evolving as the author's initial draft is appraised by a theatre company, tried out in rehearsals, shaped into a prompt-book, performed in public, and modified in changing theatrical circumstances. As chief dramatist and actor-shareholder in the most successful drama company of his age, Shakespeare, until his retirement around 1612, would surely have participated in every phase of this process.

Their conviction that he did so influences the editors' handling of several plays in the Oxford *Complete Works*. By now their provision of two versions of *King Lear*, one based on the Quarto and another on the Folio, will occasion no surprise. Shakespeare's postulated revision of this tragedy is not only held to have been undertaken some four or five years after it had first been written and performed but also affects the whole structure: hence the need for this special editorial treatment.[2] Folio excisions amounting to some two hundred and seventy lines altogether in *Richard II*, *2 Henry IV*, and *Hamlet* – all preserved in good quartos – are judged to be cuts initiated or approved by

---

[2] G. B. Shand's 'Lear's Coronet: Playing the Moment', *Shakespeare Quarterly*, 38 (1987), 78–82, is interesting but does not mention that Q's 'one bearing a Coronet' in Scene 1, line 34.1 is absent from F.

Shakespeare, and the passages peculiar to the quartos are therefore relegated to appendices.[3]

The same respect for the theatre's contributions to the evolution of Shakespeare's scripts also motivates some editorial departures from the Folio when it furnishes the control-text. Sharing the orthodox belief that the 1594 Quarto of *The First Part of the Contention* and the 1595 Octavo of *The True Tragedy of Richard Duke of York* (which the Folio entitled *The Second and Third Parts of King Henry the Sixth*) and the 1597 Quarto of *Richard III* are all memorially reconstructed texts, Montgomery and Taylor draw on them in the same liberal way that Taylor drew on the bad Quarto of *Henry V* to supplement, modify, and correct the Folio in his Oxford English Texts edition of *Henry V*.[4] Their assumption is that these imperfect reports, besides preserving Shakespearian readings that have become corrupted in the transmission of the Folio text, sometimes bear witness to authorial readjustments made subsequent to the foul papers that lie behind the Folio versions of these histories.[5] In all three cases the textual situation is complicated by the Folio's being contaminated, to varying degrees, by derivative quartos. Montgomery and Taylor tackle the consequent problems with vigour and flair. Eleven passages, totalling one hundred and forty lines, contained in Folio *Richard III* but absent from the Quarto, are deemed to have been cut, with Shakespeare's approval, from the official prompt-book, and are thus transferred to a section of 'Additional Passages' appended to the basic Oxford text of the play.

Similarly consigned to appendices are duplications and false starts in such foul-papers-based control-texts as *Titus Andronicus* (Q 1594) and *Love's Labour's Lost* (Q 1598); and in general when the control-text has clearly been set from a pre-theatrical manuscript, the editors do their best to work out how loose ends would have been tidied up as the play was prepared for the stage:[6] when the control-text is a quarto and the Folio offers little more than a straight

[3] Naturally a revaluation of the authority of F affects the editorial choice of substantive variants. For example, Jowett admits to his text of *Richard II* over forty Folio readings that have been rejected by modern editors. Many of the changes from Quarto to Folio in *Troilus and Cressida* and *Othello* are also seen as resulting from Shakespeare's second-thoughts; for these plays F is taken as the control-text for substantives (but not for incidentals). In 'The Three Texts of *2 Henry IV*', *Studies in Bibliography*, 40 (1987), 31–50, John Jowett and Gary Taylor substantiate their conclusion that F *2 Henry IV*, though set from 'a highly sophisticated scribal transcript', nevertheless represents 'the culmination of a process of conscious revision initiated even before a fair copy was begun' (p. 50). They detect bibliographical signs of this process in the second issue of Q (1600), and argue that six passages peculiar to F are Shakespeare's expansions of the political plot, not material accidentally or deliberately dropped from Q.

[4] Steven Urkowitz, 'Reconsidering the Relationship of Quarto and Folio Texts of *Richard III*', *English Literary Renaissance*, 16 (1986), 442–62, argues that Q *Richard III* is based not on a memorial reconstruction, but on an earlier state of the play than that printed in F. The Oxford editors reject this theory. In '"This Son of Yorke": Textual and Literary Criticism Again', *Shakespeare Quarterly*, 37 (1986), 359–65, James P. Hammersmith considers 'the problem of words which are *both* substantive variants and spelling variants in early modern English' (p. 359), with special reference to the 'sons' and 'suns' of *Richard III*.

[5] Jowett's carefully considered edition of *Romeo and Juliet* – for which there are the 'bad' Q1, the 'good' Q2, and F, which reprints a lightly annotated copy of the derivative Q3 – 'allows for the potential presence in the Q1 text of Shakespeare, as possible reviser of details of the final theatrical text, but recognizes the presence of another hand, probably that of Chettle, contributing material which might be difficult to distinguish from the authorial' and accepts 'that a small number of reliable emendations may have been introduced in F' (*TC*, pp. 289–90).

[6] For example, in Folio *1 Henry VI* there is a glaring inconsistency in the presentation of Winchester as cardinal, then bishop, and then newly promoted cardinal. 'It appears that the foul papers left the matter temporarily unresolved, and since we do not possess a text of the fair copy which presumably resolved it, we must either print a text that is incoherent in its treatment of Winchester or we must conjecturally make the minimum of necessary alterations in 1.4/Sc. 4. Since the play can be made coherent by the omission of two lines and the alteration (mostly obvious) of eight words of dialogue, we have adopted the second of these options' (*TC*, p. 218).

reprint, even trivial Folio changes – mainly to stage directions and speech prefixes – may have the authority of a prompt-book endorsed by Shakespeare and so afford clues to the play's theatrical realization.

Of course Shakespeare cannot have approved all the modifications to which his scripts were subject in the theatre. In the introduction to his account of the text of *Measure for Measure* Jowett, citing a forthcoming study by Taylor and himself, suggests that after Shakespeare's death the play had undergone theatrical adaptation that included insertion of the song at the beginning of 4.1 and the addition, perhaps by Thomas Middleton, of the first eighty lines or so of 1.2. He details the editorial changes that 'would restore the text as Shakespeare conjecturally first wrote it', but since the Jowett–Taylor hypothesis is as yet 'untested by scholarly opinion at large, and its consequences for a restored text are radical', while 'the distinction between adapted and original material is not unequivocally clear' (*TC*, p. 469), he prints the conjectural reconstructions of Shakespeare's original only in an appendix. In editing Folio *Macbeth*, another text that has suffered late adaptation, Wells, far from aspiring to purge the play of spurious material, draws on Middleton's *The Witch* to give us the full text of the songs referred to in the Folio in 3.5 and 4.1 only by their opening phrases. 'It is clear that, in our present state of knowledge, we cannot hope to recover the text as originally performed . . . But the songs are extant, and there is at least presumptive evidence that they were sung in full in pre-Restoration performances of *Macbeth*' (*TC*, p. 543).

Wells and his fellow editors have thoroughly reconsidered the principles that should govern the modernization of spelling and punctuation and the presentation of their text – scene and act divisions, verse lineation (including the treatment of short lines), the spacing and normalization of contractions, and so on. They devote special attention to a more consistent and generous provision of stage directions than has been customary; these are neither Shavian nor novelistic, but designed to help readers visualize the plays in production on the Shakespearian stage.[7] Names may appear in unfamiliar forms: Petruccio, Biron, Mote, Capulet's Wife (rather than Lady Capulet),[8] Owain Glyndŵr, Ensign Pistol, Valtemand, Brabanzio, Thaliart, Giacomo, Innogen. There is a rationale for all such novelties. The modern-spelling edition is free from the archaisms – 'murther', 'vild', 'bankrout', and the like – that spatter the pages of *The Riverside Shakespeare*.

As well as recording the Oxford editors' substantive departures from control-texts and the more plausible of those variants and emendations that they have rejected, the *Textual Companion* serves as an up-to-date compendium of information about key issues in Shakespearian textual criticism, since the aim has been 'to determine the nature of the manuscript or printed copy that lies behind each substantive edition' (*TC*, p. 61).[9] A table summarizes the conclusions that are reached in the separate discussions for each poem and play. No previous scholarship of substance seems to have been neglected, and the documentation is ample. Stemmas reveal the postulated relationships between significantly variant texts. There is a useful chart of currently accepted attributions to First Folio compositors, with reference to Folio pages, the

---

[7] They allow themselves a little more freedom in the modern-spelling than in the old-spelling edition. Theirs is the sort of policy advocated by Arthur H. Scouten, 'Designation of Locale in Shakespeare Texts', *Essays in Theatre*, 2 (1983), 41–55.

[8] David Bevington's *Complete Works of Shakespeare*, 3rd edn (Glenview, Illinois, and London: Scott, Foresman, and Co., 1980) made the same choice.

[9] MacD. P. Jackson's chapter on 'The Transmission of Shakespeare's Text' in *The Cambridge Companion to Shakespeare Studies*, ed. Stanley Wells (Cambridge: Cambridge University Press, 1986), pp. 163–85, offers a briefer introduction.

through line numbering of Hinman's *Norton Facsimile*, and the continuous line numbering of the Oxford old-spelling edition.

Questions raised by the probable or possible use of marked-up quartos in the printing of certain plays have been variously answered in recent years. The Oxford editors are often driven to postulate sporadic consultation of an earlier edition by a compositor or scribe who used it as a crib to decipher a difficult manuscript. Taylor now suspects that the Folio compositors of *Henry V* may have employed Q3 (1619) in this way, and that Folio *Hamlet*'s enigmatic links with Q2 are most likely to have been mediated through a copy of Q3 (1611), to which the compositors haphazardly referred. Jowett agrees with the new Arden (London, 1965) editor A. R. Humphreys that the scribe who prepared the manuscript that served as copy for Folio *2 Henry IV* had occasional recourse to Q (1600) as he transcribed a prompt-book. There will be more ink spilt, and computer print-out generated, on these matters.

Indeed there already has been. In 'Q1 and the Copy for Folio *Lear*' T. H. Howard-Hill argues that 'the only influence of Q1 in the Folio was intermediated through its reprint, Q2'.[10] I agree with him that the item of evidence supposed to prove otherwise – the absence from Q1 (uncorrected) and F, and the presence in Q1 (corrected) and Q2, of the phrase 'and appointed guard' – can plausibly be explained as due to Shakespeare's ambiguous interlineation or marginal insertion of the phrase in the foul papers, causing it to be overlooked or deliberately omitted by the Q1 compositor and the scribe who fair-copied the foul papers to create the basis for the original prompt-book; but I do not understand the reasons for his belief that the phrase was later restored (ambiguously) to the prompt-book. In the *Textual Companion* (pp. 529–32) Taylor, while continuing to hold that Q1 affected a manuscript used to annotate an exemplar of Q2, finds some grounds for sharing Howard-

Hill's view that marked-up Q2's influence on F *King Lear* was exerted through an intervening transcript. MacD. P. Jackson's 'Printer's Copy for the First Folio Text of *Othello*: The Evidence of Misreadings',[11] offers as confirmation that Folio Compositors B and E set *Othello* from manuscript, the fact that a grossly disproportionate number of F's misreadings occur within the inexperienced Compositor E's stints; this unequal distribution is inexplicable if the two men were setting from a marked-up quarto.

A long chapter in the *Textual Companion* expertly reviews the state of our knowledge about 'The Canon and Chronology of Shakespeare's Plays' (69–144). The discussion of chronology uses, among other internal evidence, some valuable but little-known metrical data published by Ants Oras, Eliot Slater's statistical study of vocabulary links between plays, a highly technical investigation by statistician Baron Brainerd of high-frequency words in Spevack's *Concordance*, and a new index, devised by Taylor, of the rate at which certain colloquial contractions appear within Shakespeare's verse. The old-spelling and modern-spelling editions themselves present the works in their likely order of composition. Greatest uncertainty attaches to the sequence in which the early plays were written, and doubts over Shakespeare's sole authorship of *1 Henry VI*, *The First Part of the Contention*, *The True Tragedy of Richard Duke of York*, *Titus Andronicus*, and even *The Taming of the Shrew* complicate the picture. The writing of plays in collaboration was a prominent feature of the Elizabethan–Jacobean entertainment industry, and the Oxford editors' attitude to the canon manifests the same sense of Shakespeare as practical man of the theatre that determines their attitude to the texts. God the Creator needed no help. But the Oxford team see no

---

[10] *Papers of the Bibliographical Society of America*, 80 (1986), 419–35, p. 421.
[11] *The Library*, 9 (1987), 262–7.

reason to suppose that Shakespeare, for all his supremacy among dramatists, would have shunned collaboration; at the beginning of his career it may well have been a necessity, as it was for virtually every other tyro playwright of the time. The editors assign *1 Henry VI*, which they date later than the other two Henry VI plays, to 'William Shakespeare and Others'; recognize that *All Is True (Henry VIII)* and *The Two Noble Kinsmen* are (like the lost *Cardenio*) the joint works of Shakespeare and Fletcher, and that Middleton had a substantial share in *Timon of Athens*; and regard the first two acts of *Pericles* as the probable handiwork of George Wilkins.[12] They accept that Addition II Hand D, and Addition III of *Sir Thomas More* are Shakespeare's.[13] On suspect early plays other than *1 Henry VI* they reserve judgement. This is one area that remains adequately to be explored. The development of objective tests capable of discriminating between the undoubted products of Shakespeare's pen in the period 1585–1595 and plays by all other known dramatists active at that time would also aid assessment of the claims of *Edward III* (1596) and *Arden of Faversham* (1592) for admission to the canon. Although these anonymously published plays are excluded from the Oxford *Complete Works*, the editors acknowledge that there exists a case for Shakespeare's at least partial authorship of *Edward III*, in particular.[14]

With the help of Marvin Spevack and the computer, the Oxford team have calculated the relative frequencies of ten function words that occur at tolerably consistent rates within Shakespeare's works, and, after testing the findings on a control group of non-Shakespearian poems and plays, have applied them to disputed and pseudo-Shakespearian works. 'The function-word test distinguishes with remarkable clarity between the two shares of both *Timon of Athens* and *Pericles*' (*TC*, p. 86), and emphatically excludes *Edmund Ironside* from the canon. It is a pity that the figures for non-Shakespearian and dis-

puted works in Tables 3 and 4 are not given in the same form as those for the undoubted Shakespearian works in Table 2; a figure such as 0.07, as a proportion of 1.00, is far less informative than 6.79 as a proportion of 100.[15]

A subsidiary aim has been 'to begin a re-examination of the non-dramatic canon, and of manuscript sources generally' (*TC*, p. 61).

---

[12] All these ascriptions are boldly made on the title-pages preceding the plays in the Oxford *Complete Works*.

[13] Important new publications on this play are Giorgio Melchiori, 'Hand D in *Sir Thomas More*: An Essay in Misinterpretation', *Shakespeare Survey 38* (Cambridge: Cambridge University Press, 1985), 101–14, and 'The Booke of Sir Thomas Moore: A Chronology of Revision', *Shakespeare Quarterly*, 37 (1986), 291–308; and Scott McMillin, *The Elizabethan Theatre and 'The Book of Sir Thomas More'* (Ithaca and London: Cornell University Press, 1987). See also Thomas Merriam, 'Was Munday the Author of *Sir Thomas More*?', *Moreana*, 24 (1987), 25–30.

[14] In 'The Reign of King Edward the Third (1596) and Shakespeare', *Proceedings of the British Academy*, 71 (1985), 159–85, Richard Proudfoot, though not primarily concerned with authorship, asserts that '*Edward III* now stands squarely on the frontier of the Shakespeare canon' (p. 184) and inclines to the view that it should be allowed provisional entry. Toby Robertson, who directed a notable revival for Theatr Clwyd, Mold, 26 June–25 July 1987, tends to concur, and reports that the play stood firmly 'on its own dramatic feet'.

[15] Marina Tarlinskaja's meticulous study of 'stress profiles', *Shakespeare's Verse: Iambic Pentameter and the Poet's Idiosyncrasies* (New York: Peter Lang, 1987), contains a wealth of metrical data pertinent to problems of chronology and attribution; the figures confirm the presence of a collaborator in *Pericles* and *All Is True* (she does not consider *The Two Noble Kinsmen*) and distinguish two strata of composition in *Titus Andronicus*, one being either earlier than any other Shakespearian dramatic verse or by a different playwright. M. W. A. Smith continues his statistical work on problems of attribution in Renaissance drama in 'The Revenger's Tragedy: The Derivation and Interpretation of Statistical Results for Resolving Disputed Authorship', *Computers and the Humanities*, 21 (1987), 21–55; 'Merriam's Applications of Morton's Method', *Computers and the Humanities*, 21 (1987), 59–60; and 'Hapax Legomena in Prescribed Positions: An Investigation of Recent Proposals to Resolve Problems of Authorship', *Literary and Linguistic Computing*, 2 (1987), 145–52.

There will doubtless be less contention over the brief epitaphs and impromptu trifles included in the *Complete Works* than there has been over 'Shall I die?' Donald W. Foster renews his attack on this lyric, on Taylor's ascription of it to Shakespeare, and on Taylor in an article prematurely entitled ' "Shall I Die" Post Mortem: Defining *Shakespeare*'.[16] There is general agreement that if Shakespeare wrote the poem he must have done so in the earlier half of his career. Foster seeks to establish a Jacobean or Caroline date of composition, but his arguments are not decisive. He considers the frequency with which 'is' is elided in 'Shall I die?' to be incompatible with Shakespeare's authorship before 1596. But of the five examples he cites in the poem – 'hope's', 'fancy's', 'that's', 'She's', and 'pleasure's' – 'that's' and 'She's' belong, on his own admission, to a group of contractions common in the early 1590s (there are twenty-two examples of 'that's' in *The Two Gentlemen of Verona*, for example), and 'that's' is, at any rate, nonsensical in the context: the alternative emendations proposed by Wells and Taylor – who were attempting merely to restore meaning to the line in which 'that's' occurs – both eliminate the word; and Foster's interpretation of the manuscripts' 'hopes' and 'pleasures' as 'hope's' and 'pleasure's' is doubtful and not shared by the Oxford editors. (I think myself that he is right about 'hope's', but the syntax is thoroughly ambiguous.) This leaves one certain instance in 'Shall I die?' of the contraction of 'is' after a noun. There are five examples in *The Two Gentlemen of Verona*, five in *The True Tragedy of Richard Duke of York* (*3 Henry VI*), which also affords 'yonder's' (for 'yonder is'), and six in *Romeo and Juliet*, which also has 'dun's' (for 'dun is').[17] So one or two instances in a short early poem by Shakespeare would be in no way anomalous; and the tight short-lined stanzas might encourage contraction. Foster's other main argument – that the poem's description of the mistress's 'pretty bare' alludes to a late-Jacobean fashion for

plunging necklines that fully exposed women's breasts – is rebutted by Taylor in the *Textual Companion*; to him 'it is clear that this passage does not refer to totally exposed breasts, but only to the exposed cleavage' (p. 454), which was on display in Elizabethan times to 'besot' the susceptible male.[18] And whatever the weaknesses of the stylistic evidence that has been accumulated in support of Shakespeare's authorship of 'Shall I die?', the Oxford editors' decision to admit the poem to their pages rests firmly on the Bodleian manuscript's attribution. The *Complete Works* 'includes all those poems – and only those poems – attributed specifically to "William Shakespeare" in contemporary documents which are not contradicted by other contemporary documents. As editors, we can only modestly defer to the testimony of the extant witnesses, when we lack any other evidence more substantial than our own aesthetic judgement' (*TC*, p. 89).

'Just about every emendation has been proposed that is likely to be adopted, and editing has largely resolved itself to the exercise of personal choice among the known alternatives', wrote Fredson Bowers over twenty years ago.[19] But the Oxford editors introduce hundreds of readings that they have thought up themselves. Most fertile in invention is Taylor, but none of the four is reluctant to diagnose corruption and prescribe a fresh cure. Occasionally they gain assistance from the

---

[16] *Shakespeare Quarterly*, 38 (1987), 58–77.

[17] Foster does not mention these three plays, although he lists eight other early plays with no contractions of 'is' or with only 'one or two'; in fact *1 Henry VI*, said to have none, has at least four.

[18] One of Foster's minor points – that the first two recorded examples of 'admiring' as a noun, as in 'Shall I die?', are both Jacobean – serves to illustrate *OED*'s unavoidable imperfections: I can think of at least one Elizabethan instance, in Campian's famous lute-song, 'Fair, if you expect admiring', published in Rosseter's *Book of Airs* (1601).

[19] *On Editing Shakespeare and the Elizabethan Dramatists* (Charlottesville, 1966), p. 167.

material bequeathed them by McKerrow and Walker.

In judging these emendations we need ask ourselves just the one simple question: is the new reading more likely than any other available, either in the primary texts or among subsequent conjectures, to represent what Shakespeare intended?[20] A simple question, but the factors pertinent to an answer may be extremely complex. Among them will be the nature of the extant quarto and/or Folio texts, the relationships between them, and the circumstances of their transmission. The Oxford volumes are unique among modern *Complete Works* in exhibiting a clear relation between the textual theory arrived at for a particular play and the amount and kind of emendation attempted.[21] Thus *Othello*, which exists in good quarto and Folio versions held to have been set from a scribal transcript of Shakespeare's foul papers and a scribal transcript of Shakespeare's revised manuscript, is conservatively edited by Wells, since the postulated genealogy of the two substantive texts comes close to precluding the possibility that a reading in which they concur is erroneous. But when incorporating into his Folio-based edition of *The First Part of the Contention* (2 *Henry VI*) patches of dialogue from the memorially reconstructed Q1 (1594) or editing passages in which F was printed from Q3, Montgomery emends freely.[22] Likewise, since Folio *Troilus and Cressida* was set from a marked-up exemplar of the 1609 Quarto, errors common to the two texts are legitimately sought by Taylor and corrected. *All's Well That Ends Well* also benefits from liberal emendation, but in this case it is compositorial error that needs correction. The old Cambridge editors stigmatized *All's Well That Ends Well* as the worst-printed play in the First Folio – an inadequacy attributable to the fact that two somewhat careless compositors, B and C, were, for the first time in their work on F, encountering the 'really foul autograph' of a verbally intricate comedy (*TC*, p. 493).

The most elaborate and ambitious restoration-work is devoted to *Pericles*, which survives only in a grossly corrupt text that appears to have been largely, if not wholly, concocted from memory. Previous modern editors, despairing of recovering the authors' original, have adopted the cautious policy recommended by Fredson Bowers as appropriate to bad quartos, concentrating on the rectification of compositorial mistakes and perpetuating the reporters' more serious confusions. The real editing of *Pericles* has been left largely to producers, who have laboured to make dramatic sense of a muddled script, with occasional borrowings from George Wilkins's *The Painful Adventures of Pericles Prince of Tyre* (1608), a novella that openly proclaims its heavy indebtedness to the play as performed. The Oxford approach to *Pericles* again reflects concern for theatrical values. As Taylor insists, an experienced editor, equipped with Spevack's Shakespeare *Concordance* and computer-generated concordances to Wilkins's *Painful Adventures* and his one unaided play, a familiarity with the workings of reporters' memories in other bad texts, and a detailed knowledge of the dramatists' sources in Gower's *Confessio Amantis* and Lawrence Twine's *The Pattern of Painful Adventures*, 'is in a far better position than the ordinary reader or actor to attempt to reconstruct something

---

[20] Some general principles are outlined in the *Textual Companion*, pp. 57–61. P. W. K. Stone's chapter on 'Editorial Principles' in his book *The Textual History of 'King Lear'* (London: Scolar Press, 1980) issued an eloquent and well-reasoned challenge to the more extreme forms of editorial conservatism.

[21] The relationship is thoroughly mutual: the theory determines the kind and amount of emendation allowable, while convincing emendations of a particular kind may serve to vindicate the theory.

[22] Montgomery has prepared a useful photographic facsimile of *The First Part of the Contention 1594* in the Malone Society Reprints series (Oxford: The Malone Society, 1985); *Norton Facsimile* through line numbers, together with a system of marginal braces and plus signs, aid comparison with Folio *2 Henry VI*.

closer than Q to an authentic text of the play' (*TC*, p. 559). He thus tackles the job that producers have hitherto been forced to do for themselves. Wilkins's 'novel of the play' is essentially, like the Quarto, a 'report', though rendered as prose narrative. The Oxford *Pericles* draws on it to an unprecedented degree, especially for the play's first two acts, which Wilkins himself probably wrote, and emends Q liberally in the interests of 'a reconstructed text'. A diplomatic reprint of the 1609 Quarto is included in the old-spelling volume for readers who prefer unadulterated adulteration.[23]

How many of the new emendations scattered through the *Complete Works* will be admitted to subsequent editions? Many, perhaps most, seem to me worthy of adoption. Some are brilliant. A strength of the textual notes in support of new readings is the extent to which they appeal to Shakespeare's practices elsewhere: the concordance has repeatedly been employed to demonstrate the persistence within the canon of certain complexes of imagery, associations between words and ideas, and linguistic habits. Even the choice of indifferent variants from collateral texts – of 'Ah' or 'Oh', 'and' or 'if', 'Yea' or 'Ay', ''Tis' or 'It's' – is governed by knowledge of Shakespeare's normal preferences and the prejudices of identifiable compositors or scribes. There are many transpositions, substitutions, interpolations, or omissions for the sake of metre: these rest on intensive study of Shakespeare's metrical practices, and the changes tend to tighten the rhetorical structure as well.

The textual note on *1 Henry VI*, 5.1.59 will serve to illustrate the weight of evidence adduced in support of such minor alterations. There it is claimed that grammatically Elizabethan English permitted either 'neither . . . nor' or 'nor . . . nor', that 'neither' is used in this position forty-seven times in the Shakespeare canon when a two-syllable word is clearly required, but occurs only three times when a single syllable is required, and that all

the anomalies are in Folio pages set by Compositor B. So the Oxford edition emends three instances of 'neither' to 'nor' on the assumption that they result from Compositor B's 'unconscious modernizing'. As it happens, the two other examples are less problematical than that in *1 Henry VI*: 'I see she's like to have nor cap nor gown' in *The Taming of the Shrew* 4.3.93, though it would be possible to retain F's 'neither cap nor gown' and still achieve metrical regularity by eliding 'to have' in pronunciation; and 'And nor by treason nor hostility' in *Richard Duke of York*, 1.1.200. The *1 Henry VI* line reads in F: 'That neither in birth, or for authoritie'. This is a case neither of 'neither . . . nor' nor of 'nor . . . nor' but of 'neither . . . or'! Moreover, it occurs within a scene that the *Textual Companion* (p. 111) assigns to a playwright other than Shakespeare. The Oxford text emends 'neither' to 'nor', but leaves 'or' as it is. The F line sounds regular enough to me when the 'er' ending of 'neither' merges with 'in' to form a single unstressed syllable.[24] Besides, *The Merchant of Venice*, 1.1.178, reads 'Neither have I money nor commodity' in the Oxford edition; here the control-text is Q (1600), and 'Neither' seems to be regarded as metrically monosyllabic.[25]

---

23 MacD. P. Jackson's 'Compositors' Stints and the Spacing of Punctuation in the First Quarto (1609) of Shakespeare's *Pericles*', *Papers of the Bibliographical Society of America*, 81 (1987), 17–23, refines earlier bibliographical analyses of the Quarto.

24 See E. A. Abbott, *A Shakespearian Grammar* (London: Macmillan, 1883 edn), sec. 465, for such dropping of 'er' before a vowel.

25 See Abbott, 466. A few other metrical emendations are to my ear unnecessary: *Cymbeline*, 1.6.126 (where the middle syllable of 'rottenness' can disappear in pronunciation) and 4.2.2 (where 'to you' may be elided), for example. Elsewhere defence of the control-text's metre and refusal to emend seem mistaken: *The Two Gentlemen of Verona*, 5.4.67 (read 'one's own'); *Love's Labour's Lost*, 3.1.199 (read 'and groan'). While quibbling over minor decisions I might add that Taylor's choice in *Richard III*, 1.1.65 of F's 'That tempts him to this harsh Extremity' over Q1's 'That tempers him to this extremity' – even though the F line

Traditional emendations are willingly accepted, but not if they can be improved upon. In *Timon of Athens*, 2.2.129–32, Timon's steward Flavius explains that he had often tried in vain to bring his lord's debts to his attention. In the Folio he says:

> O my good Lord,
> At many times I brought in my accompts,
> Laid them before you, you would throw them off,
> And say you sound them in mine honestie.

Nearly all editors have followed the Second Folio in the obvious alteration of 'sound' (with a long 's' in F) to 'found'. Jowett adopts Wells's 'summed' ('sumd' in old spelling), which is graphically almost as close to F1's word as is F2's guess, and is markedly stronger; and Shakespeare's three other uses of the verb 'sum' without the preposition 'up' all link with 'count', 'account', or 'counters', as do two of the three instances of 'sum up'. The textual note establishes that 'Neither F1 nor F2 is satisfactory'.

In *Timon of Athens*, 4.3, Phrynia and Timandra ask Timon whether he has more gold, to which he replies in F: 'Enough to make a Whore forsweare her Trade, / And to make Whores, a Bawd' (lines 134–5). *The Riverside Shakespeare* interprets the last five words as meaning 'make a bawd retire from her trade of turning women into whores', and Bevington's *Complete Works* repeats the gloss, though neither editor inserts the comma after 'And' that such tortuous syntax as could deliver this meaning would seem to require. But the interpretation is, at any rate, hopelessly strained. As the *Textual Companion* notes, the imperfect repetition 'make a Whore . . . make Whores' and the plural-to-singular of 'Whores, a Bawd' combine to render the passage highly suspect. What seems to be needed is 'an example, in Timon's misanthropic vein, of nature turned to vice, to contrast with that of gold's reformative power' (*TC*, p. 505). Taylor proposes 'wholesomeness' ('Wholsõnes' in old spelling), to which the Oxford edition emends:

'Enough to make a whore forswear her trade, / And to make wholsomeness a bawd'. Although the emendation turns the complete line 135 into an hexameter, it persuades by its characteristically bold Shakespearian use of an abstraction with concrete force; the abstract word 'wholsomeness' suits the universal sweep of Timon's satire, but in close juxtaposition to 'a bawd' it assumes the concreteness of, let us say, 'a virtuous person, free from sexual disease'. As Taylor points out, 'Elsewhere Shakespeare describes several abstract conditions corrupted to bawd' – mercy, majesty, virtue, reason, reputation, and (he might have added) honesty in *Hamlet*, 3.1.114.

The most exciting emendations are those by which inert phrases are restored to a vigorous metaphorical life that energizes a whole passage. In *Troilus and Cressida*, 1.3 Aeneas enters as envoy from the Greeks and addresses them in 'high-falutin' terms that arouse Agamemnon's suspicions: 'This Trojan scorns us, or the men of Troy / Are ceremonious courtiers' (lines 231–2). Aeneas replies in the Quarto, which the Oxford editors judge to have been set from autograph:

> Courtiers as free as debonaire, vnarm'd
> As bending Angels, thats their same in peace:
> But when they would seem soldiers, they haue galls,
> Good armes, strong ioints, true swords, & great *Ioues* accord
> Nothing so full of heart.   (lines 233–7)

---

is judged to have been set from marked-up Q3, which corrupts 'tempers' to 'temps' (Q6 has 'tempts') – strikes me as perverse. Taylor's choice implies (a) that F's version of the line derives from a manuscript used to annotate Q3 here, (b) that that manuscript reproduced Shakespeare's final intentions for the line (though elsewhere Taylor accepts Q readings as authorial second-thoughts transmitted by the reporters), and (c) that Q1's line is memorially corrupt (though the Q reporting is virtually perfect hereabouts). Yet Q1's is much the better line. In the somewhat similar situation at 4.4.465 the variants are genuinely indifferent and preference for the F reading is reasonable.

The Folio corrects 'same' to 'Fame', omits 'great', and repunctuates:

> Courtiers as free, as debonnaire; vnarm'd,
> As bending Angels: that's their Fame, in peace:
> But when they would seeme Souldiers, they
>   haue galles,
> Good armes, strong ioynts, true swords, &
>   *Ioues* accord
> Nothing so full of heart.

In his New Penguin edition (reviewed below), R. A. Foakes modernizes the last two-and-a-half lines as follows:

> But when they would seem soldiers, they have
>   galls,
> Good arms, strong joints, true swords; and –
>   Jove's accord –
> Nothing so full of heart.

He explains the last eight words: 'this is as much as to say "God willing, no one is as courageous as they are"'. This is the standard modern interpretation, though many editors retain Q's 'great', leaving the line unmetrical, and render the supposed parenthesis less obtrusive by marking it lightly with commas. Q and F can thus be made to yield tolerable sense. But it is not Shakespeare's sense, as Taylor demonstrates by the alteration of a single letter:

> But when they would seem soldiers they have
>   galls,
> Good arms, strong joints, true swords – and
>   great Jove's acorn
> Nothing so full of heart.

In the old-spelling edition 'accord' is emended to 'accorn'.[26] The oak is Jove's tree, as in *As You Like It*, 3.2.231–2 and *The Tempest*, 5.1.45, and Aeneas' rather precious metonymy (acorn = oak) enhances the affected quality of his rhetoric. The image of the oak is the node for an outgrowth of puns in 'arms', 'strong joints', 'full of heart', and 'galls', which (as Shakespeare well knew) are, among other things, excrescences that grow on oaks.[27] As so often in Shakespeare, proverb lore and the figurative language of everyday speech lie behind the wordplay: from tiny acorns mighty oak-trees grow, and stout courageous spirits have hearts of oak. English oaks and the sturdy inhabitants of Troynovaunt who fought with King Harry on Saint Crispin's day are not far below the level of Shakespeare's consciousness. Taylor's textual note on 'accord' spells out what is wrong with the QF text and the way it has been interpreted: most importantly, a parenthetical 'God willing' would more naturally qualify an action intended than an attribute possessed; and what ought to be the climax of Aeneas' boastfulness is weakened by a lame anticipation of his later retraction of it in the second half of his speech (lines 237–42). But for anybody who appreciates the way Shakespeare's poetic imagination works, the arguments are superfluous: the emendation, which has the added advantage of restoring metrical regularity to Q's line, carries immediate conviction.[28]

For the merest sampling of such inspired substitutions one might turn to *Titus Andronicus*, 3.2.62 'dirges' for F 'doings'; *Julius Caesar*, 3.1.175 'unstrung' ('unstrunge' in old spelling) for F 'in strength'; *Macbeth*, 4.1.114 'on's high place' for F 'our high plac'd'; *Antony and Cleopatra*, 5.1.15 'rivèd' ('reaued') for F 'round'; *Coriolanus*, 2.3.115 'womanish' for F 'Wooluish'; *The Winter's Tale*, 5.1.58 'mourn' ('morne') for F 'now' – with consequent repunctuation; *The Winter's Tale*, 5.3.5 'young' for F 'your'; and *The Two Noble Kinsmen*, 5.4.39.1 'mad' ('Madde') for Q 'Maide'.

---

26 Taylor compares the Q error 'boord' for 'boorn' at 2.3.244, and points to the possible corrupting influence of 'swords' earlier in 1.3.236.

27 Ink was made from them. See *OED*, *Gall*, *sb.*[3], and Alexander Schmidt's *Shakespeare Lexicon*, which cites *Twelfth Night*, 3.2.46–8 and *Cymbeline*, 1.1.102. 'Nothing' is idiomatically used as an intensive form of 'not', as very often in Shakespeare.

28 The emendation also vindicates Q's punctuation of line 236. F was printed from an annotated exemplar of Q. Taylor is understandably suspicious of 'vnarm'd' in line 233, since it seems pointlessly to anticipate 'that's their fame in peace'.

There are many incisive notes defending traditional emendations against recent attempts to reinstate quarto or Folio readings, as at *Sonnets*, 111.1, *The History of King Lear*, 7.163, and *The Tempest*, 4.1.123. Others argue equally well for retention of control-text readings that have incurred suspicion: in *Timon of Athens*, for example, a notorious muddle over the value of a talent seems to be reflected in a reference in F at 3.2.39 to 'fifty fiue hundred Talents', where 'fifty' and 'fiue hundred' look like alternatives from which the playwright intended to choose whichever turned out to be the most appropriate sum; but Jowett, accepting that Thomas Middleton wrote *Timon of Athens*, 3.2, points out that F is supported by Middleton's curious fondness for the number fifty-five. Henrietta and Thomas Bowdler would have been puzzled by the assiduity with which profanity is restored to texts deemed to have suffered expurgation. And of course Oldcastle, Russell, and Harvey – whose replacement in *1 Henry IV* by Falstaff, Bardolph, and Peto can be blamed on the censor – rejoin the *dramatis personae*.[29]

Turning to famous cruxes one is seldom disappointed. Antony's 'Arme-gaunt' steed in *Antony and Cleopatra*, 1.5.47 becomes 'arm-jaunced' ('Arme-iaunct'), which is perhaps the best proposal so far. It is a relief to find that Wells declares end of term for the 'School of Night' (*Love's Labour's Lost*, 4.3.253), though I prefer 'suit' to the Oxford edition's 'style' ('Stile'). Wells notes that 'Stile' could have been misread 'Scole' and respelt 'Schoole' by the Q compositor. Likewise, 'shute' or 'suite' might have been misread 'schule' or 'scule'. In *Romeo and Juliet*, 3.2.10–11, night is a 'sober-suited matron all in black', while the Dark Lady of the Sonnets has a brow ('eyes' in Q) 'suited' in 'raven-black' (*Sonnets*, 127.10), and in *Love's Labour's Lost* the topic is Biron's dark lady, Rosaline.

Some emendations seem misconceived. In *Much Ado About Nothing*, 2.3, Benedick hides himself in the arbour to eavesdrop on Claudio,

Don Pedro, and Leonato, who, knowing he is there, are about to play a trick on him. Claudio says in Q: 'the musique ended, / Weele fit the kid-foxe with a penny worth' (lines 40–1). Wells adopts Warburton's 'hid-fox', because a kid-fox is unknown ('a young fox is a cub') and Benedick is at any rate not particularly young. But 'kid-fox' is presumably an oxymoron, like 'niggard prodigal' and 'cursed-blessed' in lines 79 and 866 of *The Rape of Lucrece*, but here deliberately comic: Benedick, who thinks he is the sly fox of beast fable, is really the duped kid. In *The First Part of the Contention*, 4.7.87–8, the captured Saye protests in F that he is 'full of sicknesse and diseases', to which Cade retorts, 'Ye shall haue a hempen Candle then, & the help of hatchet'. Obviously 'Candle' should be 'caudle', and one might expect an article before 'hatchet' – unless its suppression was meant to indicate dialect. Montgomery emends to 'the health o'th' hatchet'. But 'help' could have a specialized medical sense in Shakespearian English, meaning 'relief, cure, remedy'.[29] In F *Richard III*, 3.1.132, Buckingham comments on the young Duke of York's precociously clever words: 'With what a sharpe prouided wit he reasons'. Editors follow Theobald in hyphenating 'sharp-provided' and glossing 'keenly thought out'. Taylor objects that no parallels have been offered for such an interpretation, and that 'supplied with sharpness' would mean no more than plain 'sharp'. He emends to 'a sharp, prodigal wit'. But what the young duke displays is a *ready* wit, like that of the man

---

29 The case for replacing the names Bardolph and Peto with Russell and Harvey is made by John Jowett in 'The Thieves in *1 Henry IV*', *Review of English Studies*, 38 (1987), 325–33, a full discussion of the Quarto's confusions in nomenclature. In the same journal Gary Taylor's 'William Shakespeare, Richard James, and the House of Cobham' (pp. 334–54) is relevant to the Oldcastle problem and to censorship in the 'Falstaff' plays.

30 See *OED*, *Help, sb.*⁵, and Schmidt, *Shakespeare Lexicon*, *Help, subst.* 4.

whose breeches caught fire when the Globe burned down in 1613 during the playing of *All Is True*: 'by the benefit of a provident wit' he doused the flames with 'bottle ale'.[31] We should read either 'a sharp, provided wit' or perhaps 'a sharp, provident wit'.

Yet even the less compelling new emendations in the Oxford *Complete Works* are a stimulus to further thought. *The Rape of Lucrece* (Q 1594) contains a long descant on the power of Time, whose glory is:

> To fill with worme-holes stately monuments,
> To feede obliuion with decay of things,
> To blot old bookes, and alter their contents,
> To plucke the quils from auncient rauens wings,
> To drie the old oakes sappe, and cherish springs:
> To spoile Antiquities of hammerd steele,
> And turne the giddy round of Fortunes wheele.   (lines 946–52)

There are several stanzas in this vein. Many editors have doubted 'cherish', since the otherwise unrelievedly negative series 'fill . . . feed . . . blot . . . alter . . . pluck . . . dry . . . spoil' leads one to expect a verb describing some action hostile to springs. Wells and Taylor do not bother to record Warburton's conviction that what Shakespeare 'certainly wrote' was 'tarish', Warburton's own coinage from the French *tarir* = to dry up. But they mention Johnson's 'perish', although the verb is never transitive in the Shakespeare canon. Wells adopts Taylor's 'blemish', which 'is used by Shakespeare, and might be misread as "cherish" in a blotted or smudged manuscript' (*TC*, p. 265). This sets one thinking. 'Blemish' does not seem apt to 'springs', and it bears little graphical resemblance to 'cherish'. A search for more plausible synonyms of 'pollute' or 'dry up' proves fruitless. However, the springs need not be of water at all. Every other line in the stanza deals with a single instance of Time's ravages, and the Oxford version of line 950 overloads it with two. My own suggestion is 'To dry the old oak's sap and check his springs' – where 'springs' are young shoots or sprigs, as in *Venus and Adonis*, line 656, and *The Comedy of Errors*, 3.2.3.[32] Sonnet 5 similarly describes the effects of 'never-resting time' on trees: 'Sap checked with frost, and lusty leaves quite gone'; and Queen Elizabeth in *Richard III*, 2.2.42, asks 'Why wither not the leaves that want their sap?'[33]

'Cherish springs' may nevertheless be correct. The Quarto is remarkably well printed, and other stanzas contain examples of the repairs, as well as the decays, of time. Q's version of the line might be thought of as leading into the paradoxes of the next stanza, and would roughly parallel 'To make the child a man, the man a child' (line 954), if 'springs' were understood as saplings. Even if the springs are of water, Q's line is neatly paradoxical: 'It is the office of Time . . . to dry up the sap of the oak, and to furnish springs with a perpetual supply; to deprive the one of that moisture which she liberally bestows upon the other', explained Malone.[34] If I were editing

---

[31] The *Textual Companion*, p. 30, prints a facsimile of the letter in which the anecdote was first told.

[32] Perhaps also *The Rape of Lucrece*, line 869. See Schmidt, *Shakespeare Lexicon*, *Spring*, subst. 3, and *OED*, *Spring*, sb.¹, III.9.

[33] 'Check' occurs frequently in Elizabethan poetry and drama in connection with plants, as in *The Tragedy of Master Arden of Faversham*, ed. M. L. Wine, The Revels Plays (London, 1973), scene 8, line 6 where the northeast wind is said to 'check the tender blossoms in the spring'. 'Checked' is applied to 'plants' and 'sap' in Sonnet 15, and 'checks' and 'sap' join in a tree image in *Troilus and Cressida* (1.3.4–6); and *The Rape of Lucrece* (line 1168) and *1 Henry VI* (2.5.11–12) connect lack of sap and absence of leaves. Misreading of 'check his' as 'cherish' might have been facilitated by a compositor's association of the two verbs as antonyms; they are antithetically coupled in *King John* (3.4.152). Support for the conjectured pronoun 'his' may be found in *The Tempest* (1.2.296–7) 'I will rend an oak, / And peg thee in his knotty entrails'.

[34] See the Variorum edition of *The Poems* (Philadelphia, 1938), ed. H. E. Rollins. Another eighteenth-century commentator turned 'cherish' into an adjective, so that

The Rape of Lucrece, partiality for my own bright idea would war with an uneasy suspicion that Q's text is satisfactory as it stands. The Oxford editors must sometimes have found themselves in this predicament.[35]

Both the modernized and original-spelling volumes include Wells's stylish general introduction to Shakespeare's career and the conditions in which his plays were staged and printed, brief one-page introductions to individual plays, an inventory of contemporary allusions to Shakespeare, and a glossary. The original-spelling volume has an essay by Vivian Salmon on 'The Spelling and Punctuation of Shakespeare's Time' (xlii–lvi).

The Oxford team have, in books, articles, and notes, been busily revolutionizing Shakespearian textual criticism in recent years. The *Complete Works* and the *Textual Companion* are the culmination of their efforts, and serve also as a 'synthesis of the disparate work of many fine scholars' over the last few decades. As Taylor observes, 'Such a synthesis in itself provokes and makes possible future progress, by identifying unsolved problems and undeveloped opportunities. A successful work of scholarship stimulates the very research which will make it obsolete, and, with our own task now behind us, we look forward to our future obsolescence' (*TC*, p. 62). Though not for all time, but of an age, the *Complete Works* makes a massive contribution to the continuing editorial tradition.

Harold Jenkins based his fine new Arden *Hamlet* (London, 1982) solidly on Shakespeare's foul papers as printed in Q2 (1604/5). G. R. Hibbard agrees with Taylor and Wells that the Folio reproduces the playwright's own substitutions, amplifications, and abridgements, and so uses it as his control-text and banishes to appendices the Q2 passages absent from F.[36] His 'Textual Introduction', occupying some sixty-five closely argued pages, presents a strong case that F's changes reflect 'a logical and coherent process of revision designed to make a better acting version with a wide appeal' (p. 109). Hibbard thinks that F was printed directly from autograph fair copy, whereas the *Textual Companion* posits the intervention of a late scribal transcript between F and the possibly-autograph original prompt-book. Taylor's evidence against F's having been set from autograph is compelling (*TC*, p. 399), and in practice Hibbard's alternative theory tempts him into a docile deference to F, even when its departures from Q2 are almost certainly due to scribal or compositorial interference. At 3.1.87–9 Hibbard reads: 'And enterprises of great pith and moment / With this regard their currents turn away / And lose the name of action'. Jenkins believed, rightly in my opinion, that F's 'pith' and 'away' were both corruptions of Q2's 'pitch' and 'awry', but 'pith' could conceivably be an authoritative substitution ill-advisedly made by Shakespeare as he fair-copied his foul papers; Taylor accepts it, but balks at 'away', which must surely be a misreading of the more difficult word.[37]

---

the springs could become, like the oak's sap, the direct object of 'dry'; his ludicrous proposal was 'cheerish': 'cherished' would have been better. Q is defended by F. T. Prince in his new Arden edition of *The Poems* (London, 1960).

[35] R. J. C. Watt offers well-considered solutions to 'Three Cruces in *Measure for Measure*', *Review of English Studies*, 38 (1987), 227–33.

[36] *Hamlet* (Oxford: Clarendon Press, 1987).

[37] Both Hibbard's text and the *Complete Works* follow F several times when Q1 and Q2 are in agreement against it. Neither Taylor's nor Hibbard's stemma allows for a second round of Shakespearian revision subsequent to preparation of the original prompt-book, which lies behind Q1. So if these F readings are authoritative, either (a) Q1's variants must be memorial corruptions that have contaminated Q2, or (b) Q1, in failing to transmit an authoritative prompt-book revision, has coincidentally reverted to a foul papers reading, or created a reading coincidentally corrupted in the same way by the Q2 compositors. Yet it seems unlikely that sporadic consultation of Q1 by the Q2 compositors to help them decipher their manuscript copy – which is what Hibbard and Taylor postulate – would cause them to set

However, Hibbard's edition is obviously a milestone in *Hamlet* studies. It includes an excellent commentary and a sane critical account calculated to show that understanding of Hamlet's tragedy has been befuddled by the familiar conflated text. Hibbard's attitude to problematical episodes and speeches is consistently determined by their 'theatrical dimensions and impact' (p. 56), their 'function in the play' (p. 42), as it arouses 'the curiosity of its audience' and engages us in the battle of wits between two 'mighty opposites' (p. 28). And Hibbard, who knows whose side he is on, has little inclination to carp at the hero: the play is no allegory, but if it were its conflict might be seen 'as a struggle between Falsehood and Deception, embodied in the King, and Truth, embodied in the Prince' (p. 63). Moreover, though Hamlet forfeits his life, his 'resistance to the King and to all that the King stands for is crowned with success' (p. 66).

No serious student of Shakespeare's Sonnets can afford to be without John Kerrigan's New Penguin edition, which is unfailingly intelligent, learned, and sensitive.[38] Kerrigan seems to have read everything on the Sonnets, without losing his sanity. Every part of his edition is informed by sound scholarship and critical acumen. The copious commentary strikes a happy medium between the over-hospitable clutter of Stephen Booth's (New Haven, 1977) and the chaste resistance to ambiguities that characterizes Ingram and Redpath's (London, 1964, rev. 1978). And the introduction places the Sonnets within their Renaissance context and accurately defines the kind of poetry they are. Many recent commentators have misheard the tone of the Sonnets, exaggerating their Donne-like intellectual and linguistic busyness at the expense of their 'cantabile' (as Auden put it) and their emotional resonance. Kerrigan gets the balance right. His edition is the first to incorporate 'A Lover's Complaint' into an account of the 1609 Quarto as an organized sequence. He assigns Sonnet 107 to 1603 (pp. 313–20),

and recognizes that the last twenty or so of the sonnets to the Friend belong stylistically to the seventeenth century. There is a good new emendation ('prived' for Q 'proud') at 67.12.

David Bevington has read as much on *Henry IV* as Kerrigan has read on the Sonnets.[39] But he wears his learning less lightly. And, unlike Hibbard, he communicates little in the way of a personal point of view as he meticulously processes for us a superabundance of diverse critical comment. 'Tillyard, as we have seen, has argued that the Prince . . . Yet in one sense, it has been suggested, Hal . . . In his most self-revealing speeches, notes Allan Gross, the Prince . . . Yet, we gradually realize . . . Undoubtedly Hal . . . Still, as W. Gordon Zeeveld insists, he . . . ' (pp. 61–2). Bevington zig-zags along like a New Year's Eve driver. But the introduction has its subtleties, and the stage history is full and informative. Bevington refuses to follow the editors of the *Complete Works* in reinstating 'Oldcastle', urging that Shakespeare's intention to give Sir John the same name in both Parts of *Henry IV* and in *The Merry Wives of Windsor* should prevail over his initial intention, when he wrote *1 Henry IV*, to christen him 'Oldcastle'. About the nature of the manuscript that served as copy for the 1598 Quarto Bevington wavers; apparently he inclines to believe that it was 'Shakespeare's foul papers . . . corrected by him or some other person for the press with a view to publication', but sometimes veers towards recognition that it must have been a scribal transcript (p. 90).[40] The *Textual Com-*

'Hast me' at 1.5.29 and 'My tables' at 1.5.107–8, if 'Hast, hast me' and 'My Tables, my Tables' appeared in their manuscript; in each case Q1 and Q2 agree against F, whose duplication is extra-metrical. The alternative explanation of Q1/Q2 agreement does not seem wholly satisfactory either.

[38] *The Sonnets and A Lover's Complaint* (Harmondsworth: Penguin Books, 1986).
[39] *Henry IV, Part 1* (Oxford: Clarendon Press, 1987).
[40] On p. 106 it is unequivocally 'Shakespeare's manuscript' with which the Q compositors are dealing.

panion (pp. 329–30) assembles incontrovertible evidence that printer's copy was scribal, not autograph. On the crucial question of whether any Folio variants derive – via a manuscript or an editor's knowledge of stage tradition – from Shakespeare himself, the indications are 'inconclusive and even contradictory' (p. 99). At 1.3.23–8 Northumberland defends Hotspur's conduct; Bevington, following Q, has him say:

> Those prisoners in your highness' name
>   demanded,
> Which Harry Percy here at Holmedon took,
> Were, as he says, not with such strength denied
> As is delivered to your majesty.
> Either envy, therefore, or misprision
> Is guilty of this fault, and not my son.

The *Complete Works*, deferring to F's changes, prints the last three lines as follows:

> As was delivered to your majesty,
> Who either through envy or misprision
> Was guilty of this fault, and not my son.

Jowett sees the F reading here as the first of a series of trivial but 'deliberate authorial changes incorporated from the manuscript', changes that make the rebels 'more defiant and accusatory' (*TC*, p. 333). But F's version of Northumberland's speech seems incoherent. In Q Northumberland claims that the 'strength' of Hotspur's refusal to render up his prisoners to the king has been misreported, either through malice or misunderstanding; guilt is conveniently transferred to abstractions, 'envy', or 'misprision'. In F Northumberland's improbably bold assertion of the King's own guilt is at odds with his otherwise conciliatory tone (Worcester having already been dismissed for mere innuendo), with Hotspur's own ensuing attempt at self-justification, and, above all, with Northumberland's (and Hotspur's) denial of the accuracy of the information that 'was delivered' to the King. Nor is there any clear referent in F for 'this fault', which in Q is Hotspur's failure to yield his prisoners. The editors of the *Complete*

Works concede that Shakespeare's putative second-thoughts as he copied his scripts or modified them for the theatre do not always make for subtlety, but in this case Bevington seems to me right to doubt the playwright's involvement in the changes. Bevington's account of his 'Editorial Procedures' (pp. 111–16) is commendably explicit, and his very full commentary is supplemented by an appendix referring details of the text to Shakespeare's chronicle sources.

R. A. Foakes is convinced by Taylor's demonstration that the 1609 Quarto of *Troilus and Cressida* was set from foul papers and the Folio text from an exemplar of Q annotated with reference to a prompt-book incorporating Shakespeare's revisions, and so in his New Penguin edition F is 'preferred generally for substantive readings' (p. 231).[41] But he rejects F's early dismissal of Pandarus (at the end of 5.3), finding 'the sourly comic ending with Pandarus complaining to the audience . . . much the more appropriate to the general tone of the play, and the nature of its action' (p. 9). He sees the play as naturally falling into two halves, 'one predominantly comic, and culminating in Pandarus's address to the audience at the end of III.2, the other harsher, and ending on a more bitter note, but also with Pandarus addressing the audience, so paralleling the first part' (p. 9). His brief critical introduction is a lively exploration of the way in which *Troilus and Cressida* open up 'conflicting perspectives . . . on love, chivalry, honour, order, and policy' (p. 22), while resisting simple moral judgements. The play is not disillusioned or nihilistic, but 'notably realistic' (p. 29).

Textually Stephen Orgel's edition of *The Tempest* is conservative,[42] but remarkable for the helpfulness of its many additional stage directions and for a new emendation – a transposition so simple that one marvels it has not

---

[41] *Troilus and Cressida* (Harmondsworth: Penguin Books, 1987).
[42] *The Tempest* (Oxford: Clarendon Press, 1987).

been made before – at 4.1.9, where Orgel reads 'Do not smile at me that I boast of her', instead of F's 'her of'; editors have been beguiled by F2's silly 'boast her off', which they interpret as 'praise her highly', but there are no Shakespearian parallels for such a usage. Orgel's challenging critical account stresses the 'openness of the text' and aims 'to indicate the range of the play's possibilities' (p. 12). He is especially anxious to correct Victorian tendencies to 'sweeten and sentimentalize' *The Tempest*. 'Power' turns out to be the major preoccupation of the play; the adjective 'libidinous' is attached not only to Caliban (pp. 27 and 28), but also to Ferdinand (p. 18) and Prospero (p. 48); Prospero's forgiveness of Antonio and his renunciation of magic are double-edged; and when Miranda in 5.1 teasingly accuses Ferdinand of cheating at chess (if that is indeed what her words mean), the affectionate banter 'seems to foretell in their lives all the ambition, duplicity and cynicism of their elders . . . Italian *Realpolitik* is already established in the next generation' (pp. 29–30)! Orgel's very modern, anti-romantic reading of the play includes interesting observations on its Renaissance political context and how this illuminates the masque and Prospero's arrangement of his daughter's marriage. For Orgel, the most satisfying modern productions 'bring into the theatre a recognition of how powerfully subversive much of the play's energy is, how incompletely it controls its ambivalences and resolves its conflicts' (p. 87). Orgel fully integrates into his introduction twenty-two well chosen illustrations.

'*The Merchant of Venice* is a play which calls for unobtrusive editing' (p. xi), declares M. M. Mahood, and the only textual surprise in her New Cambridge edition is that it returns Salarino to the play, along with the 1600 Quarto's other two 'Sallies', Salerio and Salanio.[43] In the *Textual Companion* Montgomery echoes the judgement of editors over the last sixty years: that Q's 'Salarino' and 'Salerio' comprise a single character, whom Shake-speare, whose foul papers were responsible for the muddle, decided in the course of composition to name 'Salerio'. Although Mahood puts forward several reasons for suspecting that Shakespeare may have had three separate personages in mind all along, she concludes her discussion of the matter as follows: 'It is always open to the director to identify Salarino with Salerio, thereby economising on minor parts and very probably fulfilling Shakespeare's final intention into the bargain. But the printed text must, I believe, retain three Venetian gentlemen with similar names because, whatever his intentions, Salarino, Solanio, and Salerio all figured in the manuscript that Shakespeare actually gave to his actors as *The Merchant of Venice*' (p. 183). With these words Mahood places herself in a very different ideological camp from that of the editors of the Oxford *Complete Works*. She exalts the hypothesized physical document above the final authorial intentions that can be inferred from it – intentions that would presumably have been realized in a prompt-book overseen by Shakespeare.

Her introduction examines 'Some Attitudes and Assumptions Behind the Play' under the sub-headings: 'Kinds of Comedy', 'The Myth of Venice', 'The Law', 'Jews and Usurers', and '"God-Like Amity"'; describes 'Experiencing the Play' under the sub-headings: 'Belmont and Venice', 'The Elopement', 'Debit and Credit', 'Dr Balthazar', and 'The Renewing of Love'; and recounts 'The Afterlife of *The Merchant of Venice*' on stage, ending with a brief account of John Barton's fine attempt 'to restore an equal balance of interest between Bassanio, Shylock, and Portia' (p. 52) at The Other Place, Stratford, in 1978. Towards the end of an appendix on 'Shakespeare's Use of the Bible in *The Merchant of Venice*' Mahood writes: 'Though the mind of the individual auditor preserves some total effect of a play, he

---

[43] *The Merchant of Venice* (Cambridge: Cambridge University Press, 1987).

or she does not go home nursing some nugget of "meaning", but animatedly recalling this or that moment of the action' (p. 188). Her concern for 'the theatrical experience' afforded by the play makes her a most congenial guide.[44]

The last word this year should go to Randall McLeod, who continues to detonate his puns against the kind of 'editorial behaviour' that has created all the volumes surveyed above – the kind 'that perfects Shakespeare's text by righting and rewriting it for him' (pp. 167–8).[45] His entertaining and instructive article compares the 'variations of title and name in stage direction and speech prefix' in some Shakespeare quartos (the 'anarchic aspects of early Shakespeer printings') with the meaningful 'fluidity in naming' to be found in plays by Bernard Shaw and the 'fertile confusion' of the prompt-book for John Barton's Royal Shakespeare Company production of *Richard II* in the mid-1970s. McLeod likes 'authorial inconsistencies' and dislikes 'normalizations'. His interest is in 'dramaturgic criticism', which 'countenances the integrity of every state of a play, or a part of it, as we can discern it . . . in authorial notes, foul papers, prompt copies, revisions, adaptations, etc., and which focuses particularly on the transformations of a play (or the play of transformations) through successive drafts, or from written text to enactment – or back again'

(p. 104). Or so he says in that state of his article submitted for review.

---

[44] Other editions received are: *Troilus and Cressida*, ed. Werner Brönnimann-Egger (1986); *The Winter's Tale*, ed. Ingeborg Boltz (1986); and *Julius Caesar*, ed. Thomas Pughe (1987); all with English and German texts on facing pages, and published by Francke Verlag, Tübingen, under the general editorship of Werner Habicht, Ernst Leisi, and Rudolf Stamm for the Deutsches Shakespeare-Gesellschaft West; introductions, annotations, and commentaries are in German and very full; there are long bibliographies. *Julio César* is a Spanish translation with introduction and notes by Ángel-Luis Pujante (Universidad de Murcia, 1987). Milan Lukeš, *Základy Shakespearovské Dramaturgie* (Praha: Univerzita Karlova, 1985) includes summaries in Russian and English: *The Foundations of Shakespearean Dramaturgy*; the main theme is that the so-called 'bad quartos' are not memorial reconstructions, but include 'Shakespearean prototexts and metatexts' that capture 'different stages in the process of development' of Shakespeare's scripts. Arthur Sherbo's *The Birth of Shakespeare Studies: Commentators from Rowe (1709) to Boswell-Malone (1821)* (East Lansing: Colleagues Press, 1986) is a solid piece of cultural history. Richard Knowles provides 'Dates for Some Serially Published Shakespeares', *Studies in Bibliography*, 40 (1987), 187–201.

[45] Random Cloud (Randall McLeod), 'The Psychopathology of Everyday Art', in *The Elizabethan Theatre IX*, ed. G. R. Hibbard (Waterloo, Ontario: University of Waterloo, 1986), 100–68. The expression 'Shakespeare's text' begs the question; as Taylor insists in the *Textual Companion*, 'All texts of Shakespeare are editions . . . all have been mediated by agents other than the author' (p. 1).

BOOKS RECEIVED

This list includes all books received between 1 September 1986 and 31 August 1987 which are not reviewed in this volume of *Shakespeare Survey*. The appearance of a book in this list does not preclude its review in a subsequent volume.

Clemen, Wolfgang. *Shakespeare's Soliloquies.* Translated by Charity Scott Stokes. London and New York: Methuen and Company, Ltd, 1987.

Gibson, Colin, ed. *The Selected Plays of John Ford.* Plays by Renaissance and Restoration Dramatists. General Editor, Graham Storey. Cambridge: Cambridge University Press, 1986.

Jackson, MacD. P. and Michael Neill, eds. *The Selected Plays of John Marston.* Plays by Renaissance and Restoration Dramatists. General Editor, Graham Storey. Cambridge: Cambridge University Press, 1986.

Mathis, Gilles. *Analyse stylistique du Paradis Perdu de John Milton: l'univers poétique: echos et correspondances.* 3 vols. (vol. 1 in two parts). Université de Provence, 1987.

Nagarajan, S. and S. Viswanathan, eds. *Shake-speare in India.* Delhi: Oxford University Press, 1987.

Orkin, Martin. *Shakespeare Against Apartheid.* Craighall, South Africa: Ad. Donker, 1987.

Person, James E., Jr, ed. *Literature Criticism from 1400 to 1800.* Volume 5. Detroit: Gale Research Company, 1987.

Rigaud, N. J. *La Veuve dans la comédie anglaise au temps de Shakespeare: 1600–1625.* Université de Provence, 1986.

Sales, Roger. *Much Ado about Nothing: A Critical Study.* Penguin Masterstudies. Harmondsworth: Penguin Books, 1987.

Scott, Mark W., ed. *Shakespearean Criticism.* Volume 5. Detroit: Gale Research Company, 1987.

Velz, John W. and Frances N. Teague, eds. *One Touch of Shakespeare: Letters of Joseph Parker Norris, 1875–1878.* Washington: The Folger Shakespeare Library; London and Toronto: Associated University Presses, 1986.

Watson, Robert N. *Shakespeare and the Hazards of Ambition.* Cambridge, Massachusetts and London: Harvard University Press, 1984.

INDEX

INDEX

INDEX

INDEX

Huston, J. Dennis, *31*, 165; *37*, 15n, 37n
Hutchings, Geoffrey, *33*, 169, 170; *35*, 148
Hutchings, W., *40*, 204
Hutt, William, *31*, 146; *34*, 156–60; *37*, 85; *39*, 188
Hüttner, Johann, *35*, 23n
Hutton, J., *31*, 136n
Huxley, Aldous, *34*, 145; *38*, 173
Hyde, Jonathan, *34*, 151; *36*, 151; *37*, 173
Hyde, Thomas, *40*, 221
Hyland, Frances, *36*, 58
Hyland, Peter, *32*, 216; *37*, 55, 58n; *40*, 209
Hyman, Stanley E., *34*, 68n; *40*, 127n
Hynes, Samuel, *31*, 14n
Hysel, F. E., *32*, 190n
Hytner, Nicholas, *40*, 174

Ibsen, Henrik, *34*, 2, 6; *35*, 21; *36*, 65, 125; *37*, 207; *39*, 94, 170
'I.C.', *34*, 88
Iden, Peter, *37*, 161n
Iffland, August Wilhelm , *35*, 25
Ingram, Angela J. C., *38*, 230
Ingram, Anthony, *35*, 176–7
Ingram, M., *38*, 30n
Ingram, R. W., *39*, 215, 228
Ingram, W. G., *31*, 164; *34*, 180; *40*, 41n, 218
Innes, Christopher, *38*, 236
Innocent, Harold, *38*, 207, 211, 213
Innocent III, Pope, *32*, 132n
Irby, James E., *34*, 161n
Irons, Jeremy, *40*, 177, 180–1
Irving, Sir Henry, *31*, 188; *32*, 18, 19, 21, 27n, 29, 30, 31, 32, 33n, 35; *34*, 115; *35*, 2, 3, 8, 9, 12, 14, 16, 17, 19, 34, 175; *36*, 74; *38*, 209; *40*, 1, 12, 39
Irving, Lawrence, *35*, 9
Irving, Washington, *35*, 104n
Isabella, sister of Philip II, *33*, 162
Isaiah, *36*, 15
Iser, Wolfgang, *37*, 159
Isherwood, Christopher, *36*, 30
Ives, E. W., *38*, 21n
Iwasaki, Soji, *38*, 10

Jackson, B. W., *31*, 6n
Jackson, Sir Barry, *35*, 2; *38*, 17; *40*, 16

Jackson, Berners A. W., *32*, 63n, 223; *34*, 106n
Jackson, Gabriele Bernhard, *34*, 131, 135n
Jackson, Glenda, *33*, 178
Jackson, Holbrook, *33*, 86n
Jackson, Howard, *35*, 169–70
Jackson, James L, *35*, 178, 189
Jackson, Macd. P., *32*, 237, 243–4; *34*, 190, 193; *35*, 190; *36*, 184n, 192; *40*, 156, 224, 235n
Jackson, Russell, *31*, 187; *32*, 19n; *34*, 172; *37*, 198, 199; *39*, 13, 220
Jackson, W. A., *31*, 191
Jackson, William, *36*, 140
Jacobi, Derek, *36*, 152, 154; *39*, 93, 105
Jacobs, Edward C., *32*, 235
Jacobs, Henry E., *33*, 188n
Jacobs, Richard, *34*, 185, 195–6
Jacobs, Sally, *33*, 177
Jacobson, Claire, *35*, 66n
Jaggard, William, *32*, 108; *33*, 2, 205; *34*, 186; *36*, 191; *37*, 206, 209; *38*, 91n
Jago, David M., *32*, 217
Jakobson, Roman, *31*, 54n, 56n; *35*, 117n
James, Clive, *36*, 23n
James, D. G., *33*, 7, 8
James, Emrys, *31*, 147, 149, 150; *32*, 223; *37*, 165, 172
James, Henry, *31*, 62n; *32*, 183; *34*, 65; *35*, 33; *36*, 32, 33n, 36
James I, King (James VI), *31*, 41, 101, 102, 103, 104; *32*, 134, 198, 231, 245; *33*, 147, 162, 168; *34*, 142, 180, 183; *35*, 72, 129, 130, 131, 132, 133, 136, 138, 178; *36*, 139, 165, 174; *37*, 197; *38*, 19, 20, 24, 59, 85, 128, 215; *39*, 219; *40*, 138–9, 199, 218
James VI, King, of Scotland, *38*, 21; *see also* James I, King
James, Louis, *35*, 12n
James, Oscar, *35*, 151
James, Richard, *38*, 86, 87, 94, 97, 98n, 99
Jameson, Anna, *32*, 15, 16, 17; *38*, 198
Jamieson, Michael, *32*, 2, 9
Jamieson, T. H., *32*, 165n
Janakiram, Alur, *32*, 213, 215; *34*, 184
Janson, H. W., *37*, 134n, 136, 137, 139n

Janssen, Gheerart, *40*, 216
Jardine, Lisa, *38*, 224
Jarman, Derek, *39*, 77
Jauch, Sharon L. Jansen, *38*, 231
Jauslin, Christian, *37*, 200n
Jauss, H. R., *37*, 159
Javitch, Daniel, *40*, 123n
Jayne, Sears Reynolds, *34*, 94n; *36*, 90n
Jeaffreson, J. C., *36*, 137n
Jeans, H. R., *39*, 43n
Jefferson, D. W., *36*, 103n; *39*, 171n
Jeffes, Agnes, *33*, 157
Jeffes, Anthony, *33*, 157, 158, 159; *38*, 227
Jeffes, Elizabeth, *33*, 157
Jeffes, Humphrey, *33*, 157, 158, 159
Jeffes, John, *33*, 157
Jeffes, Richard, *33*, 157
Jeffes, Richard, Jr, *33*, 157
Jeffes, William, *33*, 157
Jefford, Barbara, *31*, 160
Jeffrey, Peter, *39*, 196, 197, 202, 203
Jemie, Onwuchekwa, *39*, 175
Jenkins, Anthony W., *31*, 189, 197
Jenkins, Harold, *31*, 35; *32*, 8, 45n, 64n, 80, 82, 83–4; *33*, 73; *34*, 105n, 188, 196; *35*, 119n, 177, 184; *36*, 23n, 55, 181–2, 186n; *37*, 198; *38*, 1, 11, 13, 81, 101, 104; *39*, 244, 245
Jensen, Soren Elung, *39*, 79n
Jerrold, Blanchard, *38*, 189
Jewers, Ray, *35*, 148
Joan of Arc, *38*, 223
Jobin, Sybille, *37*, 158n
Jochum, Klaus Peter, *33*, 196–7
John de Trevisa, *37*, 86
John, Errol, *38*, 213
John Sigismund, Elector of Brandenburg, *36*, 139
Johnson, Anthony L., *40*, 205
Johnson, Celia, *39*, 105
Johnson, Charles, *32*, 37–48; *34*, 173
Johnson, David, *39*, 189
Johnson, Gerald D., *35*, 186
Johnson, Henry, *33*, 146n
Johnson, Richard, *38*, 249; *39*, 108
Johnson, Robert, *40*, 220
Johnson, Samuel, *31*, 1, 5, 9, 10, 105, 111n, 112; *32*, 71, 154n; *33*, 18, 32, 39, 53, 190, 192; *34*, 6, 11, 14, 15, 16, 19, 51, 54, 93n, 104, 144, 168, 170; *35*, 45; *36*, 28, 163,